About the author

Catherine Davies is professor of Spanish at the University of Manchester. She is the author of *Contemporary Feminist Fiction in Spain* and editor of *Women Writers of Spain and Spanish America* among many other books.

A PLACE IN THE SUN?

Women Writers in Twentieth-century Cuba

CATHERINE DAVIES

Zed Books Ltd
LONDON & NEW JERSEY

A Place in the Sun? Women Writers in Twentieth-century Cuba was first published by Zed Books Ltd, 7 Cynthia Street, London N1 9JF, UK and Room 400, 175 Fifth Avenue, New York, NY 10010, USA in 1997.

Distributed exclusively in the USA by St Martin's Press, Inc., 175 Fifth Avenue, New York, NY 10010, USA.

Cover designed by Andrew Corbett
Set in Monotype Garamond by Ewan Smith
Printed and bound in the United Kingdom
by Biddles Ltd, Guildford and King's Lynn

A catalogue record for this book is available from the British Library

US CIP has been applied for from the Library of Congress

ISBN 1 85649 541 8 cased
ISBN 1 85649 542 6 limp

Contents

Acknowledgements

This book has been some seven years in the making and many people have helped me along the way. It first took shape during a conversation with Verity Smith in a pub in Glasgow where we were attending a conference on Latin American women writers organized by Catherine Boyle. Inspired by the warm vapours of highland malt, we discussed a joint-authored volume on Cuban women writers and research for it began in 1990. Although our paths have somewhat diverged since then my greatest debt is to Verity. Her expert knowledge of things Cuban and her unfailing encouragement have proved invaluable over the years. I also thank her for reading the manuscript and for her useful advice.

Information on the constantly shifting Cuban scene is not always easily come by. I thank in particular Conrad James, Stephen Wilkinson and Miguel Arnedo for their generosity in providing information and for sharing their research interests. Many other friends and colleagues have assisted with ideas, books, material, or a personal postal service to Cuba. I thank especially: Clara Allen, Joan Anim Addo, Anny Brooksbank Jones, Peter Bush, Evelyn Fishburn, Omar García, Michael Gilsenan, Toni Kapcia, Jane King, Jeremy Lawrance, Bernard McGuirk, Pedro Pérez Sarduy, Paul Julian Smith, Jean Stubbs, Philip Swanson, Keith Ellis, and my colleagues – past and present – in the Universities of St Andrews, London, and Manchester for their kind support.

The book would not have been possible at all without the remarkable generosity of the Cuban women writers themselves: Dora Alonso, Omega Agüero, Cira Andrés, Marilyn Bobes, Rafaela Chacón Nardi, Lina de Feria, María Elena Llana, Dulce María Loynaz, Fina García Marruz, Georgina Herrera, Soleida Ríos, Reina María Rodríguez, Excilia Saldaña, Cleva Solís, Zoe Valdés, and Enid Vian. All of them, without exception, showed a keen interest in the project and were obliging in every way. They gave me material, hospitality and friendship even though they were undergoing extreme hardship. All I could offer in return was serious interest (and perhaps a teabag or two). I am indebted to Nancy Morejón for her encouragement from the very start, to Olga Fernández (and her husband Agenor Martí), and to Aida Bahr for their friendship. A warm thanks goes to Mirta Yáñez, who has been a key element in the project since her visit to Scotland in 1991. I also wish to thank the following Cubans for their much appreciated cooperation: Nara Araújo, Julia Calzadilla, Victor

Fowler, Ignacio Granados, Manolo Granados, Araceli García Carranza, Carmen Gonce, Tomás Robaina Fernández, Elena Jorge and, the first person I contacted in Havana, César López. Any errors in the book are, of course, mine entirely.

The research trips to Cuba in 1990 and 1992, and the associated activities organized in this country, would not have been possible without the generous assistance of the British Academy. Long may its hard-come-by bounty flow. I would also like to acknowledge the financial assistance of the Carnegie Trust, Scotland, and the Research Committees of the University of St Andrews and Queen Mary and Westfield College, University of London. I am grateful to the University of Manchester for the six months' sabbatical leave which enabled me to finish the book. Thanks to the librarians at QMW; Senate House (University of London); the Biblioteca Nacional, Madrid; the Biblioteca José Martí, Havana; the Centre for Cuban Studies, New York, especially Irving Kessler; the UNEAC offices in Havana, primarily Gema Suárez; to Geoff West, Barry Taylor and Carol Holden at the British Library, and to Louise Murray for her encouragement. Finally, thanks to Richard Fardon, my right hand, and my children Sarah, Anna and Tom for keeping the home fires burning.

Earlier versions of parts of Chapters 2, 5, 6, 7 and 8 have appeared in print: (in 1993) 'Beastly Women and Underdogs: The Short Fiction of Dora Alonso', in C. Davies (ed.), *Women Writers in Twentieth-Century Spain and Spanish America*, Edwin Mellen Press, pp. 55–69; 'Writing the African Subject. The Work of Two Cuban Poets' in *Women. A Cultural Review*, Vol. 4, no. 1: 32–48; (in 1995) 'Women Writers in Cuba 1975–1994. A Bibliographical Note', *Bulletin of Latin American Research*, Vol. 14, no. 2: 211–15; (in 1996) 'National Feminism in Cuba: the Elaboration of a Counter-discourse 1900–1935', *Modern Language Review*, Vol. 91, no. 1: 107–23; 'Women Writers in Twentieth-Century Cuba. An Eight-Point Survey', in J. Anim Addo (ed.), *Framing the Word. Gender and Genre in Caribbean Women's Writing*, Whiting and Birch, London, pp. 138–58. Thanks to Fondo de Cultura Económica for permission to quote excerpts from: Dulce María Loynaz (1993c) *Poemas escogidos*, ed. Pedro Simón, Madrid/Alcalá de Henares, and to Ediciones Universal from whom permission was sought to quote from: Ana Rosa Núñez (ed.) (1993) *Homenaje a Dulce María Loynaz*, Ediciones Universal, Miami.

All translations into English are my own unless otherwise stated. Where translations are more obviously approximations (as in poetry and poetic prose), the original Spanish text has been provided.

To the memory of my mother
(1928–73)
and my little brother John
(1970–96)

'Twixt the Green Sea and the Azured Vault'

Picture a single-storey house on a quiet street in old suburban Havana. The patrician house, dark and shuttered, is built in colonial style and encircled by black, iron railings. An elaborate wrought-iron gate gives way to steps leading to a wooden balcony. Around the back and the side of the house tall trees and thick undergrowth rustle in the afternoon heat. The grey-green walls, heavy like a threatening storm, are stained and damp. Inside the house lives an old lady; in order to see her, visitors must make an appointment. She often declines. When a visitor does call – as on this sultry July afternoon in 1990 – the barking dogs must be tied up before the iron gate is unlocked. The old lady goes down to open the gate herself; she wears heavy rimmed spectacles, a blue summer frock with long sleeves and a high collar, and a shawl. Her white hair is neatly coiled in a bun. She greets her visitor politely but not before examining her carefully with keen, blue eyes, as sharp as needles. This old lady is very particular about whom she allows into her home; she does not suffer fools gladly. In the cool half light of a room cluttered with leather-bound books, small wooden figures, a cross on the wall, dried flowers and faded silk cushions, she and the foreign visitor take tea, served from porcelain cups on a silver tray. Sipping their tea, they speak quietly of distant places – Spain, Egypt, Scotland – and literature: Shakespeare, Rosalía de Castro, García Lorca, Gabriela Mistral. The old lady, now in her eighty-seventh year, has travelled far and known many famous authors; she may be shrewd but today she is also strangely sad, as if she were aware of living on borrowed time. She speaks of her own work only when asked and with reticence. The visitor is struck by her assuredness and unimpeachability. This is Dulce María Loynaz, the doyenne of Cuban letters, the daughter of a general, a living legend, a semi-recluse, an international figure, winner of the 1992 Cervantes Prize for Literature, cultured, witty, and unshakeable in her conviction that Fidel Castro has brought ruination to Cuba. Dulce María Loynaz, emblem of traditional Cuban values and personification of Cuba as it was before the Revolution, was not born yesterday.

Now picture a tall, modern building that stands a few blocks east, facing the Malecon promenade and looking out to sea, in the middle of a row of undistinguished apartments. Shining white in the early morning sun, its clean architectural lines, glass and steel doorways, and sparkling uniformity dazzle the onlooker. Inside the building is the office of a young, black woman. In order to see her, visitors must make an appointment, though she often declines. When a visitor does call, as on this bright July morning in 1990, a seat is made available in the reception lounge. The young, black woman comes down the staircase to meet the visitor herself. She wears tight, white cherry-printed slacks and a red blouse, her curly hair is short and neat, she rattles her bracelets. She greets her visitor politely but not before examining her carefully with dark, inquisitive eyes; she knows the score. In the young woman's spacious office, painted white and pale yellow like a diaphanous cube, tastefully decorated with contemporary paintings and Santería figurines, she and the foreign visitor sit round a glass table sipping coffee. They speak loudly, even boisterously, of foreign places – the United States, South Africa, London, the Caribbean – and literature: Alice Walker, Derek Walcott, Jean Rhys, Aimé Césaire. The young, black woman has travelled widely and met the cream of contemporary poets. Sociable, *au courant* and unperplexed she answers her visitor's questions tactfully, speaking freely of her own work. The visitor is struck by her assuredness and mental poise. This is Nancy Morejón, director of the Casa de las Américas, internationally the most famous of young Cuban writers, the first black Cuban woman to make her mark, energetic, expansive, smart, a globe-trotter, the representative of her country abroad, unshakeable in her conviction that the Revolution is a good thing. Nancy Morejón is the personification of socialist achievement; she knows what it takes.

Together, these two scenes are indicative of the larger Cuban picture. They illustrate the heterogeneity of the Cuban cultural field even within the more restricted arena of women's literature. It would be facile to suggest that Dulce María Loynaz represents the old and Nancy Morejón the new. Together, their writings constitute cultural forms which are complementary representations of the past inherent in the present, the hybrid interrelations of the traditional and the modern. Despite their obvious differences in age, class, skin colour and political persuasion, these two women share a great deal, not least a gender, a language and a love of literature. Above all, they share a national identity because both consider themselves Cuban; they have lived their entire lives on the island despite opportunities to leave. In Cuba, staying home is a conscious, political decision. The task of the outsider is to make connections between these apparently heterogeneous spaces without reducing the complex cultural map to a monochromatic transparency.

This book is about opening windows on to interior spaces: the inner spaces of women's lives, offices and homes but also the inside pages of their books. The greatest homage a critic can pay to a writer is to open her book and read her work attentively, to enter not only the shade of the living space to take tea, but to enter the often unvisited, unread world in the book. To read literature seriously means to tread carefully, to avoid the obvious. My aim is to enter into dialogue with the texts to which I had access, to examine their multiple layers of meaning, to communicate their discursive universes to other readers, to create ripples. It is, perhaps, the greatest and the riskiest form of cooperation with a writer. I invite readers to open these windows and look through them with me. The woman writer may be surprised at what I see between the casing of her book. Where she sees patriotism I see sex; where she sees love I see horror; where she sees God I see mother. She sees animals, I see woman; she sees revolt, I see conformity; she sees sex, I see revolt.

What I have tried to suggest in this mildly fictionalized account of two figures in a Cuban landscape is the simultaneity of their dissimilar lifestyles and worlds. On a time-map these may be pictured as synchronous worlds of different factual and symbolic content, each as contemporary as the other (Gell 1992: 259). The subtitle of this book, however, referring to twentieth-century Cuba, and its organization into pre-revolutionary and post-revolutionary subdivisions immediately denotes historical time, the temporal succession of the same kind of world. Cuba is a 'hot' society in more than one sense. Following Lévi-Strauss, it is 'hot' because it has filed away events for collective remembrance, it has internalized its own historicity. It obsessively dwells not just on but in its reflexive historicity (Gell 1992: 23). This is the legacy of revolution. But despite the book's subtitle and organization my aim here is not primarily empiricist data collection or Cuban history.

I have not wished to write just another Cuban literary history, not even a woman's literary history. One-way historical or objective time plotted along a horizontal axis, a time-map according to which worlds are temporally different but continuations of the same, is the map of standard Cuban literary history. It has been argued that developmental models of time such as this are closely associated with colonialist expansion (Fabian 1983: 144). Accounts of the Cuban cultural scene have been circumscribed too often by evolutionary models or by the temporal affixes pre- and post- indicating a space-like, physical view of time. I am more interested in the dynamic, subjective, stream of experience aspects of time (Gell 1992: 151) central to the phenomenological project and to productive, creative imagination. My approach indicates not only a preference for what might be termed a good postmodern hermeneutic (a bad one having collapsed into pure simulation) but, more importantly, a feminist agenda. Feminist scholarship aims to deconstruct androcentric cultural paradigms, to unmask the false coherence of male-humanist ideologies and cultural practices. Conventional accounts of Cuban literary history with their fixation on particular cliques, generations and periodization have found little time or space for women authors, hence my attempt to view the scene differently. However, persuaded by Alfred Gell that experiental time, the flow of process and transition, is intelligible only with a 'back up' temporal map of the objectivist type (Gell 1992: 320) I have provided two long chapters which sketch with broad strokes the typologies of women's creative writing before and after the Cuban Revolution of 1959. These chapters (Chapters 1 and 5) provide no more than an aerial view whose details may be lost; and distancing, according to Fabian, is another form of collusion with 'the forces of progress' (Fabian 1983: 146). Much more interesting is to present close readings or blow-ups of selected features of the cultural map. As Henri Lefebvre argues, with reference to space:

> how many maps, in the descriptive or geographical sense, might be needed to deal exhaustively with a given space, to code and decode all its meanings and contents […] What we are most likely confronted with here is a sort of instant infinity […]. It is not only the codes that are liable to change, but also the objects represented, the lens through which they are viewed, and the scale used. The idea that a small number of maps or even a single (and singular) map might be sufficient can only apply in a specialised area of study whose own self-affirmation depends on isolation from its context. (Lefebvre 1991: 85)

In other words, contextualized interpretations are plenteous and no detail (a word, an image) is too small to be of significance. Whereas a horizontal schema extending from 1900 to the mid-1990s may serve as a facilitating framework indicating historical time, more space will be dedicated in this study to particular events plotted along that line. I understand these world events to be books the contents of which may be believed in, half-believed in, or hardly believed in (Gell 1992: 258). Unopened, unread books are objects, things extended in space but not in time. Writing and reading a book turns it into an event, inasmuch as events are the changes that happen to things. Although this study grounds the books in their social and cultural contexts, I have read them as meaningful in their own right, as free-standing world events with the potential for releasing their own time–space sequences of intense imagining.

Readers familiar with postmodern theory will recognize the suspicion of the Grand or Master Narrative, the official versions of Cuban (literary, cultural, social) history with periodizations according to war, revolution, achievement and decline. This book features the small narratives (Lyotard's 'petits récits'), the plurality of stories the Master Narrative might conceal which restore ambiguity and conflict to the historical process. The aim is not so much to unmask the constraints and contradictions of ideologies of liberal humanism or Marxist Leninism, but rather to disclose the ideology of gender, the androcentric even misogynistic premises on which the Master Narrative is based no matter what political and economic theory it confirms. This book acknowledges the presence of just a few of those troublesome 'petits récits' (traces perhaps of female sub- or counter-cultures which rework questions of gender, race, religion, home, nation and political regime from a woman's point of view), pays them attention and gives them an audience. In so doing it will become apparent that the momentous changes taking place in Cuban history may not have been quite so momentous for some women. Despite intentions to the contrary, as far as the interplay of gender and culture are concerned, the Cuban Master Narrative has altered over the last hundred years, but not quite as much as expected.

Cuba is the biggest Caribbean island with a population in 1992 of 10.5 million, over half of whom are women. It is a Spanish-speaking, multicultural society (about a third of the popluation are black or mixed) whose hybridity (European, North American, Latin American, African) is difficult to fix. It is a postcolonial society, dependent on Spain until 1898, and a quasi-dependency of the United States until 1959.[1] After the 1959 Revolution, Cuba became a socialist republic under Fidel Castro, economically dependent on the USSR until 1989. Today (1996) it is still a multiracial, multicultural, postcolonial, socialist society in the throes of painful economic reform. The plantation economy of colonial Cuba was broadly similar to that of other parts of the Caribbean; slaves were imported mainly from West Africa (Yorubaland of today's Nigeria) and their cultures survived in religions such as Santería. But Cuba was a settler society; links with the Spanish metropolis continued to be strong while a syncretic culture emerged which distinguished Cuban society from the European. Before the 1959 Revolution, many wealthy Cubans looked to the United States as a model of cultural modernity; Havana was an extremely sophisticated and cosmopolitan city. After the Revolution cultural ties were extended to Eastern Europe and Africa. Arguably, the strongest ideological force in Cuba this century has been nationalism or 'Cubanidad' which has resulted in a fairly homogenous national culture, despite differences of class, race and gender, always defined in opposition to somewhere else (Spain, the United States, the Soviet Union).

Twentieth-century Cuban history is embedded in a discourse of modernity, modernity as understood by Peter Osborne as a 'culture of time', a distinctive way of temporalizing historical time informed by nineteenth- and twentieth-century European philosophy with a political agenda (Osborne 1995: x). Modernization, the latest version of the ideas of progress and development, supposes a totalizing, homogenizing view of global time associated with emergent capitalism; spaces may be geographically different but have chronologically simultaneous times. Marxism offers a political alternative grounded on modes of production rather than on a division between the traditional and the modern, but it has not changed the temporal structure of modernity. In Sartre's words: 'Marxism caught a glimpse of true temporality when it criticised and destroyed the bourgeois notion of "progress" [...] . But [...] renounced these studies and preferred to make use of "progress" again for its own benefit.'[2] At issue then are two problems: the question of the gendering of both modernity and Marxism as forms of historical time, and the question of mediating historical periodization with phenomenological forms of time consciousness, that is, with notions of individual everyday experience and psychoanalytic accounts of identity formation. Osborne explains why:

> If structural categories of historical analysis, like 'capital', are to be rendered effective at the level of experience, they will have to be mediated by the phenomenological forms through which history is lived as the ongoing temporalization of existence. 'Modernity' is one such form; 'progress', 'reaction', 'revolution', 'crisis', 'conservation', 'stagnation' and 'the new' are others [...] These are not the products of competing totalizations of historical material across a common temporal frame. [...] They represent alternative temporal structures, alternative temporalizations of 'history' which articulate the relations between 'past', 'present' and 'future' in politically significantly different ways. (Osborne 1995: 200)

Of particular relevance to multiethnic, postcolonial Cuba are his following remarks:

> Born, like capitalism, out of European colonialism and the world market, as a structure of historical consciousness 'modernity' predates the development of capitalism proper. [...] modernity is our primary secular category of historical totalization. But what justifies this totalization of history, theoretically, if such an operation of necessity homogenizes and represses, reduces or forgets, certain forms of difference? And if we are to totalize history, how are we to do it in such a way as to preserve a sense of what is lost in the process? (Osborne 1995: 29)

My reservations about writing a historical account of women's writing in twentieth-century Cuba are as follows. First, the contextualization of these texts demanded a chronological approach which, in turn, appeals to conceptions of historical time firmly inscribed in the process of modernity, be it the capitalist form or the communist alternative. Julia Kristeva has argued that the kind of linear historical accounts associated with historiography, the charting of public events and political and economic developments, is men's time from which women were excluded (Kristeva 1989). According to Kristeva, linear temporality is predicated on female subjectivity signifying eternity and repetition. However, as Osborne points out, by prolonging the division between men's and women's time Kristeva is unable to advance towards a notion of transformation of historical time *per se*. In other words, neither feminism nor Marxism nor postmodernism has transformed the temporal structure of modernity. Extending Kristeva's hypothesis, I would like to suggest that while Cuban women did participate in the public and political life of the nation (indeed, in most cases their work would not have been published if they had not been in some way associated with the public sphere), it is the case that public life is not the staple of their work. Their writing inscribes everyday life, and Cuban women's everyday life is dissimilar to men's. Even if an individual woman's lifestyle is comparable to an individual man's, her positioning in society regarding role, attitudes and expectations is radically different. Moreover, in their writings women focus on certain kinds of gendered everyday experience relating to family (as mothers, daughters and sisters) and sexual relationships (as wives and lovers).

The question I ask is not what those experiences are, although that in itself is a crucial question which has not been sufficiently posed in the past, but rather how women's writing has shaped notions of a collective Cuban identity and how women's writing has glimpsed transformations of the historical time of Master Narratives. If Cuban history can be made sense of by recourse to modernization projects and Marxist politics, I suggest (indebted to Osborne) that it is at the level of phenomenological and psychoanalytic perspectives that women's writing can offer alternative forms, other versions of historical time and time-consciousness which counter, in a postmodern way, the 'single, historical' view of modernity. Women's writing inscribes affection and disaffection, love, desire and relationships with others (other people, God, animals). It seems to me, following Irigaray, that not only are these relationships viewed by women in a specific way, but that in order to think through sexual difference, 'we must reconsider the whole question of *space* and *time* [sic]' (Irigaray 1988: 119). As Osborne shows, a sense of time has to do with the individual's sense of no-time, death and eternity and this, in turn, is related to the process of identity and subject formation. Literature makes for a sense of time which is inextricably tied up with subjectivity and language. How does this engendered creative practice shape cultural development in Cuba, how does it alter the contours of the Cuban cultural map?

The texts I have chosen are similar in certain ways. They have been written by Cuban women whose names have often featured in Cuban literary histories. In Cuba the women's names are known, but their books have seldom been opened, critically read or seriously commented on abroad. Apart from the writers mentioned in Chapter 2, all the women are alive today and I have met almost all of them.[3] As pointed out with reference to Dulce María Loynaz and Nancy Morejón, however, these woman are very different and one of the purposes of this book is to show the plurality of women's voices, without resolving conflicting interpretations or reducing textual complexities to a synthesis. In this I am persuaded by Vattimo's concept of 'fragile thought', the refusal to reduce cultural complexity to systematic coherence (Kearney 1991: 182).

More importantly, all the chosen texts are examples of productive, creative imagination rather than mere mimesis. They have been chosen because they are less overtly concerned with political developments. As such they present imaginary possible worlds grounded in, yet released from, everyday reality, empirical facts and objective time. In Gaston Bachelard's terminology each is a 'reverie', a re-creation of reality, which is newly discovered and at the same time invented through the poetic power of imagination. Each text is considered as a world unto itself, separate (though not divorced) from Cuban historical narratives. I am more interested in the idea that the free play or free variation of the conscious act of imagining presents infinite horizons and many possible life-worlds not tied to actuality but rather positioned at the intersection between the self and the world, what Bachelard calls the 'fertile interlacings between the human subject and reality' (Kearney 1991: 103). I am less interested in mind-maps, in an author's psychological motivation or in Freudian concepts of the imaginary as the sublimation of repressed instincts. Nor am I interested primarily in an author's intentions. I consider the imaginary as a process of communication, a dialogical interaction between the author and the reader who, in turn, re-creates the world in the text. Imagination transforms received meanings and creates new ones: in Paul Ricoeur's words: 'Imagination comes into play in that moment when a new meaning emerges from out of the ruins of literal interpretation' (Kearney 1991: 140). This hermeneutic approach, a deciphering of indirect meanings, is concerned with the worlds opened up by authors and texts. But these new imagined worlds cannot be divorced from tradition. Rather, tradition is reactivated by poetic imagination and, conversely, innovation cannot exist without being grounded in tradition.

The selected texts, rather than preserve order by reaffirming a shared identity and common experiences, tend to trouble ideological stability and consensus. They query dominant versions of religion, racial and national identity, private and public space, and gender and sexuality, as well as political regime. Thus from among the collective stories which make up the social imaginary these texts can be be positioned as potential dissensus inasmuch as they resist absorption into 'la grande histoire'. According to Richard Kearney, one of the outcomes of 'good' postmodernity might be to reactivate the potentialities of modernity, to reinscribe or retrieve the betrayed stories of history through a 'critical redeployment of imagination' (Kearney 1991: 215). One of the betrayed promises of modern history has to do with female access to independent authority and subjectivity. What my readings all have in common is a critical, feminist perspective which foregrounds this problem which, in the end, is an ethical one. As Kearney states: 'ethics without poetics leads to the censuring of imagination; poetics without ethics leads to dangerous play [...] today we rely more than ever on the power of imagining to recast other ways of being in the world, other possibilities of existence' (Kearney 1991: 228); or, in the words of

Mexican feminist author Rosario Castellanos, 'another way of being, human and free / another way of being' (R. Castellanos 1988: 49).

The title of this preface is taken from Shakespeare's *The Tempest*. A woman version (O'Callaghan 1993) of *arielismo*, Latin America's cultural response to the seizure of Spain's last colonies, including Cuba, by the United States, might be to identify women writers on the island of Cuba with the brave spirit, Ariel, herself. For José Enrique Rodó, who identified Caliban with the brutish uncivilized North, however, Ariel represented the Latin American (male) intellectual who mediated between the cultures of Anglo and Hispanic America. From a gendered perspective, Ariel is emblematic of the creative, productive imaginations of Cuban women writers. Like Ariel they represent genius, intuition and ingenuity trammelled by (white, colonizing, modern) man (Prospero) and ancient (indigenous, traditional) female lore (Sycorax). Their incorporeal spirits, captured not by Sycorax (mother nature) in a tree but by Prospero's language in books, flashes their displaced presence to astonished onlookers across the miles. Books lack bodies but they disclose a voice, a woman's voice, a presence to reckon with. Books are the material presence of imagined spaces in real time. As with Ariel, the same language which charms the brave spirits into servitude eventually sets them free. The analogy can be drawn only so far, of course, but it serves as a means of problematizing the temporal complexities and equivocal links between the discursive universes of Cuban women, their foreign readers and the written word. As Virginia Woolf wrote in 1929:

> fiction is like a spider's web, attached ever so lightly perhaps, but still attached to life at all four corners [...] these webs are not spun in mid-air by incorporeal creatures, but are the work of suffering human beings, and are attached to grossly material things, like health and money and the house we live in. (Woolf 1984: 39)

It is the task of women critics to make opportunities, 'the opportunity will come and the dead poet who was Shakespeare's sister will put on the body which she has so often laid down [...] she would come if we worked for her' (Woolf 1984: 106).

This book, 'delaying not forgetting', attempts just that. It has taken some time. It has been written with care and respect, and out of a sense of increasing exasperation with the profound injustice perpetrated against people in Cuba by ignorant if not malevolent forces abroad. It is meant as a gesture of recognition for those Cuban women who, dead or alive, have found (or were able to find) the time and the space to write.

Notes

1. The Platt Amendment (1902) allowed the USA to intervene unconditionally in Cuban internal affairs. The Amendment was revoked in 1934 after the downfall of the dictator Machado by the same revolutionary government which gave women the vote. The Bastista Dictatorship (1952–59) again privileged US interests.

2. Jean-Paul Sartre, *Search for a Method* (1960), quoted in Osborne (1995: 3).

3. Sadly, Dulce María Loynaz died in April 1997 and Cleva Solís in August 1997, after this book had gone to press.

CHAPTER I

Contexts: Women Writers in Neo-colonial Cuba, 1900–59

A retrospective view of the incidence of women writers on the Cuban cultural map during the first half of this century is crucial for contextualizing the work of the writers considered in more detail in later chapters. Although the literary works themselves may not directly refer to this social and political scenario, it can hardly be dispensed with. What follows is a sequential narrative of the presence of Cuban women writers rather than their writings and a critical look at some of the canon-forming histories of literature and anthologies where their work is discussed. In this chapter, an act of remembrance and accreditation to many women writers, description takes precedence over theoretical reflexion. First, though, a short account of the earlier years of the Cuban women's literary tradition.

Creole women in colonial Cuba are first recorded as writers in the Romantic period. The childhood memories of the Countess Merlin (1789–1852), who spent her first twelve years in Havana before settling in Spain and France, were published in Paris in 1831 (in Spanish in 1833).[1] Max Henríquez Ureña (1963) cites the few extant verses of an eighteenth-century mulatta woman teacher, Juana Pastor (see Cervantes 1985). The Cuban woman writer who has received most recognition ever, to the extent that she has been conceded prime place even in Prospero's literary canon, was the nineteenth-century poet, novelist and dramatist Gertrudis Gómez de Avellaneda (1814–73). Avellaneda left Cuba for Spain in her early twenties and returned to live there between 1859 and 1864. Her much acclaimed anti-slavery novel *Sab* (1841), published eleven years before H. Beecher Stowe's *Uncle Tom's Cabin* (1852), was considered highly subversive. Both *Sab* and a later novel *Dos mujeres* (1842–43), published in Spain of necessity, were prohibited in Cuba and all imported copies were seized by customs at the ports of entry. In *Sab* a mulatto slave, Sab, falls in love with his white mistress, Carlota. She, in turn, loves and marries the unscrupulous son of an English merchant. Sab dies of a broken heart and a disillusioned Carlota realizes how much more worthy the Cuban slave was than his English master. The novel is sentimental but unique for its times. In the other Cuban anti-slavery novels, written by men, the catastrophic denouement is often attributed to the white mother who takes on the masculine role of racist authoritarian; the feminized, black male slave represents the oppressed but virtuous woman. In this way, one subaltern subject becomes the victim of another and the patriarch is blameless. In *Sab* the mother figure is absent and all blame is placed squarely on the shoulders of the Englishman who represents not only masculinity but also immorality, materialism and expropriation. A clear analogy is drawn between the slave's lack of freedom and that of the married woman. The novel also articulates fears of encroachments from the anglophone 'North' on Hispano-Cuban society. This identification of women, slaves and Cuba enmeshed in complex power relations, subjected to and exploited by the white man of the North is a theme which recurs in women's writings throughout the nineteenth and twentieth centuries (Picón Garfield 1994). Although implicated in the colonizing project, Avellaneda consistently undermines concepts of centralized power in her novels, plays and women's magazine and rewrites official versions of history from a subaltern point of view.[2]

The many other successful women writers in nineteenth-century Cuba all belonged to the white creole elite: the poets Luisa Pérez de Zambrana (1835–1922) and Juana Borrero (1877–96) are two of the better known.[3] Antonio González Curquejo's splendiferous three-volume *Florilegio de escritoras cubanas* (Havana, 1910–19) includes the work (poetry and short essays) of over 120 women writing and publishing between 1833 and 1919. Another anthology, *Arpas cubanas* (1904) included poems by four women (out of twenty-nine contributors): Dulce María Borrero, Nieves Xenes, Aurelia del Castillo and Loló Rodríguez de Tió.

Unlike their foremothers, the women writers publishing in the first half of the twentieth century belonged not so much to the aristocracy or plantation oligarchy as to the white, educated, urban middle classes. Many were politically conscious and extremely patriotic. But the 1901 Constitution did not give women the vote and a strong women's movement developed, one of the most advanced of its kind in Latin America. It culminated in the First National Women's Congress of 1923. A Second National Women's Congress was held in 1925 and a third in 1939. Several feminist journalists and writers participated in this first-wave feminism. By the 1930s and 1940s a number of women writers held important public posts, particularly in education and the diplomatic corps. Of course, not all women writers were feminists or politically aware. As we shall see, some led very sad lives, others were more fortunate. Some of the most prestigious women writers of twentieth-century Cuba belong to this pre-revolutionary period. These are all Hispano-Cuban writers and show little interest in African traditions, referring not to the Caribbean but to the Antilles. They none the less inscribe in their literature the kind of ambivalent relationships with Europe (particularly the Spanish metropolis) evidenced in the work of women from other parts of the Caribbean. Standard intellectual histories of the Cuban Republic divide the period into three generations (Lazo 1974). In what follows I will sketch the salient political events, including the development of the women's movement, and briefly account for the women writers pertaining to each.

First generation of the Republic: 1900–23

The 1898 Treaty of Paris marked the end of the Spanish–American War and, theoretically, the end of Cuban colonial dependence (Suchlicki 1974). The first Constitution of the new Republic (1901), which provided the framework for universal male suffrage, was liberal for its time but seriously curtailed by the Platt Amendment which permitted US intervention in Cuban affairs. It also failed to give women the vote. The period from 1902 (when US military occupation ended) to 1924 (when Gerardo Machado came to power) was one of nation-building and modernization in which women actively participated. But the early optimism and enthusiasm for the national project faltered in the face of increasing economic dependency and repeated intervention by the United States in Cuban internal affairs, resulting in political instability, corruption, frustration and scepticism among the governing classes and the populace. The economic crisis of 1920, following the sugar boom, brought about great hardship and fuelled xenophobia and anti-US feeling as well as calls for social reform.

From the point of view of women, despite the fact that they were denied the vote, there were a number of important developments during these first two decades of national independence. As K. Lynn Stoner writes: 'Male legislators advanced women's rights in their desperate efforts to consolidate their own power and modernize Cuba' (Stoner 1991: 53). In other words, the advances in women's rights were due not so much to pressure from women but were part of the modern, nationalist, post-colonial project. The move was away from Spain and the Catholic Church towards US or French models of social development and political organization.

The end of colonial rule augured well for women. The 1901 Constitution laid the foundations for the women's movement, although many reforms were postponed until later. The separation of church and state was fundamental in this respect as was the planned provision for public education and for a health service. Secular, public, coeducational schools, based on the US system (anathema in Spain) were set up from 1901 onwards. For women of the elite, however, an expensive, secular, private education had been available as early as the 1870s thanks to the pioneering work of María Luisa Dolz, Professor of Education at the Colegio Isabel la Católica where women were taught science and technology and instructed in the values of national liberation. By the late 1920s some 25 per cent of the students at Havana University were women (Smith and Padula 1996: 17). Legal reform (for example, of the infamous 1889 Spanish Civil Code), symbolic of the break with the colonial past, was extensive and enabled traditional male privilege ('patria potestas') to be questioned if not changed immediately.

The legal situation of Cuban women was infinitely more favourable than that of their Spanish counterparts. In 1917 Cuban married women were given the right to administer and dispose of their own property, authority over their children, and legal representation. The much debated no-fault divorce law was passed the following year. Between 1918 and 1927, 2,500 divorces were filed (Stoner 1991: 45–6). Women also entered the white-collar workforce in increasing numbers: there were more teachers, nurses and clerks and for the first time women took jobs as government employees, office workers, merchants and pharmacists.[4]

Cuba was an emerging nation and women, who had recently taken a major part in the Wars of Independence (1895–98), to the extent that it was known as the 'women's war' (Smith and Padula 1996: 11–13), expected to participate actively in the national programme. The 'mambisas' (women who fought for Cuban independence) embodied 'maternal nationalism': the warrior-mother who was both brave and vulnerable became a powerful icon symbolizing national independence, the struggle for social justice and women's rights. Indeed, women such as Rosario Sigarroa who had founded the newspaper *Cuba Libre* (1899–1912) went on to be active feminists. Conversely, all demands for reform, including those of women, would be perceived as nationalist. The cultural influence of the United States familiarized Cuban women with the ideas of US feminists and they invited a number to speak in their organizations. However, the aims and values of Cuban feminists were markedly different from those of their Northern sisters (Stoner 1991: 1–8) and at least on one occasion US feminists actively curtailed the introduction of women's rights in Cuba. In the 1926 Inter-American Women's Congress held in Panama, US feminists, in particular Carrie Chapman Catt, took the view that women in Latin America were not sufficiently prepared to vote.

A thriving Cuban feminist movement, consisting overwhelmingly of white middle-class women taking full advantage of the legal and educational reforms, was active on several fronts from 1917 onwards. These women had been disappointed by the 1901 Constitution that denied them suffrage and few condoned the Platt Amendment; the majority were fiercely patriotic. Resonances of the suffragette movement appeared in the occasional work discussing feminism, such as Luz Rubio's *Consideraciones sobre feminismo* [Consideration on Feminism] (1914). Several women's clubs: the Committee of Women's Suffrage (1912); the Feminist Party of Aspirations (1914) with their own magazine *Aspiraciones. Periódico cívico-*

patriotico, defensor de los intereses de la mujer y del débil y vejado [Aspirations. Civic-patriotic newspaper, defender of the interests of women, the weak and the molested] edited by Pio de Lara y Zaldo and his wife; the Feminine Association of Camagüey with their own *Review* (1921) and, most importantly, the progressive Club femenino [Feminine Club] of Cuba (founded in 1917) whose membership included the leading lights of Cuban radical feminism: Hortensia Lamar, Mariblanca Sabás Alomá, Loló de la Torriente and Rosario Guillaume. Many other women's organizations existed in the first decades of the century (FNAF 1949: 14, 37) and they worked hard to put women's rights on the cultural and political agenda. Their activities culminated in the high point of the women's movement, the First National Women's Congress of 1923 organized by the Feminine Club in Havana whose president at the time was the former 'mambisa' Fela [Elena] Mederos de Fernández.[5]

The National Federation of Feminine Associations (FNAF), was created as an umbrella organization for the purpose of arranging the 1923 Congress under the presidency of Pilar Morlón de Menéndez. Thirty-one women's associations of all types sent representatives and forty-three women spoke (Stoner 1991: 53). In her opening speech, the president of the FNAF called on women to see themselves as representatives and defenders of the inseparable values of national independence and moral virtue:

> We declare ourselves always on guard against evil, wherever and in whatever form it may be. We shall give our activities the plain title of 'Nationalism', nothing more, which embraces men and women of all classes and beliefs. It will be the emblem of those who are pure, good, and true patriots. The Cuban Revolution [Independence War] has not ended with the sight of the Cuban flag raised on the Morro [the fort in Havana], no, because in the wake of political freedom we have now to conquer moral freedom and this will not be achieved without the corresponding virtues. (FNAF 1923: 34)

Themes broached during the Congress included women's rights, nationalism, the protection of children, women's participation in the Wars of Independence, women journalists, women's employment rights, the adultery laws, women's suffrage, women in the home, the Civil Code, education, health reforms, prostitution and the white slave trade, kindness to animals, cleaning up Havana's streets, and the fight against drug abuse; 'Most speeches were patriotic and passionate' (Stoner 1991: 62). A minority of radical feminists introduced the more controversial topics such as equal rights for illegitimate children. The FNAF published all these contributions in an invaluable document, the *Memoria* (1923), and selected papers were also published in the press. Among the various feminist groups which met at the First National Women's Congress were several creative writers and journalists who would make their mark in these and the following decades: Ofelia Domínguez Navarro, Ofelia Rodríguez Acosta, Mariblanca Sabás Alomá, Loló de la Torriente and Renée Méndez Capote.

WOMEN WRITERS A clear indication of the wealth of literary writing by women during these years is the *Florilegio de escritoras cubanas* (3 vols) edited by A. González Curquejo. Included in that anthology is a selection of the work of several writers who would later establish their literary reputation, and who will be discussed at greater length in the next chapter. In addition, Ana Núñez Machín (1989) lists the names of 105 women journalists publishing during the period 1814 to 1912. One of the most important authors of the first years of the century was Dulce María Borrero de Luján (1883–1945) (poet laureate). She was the younger sister of Juana Borrero (1877–96), the idealized love of the acclaimed Cuban poet Julián del Casal. The early poetry of Dulce María was in the new modernista style and she became one of the leading members of the first generation of Cuban poets represented by the anthology *Arpas cubanas* (Kostia 1904). She was also among the first generation of feminists and wrote a number of works on the role of women in society (González Curquejo 1910: 299–306). According to María Collado, a leading conservative feminist and journalist writing in *La Mujer* (November 1929), the organ of the Feminist Party, Dulce María was 'the most outstanding female figure in the Cuban intellectual world [...] her poetry surpasses that of all contemporary Cuban women poets'. As well as poetry, Dulce María published *El matrimonio en Cuba* [Matrimony in Cuba] (1914) and testified in Congress in support of the divorce bill. She wrote numerous articles in the press in the 1920s on the need for the protection of women, especially pregnant women, in the workplace and she attacked the isolation of women in the home. In a speech entitled 'Women indirectly responsible for the progressive degeneration of the Cuban soul' (FNAF 1923: 110–19), she declared that Cuba needed women to take part in its national reconstruction otherwise they were doing society a disservice because the nation would decline. In this way, modernization was identified with women's emancipation. In 1935 Borrero became Director of Culture in the Ministry of Education.

Not included in González Curquejo's anthology is the poetry of María Luisa Milanés (1893–1919). Milanés, who used the pseudonym Liana de Lux, had been educated in a convent and wrote seven volumes of poetry and other works before committing suicide. The cause of her unhappiness was an unfaithful husband to whom she was married for seven years. Only some 300 poems were saved from destruction by her mother and were finally published; they are dramatic and heart-rending, comparable to those of the contemporary Uruguayan poet María Eugenia Vaz Ferreira. Although Milanés was not involved in the feminist movement, her poetry inscribes national feminist motifs similar to those of her more militant peers as we shall see in Chapter 2 (Valdés Roig 1930).

Second generation of the Republic: 1923–40

The chaotic period between 1923 and 1940 demonstrated that Cuba was an underdeveloped country that could not shake off the colonial legacy. These two tempestuous decades witnessed a violent push for change, economic chaos, increasing political activism and polarization, the flowering of first-wave feminism and, in 1934, women's emancipation. The second generation of intellectuals of the Cuban Republic, whose radical cultural and political activities centre on two key dates, 1923 (marking the start of their revolt) and 1933 (when the Revolution of that year finally ousted Gerardo Machado) attempted to reshape Cuba as an independent nation with a democratic government.

The centre of this thrust for democratic reform was the University of Havana. In 1923 the first National Congress of Cuban Students took place; the Cuban Communist Party and the Cuban National Workers' Confederation were founded in 1925, and the University Student Directory and the Marxist avant-garde 'Minorista Group' in 1927. After the fraudulent elections of 1928 which extended Gerardo Machado's original four-year mandate, political oppression, violence and anarchy spiralled out of control until Machado was forced to quit in 1933. But the 1933 Revolution, led by army stenographer Fulgencio Batista, was frustrated. Grau's reformist government, which cancelled the Platt Amendment (and thus was not recognized by the United States) lasted no more than a year. The years 1934 to 1940 were ones of disillusion. Batista controlled a series of puppet presidents until he took over the executive himself in 1940. The opposition was muted, disbanded or in exile. In response to these national and ethical problems, the Cuban independence fighter, thinker and poet José Martí (1853–95) was presented as a national icon culminating in the 1953 centennial celebrations of his birth. The role of women in the political and cultural activities leading up to the reformist constitution of 1940 proved to be crucial and their political manoeuvring paid off.

The Second National Congress was held in April 1925, again organized by the Feminine Club and the FNAF shortly after Machado came to power. By then, however, the winds of political change were less favourable and the Congress was hi-jacked by right-wing Catholic groups.[6] The themes discussed in the Second Congress were similar to those in the first, although there was a tendency to show more concern for the working classes, women's education, children and health provision. After these first two National Congresses women became increasingly organized and politically active. They lobbied politicians for reform and sometimes joined forces with student and revolutionary groups. The Assembly of 1928, which extended Machado's power, once again refused to give women the vote despite Machado's promises to the contrary. The Sixth Pan-American Conference was held in Havana in 1928 during which the Inter-American

Women's Commission was founded. This consisted of delegates appointed by the various South American republics and an elected Executive which met in Washington. That same year Pilar Jorge de Tella and Ofelia Domínguez Navarro merged the 'Committee for Civic Action' and the 'Committe for Women's Suffrage' to form the National Feminist Alliance and keep the question of women's votes in the public eye. The Alliance was a conservative association which met in the Havana Yacht Club consisting of wealthy upper-middle-class women. In 1930 Ofelia Domínguez Navarro stood for the presidency and when not elected left the Alliance to found the socialist Labour Union of Women whose socialist–feminist manifesto was added to that of the Communist Party of 1928 (Stoner 1991: 75). Unlike all other feminist groups, the Union finally denounced Machado's promise of women's suffrage as a ploy to keep women in his camp. Thus, by 1930, women's suffrage became a 'metaphor for constitutional democracy' (Stoner 1991: 108) and Machado's betrayal of women a symbol of his undemocratic dictatorship.

Several important feminist magazines were founded in the 1920s which often divulged feminist ideas and brought women together into groups of varying political persuasion. Núñez Machín lists twenty-seven women chief editors of newspapers and magazines for the period 1909 to 1939 (Núñez Machín 1989: 194–5). Some of the more important magazines in the 1920s were *La mujer moderna* [Modern Woman] (1926), the official organ of the Club Femenino de Cuba, subtitled 'Liberty, Education, Work', edited and owned by the radical feminist Hortensia Lamar. This was the most politically radical of the journals of its time, containing a section entitled 'Thoughts of Martí' which indicated the moral import of its programme. *El sufragista* (1922–26), organ of the Partido Nacional Sufragista (formerly Feminista), edited by Amalia E. Mellén de Ostolaza, was significantly retitled *La sufragista* in 1926 and under the editorship of Luisa M. de la Cotera O'Bourke ran until 1934. *La sufragista*, which published the 'Suffragist Hymn' (no. 1, March 1928, p. 3), featured articles on politics, children and poetry while overtly pandering to the government by publishing endearing photographs of General Menocal (no. 29, October 1928), of Machado's wife Elvira (no. 41, June 1934), and even of Machado's granddaughter. Interestingly, opposite the photograph of Elvira Machado is one of the young Lydia Cabrera (no. 29, October 1928) who was about to leave for Paris to make her fortune in the art decor trade. The more sober *Boletín de la Alianza Nacional Feminista* [Bulletin of the National Feminist Alliance] (1931–35) published articles on science and biology, an example being 'The Position of Woman in Biology and Juridical Science' by Emilio Camus (September 1932), and on political reform, women's emancipation and women's activities in the United States. This review was clearly more interested in parliamentary lobbying than most and published a list of the names of parliamentary representatives who voted for and against women's suffrage in 1932. Far more interesting and entertaining was the beautifully produced *La Mujer* [Woman] (1929–42), subtitled 'A fortnightly magazine for the family and the home', directed by María Collado (b. 1899) who was president of the right-wing Democrat Suffragist Party and used the journal to launch virulent attacks on the radicals Mariblanca Sabás Alomá and Ofelia Domínguez Navarro.[7] Here readers could find a rich mixture of quality articles on, for example, 'Women in the Revolution' (the Independence War) and 'Women of Merit', up-to-date fashion designs and patterns, hairstyles, recipes, various literary sections which included the work of Latin American women poets such as Gabriela Mistral, Alfonsina Storni and Juana de Ibarbourou, articles on the Spanish contemporary writer Concha Espina, and the Cuban Dulce María Borrero, a section for young readers, and numerous advertisements for the latest products and garments, mostly imported from the United States. Despite the conservatism of its editor, this was by far the most open journal as far as sex was concerned with daring photographs of the latest models in bras and suspender belts placed next to pictures of Gary Cooper. Female journalists of some repute, such as Anita Arroyo, collaborated on *La Mujer*, while others, such as Mariblanca Sabás Alomá or Ofelia Rodríguez Acosta, wrote for the more widely circulated *Carteles* (after 1927) and *Bohemia* (1929–32) respectively.

As mentioned previously, the most long-running and influential women's cultural organization in Cuba for the next forty years was the Havana Lyceum.[8] It was founded in 1929 by several women, in particular Berta Arocena de Martínez Márquez, Elena Maderos and Renée Méndez Capote. The range and quality of the activities organized by the Lyceum well into the 1960s – public lectures, conferences, courses, public library holdings, classes for women (including evening classes for working women) and for children (languages, typing, literature), art exhibitions and social welfare – were truly impressive. The Lyceum lobbied for women's votes, education and culture. Numerous world-famous intellectuals and writers lectured there. In the 1930s, for example, the poets Federico García Lorca (Spain) and Gabriela Mistral (Chile), and the novelist Teresa de la Parra (Venezuela) gave talks or taught courses. Apart from its obvious cultural and intellectual benefits, this politically neutral institution provided a focus for women's pursuit of political and social reform.

In such times of chaotic instability and institutional weakness the power of pressure groups (students, the church, intellectuals) increased. Both moderate and revolutionary feminists acted as 'power brokers' among the vying political factions (Stoner 1991: 10). Female suffrage was promised throughout the 1920s but was not introduced until 1934, after the anti-Machado Revolution. The provisional constitution of that year (introduced by a revolutionary government not recognized by the United States) gave women the vote. This was ratified formally in the Constitution of 1940 under Batista. Women's emancipation was thus secured. Women voted for the first time in the federal elections of 1936 and six women were elected to the House of Representatives. In the latter half of the 1930s women's activities switched focus from female emancipation to wider social issues such as social welfare, literacy, health provision and moral regeneration. They made great advances; the Maternity Code of 1937 was 'one of the first and most progressive legal provisions for women in the Western Hemisphere' (Stoner 1991: 178) and the Equal Rights Article of the 1940 Constitution, which prohibited discrimination on the grounds of race, sex and class, stipulated full legal equality for women. Paradoxically, Fulgencio Batista proved to be women's greatest ally in matters concerning political and legal reform. By 1940 the 'feminist movement for legal change was over' (Stoner 1991: 192).

WOMEN WRITERS   In the 1920s and 1930s, when Marxist and socialist feminism was strong, several radical and socialist feminists representing the Feminine Club and some members of the University Feminist Union organized cultural and political activities. Some of them published literary works: Ofelia Domínguez Navarro (1894–1976), Ofelia Rodríguez Acosta (1902–75) and Mariblanca Sabás Alomá (1901–83) (one of only two women in the Marxist 'Minorista Group') were the most prominent. Both Domínguez Navarro and Sabás Alomá (known as the 'Red Feminist') were imprisoned in the 1930s for their political activities. Domínguez Navarro and Rodríguez Acosta were exiled to Mexico for several years, the former returning in 1937 after publishing *La vida en las prisiones cubanas* [Life in Cuban Jails] (Albella, Mexico, 1937) to found the Radical Union of Women. A number of distinguished women journalists and novelists, such as Loló de la Torriente (1906–83), Loló Soldevilla (1911–71), Lesbia Soravila (b. 1907) and Graciela Garbalosa (1896–1977) also made their mark during this decade and went on to write throughout the post-1959 period.[9] Renée Méndez Capote, co-founder of the Lyceum, was the daughter of Domingo Méndez Capote, vice-president of the Republic in the Estrada Palma administration who had resigned in 1907 disgusted by government corruption. Renée and her more radical sister Sara founded the review *Artes y Letras* in 1918 and travelled widely. Renée published several works of literature (mainly children's books) in Cuba after the Revolution. Her lively autobiography *Memorias de una cubanita que nació con el siglo* [Memories of a Cuban Girl who was Born with the Century] (1964) is of great significance for the insight it affords of a young, privileged girl's upbringing in the first decades of the century.[10]

Cultural nationalism was strong during these years, resulting in a plethora of books and creative works on Cuban and African Cuban culture and traditions (by anthropologist Fernando Ortiz, writer and academic Jorge Mañach, writer and political activist Juan Marinello, poet Nicolás

Guillén, novelist Alejo Carpentier and musician Amadeo Roldán) to which Lydia Cabrera (1900–91) contributed in the 1930s and later (Sánchez and Madrigal 1977; Castellanos and Inclán 1987; Hiriart 1978). It is perhaps ironic that the writer who inspired greatest interest in African Cuban culture and who dedicated her life to the recording and creative interpretation of a virtually unexplored African Cuban heritage should be a white woman, born into one of the most wealthy and prestigious families in the Cuban Republic. Cabrera's brother-in-law was the anthropologist Fernando Ortiz, the first Cuban to study contemporary African Cuban culture seriously. She had known him since childhood and it was he who initiated her into 'a taste for Afrocuban folklore' ('Prologue' to *Cuentos negros de Cuba* [1940] in Cabrera 1961: 9). Cabrera's father (the liberal intellectual Raimundo Cabrera) had founded the newspaper *Cuba y América* in New York and here Lydia published articles at the age of thirteen. She continued to write for the press when the family returned to Cuba from political exile in 1917. As a girl, Cabrera was in close contact with the black female servants of the household from whom she gathered much of her material; she was not given a formal education but was allowed to cultivate her interest in art and studied Fine Arts in Havana and Paris. During her stay in Paris (1927–38) she became acquainted with the 'négritude' movement and, in 1936, at the insistence of her dying friend, the Venezuelan novelist Teresa de la Parra, Cabrera finally wrote down her versions of the African Cuban stories she had heard. These *Contes nègres de Cuba* (twenty-two stories) were published in France in 1936 and in Cuba in 1940.

Cabrera's stories are creative versions of black oral traditions told to her by a series of informants. They are set in the past, in a recognizably tropical landscape (Cuba or Africa), and they usually involve a small number of clearly defined and individually named characters which may be human, animal or supernatural. The animals and divine beings are attributed with human emotions and failings; the narrations in which they feature, therefore, are fables and myths. Some stories incorporate words, refrains and songs in lucumí or congo (Cuban yoruba or bantu) so that a story becomes a bilingual text. It is this mixture of vivid realism, humour, myth and fantasy, the use of animals indigenous to Cuba, particularly the small turtle ('jicotea'), the boa ('majá') and the vulture ('aura tiñosa'), and the imaginative use of language which makes Cabrera's tales distinctive (see Chapter 6).

In 1938 Cabrera returned to Cuba and continued to record traditional African Cuban customs and beliefs. This material would be used in a succession of books, published first in Cuba and, after her departure from the island in 1960, in Miami. Clearly, the daughters of white creole families proved to be valuable instruments in the gathering and dissemination of subaltern cultures. Having said this, Menéndez (1993) mentions a small group of (possibly) black women writers: Irma Pedroso (whose novel *Sombras de pueblo negro* [Shadows of a Black People] was published some time during the 1920s or 1930s and features a black, left-wing feminist protagonist); Cristina Ayala, who published poetry during the 1920s; and Calixta Hernández and Ana Echegoyen who collaborated on the journal *Avance* in the 1920s.

In the unstable political climate of the 1920s and 1930s, the literature of the nation was increasingly critical and non-conformist. The lyricism of the first decades gave way to social protest, engaged literature and political themes. Yet, according to Roberto Fernández Retamar (1954) and Cintio Vitier (1970 [1958]), few female poets wrote social poetry. They mention two exceptions: Emma Pérez and, more importantly, Mirta Aguirre (1912–80). Aguirre joined the Communist Party in 1932 and was the most important female academic and woman of letters in post-revolutionary Cuba. Her book *Influencia de la mujer en Iberoamerica* [The Influence of Woman in Latin America] (1948) (published by the Women's Civil Defence Service) won the Iberoamerican Floral Games, but her only volume of poems during these years, *Presencia interior* [Interior Presence] was published as early as 1938. Other poems were included in Juan Ramón Jiménez's famous 1936 anthology of Cuban poetry (Jiménez et al. 1937).[11] Interestingly, Fernández Retamar refers to Aguirre's early lyrical poetry as social poetry which nevertheless attempts to reconcile 'inner poetry' ['poesía interior'] with social themes; 'this approach produces a curious poetry in which social themes develop from spiritual intimacy' (Fernández Retamar 1954: 74). He describes the poetry of both Pérez and Aguirre as 'social intimacy, if the paradox fits' (1954: 75). Clearly, this merging of the intimate with the social, the lack of a clear distinction between private and public protest, troubled traditional categories and confused Master Narrative critics.

Raimundo Lazo (1974) situates the work of a number of female poets who, he states, were not so interested in the march of history or the politics of public life, in the notable current of intimist lyrical poetry which persisted throughout the period. Their poetry is characterized, he claims, by 'intemporality' and a preference for 'love themes in multiple forms' (1974: 222). One of the more outstanding of the poets he mentions is Emilia Bernal (1885–1964) whose work shows 'personal notes of eroticism and ideological speculation' (Lazo 1974: 223).[12] However, a close study of Bernal's work discloses a very ostensible interest in public events, discussed at greater length in the next chapter. In her autobiography, *Layka Froyka* (1925b), which describes the first fifteen years of her life and her family's participation in the Wars of Independence, and in a series of lectures (*Cuestiones cubanas para América* [Cuban Questions for America]) published in Madrid in 1928, particularly the lecture entitled 'Cuban Political–Social Study' read in Coimbra, Portugal, in 1925, Bernal shows great concern for Cuban political affairs. In the latter she publicly deplores US intervention, the Platt Amendment and government corruption.

The early poetry of María Villar Buceta (1899–1977), a journalist until 1924 and then a librarian, was included in the *Florilegio* (III: 309–13), but her most famous work was the collection of avant-garde poetry, *Unanimismo* [Unanimity] (1927). Cintio Vitier mentions Villar Buceta in his anthology and Roberto Fernández Retamar includes her among the 'posmodernistas' (Fernández Retamar 1954: 9). Her younger sister, Aurora Villar Buceta (b. 1907) wrote short fiction and won a prize in a short story competition organized by the Lyceum in 1930. Villar Buceta's poetry is certainly avant-garde, but it is no less feminist (as we shall see in Chapter 2).

Several women were writing in the 1920s and 1930s but did not publish or establish themselves as authors until later. This is the case of Dulce María Loynaz (1902–97) whose extraordinarily original work (poetry, prose, novel), much of which was published during the 1950s in Spain, 'disarms criticism' (Lazo 1974: 224). Her lyrical novel, *Jardín*, which will be discussed in detail in Chapter 3, was written between 1928 and 1933 but was not published until 1951. She was better known for her poems, *Canto a la mujer estéril* [Song to a Sterile Woman] (1938), *Juegos de agua* [Water Games] (Madrid, 1947), *Poemas sin nombre* [Poems without Name] (Madrid, 1953), and *Obra lírica* [Lyrical Works] (Madrid, 1955) and *Ultimos días de una casa* [The Last Days of a House] (Madrid, 1958). Dulce María, who belongs to a distinguished literary family (her father had been a general in the Wars of Independence and her home was a meeting place for the Cuban literati of the 1930s) is now recognized by many as Cuba's greatest female author. She won the Cuban National Prize for literature in 1987 and the Spanish Cervantes Prize in 1992. Her sister Flor Loynaz (1908–85) also preferred not to publish and her poetry was not divulged until after her death.[13] Fernández Retamar includes Dulce María and María Villar Buceta in the first 'wave' ['promoción'] of this second generation of poets of the Republic, that is, poets writing in the 1920s who bridge the period between earlier avant-garde poetry and the later social poetry of the second 'wave' of the generation (Fernández Retamar 1954: 9). However, he does no more than mention their names.

Third generation of the Republic: 1940–59

The Constitution of 1940 enshrined undeniable legal and social reform. During the following fifteen years, however, government corruption, US involvement in Cuban affairs and violence all escalated to fever pitch under the governance of a series of stooge presidents manipulated by Batista. In short, the liberal-democratic Republic failed. These were decades of intensified political, economic, and cultural 'denationalization' (Kapcia 1982: 64) and class division. While wide sectors of the population suffered appalling poverty the Cuban bourgeoisie, modernized, materialistic, philistine and consumerist, mimicked the much admired 'American way of life'.

Racism was rampant. From the end of the 1940s Havana, the 'brothel of the Caribbean', was submerged in gambling and gangsterism; Al Capone and other mafiosi set themselves up in the Hotel Nacional. As O'Connor writes in 1970:

> Coca-Cola, baseball, Standard Oil, American tourists, abstract-expressionist painting, United Fruit and Madison Avenue advertising techniques seemed to have submerged the once powerful social and political force of Cuban nationalism [...] During the six decades following political independence from Spain, Cuba imported not only investments, consumer commodities, food, technology, and business methods from the United States, but also much of its culture including many of the ideas that Cuba held about itself. (quoted in Kapcia 1982: 68)

In response, Cuban intellectuals became increasingly introspective. In 1944 the Communist Party changed its name to the Partido Socialista Popular. The students, under the guidance of Chibás's Cuban People's (Orthodox) Party and the ideas of José Martí, mounted attacks on the establishment demanding economic independence and social reform, but in 1951 Chibás shot himself while broadcasting a radio lecture so the whole country could hear. In 1952, on the fiftieth anniversary of the founding of the Republic, Batista effected a military coup thus ending a decade of social confusion but relative political stability. In 1953 Fidel Castro launched the assault on the Moncada barracks and thus began the activities of the 26th July Movement and the revolutionary war, culminating in the Revolution of 1959. Student organizations went underground and the university, the main target of repression during the mid-1950s, was closed down between 1956 and 1959.

There is no doubt that by the 1950s white, middle-class, educated Cuban women had made great advances and were clearly recognized as social and political subjects. By 1953 women made up 13 per cent of the workforce, half of them held white-collar jobs (teachers, clerks, public employees) (Smith and Padula 1996: 20). Unlike US feminists, however, the Cuban feminists were not overtly critical of patriarchy but rather celebrated motherhood, children and family life. According to Stoner (1991: 193), working alongside progressive men they had created a new form of governance, 'state familialism', which was to cross the watershed of the Revolution. Feminists never lost sight of a wider national consciousness and their relationships with US feminists were decidedly ambivalent. Stoner sums up the crucial difference thus:

> An equal rights constitutional provision declared all Cuba citizens to be equal, but the conception of equality was Ana Betancourt's and José Martí's, not Susan B. Anthony's or Thomas Jefferson's. Cuban society still rested on Hispanic corporate models in which social groups, not individuals, held power [...] Blacks and women demanded rights. But they struggled as members of groups, not as

isolated individuals. Women made up the group of women-mothers. As group members, they derived the same rights as members of any other social group [...] but as mothers they required special provisions. Thus, Cubans viewed women in two dimensions; they were at once equal with and distinct from men. (Stoner 1991: 192)

It was against this background that the Lyceum (and Lawn Tennis Club after 1949) continued its laudable work providing a cultural haven for women. Politically, it professed to strict neutrality. It supported the United States and the Allies in the Second World War (1941–43) while inviting leading Cuban and foreign writers and intellectuals such as José Antonio Portuondo (1941–43), Camila Henríquez Ureña (1939–40), Pablo Neruda (1942), Dora Alonso (1949), Mirta Aguirre (1950), María Zambrano (1952) and Fina García Marruz (1952) to speak or teach courses. It arranged a series of conferences such as 'The Letter as a Feminine Literary Form of Expression' in July 1950, and discussions, for example, of Simone de Beauvoir's *The Second Sex* (1950). By 1943 the Lyceum had over 6,000 pupils registered for its classes and expanded the public library (over 10,000 volumes for adults and 5,000 for children) and borrowing service. There were a further two dozen women's associations, most of them set up around the time of the First World War or in the mid-1930s.

Wealthy women owned or directed several newspapers; Esther Hernández owned *Avance* and Josefina Mosquera edited *Vanidades* although its content was hardly feminist (Smith and Padula 1996: 20). One of the most impressive women's magazines of the period was the bi-monthly *Mujeres cubanas* [Cuban Women], subtitled 'For peace, for life', the organ of the Democratic Federation of Cuban Women, edited by Edith García Buchaga, and running between 1950 and at least 1955. This magazine is a clear example of the multiple discourses informing women's oppositional politics, even after Batista's coup in 1952. Steering a path between the bourgeois status quo, socialist, and nationalist politics, it attempted to confirm traditional concepts of woman, motherhood and the home while at the same time informing its readers of global events with the clear purpose of fomenting socialist, feminist political awareness. The result is an almost schizophrenic mixture of the equivalent of the *Socialist Worker* and *Woman's Own*. While the cover of each issue featured rosy-cheeked children and smartly-dressed women, and at least half of the spreads were given over to fashion, cookery, household tips, child care, hobbies and children's sections and short stories, the magazine might also include articles on topics such as poverty in post-Civil War Spain, Rosa Luxemburg, a Russian woman doctor, oppressed peasant women in Mexico and the asylum provided in Romania for Korean children, as well as diatribes against the imperialist politics of Great Britain and the United States. A regular feature was the 'Martí Corner', where apposite thoughts of the 'Apostle', usually to do with the family and the role of the mother in nation-building, were brought to the reader's attention. The November–December 1953 issue features national icon Mariana Grajales, the mother of mulatto Independence fighter Antonio Maceo, and various 'Greetings' from women across the world (China, USSR, Romania, India) to the women of Cuba, as well as pieces on how to tie bows on Christmas presents, a story by Bennet Arnold (sic), and what to do with a stuffed pig. Of particular interest in the June 1951 issue are the denunciation of Pilar Primo de Rivera's fascist women's organization in Spain and the vicious invective against Dulce María Loynaz for attending its congress as the self-appointed Cuban delegate. In the same issue, Loynaz (elected to the Academia de Artes y Letras) is said to be in 'full decline' and her latest work (*Jardín*) 'aesthetically retrogressive' (pp. 2, 4). Mirta Aguirre was a regular contributor to the magazine which also featured a special article, with a photograph, on the young Rafaela Chacón Nardi. On the first page of that issue a short paragraph reads: 'Because you now have the right to vote they tell you you're equal to men. This isn't true […] There are still many inequalities to erase and the FDMC will fight with you to make sure equality is really put in practice.'

The many achievements of the feminists, then, were limited. They were always a significant minority, counting no more than 950 at the peak of their activity in 1932 (Stoner 1991: 208) and few working-class women were among their ranks. Although working-class women experienced improvements in domestic and working conditions and participated in political activities in the workplace, they did not take an active part in bringing about gender-specific reforms. The feminists were comfortably well-off, educated at least to university level, many were professionals, and over half of the leaders remained single. Class differences were only reinforced. Similarly, black women were not a part of the early feminist movement. The Third National Women's Congress of 1939 was the first to include a 'black' section, while the well-meaning collaborating white feminists only partially understood the full implications of racial discrimination.

This is demonstrated in the acrimonious polemic between the radical white feminist Mariblanca Sabás Alomá and the mulatto socialist Angel César Pinto Albiol regarding the participation of black women in the Third National Women's Congress.[14] This extraordinary document (published by Pinto Albiol) consists of an article, 'Black Women in the Women's Congress', published in the *Pueblo* newspaper by Sabás Alomá in April 1939; Pinto Albiol's response; her reply; and his second response, which was rejected by *Pueblo* and published in *Hoy* instead. The gist of the debate is this: Pinto Albiol believes that Sabás Alomá is racist and has no right to speak on behalf of black women or blacks; Sabás Alomá believes that, as a woman, she has every right to express her feelings of solidarity with black women. Pinto Albiol takes Sabás Alomá to task on what may appear to be minor issues, such as her use of the term 'mestizo' instead of 'mulatto' and the fact that she states white women have no specific feminist demands when she should have written that white women have no specific feminist demands in so far as they are white. However, Sabás Alomá does seem to be of the opinion (although she rejects this interpretation in her response) that miscegenation is bad and that the mulatto population is somehow an impoverished version of the 'pure' black race. She strongly criticizes Cuban society which condones sexual relations between white men and black women, but not sexual relations between white women and black men which were taboo. She is critical of white men who thus enjoy sexual relations with both white and black women, but are not so keen to legitimize their relationships or their children with the latter, and black women for preferring relationships with white men. She insists that black women are victims of racist whites and racist (by which she means masculinist, selfish, uncaring) black men, and laments the fact that the 'pure' black race is therefore weakened ('empobrecimiento') by the white man.

Albiol, not unjustifiably, believes she is implicitly condoning evolutionist, racist theories. More importantly, he disputes her clearly uninformed statement that Cuba has always consisted of a majority of 'pure' whites and a minority of 'pure' blacks who lived together in peace. Cuba, he argues, quoting figures from the 1822 and 1882 population censuses, is not only perceived by foreigners as a mulatto society but in the nineteenth century the black population far outnumbered the so-called whites ('from Andalusia'). Moreover, the two populations hardly lived together happily: the blacks were the violently oppressed slaves of the whites. The history of Cuba, he states, is one of a majority of black slaves working for a minority of white slave-owners. He is also furious at Sabás Alomá's remarks about black women preferring white men to black men on the supposition that the former are racially superior. What about all the black and mulatto marriages, he asks? Sabás Alomá does not reply. Black women themselves, of course, are not given a voice in this debate which confirms their double marginalization. But the fact that even an informed, radical feminist such as Sabás Alomá should endorse, albeit unwittingly, a racist, classist ideology in this way indicates how far attitudes would have to change in Cuba if discrimination were ever to be attenuated.

WOMEN WRITERS It is not surprising that women writers of the 1940s and 1950s were white and middle class. The process of publishing books in Cuba at the time was yet another obstacle to black or working-class women who not only lacked education, incentive, time and space but, crucially, money.[15] Only after the Revolution would they be given the opportunity to publish more readily. One book where black women's voices are heard clearly is Lydia Cabrera's El Monte [The Mountain] (1954). Cabrera's greatest contributions to Cuban culture and anthropological scholarship were the two monographs she published in this period – *El Monte* (1954) and *La sociedad secreta Abakuá* [The Secret Society Abakua] (1959) – and the linguistic study *Anagó. Vocabulario lucumí* [Anago. Lucumi Vocabulary] (1957). These works incorporate the discourses of fiction, song, autobiography, ethnography, linguistics and 'testimonio'. *El Monte*, read as testimony, is a remarkable book because it is here that the lost voices of the black Cuban women of the first half of the century are recorded. One of the most poignant stories in the book is an account of how Teresa M. Omí Tomí lost her baby daughter because of black magic. Omí Tomí, daughter of a slave from Dahomey and over a hundred years old when Cabrera wrote the book, had been the Cabrera family's seamstress. Before she joined their household she had been brought up among white children and had little knowledge of black religions; consequently, she was unable to protect her child from evil. What she subsequently learned was passed on to Cabrera. In the prologue to the book, signed April 1954, Cabrera states categorically that the black people she interviewed, including Omí Tomí, are 'the real authors' (Cabrera 1986: 10). Among them are various women whose words (opinions, memories, knowledge, stories) are presented as direct speech without the mediation of the narrator. They are Calixta Morales or Oddeddei, Francisquilla Ibañez and her two daughters Petrona and Dolores, the old 'conga' Mariate, the hundred-year-old Anón and Enriqueta Herrera.

Cabrera's work served as inspiration for poets such as the teacher Pura del Prado (b. 1932), who published 'black poetry' ['poesía negra'] in the 1950s. Her poem 'Abuele' is dedicated to 'Leonor, the sweet black washerwoman'. Other similar poets are Ana González ('The negro's black ballad') and Ana Rosa Núñez (b. 1926) ('Drops of ebony'). Like Cabrera, all these women left Cuba after the Revolution (Ruíz del Vizo 1972).[16]

Generally speaking, Cuban literature published in the 1940s and 1950s was pessimistic, escapist and often esoteric. Lyrical poetry (in verse and prose) and the short story were the preferred genres. These were the decades of the 'Orígenes' (1944–56) group, discussed in Chapter 4, and its ultra-aestheticism. Fernández Retamar refers to this poetry as 'transcendental' but not totally escapist; 'instead of avoiding circumstances, it faces them, transcending them, to reach more secret, inner truths' (Fernández Retamar 1954: 118–19). Guillermo Rodríguez Rivera suggests that poetry compensated for a disappointing historical reality: 'Art as the fulfilment of a national culture, which cannot be attained in history' (quoted in Arcos 1990a: 29). Art enabled the transcendence of the chaotic and disagreeable society. Cintio Vitier divides the 'Orígenes' group itself into two further groups: the earlier and most uncompromisingly impersonal is that of José Lezama Lima; the poetry of the second is characterized by intimist themes and a reaching out to everyday reality. Here Vitier includes himself and his wife Fina García Marruz (b. 1923) (Vitier 1970: 501). According to

Vitier, her poetry comprises three themes: personal experiences and memories, Catholicism, and Cuba. Fernández Retamar refers to the 'delicate tenderness, that keeps a soft feminine feeling in her poems'(1954: 115). However, as with Mirta Aguirre, critics betray a preoccupation with García Marruz's poetry, which does not fit into their neat categories, because it is both intimist and social, personal and collective. García Marruz's first collection, *Poemas*, was published in 1942, and her outstanding collection *Las miradas perdidas* [The Lost Gazes] in 1951 (written from 1944 onwards) and she continued to publish in the 1990s.

Younger women poets started publishing in the 1940s and 1950s and continued to write throughout the twentieth century. Three of the most important are Carilda Oliver Labra (b. 1923), who has lived in Matanzas all her life, whose first poems appeared in the 1940s and who won the National Prize for Poetry in 1950, Cleva Solís (1926–97) (a close friend of the Vitiers' and loosely associated with the 'Orígenes' group) who published her first book of poetry, *Vigilia*, in 1956, and the mulatta poet Rafaela Chacón Nardi (b. 1926), who won a Lyceum scholarship in 1950 to study the school system in Mexico and became one of Cuba's most outstanding educationalists. Her *Viaje al sueño* [Journey to Dream] (1948) is of particular interest because it makes no reference to an African Caribbean tradition but suggests an obsession with the colour white. There are poems about the white carnation, the white butterfly, white clouds, white handkerchiefs, the white lily, the white page. Love is a 'rose without colour'; her mother 'a flower of white petals'; Cuba, an island 'small and white'; and the stars, white flowers in the sky. These sonnets – written with great delicacy and flair – draw on the tradition of the French Parnassians and Symbolists who also delighted in the symbolical connotations of the colour white. It would be of interest to read Chacón's early poetry in the light of Frantz Fanon's ideas on the cultural and psychological alienation of black and mulatto writers in a racist society.

Literature written specifically for children became increasingly important as the educational needs of future generations became more apparent and the state assumed this responsibility. José Martí himself had always stressed the role of education in achieving national prosperity and had written various story books for children. Haydée Arteaga, a member of the PSP and of the organizing committee of the 'First Convention of Women of the City of Havana for the Security and Happiness of Women', 1955, had founded the 'Day of the Child' in 1936 and organized a series of 'cultural talks for children', open to children of all skin colours, during the 1950s.[17]

The first woman to establish herself as a novelist and short story writer rather than a poet was the journalist Dora Alonso (b. 1910) who, like the three poets mentioned above, continued to publish extensively throughout the post-1959 period and whose work will be discussed in detail in Chapter 6. She was brought up on her father's large country estate and her novels of the creole realist genre are set in the Cuban countryside. Other journalists and writers of short stories of the immediate pre-Revolutionary period were: Ana María Simó (b. 1943), who moved to Paris in the late 1960s,[18] Anita Arroyo, and Hilda Perera Soto. Continuing in the tradition of Mirta Aguirre, essayist and university academic Camila Henríquez Ureña (b. 1894, Santo Domingo, Dominican Republic, d. 1973), the sister of the more internationally renowned Max and Pedro, returned to Cuba in 1960 after several years of exile in the United States.[19] Her lectures on 'Feminism' and 'Women and Culture' were delivered in 1939 in the Hispano-Cuban Cultural Institute and the Lyceum respectively and throughout the 1930s and 1940s she published studies of women's writing.[20] It was she who co-edited with Juan Ramón Jiménez *La poesía cubana en 1936* (1937). Henríquez Ureña went on to become one of the most inspiring professors at Havana University in the post-1959 period.

Given the increasing importance of the urban, middle-class consumer society seeking entertainment, it is not surprising that several women playwrights should make their names in the 1940s and 1950s. María Alvarez de los Ríos (b. 1919) staged many popular comedies.[21] Nora Badia (b. 1921), a secretary by profession, became famous for her drama *La alondra* [The Lark] (1947) and the one-act monologue, *Mañana es una palabra* [Tomorrow is a Word] (1947) in which a woman, who thinks her husband no longer loves her, justifies her infidelity to him at length only to discover at the end of the play that she has been speaking to a dead body: he has committed suicide. Like Badia, Gloria Díaz Parrado (*Un día de agencia* [Day of Agency], 1957) and Flora Díaz Parrado (*El velorio de Pura* [Pura's Party], 1941) went on to stage plays after the Revolution. Isabel Fernández de Amado and Cuquii Ponce jointly authored comedies such as *El que dirán* [What Will They Say] (1944), and *Lo que no se dice* [What Can't be Said] (1945). Poet, journalist and teacher Renée Potts (b. 1908), the most prolific of the women dramatists at this time, staged dozens of plays between the 1930s and the 1960s. She is best known for *Habrá guerra mañana* [There Will be War Tomorrow] (1935), *Cocoa en el Paraíso* [Cocoa in Paradise] (1951), and *Domingo de Quasimodo* [Quasimodo Sunday] (1952). *Imagíname infinita* [Imagine Me Infinite] is set on a passenger liner where professional and middle-class women, pulled between their professionalism, home-life and love, face the contradictions in their lives.[22] Dora Alonso and Dysis Guira published plays in the early 1950s. María Julia Casanova and Olga Blank wrote the librettos and music respectively for several musical comedies, such as *Cuento de Navidad* [Christmas Tale] (1954). These works are often drawing-room dramas or comedies tailored to the tastes of the conventional middle classes; sometimes they are merely escapist, but they deserve to be studied no less (see Allen [1987]; Herdeck [1979]; and González Freire [1961]).

Women writers on the neo-colonial cultural map

A number of points can be made in the light of this brief survey. Apart from one notable exception (Rafaela Chacón Nardi) virtually all the women writers mentioned above are white. They were all middle class, educated and often wealthy. Several were journalists or teachers; most preferred to write poetry or lyrical prose rather than narrative. Their political and feminist persuasions varied from the conservative (Lydia Cabrera, Dulce María Loynaz) to the radical (Mariblanca Sabás Alomá, Mirta Aguirre). Their life trajectories and works vary enormously but often point up the contradictions of their class: the bourgeoisie. They helped pioneer the almost frenetic search for collective and national identity in the face of US encroachment, but on the basis of traditional family icons and gender roles while enjoying the wealth and privileges capitalist consumer society provided. Their social politics were frustrated either by inner contradictions, the traditional oligarchy or foreign capital. Above all, they shared their class's sense of neo-colonial inferiority and impotence but were often unable to make the break with the developed North.

After the 1959 Revolution the majority of these writers remained in Cuba; many did not (Emilia Bernal, Lydia Cabrera, Ana Maria Simó, Hilda Perera Soto, Teté Casuso and Rita Geada all left).[23] Those who stayed were sometimes alienated (Dulce María Loynaz became a recluse). Others (particularly the socialist feminists) were almost totally ignored. Only a handful continued to write and to carve out a place for themselves in the literary establishment of the 1960s and these tended to be among the youngest generation. The Revolution was a young Revolution and women writers and intellectuals of the past were overlooked in the enthusiasm to construct something new. Mirta Aguirre, the intellectual spearhead of the 1940s and 1950s, and Camila Henríquez Ureña continued in their university posts profoundly influencing younger generations of women.

At the risk of exaggerating, I would say that during the first fifty years of this century women's writing flourished in Cuba on an unprecedented scale. Anthologists of poetry, such as Félix Lizaso, José Antonio Fernández de Castro and Juan Ramón Jiménez, made a point of including women poets. No anthology of women's work comparable to González Curquejo's three volumes has been published since 1919. Yet, for multiple reasons, the literary works of all these writers have received relatively little critical commentary. What becomes apparent after reading through histories of Cuban literature and introductions to anthologies is that (male) critics insist on applying generational schema to these women and are worried when these classifications do not easily apply. The grouping of authors and their works into 'generaciones' and 'promociones' is guided by historical developments and events in public life which, as I have suggested, are not always entirely appropriate to women writers.[24] Having said that, the social protest writings of the women of the 1920s and 1930s did form part of a generational push for change. Whatever the political persuasion of the authors, common themes recur repeatedly in their creative literature: the home, the house, the family (mother and children), love, sex, friends and neighbours, travel, urban and rural landscape, Cuba (in other words, everyday life) – and these themes remain constant despite social and political ideologies and change. Of the ten characteristics listed by Cintio Vitier which indicate 'Cubanness' in poetry, one in particular might apply to these women writers: 'endearment', that is, criollo life and 'the shaded, sheltered family circle' (Vitier 1970: 573). But women writers perceived motherhood and the family not just as a site of protection but also as a site of political resistance, moral integrity, and future improvement for the nation. Their poems about love and sexual relations are often extremely subversive, irrespective of whether they considered themselves feminist or not. In other words, for women authors the distinction between social and intimist writing does not hold. Perhaps there is nothing new in this observation. What is new is a refusal on the part of the critic to trivialize or ignore this thematics, to dump women's works in boxes labelled 'delicacy', 'sensitivity' and 'feminine concerns', an attitude possibly even more entrenched after the Revolution.[25] Instead, their writings should be considered exceptionally important not only from the point of view of nation-building and social cohesion but also from the perspective of the inscription of a profoundly humanist and gender-specific 'inner life' (Fernández Retamar 1954: 75) informing an often contentious discourse. This will be the subject of the next chapter.

Notes

1. *Mes douze premières années* (Paris, 1831). This is possibly the first account of childhood memories in Spanish American literature. See Molloy 1991: 85–96.

2. For a good English translation of *Sab* and Avellaneda's epistolary auto-biography, see Gómez de Avellaneda (1993). Also Harter (1981) and Kirkpatrick (1989) for an appreciation of Avellaneda's poetry.

3. For more details of these and other nineteenth-century women poets see the introduction to Randall (1982).

4. In 1907 there were 6,388 women in white-collar jobs and in 1919, 11,079 (3,800 teachers in 1907 and 5,000 in 1919). The number of women in blue-collar jobs decreased from 41,205 in 1907 to 34,253 in 1919 (there were 24,016 laundresses in 1907 and only 8,680 in 1919). The great majority of working women were laundresses, seamstresses and agricultural workers. The greatest area of female employment throughout the period was domestic service: there were over 23,000 domestic servants in 1907 and over 39,000 in 1939 (Stoner 1991: 197). Many women worked in the tobacco industry. By the 1950s, 90 per cent of stemmers were women, nearly half of them black (Smith and Padula 1996: 12).

5. Elena Mederos (b. 1900) was a pharmacist. She became Minister of Health and Welfare in Fidel Castro's first cabinet (Smith and Padula 1996: 17).

6. Seventy-one organizations registered in the 1925 Congress, many were Catholic and conservative. The delegates did not pass Ofelia Domínguez Navarro's resolution on equal rights for illegitimate children (23 per cent of the total population was illegitimate in 1919). As a consequence she, Dulce María Borrero, Mariblanca Sabás Alomá, Ofelia Rodríguez Acosta and other feminists walked out of the Congress. The argument led to a serious split between conservative and radical feminists who did not reconcile their differences until after 1940 (Stoner 1991: 65–70).

7. María Collado had begun her feminist career as a member of the Club Femenino in 1920 when she was the club's director of publicity. She was vice-president of the National Suffragist Party in 1924 and then broke with this in 1925 to form her own Democratic Suffragist Party. *La Mujer* ran until 1942.

8. In 1949 the Lyceum, founded in 1929, merged with the Lawn Tennis Club, founded in 1913. An earlier Lyceum had been established in 1844.

9. Lesbia Soravila, a feminist, published *El dolor de vivir* [The Pain of Living] (1932) and *Cuando libertan las esclavas* [When They Free the Slave Women] (1935). The latter, according to Menéndez (1993: 58–66) is about a young unmarried woman, a left-wing activist under Machado's dictatorship. Menéndez cites five novels written by Garbalosa published between 1922 and 1941.

10. See Barnet (1963) and Oliver (1964).

11. Aguirre was a Golden Age specialist and published works on Cervantes and Sor Juana Inés de la Cruz as well as numerous studies on children's literature. See *Juegos y otros poemas* [Games and other Poems] (1974) and *Canción antigua a Che Guevara* [Old Song to Che Guevara] (1970). Fernández Retamar (1954: 79) includes her among both the social poets and the neo-romantics. Her collection of poetry *Ayer de hoy* was published in 1980.

12. See *Homenaje* [Today's Yesterday] (1986) for secondary bibliographies. Her poems are also in the Carbonell anthology (1928) and the Lizaso anthology (1926).

13. Flor Loynaz refused to contribute to Juan Ramón Jiménez's anthology of 1937. She was Federico García Lorca's closest friend during the poet's visit to Havana in 1930 and she took an active role in the struggle against Machado. She married in 1936, later divorced, and lived her last years in almost total isolation near Havana.

14. Reel 2 of the Stoner Collection. I surmise, perhaps incorrectly, from the import of Pinto Albiol's remarks that he is mulatto and of socialist persuasion.

15. Before the 1959 Revolution there were no publishers in Cuba, only printers. About a quarter of the 5 million Cubans of 1959 were illiterate. The majority of them were working-class and coloured women.

16. These poems were brought to my attention by Miguel Arnedo.

17. See 'Simplemente Haydée: la maravilla de la poesía', *Mujeres*, June 1987: 6–7.

18. Simó trained and worked as a journalist after the Revolution and published *Las fábulas* in 1962.

19. Camila Henríquez Ureña was born in the Dominican Republic, came to Cuba in 1904 and took Cuban nationality in 1926. A Doctor of Philosophy and Letters and Pedagogy at Havana University, she studied in the USA and Paris, was appointed Professor of Spanish Literature and Language at Vassar College and Havana University, and became Emeritus Professor of the latter in 1970. She was imprisoned by Batista in 1935 and exiled between 1945 and 1960 in the USA.

20. Collected in Henríquez Ureña (1985) and *Casa de las Américas*, Vol. 11, nos

65–66, May–June 1971; Vol. 14, no. 84, May–June 1974; Vol. 14, no. 88, February 1975.

21. Including *El maridito de Beba Fraga* [The Husband of Beba Fraga] (1948); *No quiero llamarme Juana* [I Don't Want My Name to be Juana] (1948); *Martí 9* [Marti 9] (1949); *Según el color* [Depends on the Colour] (1955); and *La víctima* [The Victim] (1959).

22. See (1962) *Teatro cubano. Teatro contemporáneo*, Aguilar, Madrid: 253–300. Renée Potts also published a book of poetry, *El Romancero de la Maestra* [Ballads of a Teacher] which won the Lyceum Prize in 1936, and two prize-winning collections of stories in the early 1950s – *La ventana y el puente* [The Window and the Bridge] (1953) and *Camino de herradura* [Horseshoe Road] (1955) – as well as writing screenplays for television.

23. Teté Casuso sheltered arms for Fidel Castro in her flat in Mexico in 1955. Her 1944 novel is about Cuban women in exile in New York under Machado (Menéndez 1993: 87). She published *Cuba and Castro* in New York, 1961.

24. See Lazo (1973) and Portuondo (1981). For Lazo, a new generation appears every fifteen years and for Portuondo every thirty years.

25. Note the following comment by Eduardo López Morales, who wrote the prologue to Suardíaz and Chericián (1984) in which he refers to male poets only: 'these investigations [into human existence] should not pertain exclusively to the unconscious and should not be expressed in purely "lyrical" poems, even if these (as might be the case of Rafaela Chacón Nardi, Carilda Oliver Labra or Cleva Solís) have an existentialist content' (Suardíaz and Chericián 1984: 39).

CHAPTER 2

Mother Nation: Female Subjectivity and National Identity in Cuba, 1900–35

Women and Cuban nationalism

The aim of this chapter is to enlarge the scale of the Cuban cultural map and study in more detail the work of women writers publishing during the first thirty-five years of nation-building leading up to women's emancipation in 1934. I will argue that women's writing during these years is predominantly oppositional, inscribing a plurality of discourses which contest the ideological and cultural hegemony of the governing elites with a view to changing civil society. Apart from the political speech and the manifesto, women voiced their discontent in other genres and less obviously political and feminist texts: the literary essay, the novel and lyric poetry. Poetry is possibly the most oppositional discourse of all in that it may inscribe sexual difference through a radically different feminine view of time, space and subjectivity, and thus offer a glimpse of other conceptualizations of historical time.

LIBERAL FEMINISM The following words, mentioned in Chapter 1, were read by Pilar Morlón de Menéndez (president of the National Federation of Feminine Associations) in her speech entitled 'Nationalism' which opened the first Cuban National Women's Congress held in Havana on 1 April 1923:

> In the year 1923, Resurrection day, the women of Cuba met to declare the Homeland was in danger and they agreed to save it. [...] We give the name of Nationalism to our action. It will be motto of the pure, good, true patriots. (FNAF 1923: 33–4)

Her words are important because they illustrate what I shall refer to as 'national feminism': feminist demands inscribed in terms of a nationalist agenda. The first four decades were years of frustration and failure for the young Republic which could not shake off the colonial legacy. Cuba was a nation in formation and women expected to participate in the nation-building project. The warrior-mother was a forceful icon symbolizing the struggle for social justice. All demands for women's rights were perceived as nationalist (Stoner 1991: 1–8). As P. Chaterjee points out with reference to India, women's emancipation is 'constrained to take on a nationalist expression as a prerequisite for being considered political' (Radhakrishnan 1996: 186). In Chapter 1, a liberal feminist movement consisting of white middle-class women was shown to be actively engaged with the politicians with the hope of prioritizing women's rights but after 1923, when the frustrated push for change led to increasing political polarization, many of them took up more revolutionary positions preferring to pursue socialist and anarchist as well as feminist objectives.

Early feminists like the moderate Pilar Morlón positioned themselves as advocates of social improvement. The social ills Morlón denounced in 1923 were: lack of national independence, corruption in public administration, selling off of state institutions such as orphanages, drug-trafficking and child murders. In other words: 'The social machine is not working properly [...] There is a desire for cleanliness, justice and honesty' (FNAF 1923: 33). National regeneration depended on the nation's mothers who personified virtue and wisdom: 'Does not motherhood give us the right to be on guard for the material and moral good of our children?' (p. 30). In March 1918 the women's magazine *Aspiraciones* (Vol. VI, no. 2) published a manifesto explaining its objectives. It aimed to rid Cuba of corruption and bribery so that mothers would no longer have to watch their children suffer.

In 1914 Luz Rubio, representing the Feminist Party, published an important booklet entitled *Consideraciones sobre feminismo* [Considerations on Feminism] dedicated to the wife of President Menocal. The gist of Rubio's argument was that a vanguard, led by the 'apostle' (José Martí) had fought for and achieved national independence, 'holy freedom' (Rubio 1914: 1) which had benefited everyone except Cuban women. Women remained subject to Spanish colonial legislation; half the population still experienced colonial rule. In this respect, the Civil Code made (white) women slaves: 'She has to be subjected, she has to be watched, her hands and feet have to be tied up. She cannot be free, she has to be a slave' (Rubio 1914: 35). The nationalist project was incomplete. Rubio advocated freedom through struggle. Women had to educate themselves to deserve emancipation and should not follow the model of the English suffragettes who wanted to master men, 'that cannot and should not be right' (p. 15), because women were biologically weaker. So why was emancipation important in Cuba? Because woman:

> represents the base, the unchanging foundation of everything that man creates. She is the starting point of all his generous efforts and the horizon of his most noble aspirations [...] She is, graphically speaking, the brain, the inspirer; man is the irreplaceable activator, the arm which carries things through. (p. 16)

In other words, men are active and women passive, but if men are the mere arm of the body politic, women are the brains. Without women, men's actions are morally unsound. Thus feminists cleverly appropriated the will and intelligence for good actions and claimed irresponsibility for the bad (such as war): 'If our brothers, because of ambition and hatefulness, have not been able to come to an agreement that would benefit the Cuban homeland [...] then we should give them an example of our capabilities and patriotism' (p. 44).

The kind of demands Rubio sets out are to do with the reform of the Civil Code; sixth on her list of seven was female suffrage. But she was most incensed by women being kept out of the workforce by men who usurped women's jobs, for example, sales assistant in women's wear:

> we often see extremely robust men dispatching hats, corsets, ribbons, for the sale of which, when it is not to the liking of the lady customer, they make use of an 'amorous dictionary', besieging their customer with compliments which are always tasteless and in bad form; they would be better occupied in other kinds of work more suited to their strapping physiques. (Rubio 1914: 32)

In 'Female Suffrage', a paper read out in the First National Women's Congress, Aida Pérez de Villaurrutia, representing the National Suffrage Party, blames the shortcomings of the Cuban 1901 Constitution on the fact that it was based on the US Constitution, which denied women the vote. Nevertheless, she points out, Cuban legislators ought not to look to a caste-ridden Europe for models. Cuba had to create something unique and new (FNAF 1923: 351). In a later article enitled 'Yara's call' [the call for independence] published in *La Mujer* (10 October 1929), she compares a feminized Cuba with Cuban women: 'The pretty little island', she writes, 'emerged beautifully with so much charm' from the Wars of Independence but, unlike the fortunate island, Cuban women 'are still left behind'. They have not been emancipated; to give women the vote would be 'a gesture of great patriotism'. Another angle was taken by Amelia de Vera de Lens of the National Feminist Association in a radio broadcast in 1930, 'In favour of Cuban women'. If, she asks, women in the USA and Germany can vote and even stand as MPs and Cuban woman cannot, does this mean that Cuban women are inferior? She reminds her audience of the patriotism of Cuban women by invoking the mythical figure Mariana Grajales, the mother of mulatto independence fighter Antonio Maceo. To give women the vote would be a gesture of strength, goodness and beauty (de Vera de Lens 1930: 4, 7).

The above are examples of explicitly white, middle-class, feminist political discourse, the feminist version of Cuban populist nationalism or 'Cubanismo'. As Antoni Kapcia (1982: 63) has argued persuasively, Cubanism is the strongest and most pervasive oppositional force in twentieth-century Cuba; it encompasses both 'a political search for ideology, articulation and identity that preceded and followed 1959; and a literary search for an individual and collective identity'. The language and ideas of the hegemonic elite in the first decades of the Cuban Republic were neo-colonialist in character, promoting collaboration with and dependency on an expanding foreign power (the United States) and the ethos this sub-sumes: secularism, amoralism, modernization, social inequality, violence and uneven capitalist growth. Cubanism survived throughout the period as a liberating counter-discourse proposing resistance, decolonization and the construction of an autonomous national and cultural identity. It made possible the short-lived Revolution of 1933–34 and the withdrawal of the Platt Amendment that same year (Thomas 1971: 453–5). Cubanism is primarily an ethics. Like all nationalist doctrine it has its roots in Kant's concept of the moral struggle for self-determination being in itself the supreme virtue: 'the good will, which is the free will, is also the autonomous will' (Kedourie 1951: 24). Thus Cubanism (as is clear in the work of José Martí) signifies the struggle to create a collective consciousness based on national sovereignty (self-determination), collective rights (justice), probity and integrity (virtue); it is secular moral regeneration.

Women's feminist writing (the writings of middle-class women claiming their rightful position as social and political subjects) is also a counter-discourse. Because women's rights were not recognized by the governing elites, feminist discourse was inserted by women into the nationalist project at least until 1934, when women's suffrage was finally introduced. National-ism is a gendered and an eroticized discourse in which the family, kinship and affection are symbols of the nation as a natural division of human society. Herder wrote: 'the savage who loves himself, his wife and child with quiet joy [...] is a more real being than that cultivated shadow [...] the idle cosmopolite' (Kedourie 1951: 57). Müller argued at the beginning of the nineteenth century: 'if we separate private from public life, even at only one point, then we can no longer see the state as [...] an idea' (Kedourie 1951: 39). In other words, the distinction between private and the public is blurred when relations between citizens are conceived as relations between heterosexual partners and members of a family. What feminist writers did was to 'feminize' Cuban nationalist ideology by appropriating nationalist symbols of purity and integrity, such as the mother and the home, as the prerogative of women. Throughout this period the extrapolation of such values to the nation as a whole formed the basis of a women's politics of resistance as decribed by Sara Ruddick: women are the participants, 'they explicitly invoke their culture's symbols of femininity and their purpose is to resist certain practices or policies of their governors' (Ruddick 1989: 222). Women writers represented them-selves as the natural, organically home-grown, resistance to injustice. They contested what was perceived as an exploitative, artificial, imported culture, and set themselves up as the agents of future redemption. Thus woman came to signify the pure and ahistorical signifier of 'interiority', the inner sanctum of national identity (Radhakrishnan 1996: 189–92).

Cubanism may well be a counter-discourse in the context of political theory (it posits autonomy rather than dependency), but it does not challenge nationalist theories as configurations of masculinity, what Francine Masiello calls the 'national masculine imagination' (Masiello 1992: 2; di Stefano 1991: 60). The nationalist–feminist discourse of these years, although articulated from a woman's view, generally confirms and strengthens many traditional myths about women, thus reinforcing patriarchal attitudes. The symbolic Great Mother, for example, is susceptible to ambivalent interpretations and manipulations of right- and left-wing tendencies. The family can be figured as both the site of the reproduction of the system and resistance to it. In the words of Iris Zavala, the paradox faced by modernist women writers was that 'they sought as individuals to oppose autonomously the authoritarianism of the social order, but the only way in which this was done was through the internalization of patriarchal authority' (Zavala 1992: 188). Also, there is an ambivalence in Cuban women's perception of modernity and capitalist growth. Inasmuch as it is foreign and artificial, it tends to be seen negatively; xenophobia was rife. But as consumers, middle-class women were not so dismissive of the benefits a modern, cosmopolitan society could offer. Nor could they ignore the increasing possibilities modernization was opening up for them in education and work. Feminism, after all, is a product of modernity. The advertisements in the women's magazines encouraged women to cook in Kokofat, use Flit to kill flies and Emulsión de Scott for TB. Scant wonder then that Cuban feminists often looked to liberated women in the United States as models of their own emancipation, as did Martí, although, like him, they decried materialist consumerism and the commodification of relations between men and women.[1]

Women's writing in postcolonial Cuba inscribed a potentially more revolutionary consciousness than that described so far, in two ways. The writings of Marxist, socialist and anarchist feminists forged connections between Cubanism, feminism, class politics and anti-racism. These works linked feminist demands to those of other subaltern groups: the blacks, mulattos and working classes. The imaginary future nation was represented as an organic, harmonious whole absorbing all relationships and working towards the common good of all society. This fitted in well with classical nationalist ideas which argued that the individual is subsumed in the whole and self-realization comes about by absorption into the collective consciousness. In this kind of revolutionary feminist writing, the target was a dominant, capitalist ideology which naturalizes white masculinity as the universal norm and the bourgeois nuclear family as the model for social organization. Socialist and anarchist feminists made it their business to fight for the rights of illegitimate children and to reform the adultery

laws and were in turn accused of being proponents of free love. They
were ostracized by liberal feminists precisely because they attacked bourgeois family values (Stoner 1991: 54–107; Núñez Machín 1989; Montero
1989).

Other kinds of women's writing which were not necessarily feminist
(writing for women's rights) but more often lyrical and subjective, questioned and undermined patriarchy and the values it subsumes in different
but no less profound ways. Women's poetry, for example, repeatedly
subverted traditional myths of femininity, including the Mother and
Domestic Bliss, by means of several discursive strategies: by refocusing
the female body and sexuality from a feminine perspective, by emphasizing
the specific experiences of women's lives, and by deflating dominant myths
of masculinity through irony, ridicule and humour. This kind of women's
writing is perhaps the most radical as it involves the writer turning private
subjectivity into the source of a collective, liberating discourse; it involves
socializing the unconscious and the inner self. This, too, is a project
inherent in Cubanism and the nationalist project inasmuch as the nation
(the collective conscious) encapsulates the individual. Moreover, poetry as
a new knowledge and ethics is what informs José Martí's work and Spanish
American modernista thinking in general (Zavala 1992: 45–7). It is in
poetry that we find the rebellion of subjectivity and desire against all
forms of institutionalized life, where we are reminded that power is played
out just as much at the level of interpersonal relationships as in the public
sphere, and that literature can produce what Bourdieu refers to as an
'accumulation of symbolical capital' which challenges the pragmatic com-
mercialism of the bourgeois state (Bourdicu 1993: 75). Women's stark
revelations and revisions of the workings of gender relations in patriarchal,
postcolonial Cuba threatened any propensity among the dominant sectors
to settle into smug satisfaction. To use Zavala's words: 'writing in occupied
territory meant breaking mirrors' (Zavala 1992: 186). The Cuban social
fabric was rotten and in tatters. What Cuban women writers attempted to
do was to sew the pieces together differently, following their own patterns
of thinking and doing.

In what follows I will pinpoint some specific strategies by means of
which women create a multiply layered counter-discourse in Cuba between
1900 and 1935. Ostensibly, there is an attempt to redefine the postcolonial
social body and that of the individual from a woman's or a feminist point
of view. At the same time, women writers engage with language. For
those writers who demanded more than equal rights, language became an
essential instrument in achieving a sexual liberation which entailed, in
Luce Irigaray's words, 'access to a status of individual and collective
subjectivity that is valid for them as women' (Irigaray 1993a: 73).

SOCIALIST FEMINISM   First, I shall refer to the revolutionary writings of socialist and anarchist feminists writing in the 1920s and 1930s. One of the most prolific was Ofelia Rodríguez Acosta, daughter of José Rodríguez Acosta, the Home Office Under-secretary. Her first book, *Evocaciones* [Evocations] (1922), a collection of short lyrical prose pieces published when she was nineteen, already shows a keen awareness of woman's restricted social role. She founded a short-lived feminist magazine in 1927 and was in charge of the feminist section of the *Revista de Habana* [Havana Review] in 1930 (Menéndez 1993: 89–90). She went on to publish many books.

Her most popular novel, *La vida manda* [Life Demands] (1929), tells the sad story of Gertrudis, an independent typist, whose passionate affair with the handsome but deceitful Damián leads to her downfall. A modern woman who wants to be 'emancipated' (Rodríguez Acosta 1929: 20) and is intent on losing her virginity, she is unaware that her lover is married with a family. Gradually, her self-confidence and will-power are worn away. Her break-up with Damián leads to a potential affair with a lesbian, a nervous breakdown, and a baby fathered by her ex-fiancé (which later dies). She loses her job and, finally, shoots herself, but she is unsuccessful in this too and ends her days blind and deranged. The moral of this tragic melodrama is that free love does not lead to women's emancipation. Female sexual desire may be natural but is also dangerous for women given the misogynistic, patriarchal society in which they live. Economic independence and emancipation in the public sphere must be matched by a radical rethink of sexual relations and women's position in the private sphere. Above all, Rodríguez Acosta criticizes women themselves, first for succumbing to pernicious romantic myths (Gertrudis falls for Damián because he is more virile than other men) and, second, for attempting to fulfil themselves through their relationships with men. In this respect, the incipient friendship between Gertrudis and the lesbian Delia, who is portrayed sympathetically, is of great significance and perhaps suggests an alternative way of life.[2]

If Gertrudis is naive, Damián is a selfish liar. He treats Gertrudis as his sex object. At one point he even accuses her of being 'a slave to your ovaries' (p. 173). None of the male characters (except the elderly Don Esteban) is portrayed sympathetically. What is surprising, given the date of publication of this lengthy novel, are the steamy sex scenes, described in great detail, and the frank expression of female desire:

> ... there was no corner of the woman's body that his mouth had not kissed; Gertrudis writhed and moaned, consumed with insatiable, relentless desire. (p. 75)
> ... he wrapped his legs around hers with a precise thrust. The man's chest touched the tips of his lover's breasts lightly. Their hips, swaying with the rhythmical movement of their love song, kissed voluptuously with a burning, intricate contact. (p. 118)

After their love-making she smells on herself the 'smell of a man's flesh' (p. 69); when she is away from Damián, 'she felt desire again, with its soft and imperious call, and faced with the impossibility of satisfying herself, tears came to her eyes' (p. 71).

Although the third-person narrative distances the narrator from these scenes, the novel is a courageous and successful attempt to chart women's erotic feelings and sexual experiences from a woman's point of view. Not surprisingly, it was much criticized by conservative and Catholic women (Menéndez 1993: 90). Although influenced more by nineteenth-century naturalism than socialist realism, the embedded subplot introduces a spirited attack on poverty and social injustice. Gertrudis's working-class cousin, who is attacked and raped in a horrifically violent scene, pours petrol on herself and dies in a blaze of fire. Few women in this novel, no matter what their class, find happiness. The exception is Damián's young wife who, protected by traditional values and social structures, suffers none of the despair of less fortunate (unmarried, emancipated or working-class) women. Yet, as Menéndez points out, in the novel there are no successful marriages or complete families. Mariblanca Sabás Alomá praised *La vida manda*, 'a novel about a woman, a *complete* woman, by a woman. A strange occurrence' (Menéndez 1993: 94).

In her essays Rodríguez Acosta explores these feminist themes in greater depth targeting not only patriarchy but also capitalism and imperialism. Her *La tragedia social de la mujer* [Woman's Social Tragedy] (1933), read as a lecture in the Lyceum in December 1932, attacks Nemilov's theories on the biological 'tragedy' of women by making a clear distinction between biological and cultural factors in shaping women's social roles. She criticizes the family and marriage and argues in favour of free love, which does not mean 'licentiousness' (Rodríguez Acosta 1933: 16) but a mature relationship free from hypocrisy. Single women, divorced women and young widows are unable to enjoy a 'free and open sex life' because of bourgeois social mores. Romantic love, privileging spiritual over physical love, results in women being submerged in 'a chaos of doubts, passions, errors' (p. 12) hinging on the equivocal notions of 'sex appeal' [sic] and 'the interesting guy' (p. 18); 'clearly the so-called biological tragedy of woman is caused by the clash between the laws of biology and a social reality fabricated by men' (p. 9). In her argument in favour of free love she points out that both sexes have medical problems (men may be impotent) and that sex may not lead to motherhood if contraceptives are used (p. 10). For Rodríguez Acosta to conceive a child is not a 'feminine tragedy', in the same way that giving birth is not a catastrophe, but the 'triumph of life' (p. 20). Giving birth is 'an affirmation of life [...] a demonstration of the biological creative capacity of woman' (p. 21). How is it, then, that birth has come to signify tragedy, 'as if the law of biology was a death sentence rather than the most awesome consecration of life?' (p. 22). The answer is because people's attitudes are formed according to the conventional lies of a capitalist system.

Having considered the matter from a feminist point of view, Rodríguez Acosta then focuses on class differences. The tragedy of working-class women's lives has nothing to do with biology and everything to do with capitalist exploitation. The following lines are of interest not only because of these socialist inflections of feminist discourse (progress is identified not with women's emancipation but with class equality) but also because – once again – a nationalist, anti-imperialist dimension is introduced where least expected:

> Today the bourgeoisie controls capitalism and culture. People, or more precisely, the workers, know that while evolution means wealth and power for some, it means misery and slavery for them. (p. 39)
>
> In every country where women's suffrage is now a decisive political factor [USA, UK], we see women's activities limited to the middle classes [...] we shall see that women, in a bourgeois political set-up, will know how to act just like men when they feel their class interests are threatened. (p. 27)

Other radical feminist texts of the times include those of journalist Mariblanca Sabás Alomá whose *La Rémora* [The Hindrance] (1921) is among the most contentious. In this invective against the Catholic Church, religion is positioned as the enemy of women and, therefore, of progress and civilization. Sabás Alomá targets convents – 'the convent is immoral' (Sabás Alomá 1921: 14) – the confessionary, and the men of the church. Catholicism, a colonial legacy, is identified with Spanish-speaking countries and is the most serious obstacle to women's emancipation.

Camila Henríquez Ureña's lectures on women's culture, which – like so many others here discussed – were first read in the Lyceum, are less aggressive but no less forceful in their argument. In 'Woman and Culture' (Henríquez Ureña 1985: 61–71),[3] part of the opening events of the Third National Women's Congress of March 1939, university lecturer Camila Henríquez Ureña discusses a point put to her by a male colleague: why are there fewer oustanding individual Cuban women now than in the past despite women's liberation and more extensive participation in Cuban culture? Is it that women's culture has improved quantitatively but not qualitatively? Henríquez Ureña argues that there was no such thing as a 'feminine culture' (p. 62) in the last century. Women, whose sole function was defined in terms of their relationships with men, could not develop their individual personalities. They were mothers, prostitutes or, if they escaped, nuns; their condition was analogous to 'that of the slave, who existed purely in relation to a master' (p. 63). In order to overcome this situation a woman had to be extraordinarily gifted, energetic and rich. Today, 'the female human being is starting to exist' (p. 65). The kind of culture women are propagating, a gender-specific 'maternal sense of existence' (p. 68), is 'a collective enterprise of great transcendence'. Women have had no time yet to isolate themselves and concentrate on 'a great personal work' (p. 67), and for this reason sisterhood solidarity is more important than ever.

Henríquez Ureña strongly criticizes Catholic women (and, even more so, the Catholic Church) for not taking part in the women's movement, but she also attacks frivolous women who 'abuse sports, drink, tobacco and sex' and refuse to treat life seriously. Of particular interest in her lecture is the analogy she draws between women and slaves (a recurrent motif in feminist discourse) and between women and the working class; 'we are, we have been, a kind of proletariat' (p. 69), obviously a key concept in socialist feminism. Her distinctively patriotic angle, 'Cuban women [...] march at the head of Latin American women' (p. 66), is also incisive in this context.

It may be thought that the arguments and motifs briefly considered in this overview of socialist feminist discourse are exclusive to the work of the more radical writers identified with Cuban first-wave feminism. This is not so.

GYNOMORPHIC REPRESENTATIONS OF THE NATION Antonio González Curquejo's *Florilegio de escritoras cubanas* (1910; 1913; 1919) included the work of over 120 women writing between 1833 and 1919. One of the prose pieces in the third volume is 'Cuban Woman' by Africa Fernández Iruela (González Curquejo 1919: 235–40).[4] Fernández Iruela was not a professional writer (unlike the radical feminists above) and probably published no more than articles in the local press. Her essay is more interesting for this reason. It indicates the extent to which traditional feminine role models were rejected in Cuba, at all levels of society. 'Cuban Woman' opens with a description of a watercolour painting the author remembers from her childhood entitled 'Cuban Woman'. The subject, she points out, was a well-known source of inspiration for 'sweet poets', presumably male, who were wont to hymn the beauty of women:

> Lying in a wide hammock stretched between two tall palm trees rests an entrancing woman, her pretty hands pillowing her head, her beautiful eyes half closed, her long, black hair falling in curly waves over her white neck, her elegant body wrapped in pure white apparel, a languid dreamer; next to her a young slave boy imprisons in his little hands of ebony a snow white fan of feathers. The scene is presided by Phoebus, with his burning face peeping between the leafy branches of a ceiba tree. (González Curquejo 1919: 235)

The woman in the painting is pure and beautiful but only half awake. She is resting passively, and her hands serve only as a pillows. She is tantalizingly desirable, but not for the one male portrayed in the picture, the child slave. Because he is a boy he is allowed to be next to her, at a slightly lower level. He imprisons in his black hands a snow-white fan, the oxymoron emphasizing yet cancelling extreme opposites. This picture of peace and harmony featuring a semi-conscious woman and an unthreatening boy is viewed by a voyeuristic Phoebus, burning – presumably with desire – and spying on them between the branches. His masculine stare 'presides the scene'. Phoebus reflects the projected and introjected image of the male viewer and consumer who is intended to look at the painting (including the painter himself) and his look could be described as the look of modernity 'covetous and erotic' (Pollock 1988: 67).

Fernández Iruela adopts this look ironically as she lingers on the woman's fragmented body in her description: hands, eyes, hair, neck, body. Thus the 'Cubana' is the image through which Cuban women who look at the painting are meant to see themselves: the passive objects of desire. The Cubana has no gaze of her own, no desire, because her eyes are half closed. And, as Pollock writes, if women cannot look they are 'denied a representation of their desire [...] and are constantly erased' (Pollock 1988: 85). Neither are the slave's eyes or face mentioned; only his hands. Indeed, although both woman and slave are subjected to the sun, it is the boy who protects the woman from Phoebus's lascivious kiss. Neither child slave nor woman is portrayed as a subject of desire; both are dominated by the phallic sun.

Fernández Iruela rejects this picture. The dismembered parts of the woman's body need to be re-membered and incorporated into an image of the whole, just as the dispersed members of the fragmented body politic need to realign for the good of the nation. In addition, the transitionary space occupied by the Cuban woman, who is disempowered outside the walls of the home and is lying suspended on a veranda – the threshold of the public and domestic domain – must be redefined. Fernández Iruela offers this painting to her women readers from a feminine perspective so they can interpret it differently. She re-presents a masculine representation of Cuban womanhood to the Cuban women themselves. She repaints the picture through verbal images thus positing a critical look; she makes her readers aware of the sexual politics of looking and invites potential female viewers actively to participate in the production of meaning. The picture is false, she writes, it is associated with her childhood and is naive because the experiences of her life have proved it to be a misrepresentation. She contrasts the colonial image of the indolent 'creole beauty', needing (like the slave boy) 'the protection given to the weak', with contemporary Cuban women who struggle for their own, independent future and for that of their semi-independent nation where a colonial economy (rural sugar estates) has been replaced by an urban, modern society. 'No more hammocks hung between palm trees, no more slaves with feathery fans to shelter us from the fiery kiss of our tropical sun', she writes; no longer are Cuban women 'luxurious dolls', 'unconscious beings' but the 'companion' and even the 'protector' of boys and men.

The roles have been reversed and this change is due, she believes, to natural evolution: from the ugly chrysalis comes the butterfly, from the shell the pearl, from coal the diamond and (note the reversal) from the goddess comes the female human being. Butterfly, pearl, diamond, female human being represent all that is natural, pure and beautiful: 'that is what we are now, *humans* after having been *goddesses*' [sic] (González Curquejo 1919: 236). In true modernista fashion aesthetic considerations take on moral values. Is the change in women's position justifiable, asks Fernández Iruela? Yes, because it is for the good of the country; women's active participation in society 'is synonymous with well-being and progress' (p. 236). Without women's emancipation there is no progress. The separate identities of the Cuban nation and the Cuban woman are further elided syntactically when, having referred previously in one sentence to 'Cuban woman', 'this Antillean pearl' and 'this beautiful land', the author declares she wants to 'sing her the song of praise she deserves' (p. 236). Whose song of praise is she singing? Cuban woman's? Cuba's? It is one and the same thing.

She uses two tropes to describe the cultural achievements of Cuban women: nature and war. Women might not be successful in the Arts but they will have sown their 'little seed in the furrow which one day will grow' (p. 236), indeed, 'the university lecture halls are now like feminist gardens' (p. 38). Woman is also the unknown heroine of a 'silent war' and may fall 'in the struggle'. Morally justifiable warfare to fulfil a natural destiny is the language of nationalism. The author points out Cuba's war effort on the part of the Allies against the 'Teuton tyrant' (p. 239) (Cuba was drawn in on the side of the Allies because of its dependency on the USA, which needed the sugar). 'In the silence of the night', she expects, 'when the mothers of the Allied forces raise their prayers to God, you can hear on their lips the Holy name of Cuba', more precisely, the name of Cuban women. Her article ends with instructions to painters in future to represent Cuban women as active, intelligent and alive. Women create their identity through social activity. In this way she calls for an end to patriarchy's disabling myths of the feminine which implicate women, slaves and children as the sectors of society most disempowered by patriarchal values. Women's struggle for freedom is a natural evolution towards moral perfection; the nation is presented gynomorphically and the destinies of the Cuban nation and Cuban women are concomitant.

This single essay inscribes a gynomorphic representation of the nation as well as several other discursive strategies outlined below. Images of nature and war recur in feminist discourse well into the 1930s. In Dr María Gómez Carbonell's 'Song of Victory and Propaganda of the National Feminist Alliance: At the Furrow-Trench' (*Boletín de la Alianza*

Nacional Feminista, Vol. I, no. 1, May 1931: 12) the struggle for emancipation is figured as a moral crusade,

Coro

¡Avanzad!: La consigna es sagrada.
Fe y valor junto al surco-trinchera.
La justicia por única espada,
Y el amor por escudo y bandera.
[...]
Triunfar sepa en la ruda jornada
La que sepa, entre angustias, dar vida.
La mujer, en el mármol plasmada,
La mujer, en los bronces fundida.

Refrain:

Forward! The watchword is sacred. / Faith and courage at the furrow-trench. / Justice is our only sword, / Our shield and flag is love. [...] The one who knows how to triumph in the hard day's toil / Is she who knows, with suffering, to give life. / It is Woman, carved in marble, / It is Woman, forged in bronze.

The battle trench is a furrow: farming and sowing (culture) and natural reproduction are the prerogative of living women who break out of the constraints of patriarchy's sculpted images. Thus the death and destruction of (men's) wars is counter-balanced by the fight for life and creation. In the preface to Luz Rubio's previously mentioned book, Elisa de Grau turns the association of woman and nature to women's advantage (Rubio 1914: Preface). Nature is wiser and more prudent than mankind, she states, and women have learned from nature by opening for themselves the 'ploughed furrows' of culture and education. Thus women's emancipation is again inscribed in nationalist images of natural, organic growth.

Complementing the kind of women's discourse which took the high moral ground is a potentially more subversive strand which eroticizes the Cuban landscape. Nieves Xenes in her sonnet 'July', written in 1907, published in *Poesías* (1915), presents a daring picture of a lascivious Cuba, literally 'on heat', caressed by the male sun (Feijóo 1964: 175). This picture clearly counters the Cubanist image of the nation as virtuous motherhood:

Ostenta el campo su verdor lucido,
de intenso azul el cielo se colora
y el Sol vierte su luz deslumbradora
ardiente como el oro derretido.
Es un amante de pasión rendido
ante la hermosa Cuba a quien adora,
que a su ávida caricia abrasadora
abandona su cuerpo enardecido.

Y en lánguidez erótica postrada,
voluptuosa, gentil, enamorada,
a sus besos ofrece incitadores,
perfumados con lúbricos aromas,
ya los erectos senos de sus lomas,
ya los trémulos labios de sus flores.

The countryside shines with brilliant green, / the sky is painted intensely blue /
and the Sun pours down his blinding light / like molten gold scorching. / He's
a lover exhausted with passion / for the beautiful Cuba whom he adores, /
who, with his eager, flaming caresses / relaxes her body burning with love. /
And spent, in erotic languor, / voluptuous, elegant, enamoured, / she offers up
to his kisses, tempting, / oiled and perfumed with aromas, / the erect breasts
of her hillsides, / and the trembling lips of her flowers.

It could be argued that Nieves Xenes simply adopts the kind of
masculine gaze much criticized by Africa Fernández Iruela. But the eroticization of the landscape by women poets[5] is interesting for the ways they
both adopt and undermine objectification; the female body becomes the
'object of a female subjectivity experiencing and identifying itself' (Irigaray
1993a: 59). This particular poem functions on various levels: in inscribing
the newly liberated nation as a woman freely exhibiting sexual desire,
Nieves Xenes not only legitimates female-authored erotic poetry and the
self-representation of the female body and sexuality, she also fulfils the
national feminist objective of associating love of woman (implying care)
and the female body (implying possession) with love of country and the
body politic.

MOTHER AND MOTHERLAND   Another common strategy was the
(self)-identification of the mother with the motherland. Dulce María
Borrero is also represented in González Curquejo's anthology. Her poem
'Our own land' represents Cuba as the Great Mother or, more precisely,
maternal practice: protection and nurturance (Ruddick 1989: 80–90). The
mother is nature, growth, shelter and natural origins; the collective body,
when it dies, is refertilized in the birthplace:

Por ella respirar, y entre sus brazos
cuando, helada, la muerte nos sorprende
dar a su seno nuestra propia vida
de nuestro amor como postrera ofrenda. (González Curquejo 1910: 301)

To die for her, and in her arms / when death comes cold, unbidden, /
give to her breast our life / and our love as our last offering.

This mother-paradise, once lost, is now rightfully (in natural law) regained
by her children, on whose behalf the daughter-poet speaks: 'Ours, at last,

is the land where we were born / The beautiful island is finally ours.' In reclaiming the mother-country the poem inscribes an organic symbiosis of people and landscape and a renewal of maternal genealogy. Dulce María Borrero's sonnet 'The Rivers', first published in *Horas de mi vida* [Hours of my Life] (1912), conjoins maternal with erotic tropes of the homeland thus cancelling patriarchal mother/whore dichotomies and positing masculinity as a threat. When the poet asks the feminized rivers where they come from and go to, their reply is telling: they flow from the mother of life to the male sea-monster of death:

> Desde los senos rebosantes
> venimos, de la tierra en viaje largo [...]
> ¡Somos el néctar de la vida pura,
> por donde va la maternal dulzura
> a la boca voraz del monstruo amargo! (Feijóo 1964: 208)

From the flowing breasts / we come, from the soil on our journey long [...] / We are the nectar of pure life, / and through us maternal sweetness goes / to the voracious mouth of the monster vile!

At times sexual and maternal representations of the nation are kept strictly apart. In the pages of *La Mujer* (10 October 1929) the red star of the Cuban flag, the symbol of the independent nation, is eroticized in a sonnet, 'The Flag', by Amable Sáez J. Venezolano:

> En el triángulo rojo, luminosa
> como la aurora que inició aquel día
> luce la Estrella Solitaria hermosa.
> Al tierno beso de la brisa ondea,
> y en un canto triunfal de epifanía
> voluptuosa y gentil surge y flamea.

In the red triangle, luminous / like the dawn that began that day, / the lovely solitary star is shining. / She flutters at the tender kiss of the breeze, / and in a triumphant song of celebration / voluptuous and elegant she rises and flames.

The hymn is followed by a long, anonymous eulogy to the wife and mother of Antonio Maceo, María Cabrales de Maceo and Mariana Grajales de Maceo respectively, in which the latter is described as 'patriot [...] and heroic mother [...] Mother without equal', and by yet another poem to the flag, 'My Flag', by Mercedes Borrero de O'Reilly, which is clearly Cubanist and makes no reference to women at all.

The identification of the mother with the motherland is particularly strong in Emilia Bernal's autobiography *Layka Froyka* (1925b) written in New York in 1919.[6] The book is an account of Bernal's childhood up to the death of her mother from TB (in 1901) when Bernal was sixteen, focusing on the mother's illness and her slow decline. A parallel is drawn between the mother's worsening situation and that of Cuba simultaneously suffering the Wars of Independence. By the time the book reaches Part X entitled 'Goodbye for ever', when the author refers to the 'sorrow', the 'worst possible situation', she is referring both to her mother and to Cuba (Bernal 1925b: 173). The mother's life and death are analogous to the recent history of the nation. Cubanness is represented in terms of mother-love, love for and by the mother that enables the author to construct an engendered familial and national identity. This is clear in the passage where she describes the destruction of her home during the Wars of Independ-ence; the courageous patriotic mother returns to the burning house to rescue the family's papers, the family-tree, the documented genealogical history. Thus the heroine-mother saves the family and the nation from oblivion. Even in her dying letter to her daughter the mother draws a contrast between her own decline and Cuba's prosperity: 'I am suffocating [...] And in the midst of this torture I think of my homeland. Oh, Cuba, from the cradle I was a martyr with you and now that you prosper and delight in expectation of the future I am once again a martyr and I feel I am dying' (p. 184).

Shifting the focus from the nation to the family, the mother-figure herself was reshaped by women writers (necessarily mothers and/or daughters) from knowledge acquired through personal experience. Women's recognition of their power as mothers, as the creators of men, and of themselves as forces of production into which they invest unacknowledged time and work is often foregrounded in the poems they write to their children. In these poems the labouring mother is not denied as she is in Western socio-political theory.

In the sonnet 'My Seraphin and I', first published by Dolores Bolio in 1917, the poet describes her little boy, associating his golden curls on the white pillow with the masculine sun. Suddenly the mother sees in the boy's 'look' her own image. In the reciprocal gaze between mother and son each sees the other's image, the unrepeatable oneness of the mother-child. Yet the mother sees herself as a moon, reflecting borrowed light from a third source, possibly the (sun) father. This will enable the male child to establish his own individual identity through separation and positions the mother as practising attentive love, a love which 'lets difference emerge [...] lets otherness be' (Ruddick 1989: 123). The mother-poet disavows possession but is fully aware of her own handiwork, her labour of love. The strength of her maternal genealogy has stamped her mark, reproduced her form in her child irrespective of biological sexual differences. The final words of the poem, 'paint', 'forge', 'imprinted', contrasting with the natural images at the beginning, indicate her knowledge that giving birth to the population and the workforce is a gender-specific mode of production:

Sobre mi corazón, tan tiernamente
he oprimido su testa ensortijada,
que se desliza el oro por la almohada
como en cumbre invernal sol refulgente
Suspiro, y al besar su pura frente
sorprendiendo mi rostro en su mirada,
me parezco a la luna extasiada
su miniatura copia en una fuente.
Y le arrulla mi voz: ¡Naturaleza
con mi sangre pintó tus encendidas
y redondas mejillas; tu cabeza
forjaron mis ideas florecidas;
tu espíritu, mi amor: yo llevo impresa
tu forma entre mi ser hace mil vidas! (Feijóo 1964: 215)

Tenderly, on my heart / I have laid his curly head. / The gold spreads across the pillow / like sun shining on a snowy peak. / I sigh, and as I kiss his forehead pure / I catch a glimpse of my face in his gaze, / I see myself like the enraptured moon / copying its miniature in a fountain. / And my voice murmurs to him: 'Nature / painted your bright, chubby cheeks / with my blood; my blossoming / ideas forged your head; your spirit, / my love; your shape was imprinted on my being / a thousand lives ago!

In a less lyrical vein, Celia Sarrá de Averhoff, in an article entitled 'To Cuban Woman' (*Boletín de la Alianza Nacional Feminista*, Vol. I, no. 1, May 1931) took this argument further. Cuban women should not consider themselves simply (re)producers of labour in a capitalist economy; they should also fulfil their role as moral educators in society:

Don't just be a human incubator, the woman-manufacturer of automatons that simply adds numbers to the population without being of any benefit or practical use to her country. Learn homiculture ['homicultura'] so that you are the promoter of women and men who are sound in conscience as well as body. (p. 12)

One of the most subversive poems of this period (but published outside the time-frame of this chapter) is Dulce María Loynaz's 'Song to a Barren Woman' (1937). This is both an impassioned defence and exaltation of woman as non-mother. The 'impossible mother' is elevated, not as mother of God, but as a self-contained entity in her own right in place of the single, masculine One. 'Let God rot the tongue of whoever speaks / badly of you!', she writes:

Y reinarás
en tu Reino. Y serás
la Unidad

perfecta que no necesita
reproducirse
como no se reproduce el cielo. (Núñez 1993: 99–100)

And you will reign / in your Kingdom. And you shall be / the perfect / One /
with no need to reproduce itself / as heaven does not reproduce itself.

María Luisa Milanés, who committed suicide because of an unhappy
marriage, wrote several powerful poems which smash the rosy myth of
domestic bliss and demystify the figure of the contented mother as pillar
of strength (Valdés Roig 1930). 'Via crucis' portrays a frail and helpless
figure who, it is revealed, is the poet's mother:

Tus dulces ojos de llorar cansados;
tu boca, que ha olvidado la sonrisa;
tu corazón, que lleva la divisa
del que murió en Salem crucificado;
tu cabeza, que el golpe de la pena
trocó, de ala de cuervo, en nieve pura; [...]
tu voz de llantos, de sollozos llena,
todo me dice a una
que andar no puedes más. Ven, llegaremos:
apóyate en mis hombros, que aún altivas
verás nuestras siluetas por la Vía;
Nos falta poco ya, descansaremos
a la sombra del roble, ¡madre mía!

(Lizaso and Fernández de Castro 1926: 303)

Your sweet eyes tired of weeping; / your mouth has forgotten to smile; / your
heart bears the stamp / of he who died in Salem crucified; / your hair, the
blow of misfortune / changed from raven black to pure snow; [...] / your
voice, filled with sorrow and sighs, / all tell me now / you cannot go on.
Come, we'll get there yet: / lean on my shoulders, and still you shall see / our
proud figures on the Via; / we have a short way to go, then we shall rest / in
the shade of an oak tree, mother dear!

This poem foregrounds the mother–daughter relationship in religious
tropes; thus the martyred mother and her daughter together resist the
humiliation of patrilinear family life.

The home itself was also often refigured. In a lecture entitled 'A Cuban
Political-social Study' read in the University of Coimbra on 24 October
1925, Emilia Bernal described Cuba as she knew it before leaving in 1919
(*Cuestiones cubanas para América*, 1928). Well-informed about Cuban history
and politics, Bernal expounds mainstream Cubanist ideas: she opposes the
Platt Amendment and US intervention exalting José Martí and Antonio
Maceo. The only way Cuba can rid itself of the Platt Amendment, she

writes, is by appealing to justice and virtue. Only self-sacrifice, the prerogative of women, within a framework of national autonomy can right the country's ills. In this context it is significant that Cuba should be figured as the home ('let us make our home free and pure, ourselves'), as well as the mother who is to be rescued from rapacious foreign (capitalist, imperialist, male) hands: 'Let us remove the foreign hands which, unfortunately, we have allowed to settle on her and then let us preserve her from all profanation' (Bernal 1928: 94–5).

REFIGURING THE HOME In the same way that women writers revised traditional representations of the mother, some presented unfavourable versions of the home which clearly challenge those of Cubanist nationalist ideology. Revealing the stark reality behind the myth of the happy family was the objective of María Villar Buceta in 'Hermeticism':

> ¡En casa todos vamos a morir de silencio!
> Yo señalo el fenómeno; pero me diferencio
> apenas del conjunto … ! Tengo que ser lo mismo!
> Dijérase que estamos enfermos de idiotismo
> o que constituimos una familia muda …
> de tal suerte en sí propio cada uno se escuda.
>
> (Lizaso and Fernández de Castro 1926: 345–6)

In our house we shall all die of silence! / I indicate the phenomenon; but I differ little / from the group … I have to be the same! / One would say we were ill with stupidity / or that our family is dumb … / each one of us wrapped up in himself.

and of Matanzas poet América Bobia (b. 1893) in 'Dolls' House' (written in 1923),

> Una casa de juguetes:
> los hermanos, la mamá
> los cenceños abuelitos
> y el laborioso papá.
>
> Prensador de corazones
> el tiempo pasa fugaz:
> se rompen los viejecitos
> y envejecen los papás.
>
> Crece el bebé sin caricias
> y se casan los demás.
> ¡Frágil casa de muñecas
> qué tristeza de jugar! (Bobia 1993: 14)

A toy house / brothers, sisters, mama / ancient grandparents / hardworking papa. // Pressing down hearts, / time swiftly goes / old people break / parents get old // baby grows, no caresses, / the rest marry, go away. / What a fragile dolls' house / how sad to play.

Here the opening picture of harmony proves to be false: passing time cracks the myth of domestic bliss. For her part, María Luisa Milanés targets the myth of the supportive husband and shows the domestic space to be one of utter hopelessness for unhappy wives. In poems such as 'You have done this to me … ' and 'I am nothing to you … ' she voices, with shocked outrage, the appalling physical and psychological effects caused by her husband's blatant indifference and infidelity:

Cuando pones tus sienes en la almohada
cuando apagas la luz para dormir,
¿no has visto entre las sombras la mirada
de unos ojos cansados de sufrir
[…]
¿No ha llegado hasta ti la voz humilde
que habla un momento y asustada calla,
que te recuerda en tus palabras mismas
'que el triunfo no autoriza ser canalla'?
 […]
¿No has sentido mi voz llegar muy dulce
a través del espacio junto a ti
para decirte, cariciosa y triste,
ESTO HAS HECHO DE MI? (Lizaso and Fernández de Castro 1926: 302)

When you rest your head on the pillow / when you put out the light to sleep, / have you not seen a look in the shadows / the tired look of eyes that weep? […] Has not a humble voice reached you, / which speaks then, frightened, is quiet, / which reminds you, using your own words, / 'success should make no one a swine'? […] Have you not heard my voice reach you sweetly / across the space at your side / to say to you, sad and endearing, / THIS YOU HAVE DONE TO ME?

Irony becomes aggressive sarcasm and anguished protest in 'I am nothing to you … ':

¿Qué soy yo para ti? Sólo un guiñapo
que el aire ondeó cual gonfalón de ensueño.
Perdió la novedad, pasaste el rato,
y hoy dejarlo de ver sólo es tu empeño […]

(Lizaso and Fernández de Castro 1926: 300)

What am I to you? Just a rag doll / which the air blew like tatters in a dream. / The novelty wore off, you had a good time, / now you desire to be rid of me.

In Dulce María Loynaz's 'Prison in the air', the entrapment of the home routine, 'A prison without jailer and without chains / where I eat my bread and I drink my water / day after day', is invisible but no less real (Núñez 1993: 65). To escape the confines of the patriarchal home women often resorted to reading. Indeed, this was generally encouraged as educated women were increasingly perceived as potential consumers. (Surely it is no coincidence that advertised in *La Mujer* are a shoe-shop named 'The World' and a clothes-shop 'Philosophy Stores'?) Thus Emilia Bernal writes in 'Inner Life'(*¡Como los pájaros!* [Like the Birds], 1922), 'I live like a nun': but her 'cell' is 'perfumed / with the exotic fragrance of "Les fleurs du mal"'. With Edgar Allan Poe as inspiration, the classical stone figure of the wise woman (Pallas Athene) is rejected in favour of the living female subject, 'Let the raven's blue wing break the glass of the cloisters, / let it enter and croak at the statue of Pallas "nevermore"'(Bernal 1922: 71).

A different view of reading is offered by Amada Rosa Rodríguez in a sonnet 'Country Life' (first published in *Poetas jóvenes cubanos,* 1907). The poem describes an erotic landscape at dusk which exudes desire. The breeze caresses the flowers, the sun is in his 'rosy bed', the phallic palm tree is 'majestic, swaying his crests on high', while darkness gradually covers 'Nature's charms'. The woman-poet, unfortunately, is excluded from the scene: 'and I alone in my silent room, / searching for entertainment in books' (Feijóo 1964: 73). María Villar Buceta, who was to become one of Cuba's most respected librarians, warns with irony in 'Bibliophobia' of the pernicious effects of reading, 'Cursed be he who drinks / of the black waters of books'. Man, Life and Nature are 'deformed' by the 'organically abnormal' senses of

> [...] artistas, poetas
> (exégetas de lo Infinito),
> filósofos, historiadores ...
> (mixtificadores de oficio,
> apóstoles de la Mentira
> tortura de eruditos) (Lizaso and Fernández de Castro 1926: 343)

> artists, poets, / (exegetes of Infinity), / philosophers, historians / (mystifiers by trade, / apostles of the Lie / torture for the erudite)

While this is clearly a critique of philistinism, from a feminist point of view it is also an indictment of patriarchal literary and philosophical discourses, an attitude which is more explicit in Villar Buceta's wry poem 'Peace':

> Un filósofo ha dicho que la mujer no es más
> que el reflejo del hombre que encuentra en su camino
> ¡He aquí una profunda exégesis! ...

Jamás
descubriste ¡oh mi dulce alma femenino!
al Hombre entre los hombre ... , y es por eso que estás
como un niño dormido en la paz de un camino.

(Lizaso and Fernándo de Castro 1926: 344)

A philosopher has said that woman is no more / than the reflection of the man she encounters on her way. / Such a profound explanation! / Never, / oh, my sweet feminine soul, did you discover / the Man among men ... , and this is why / you are like a child sleeping in peace on his way.

CRITIQUE OF MODERNITY AND MASCULINITY In women's writings, modernity (expressed in terms of metals, tools and manufactured goods) is often represented as oppressive, unjust and unnatural, and is associated with masculinity, artificiality, lack of feeling and death. This feminist critique of masculinity-as-modernity is found in Emilia Bernal's 'Yes, one day I will open up my breast' (*Alma errante* [Wandering Soul], 1916). The subject describes her 'breast' as having 'two doors closed with a hammer' in which 'a wounded dove coos and trembles' (Bernal 1916: 92). The poem 'Iron' from her *Los nuevos motivos* [New Motifs] (1925a) is exemplary in this respect and brings to mind José Martí's concept of 'the metallization of man' by which he meant man's lust for money.[7] The poem associates physical man with modern capitalist development: iron, power, rapaciousness, ignorance (he tears the roots of the tree of knowledge from Adam's hands), insensitivity, stupidity, war-mongering, madness and greed. But the poet does not feel threatened; she offers her hand in a gesture of friendship because she knows the 'civilization' he incarnates will pass. It will be replaced by a splendid civilization which will cover all 'Our America' (Martí's term). The artisan of this new imaginative construction is the idealist man from the South (America), who is precisely all the Iron Man (of the North) is not. By querying modernity and associating it with masculinity *qua* exploitation, this poem claims autonomy not just for nation and continent but also for woman. It is dated New York, 1923:

¡Un hombre de hierro ... !
De hierro las carnes del pecho invencible.
De hierro los biceps y triceps del brazo que erecta triunfante ademán.
Las manos de hierro y el vientre.
Y los muslos columnas potentes de hierro y las piernas ...
[...]
¡Gran hombre de hierro, yo os extiendo la mano cordial!
¡Yo os extiendo la mano valiente, grandioso animal!
¡Alumbra la tierra con hierro!
 ... Esa civilización pasará ... (Bernal 1925a: 60)

A man of iron ... ! / Of iron the flesh of his invincible chest. / Of iron the biceps and triceps of the arm he raises in triumphant jest. / His hands and belly of iron. / And powerful columns of iron his thighs and legs, ... / [...] Great man of iron, let's shake hands in peace. / I offer you my hand with courage, oversized beast! / Enlighten the earth with iron! / ... Your civilization will pass ...

WOMEN AND SLAVERY After the publication of Gómez de Avellaneda's *Sab* an analogy drawn between the condition of woman and that of the slave was popular in women's writing. Slavery was officially abolished in Cuba in 1886 but only after independence were black Cubans recognized by the Constitution as equal citizens and black males allowed to vote. In 1908 an Independent Party of Colour (PIC) was set up exercising a form of identity politics (no women appear in its lists of members) but it was brutally squashed in 1912 and its leader killed (Fernández Robaina 1990: 97–100). No such action was ever contemplated against the all-women's feminist organizations which posed no political threat. Women writers, however, constantly alluded to the 'enslavement' of women, reminding politicians implicitly if not explicitly that while (working-class, illiterate) black men were emancipated, (middle-class) white women were not. In her radio lecture of 1930, Amelia de Vera de Lens began with a quotation from John Stuart Mill: 'What differentiates the slave from the free man is that the first obeys laws in which he has had no part while the second obeys laws of which he is the legislator' (de Vera de Lens 1930: 1). She argues that Cuban women like herself 'belong to the category slaves'. Men see women as dolls or servants, not as human beings with equal rights (1930: 4). 'To a Slave' by Emilia Bernal (*Alma errante*, 1916) represents slaves as the brothers-in-arms of subjected women:

> ¡Esclavo! ¡Esclavo! Cuando duerma todo
> el mar, la tierra, el bosque, el llano,
> iré a la puerta de tu cárcel negra
> para llamarte, con ternura, Hermano ... (Bernal 1916: 48).

> Slave! Slave! When all the earth, / sea, woods, and plains are asleep, / I will go to your black prison door / and call you, Brother, tenderly ...

The 'Suffragist Hymn' written by Felicia Martínez Vélez de Grillo and published in *El sufragista* (Vol. II, no. 1, 18 March 1923: 3) inscribes similar tropes:

> Pasaron por siempre los días aquellos
> que esclava sumisa la triste mujer,
> fue sierva ignorante, del hombre, que, entonces

negábale fiero la luz del saber.
[...]
¡Que viva el sufragio, que viva, viva! ...
En Cuba imperioso lo exige el deber ...
¡Que viva, que viva, que ya practicarlo
Consciente y segura sabrá la mujer! ...

Those days have passed for ever / when sad woman was submissive slave, / the ignorant serf of man who fiercely denied her / the light of wisdom. [...] Long live suffrage, viva, viva! / Duty demands it in Cuba now ... / Viva, viva, to put it in practice / conscientious and certain, women will know how!

Perhaps the most moving poem in this respect is 'I'll do what Spartacus did' by María Luisa Milanés who killed herself shortly after writing it:

Ya decidí, me voy, rompo los lazos
que me unen a la vida y a sus penas.
Hago como Spartaco;
me yergo destrozando las cadenas
que mi existir tenían entristecido,
miro al mañana y al ayer y clamo:
¡Para mayores cosas he nacido
que para ser esclava y tener amo!

(Lizaso and Fernández de Castro 1926: 303)

My decision is made, I will go, I'll break the ties / that bind me to life and its pains. / I'll do what Spartacus did; / I'll rise up and destroy the chains / that have made my existence sorrow, / I look to yesterday and tomorrow / and cry: Greater things were meant for me / than a master to have and a slave to be!

IRONIC DEFLATION OF GENDER MYTHS Irony, particularly the deflation of conventional myths of masculinity and femininity, resulted in devastating poems which challenge hegemonic ideology inasmuch as they attack the very foundations of the masculine subject and androcentric thinking. Women writers, often poets, switched from mimeticism to mimicry and wrote with sarcasm and wit to target normalized assumptions of male superiority. The legitimacy of casting woman as man's other, of defining the female as an inverse reflection of the male, is questioned in poems which destabilize the myths of manhood. Many of Emilia Bernal's poems fall into this category. In 'I Wish' (*Alma errante*), she writes,

Quisiera ser la castellana amante
a quien el caballero suspirante
al galopar de su corcel guerrero
flores de amor dejaba en la ventana.
Mas ¡ay! no puedo ser la castellana

porque no existe un solo caballero! (Bernal 1916: 69)

I wish to be the lady of Castile / for whom a lovelorn knight / galloping by on his warrior steed / leaves flowers of love at her window. / But, alas, I cannot be this lady bright / because there exists not a single knight.

In an earlier poem, 'Statue Heads' (*¡Como los pájaros!*) Bernal mimics women's propensity for self-derision and turns her withering look on to the male body. The female head, 'Head of a statue', 'Crater of illusions, ashes of affection', is senseless. According to rational logic, to support such a head a girl needs a male physique, and that is no less sclerotic, 'Give me, athlete, your body of stone / to bear with pride a statue's head of my own' (p. 46). In 'Grains of fire' (*Vida. Poesías* [Life Poems], 1925c) again mimeticism undermines traditional images of womanhood:

¿Por qué no me hace santa
el cielo?
Tengo yo la culpa de vivir
acaso?
¿Y he de arrastrar este dolor perpetuo
de ser
mujer?
¡Oh Dios, compadécete de mis lágrimas! (Bernal 1925c: 3)

Why doesn't heaven / make me a saint? / Is it my fault I'm living? / Must I always bear eternal pain / for being / a woman? / Oh, God, take pity on my tears!

This poem refers tongue-in-cheek to the so-called tragedy of womanhood while at the same time relinquishing all responsibility. In 'God's will' (*Exaltación*, 1928) modernization is cast in terms of religion, thus exposing the serious rifts between the two contradictory discourses for women:

¡Dios mío, dame un empleo para mi alma!
En esta oficina no me lo quieren dar.
Que no tengo habilidad, ni disciplina, ni calma,
que tengo muy mala letra y que no sé contar ...
Oh, señor, mándame un gran sacrificio! [...]
... Que tengo mala letra y me equivoco en las cuentas ... Sin embargo
Cuán grande es mi voluntad de servirte mejor ... (Bernal 1928: n.p.)

Dear Lord, give me a job for my soul / In this office they won't let me stay. / I have no skills, or discipline, or calm, / my sums are awful, my writing in vain ... / Oh, Lord, send me a great sacrifice now [...] / ... I can't count, I have trouble with my letters / But how great is my will-power to serve thee better ...

In her poem 'I Don't Understand ... ' María Luisa Milanés deconstructs and exploits the myth of Narcissus, perhaps the most cherished of masculine myths, which underpins masculine notions of identity, self-recognition and self-esteem, and (according to Freud) homosexuality. Her quiet irony, directed at her own apparent lack of comprehension, belies a devastating attack on the shallowness of male vanity:

Me abisma no entender, bello Narciso,
la ingenua admiración que te arrebata
y te fascina en la onda azul y plata ...
Claro, que para ti es un paraíso
mirar tus ojos bellos y tu boca,
tu sonrisa, tu frente y tu figura
llena de majestad y de dulzura ...
Pero ¿no piensas que haya algo de bueno
que distraiga tus ojos y tu mente,
fije más alto tu mirar sereno
y entretenga tus horas dulcemente?
¡Quisiera comprender mi alma sencilla
la perfecta hermosura de tu frente,
donde jamás el pensamiento brilla!
                              (Lizaso and Fernández de Castro 1926: 301)

Beautiful Narcissus, I do not understand / the naive admiration that you crave, / and your fascination with the blue and silver wave ... / Of course, for you a glimpse of paradise / is to see your mouth and your lovely eyes, / your figure, your brow and your smile, / full of sweetness and majesty ... / But don't you think there's something else worthwhile / that might distract your eyes and your mind, / fix your gaze serene on something high / and give you pleasure all the while? / My simple soul would love to comprehend / the perfect beauty of your lovely head / where never a thought does shine!

The device is just as effective in a sonnet ostensibly entitled 'Anonymous' written by Nieves Xenes in 1899, first published in 1915:

No siento del amor la honda tortura
cuando contemplo con tenaz fijeza
la rara perfección de su cabeza
y su cuerpo de helénica escultura.
Como imprimiendo a su gentil figura
sello de augusta y varonil nobleza,
en su mirar de fúlgida limpieza
la luz del pensamiento no fulgura.
Al contemplarlo sin afán ni anhelo
de un artista inmortal digno modelo,
su belleza magnífica que encanta

sólo en mi alma a despertar acierta
la admiración tranquila que despierta
la belleza del bruto o de la plata. (Feijóo 1964: 174)

I feel no love or torture deep / when attentively I contemplate / the strange perfection of his head / and his body sculpted like a statue Greek. / As if to mark on his elegant frame / the stamp of noble manhood, fine, august / in the clear transparency of his look / the light of a thought never shines. / Without want or desire I look at him now, / the perfect model for an artist of fame / his magnificent beauty enraptures / yet in my soul it only captures / the calm admiration released / by the beauty of silver or a beast.

Here, once again, the female gaze objectifies the male body in a subversive reversal of patriarchal positions. In all these double-voiced poems irony exposes at least two contradictory positions: that of dominant patriarchal discourse and woman's refusal to comply.

It could be said that what is at issue in the work of women writers is, above all, the construction of female subjectivity. All the poems referred to so far are relevant in this respect. However, a number of self-reflexive poems go so far as to posit a female identity, paradoxically, through self-dissolution and woman as lack. This rebellion of subjectivity sometimes takes an ironic tone and sometimes one of resignation. Mirta Aguirre writes in 'Disorientation':

Se me ha perdido mi cuerpo
y el alma se me perdió.
¿Dónde estoy yo misma ahora?
Busco y no puedo encontrarme.
Aquí estoy en carne y huesos.
Aquí estoy y no hay nada. (Jiménez et al. 1937: 9)

I have lost my body / I have lost my soul. / I myself, where am I now? / I search but I cannot find me. / Here are my flesh and bones. / Here I am, yet nothing is here.

In this poem the subject is able to reconstruct her identity only through her relationship to others, and those others are, significantly, 'many men'.

Dulce María Loynaz, a practising Catholic, appropriates and exaggerates traditional Catholic beliefs about women to reveal their incongruity. A mimetic strategy, possibly feigning humiliation and self-degradation, enables Loynaz to undercut both Catholic and pseudo-scientific discourses on woman. If I have no place among rational beings in the world, she asks in 'Lord, Who Wished it Thus', then why bother to make me?

Señor, que lo quisiste: di, ¿para qué he nacido? ...
¿Quién me necesitaba? ¿Quién me había pedido? ...

¿Qué misión me confiaste? ¿Y por qué me elegiste?
Yo, la inútil, la débil, la cansada, la triste ...
[...]
Bien sé que todo tiene su objeto y su motivo,
que he venido para algo y para algo vivo ... ,
y hasta el más vil gusano su destino ya tiene,
que tu impulso palpita en todo lo que viene,
y que si lo mandaste fue también con la idea
de llenar el vacío por pequeño que sea ... ;
[...]
¡Oh, Dios de los mediocres, los malos y los buenos,
en tu Obra no hay nada de más ni de menos ... !
Pero ... No sé, Dios mío ... , me parece que a Ti
– !un Dios! – te hubiera sido fácil pasar sin mí ...

                    (Lizaso and Fernández de Castro 1926: 376)

Lord, who wished it thus: tell me, why was I born? / Who needed me? Who
lost me? / What mission was I given? What was I chosen for? / I the useless,
the tired one, the sad one, the weak ... / [...] Everything has its purpose, I
know, and is fixed, / I'm here for some reason, and for a reason I live ... /
even the vilest worm has its destiny here, / your impulse beats in all that
exists, / and if you gave the orders it was with the idea / of filling in an empty
space no matter how tiny it be ... [...] / Oh, God of the mediocre, the bad,
the good and true, / in Your work there aren't too many or too few / But ...
I don't know, my Lord ... it seems to me that You / – a God, after all! – could
get on fine without me!

Similarly, 'The Rose's Prayer' mimics the Lord's Prayer. The roses ask
God to forgive their sins, 'as we forgive / men, who trespass against us /
who cut us and sell us and take us away' (Núñez 1993: 44). The female
subject may be presented and then negated, leaving her trace only in
language, as in 'Quietly':

Yo me iré calladita [...]
Yo me iré en puntillitas,
y ni se habrá de dar cuenta la tierra
de que la he pisado. (Lizaso and Fernández de Castro 1926: 377)

I will go very quietly [...] / I will go on tippy-toe, / and where my steps take
me / not even the earth will know.

She may be lost in a web of hypotheses and counter-factuals, 'If I were
nothing more than one / shadow without shadows; no more than an
intimate / darkness inside out' (Núñez 1993: 63), or, like 'The Woman of
Smoke', impossible to grasp. In this poem immateriality is resistance to
entrapment, confinement and definition:

Soy lo que no queda
ni vuelve. Soy algo
que disuelto en todo
no está en ningún lado ... [...]

Hombre que me besas
tu beso es en vano ...
Hombre que me ciñes:
¡Nada hay en tus brazos! ... (Núñez 1993: 54)

I do not remain / nor return. Everywhere / I am dissolved / yet nowhere [...]
// Man who kisses me / your kisses are in vain ... / Man who embraces me:
/ Your arms are empty!

'Of Silence'

Yo no hablaré más nunca [...]
Más que la tierra voy a ser callada
y humilde y triste ...
Para siempre estoy llena de silencio,
como vaso colmado
de un vino amargo y negro.

(Lizaso and Fernández de Castro 1926: 378)

I shall never speak again [...] / More silent than the land is what I'll be / and
humble, and sad ... / I shall be for ever silent / like a cup overflowing / with
black, bitter wine.

voices, paradoxically, the renunciation of language, and self-denial is figured
as the archetypal woman-vessel, but filled with dark resentment. Interestingly, in renouncing language the poet identifies with the land: both are
humbled and silent, neither can aspire to subjectivity and agency.

In their more subjective poems, women attempt to situate their voices
and inscribe their female bodies in language. But in Loynaz's poems
androcentric assumptions of masculinity and femininity are contested by
negating the possibility of a centred identity and so leaving space for
signs of the female self. Women poets write a way out of the ideational
void, out of the restraints of social practices and cultural myths, and even
out of language altogether. Language, as Luce Irigaray points out, reduces
the value of the feminine to the non-masculine, and it is for this reason
that 'women find it so difficult to speak and to be heard as women. They
are excluded and denied by the patriarchal linguistic order. They cannot
speak as women in a sensible, coherent manner' (Irigaray 1993a: 20). Poetry
in which women consciously inscribe silence is possibly the most subversive
of counter-discursive practices.

It has been said that in Latin America the 'first generation of urban, literate women [...] appeared in Havana' between 1910 and 1950 (Berg-mann et al. 1990: 2). Cuban women's writings in the first three decades of the century would seem to bear out the view that this particular literary sub-field was indeed rich. As in all countries, there is a wealth of material in Cuba yet to be brought to light and read critically. Critical activity is imperative because, as Bourdieu has argued, works of literature exist as objects loaded with symbolical value 'only if they are known and re-cognised as such, that is, socially instituted as works of art and received by spectators capable of knowing and recognising them as such' (Bourdieu 1993: 37). Writing was one of the means by which Cuban women asserted their difference in the fraught context of a dependent, postcolonial country undergoing rapid modernization. They questioned prevailing attitudes and in so doing must have sparked off a ripple-effect among the 'occupants of other positions' in the literary world (Bourdieu 1993: 58) which have yet to be studied. It is the task of feminist critics to recognize and name what these women undertook. Only then will multicultural feminist scholar-ship be able to counter universalist claims with evidence of other ways of thinking and doing. The fact is that what Cuban women were writing between 1900 and 1935 cannot be assimilated even into women's writing of the postcolonial Caribbean. Shusheila Nasta's observation that in countries with a history of colonialism 'women's quest for emancipation, self-identity and fulfilment can be seen to represent a traitorous act, a betrayal not simply of traditional codes and practice and belief but of the wider struggle for liberation and nationalism' does not apply to Cuba (Nasta 1991: xv). Although Cuban women wrote within a cultural offensive, it is difficult to find any trace of the sentiment expressed by Virginia Woolf at the time in *Three Guineas* (1938): 'as a woman I have no country. As a woman I want no country' (Woolf 1984: 229).

Notes

1. For José Martí's ideas on women's emancipation, see Martí (1961: Vol. XXIII, 24–54) and Toledano Sande (1985: 25–41).

2. For some interesting observations on gay and lesbian sub-themes in novels authored by women at this time, see Menéndez (1993: 118–57).

3. Camila's mother, Salomé Ureña, was a leading cultural figure in the Domin-ican Republic and founded the first secondary school for girls on the island.

4. Africa Fernández Iruela (an occasional writer) was the daughter of a school teacher and had studied pharmacy. She contributed to the periodical *Letras Güineras*, founded in 1909, and set up a pharmacy.

5. See also the erotic 'Spring scene' by Nieves Xenes in *Arpas cubanas* (Kostia 1904: 409–10). Here the sun is a sultan who caresses his harem of voluptuous flowers. A plant without flowers stands in a pot on the poet's balcony and seems indifferent until the sun 'with burning desire' kisses her too, at which point she 'doubles up, with pleasure spent'.

6. Emilia Bernal's mother was a school mistress who died prematurely and her

father was completely deaf. Mother of four children, she graduated with a degree in Pedagogy and became lecturer in literature in the Schoolteachers' college. After divorcing her husband she entered the diplomatic corps and travelled widely between 1935 and 1940, publishing over twenty books. She left Cuba in the early 1960s and died soon after. See Vega Ceballos (1978).

   7. Martí (1961: Vol. XXl, 16).

CHAPTER 3

Dulce María Loynaz: Horror of House and Home

In the Introduction to this book I stated an interest in women's works of literature as examples of creative imagination less overtly concerned with political events. The previous chapter showed the various levels of social commitment in evidence in women's poetry and suggested that it was when women queried the centred subject of male humanism that they were being most radical. I will now focus on the work of one writer, Dulce María Loynaz, in particular her novel *Jardín* [Garden], to explore further the idea that a woman's text need not refer directly to political events or historical time in order to be subversive but that, as Irigaray points out, in order to think through sexual difference the whole notion of time and space must be reconsidered (Irigaray 1988: 119).

Dulce María Loynaz, daughter of Cuban Independence veteran General Enrique Loynaz del Castillo, was born in Havana in 1902 (the year of the first Cuban Constitution), the eldest of four children who were all to become writers and artists. She published her first poems in 1919 in the newspaper *La Nación* and in Lizaso and Fernández de Castro's *La poesía moderna en Cuba* (1926). After obtaining a Law degree at Havana University in 1927, the profession she would pursue for thirty years, and travelling to Egypt, Turkey and the Middle East (1929), she married her cousin Enrique (1937) but they were divorced within six years. In 1937 she travelled to Mexico and published her powerful poem 'Song to a Barren Woman' in the *Revista Bimestre Cubana* (July–October 1937). A year later *Versos. 1920–1938* appeared and the prose poem 'Love Letter to King Tut-Ank-Amen' (written in 1929) was published in a magazine. Although Loynaz's poetry was well received (Rafael Marquina lectured on her work at the Lyceum in 1938, where she later gave various poetry readings herself) (Núñez 1993: 292–316) these were to be her last works published in Cuba until the 1990s. In 1946 Dulce María married the love of her life, Tenerife journalist Pablo Alvarez de Cañas, who encouraged her to publish in Spain.[1] Thus it was that her poems *Juegos de agua. Versos del agua y del amor* [Water Games. Verses of Poetry and Love] (1947) and her novel *Jardín* (1951), written in Cuba in the 1920s and 1930s, first appeared in

Madrid. In 1951 she was made a member of the Cuban Academia de Artes y Letras. *Jardín* was followed by *Carta de amor al Rey Tut-Ank-Amen* [Love Letter to King Tut-Ank-Amen] and the collection *Poemas sin nombre* [Poems without Name] (both published in Madrid in 1953), *Obra lírica* [Lyrical Works] (Madrid, 1955), the long poem *Ultimos días de una casa* [The Last Days of a House] (Madrid, 1958) and the travel book *Un verano en Tenerife* [A Summer in Tenerife] (Madrid, 1958). She attended various official celebrations in Spain, for example, the Fifth Centennial of the Birth of the Catholic Kings and was made a member of the Spanish Royal Academy in 1968. The fact that the bulk of her work was published in Franco's Spain, where she was a celebrated figure, did not augur well for the future. After the Revolution of 1959 Dulce María refused to leave Cuba (although her husband lived abroad between 1961 and 1972, and died in Cuba in 1974) but she vowed never to publish there again. She took no part in revolutionary cultural activities and remained, ignored or forgotten, a figure of stubborn resistance to change for twenty years, until the 1980s. In 1992, at the age of ninety, she won the Spanish Cervantes Prize for Literature and her works (some previously unpublished) have been, finally, collected and re-edited in Cuba and Spain (Yglesias 1984).[2]

Dulce María Loynaz was not associated with the feminist movement. According to her own account she was taught at home by private tutors and seldom ventured into the world outside the family and the home. She was at university in the stormy early 1920s but makes no reference to this period in life. Afterwards, she was often travelling abroad. Although, as we saw in Chapter 2, her poetry destabilizes androcentric assumptions of subjectivity and, as we shall see, sometimes subverts Catholic discourse (in the *Poemas náufragos* [Shipwreck Poems] particularly), Loynaz seldom wrote what might be termed nationalist feminist poetry or explicitly feminist poetry. Having said that, three of Loynaz's most beautiful poems fall precisely into those categories. The first, 'Poem CXXIV' (1953), is a rapturous hymn of joy to Cuba, one of the most magnificent eulogies ever written to the island. In this long prose poem the island is figured as a handsome young girl, Catholic and traditional, sometimes the daughter of the poet, sometimes her mother, but always part of the family to which she belongs and with which she identifies:

Isla mía, ¡qué bella eres y qué dulce! [...] Escarchada de sal y luceros, te duermes, Isla niña, en la noche del Trópico. Te reclinas blandamente en la hamaca de las olas [...] Tú eres por excelencia la muy cordial, la muy gentil. Tú te ofreces a todos aromática y graciosa como una taza de café; pero no te vendes a nadie.[...] Isla esbelta y juncal, yo te amaría aunque hubiera sido otra tierra mi tierra [...] Isla mía, Isla fragante, flor de islas: tenme siempre, náceme siempre, deshoja una por una todas mis fugas. Y gúardame la última, bajo un poco de arena soleada. (Núñez 1993: 204)

Island of mine, how beautiful you are and how sweet! [...] Frosted with salt and stars, you sleep, child isle, in the tropical night. You recline softly in a hammock of waves [...] You are by far the gentlest, the noblest of ladies. You offer yourself to all, delightful and aromatic, like a cup of coffee; but you sell yourself to no one [...] Island, lissom and slim, I would love you even if my land were another land [...] Isle of mine, fragrant isle, flower of the islands: hold me always, let me be born of you always, scatter my flights one by one. And keep the last one safe for me, beneath a handful of sunbaked sand.

The other two poems which must be singled out, not only because of their aesthetic value but also for their feminist ideas, are 'Song to a Barren Woman' (1937), and 'The Last Days of a House' (1958) which will be referred to later. Both of these poems are powerful indictments of iniquitous patriarchal attitudes towards women and an impassioned defence of women's instrinsic worth.

Jardín. Horror of house and home

This section focuses on *Jardín* ([1951] 1993a). I shall offer a close reading of the novel and then follow through some of the ideas it raises in a selective study of Loynaz's poetry and poetic prose. *Jardín*, one of the few novels published by women in the pre-revolutionary period and certainly the most experimental, is receiving increasing critical attention. This is partly because Loynaz won the Cervantes Prize, which resulted in the publication of new, easily accessible editions of her work, but also because Loynaz has long been recognized as the most important Cuban woman author living today. She is primarily a poet; *Jardín* is her only novel. When it was first published it was received in Cuba and Spain with admiration as well as perplexity. Gastón Baquero warmly recommended the novel to readers of the *Diario de la Marina* (20 January 1952); José María Chacón y Calvo published a series of critical articles on the novel in the *Diario* (10 February to 16 March 1952); and, some years later, Emilio Ballagas wrote a short, incisive essay for the same daily (9 September 1958) (Núñez 1993: 316–38). Within the last decade the novel has been singled out as a key feminist text. The time it took Dulce María to write *Jardín* (seven years, between 1928 and 1935) and for it to be published (some fifteen years later), its fragmented structure, gaps, incongruencies and intensely haunting, lyrical prose make this a strange novel indeed. It is difficult to classify in conventional generic categories.

Not surprisingly, criticism has focused on psychoanalytic interpretations. *Jardín* has been read as a woman's version of female identity formation and development.[3] Verity Smith opened the way for feminist readings in a brilliant analysis of mirror and photograph motifs, the embedded 'Sleeping Beauty' narrative, and women's fictional archetypes in the novel some years ago.[4] For Ileana Rodríguez, *Jardín* narrates the elite white woman's fraught transition to modernity in the context of the neo-colonial Caribbean.[5] My reading situates *Jardín* in the feminist Gothic tradition which I hope will complement these critics' findings, although I intend to dwell a little longer than they do on the spookish, nightmarish aspects of Loynaz's startling tale.

Jardín is, above all, a ghost story, a tale of horror and suspense in which a young woman, enclosed in an ancient house surrounded by a menacing garden, finally meets her death. The young woman, Barbara, is isolated and alone. She spends many hours contemplating the garden through her window or wandering along its labyrinthine paths. She can glimpse the sea through the trees but, for some reason, does not leave the domestic space which hems her in. One day, in a dark corner of the garden, she accidentally discovers an overgrown wall and a secret door opening into a small pavilion, inside which there is a chest. She smashes the lock and discovers in the chest remnants of a past history and a past identity: the outmoded clothes and sundry possessions of a woman who, it seems, had packed hastily in order to make a long journey. There is also a bundle of letters tied with a ribbon. Some are ripped and crumpled, but Barbara, beset by curiosity, unties the ribbon and is impelled to read. Thus begins the heroine's adventure in what – in the way I have described it, at least – bears the imprint of the Gothic novel.

In Gothic romance a young woman (endangered, vulnerable and dependent) is trapped in a haunted house (crumbling castle, monastery or mansion) and is besieged by a cruel villain (outside force or malevolent spirit). Virtually buried alive (possibly with a maid), she is beset by cruel passions, undefined violence and evil. Her terror takes the form of dread and a vague premonition; yet she feels both fear and attraction for the macabre. Her insatiable 'feminine' curiosity impels her to explore the hidden recesses and dark passages of the building where, after wandering around interminably, she makes a crucial discovery, usually a family secret involving another woman. After a series of terrifying events, the heroine finally marries and lives happily ever after. The eighteenth-century lady reader breathes a sigh of relief.

There are several versions of this basic Gothic plot (Anne Williams, for example, distinguishes a Male Gothic and a Female Gothic, to which I will return), but the key components remain the same. The most important point to make here is that in Gothic romance everything which is supernatural and mysterious, dark and gloomy, represents the presence of the 'other'. For Williams the other is always female, for DeLamotte the 'evil Other' in women's Gothic is male (A. Williams 1995: 1; DeLamotte 1990: 163). In my reading of the first four (of five) parts of *Jardín*, I shall show how closely the novel follows the Gothic pattern and suggest a feminist reading in which the 'other' is both female and male. I shall then argue that Part V, the final part of the novel, which I split into two sections (chapters 1–5 and chapters 6–8) provides, if not a 'turn of the screw', at least a 'twist in the tail'.

Barbara is shut up (we are not sure why) in a silent house and garden near the sea. She seems to be alone; the black servant Laura appears briefly. During the first part of the novel, she spends all her time in her bedroom which is described in significant detail: whitewashed walls, a high ceiling supported by beams, and a frieze depicting fighting monsters, warriors combating dragons, and great black birds in flight; heavy furniture; stuffed birds; a clock stopped at a quarter past six; purple curtains covering the doorways; a mirror placed so high it reflects only the dragons; a window and a half-opened door, obstructed by an almond tree, looking out on to the garden.

In Part I of the novel, Barbara sifts through a series of family photographs. One of the first is of her great-grandmother or, more precisely, her great-aunt who died young (some say she was poisoned, others that she killed herself with her hat pin). The face in the photograph is blurred and, like Barbara, the figure wears a silver cross. Another photograph is of a thin young man, an overgrown boy, with fair hair flicked over his eyes. His photograph seems less worn; he does not seem dead, and Barbara thinks he is about to smile. On the reverse she reads, 'For Barbara. Passionately, A...'. The writing is almost illegible and she must decipher the message letter by letter, although the young man's name has been worn away. Was the great-grandmother's name Barbara too, she wonders? Other photographs she comes across are of a distant male ancestor (an admiral of the king), and her younger brother who died when he was three. Finally, she discovers a wad of photographs of herself. Thus begins a long process of self-identification (mis-recognition in Lacan's terms) as Barbara looks at the series of images of herself and reconstructs in her mind scenes of her childhood. Her most painful memory is when, after a serious illness (which she survives but not her brother), Barbara sees her grief-stricken mother withdraw behind a closed door. The little girl waits at the other side of the door she cannot open, sobbing, but the mother never reappears, except as a vague figure floating in white. Clearly, the brother's death was of greater significance than her own illness; Barbara sees herself as the living sacrificed to the dead.

Verity Smith associates this episode involving photographs and mother-memories with the Lacanian mirror phase and the child's entry into the symbolic. The brutal separation of mother and child, and the repression of the female imaginary, are reflected in the photographs of an older Barbara where the girl appears as a lifeless object (a hat or a doll), positioned against an artificial, painted landscape (V. A. Smith 1993: 272). Barbara's only means of escape from the law of the father are the sea, the sun and fantasy (fairy stories).[6]

These first chapters insert the heroine into the context of the traditional patriarchal family, embodied by the house in which she is enclosed, its awesome accoutrements (the dragons, warriors, the empty mirror), and the now extinguished family line (the dead admiral, the dead brother). The house traps her in its frozen silence like a cold spider's web, 'sewing up her lips' (Loynaz 1993a: 48) and she feels claustrophobic, 'in life, but inside a glass wall' (p. 76). However, there is no mention of the father, as Smith notes, and the presence of the girl within that silent space suggests the decadent, patriarchal edifice may be about to crumble. The child Barbara is very much aware that her brother's death has endowed her with a vestige of power: 'It was necessary that he should die [...] so that she could assume a little of her power and just one, the least important, of her rights' (p. 17). Although she is alone, within her confined space she does enjoy some autonomy.

According to Williams, the hierarchical patriarchal family (by extension, kinship and the nation) is the 'basic conceptual metaphor' (A. Williams 1995: 89) of Gothic romance; exploring origins of the self implies delving into the family (and society's) history. DeLamotte suggests that the women in Gothic romance suffer on account of the institutions which they feel are alien to them (the family and education) and that the interiors of the Gothic house are nightmarish because their disorder reflects 'the logic of the social order' as experienced by women (DeLamotte 1990: 151). Gothic, then, expresses anxiety not only about the family; it also challenges and disrupts the symbolic order itself. It does this by symbolizing female 'otherness' (the poetic, irrational, natural, unspeakable other), what Irigaray refers to as the maternal line, and by focusing on transitional states and dissolving boundaries. The heroine in *Jardín* hardly remembers the mother who is a mere trace, 'the ghost of a mother' (Loynaz 1993a: 24) and the death of her mother (both real and symbolic) brings terror as well as joy; the 'bittersweet' feeling of someone freed 'from a person who was, sadly, an enemy' (p. 24). Yet the break with the mother has been only partially successful (the mother perhaps lurks in the garden), and paternal authority is insecure. Barbara thus inhabits a transitional zone symbolized by the maternal-garden and the paternal-house.

In this novel, as the title suggests, the garden is the more powerful of the two. Associated with the mother (killed by a falling tree in a storm) and the womb, the garden becomes increasingly menacing as the novel progresses. It takes on a life of its own and, like a sleeping monster lurking outside her window (p. 87), lures the heroine to walk its circular paths in springtime while continually threatening her with destruction. When Barbara ventures out of the house (an enclosure but also protection) into the garden (nature run riot), wherein lies another enclosed space (the pavilion), when she goes in search of 'eyes other than her own reflected in a mirror' (p. 55), strange things start to happen. The garden is like a malignant growth threatening the heroine with non-being, barring her path to freedom (the sea and the sky).

As Rodríguez notes, in *Jardín* it is the pavilion rather than the house which is the 'centre of meaning' (Rodríguez 1994: 100). Barbara falls asleep in the garden, awakes as if in a dream, and sees the pavilion wall. The ruinous pavilion, whose hidden door she must dig out from among the vegetation, both embodies and is the repository of the 'mystery' of the novel. The pavilion she excavates has the nauseous smell of a 'tomb recently opened' (Loynaz 1993a: 63) and as night draws in she feels faint, as if her spirit separates from her body, as if she could lay down and die. Entering the pavilion-tomb, she enters herself 'going inward, going in towards herself again' (p. 64) and, like Alice in 'Wonderland', suddenly finds she is taller. Once inside the pavilion-womb ('she could see the garden's entrails hanging down inside' [p. 65]), a space which feels so familiar, the heroine retrieves evidence from the past relating to a personal history (her own) and to the history of the nation.

In view of the Gothic traits of the first part, I would like to suggest the following reading of the novel (excepting Part V). It is a reading which at first may seem implausible. My Gothic reading is as follows: Barbara is haunted by the vampire 'A...', the young man in the photograph. The vampire is let loose when Barbara, like Pandora, opens the forbidden box in the pavilion in the garden (Part II). The love letters she finds there were sent by 'A...' to Barbara's namesake, her great-aunt Barbara, many years ago. The letters are addressed to 'Barbara' and in reading them (Part III) Barbara assumes her great-aunt's identity. She finds herself identifying with memories (newspaper accounts of the 1840s plastered on the pavilion walls) which cannot be her own because she was not born then. In acknowledging the interpellation of the unknown, unidentified 'voice', in responding to this (her only) interlocutor, in thoughts if not in speech, Barbara finds herself sucked into a past life, a past love.

For DeLamotte, discovery of the other woman (in this case, the Good Woman) whose death was undeserved, is the heroine's encounter with the oppression of women (DeLamotte 1990: 154). Here the heroine becomes the 'Barbara' of the letters and, in turn, brings 'A...' back to life.[7] 'A...', the unprepossessing man of the photograph (hardly the Byronic demon), first materializes through the words in his letters, but he gradually acquires a presence, a power, which is somehow identified with the garden, the night and the moonlight. He is a revenant, a malign spirit, a shadow which haunts her room at night, a danger to which she is attracted and of which she is afraid. Thus, the garden, which is the object of Barbara's contemplation, becomes an emblem of evil despite its beauty and seasonal changes. Barbara is familiar with the garden, she spends many hours there, but it turns against her and she feels her life being sucked away.

The relationship Barbara is drawn into is one of tyrannical, devouring love. 'A...'s love for 'Barbara' was passionate and selfish. The story Barbara pieces together from the fragments of letters tells this one-sided account of an affair (there are no letters written by the great-aunt) which results, apparently, in the young man's death. Before he dies he curses 'Barbara' and vows he will never leave her; he knows she is preparing for a journey but, he tells her, there can be no escape, he will never die. This overwhelming Romantic love, bent on destroying the object of its desire (it seems the great-aunt died before she could escape [p. 93]) is now targeted on Barbara who has memorized the contents of the letters to such a degree that it seems 'A...' is speaking directly to her. She, too, senses the danger; she, too, will make plans to escape; she, too, like her foremother, will spend the night packing her things watched by 'A...' from the garden. But beforehand, in the midst of a tremendous storm, Barbara is lured to the top of a cliff where she finds herself looking out into the dark sea. Lightning flashes and with 'A...''s words ringing in her ears Barbara waits for 'him' to come:

> she [the great-aunt] had believed he had died; he had said he was dying, he had exhausted her talking about his death, but he had never died at all, he would never die. While she [Barbara] had believed he was dead, she had been reviving him with her own life, nourishing him with her own blood, feeding him with the rich sweetness of her heart. She had believed in time, but time had crumbled in her hands [...] It was him; eternally him; invincible him; obstinate, stubborn hateful him. (p. 152)

The loved one for whom Barbara waits is none other than Dracula himself, a mere 'colourless, shapeless product of the storm' (p. 155) at this point in the narrative. However, he does not appear. Instead, something unforeseen happens. At the moment of sublime exaltation and imminent transcendence of the self, Barbara sees a figure slowly making its way towards her along the beach. She knows it is not 'A...'; it is another young man (dark hair, blue eyes) who has arrived from the 'real' world. His ship, the *Euryanthe*, has come aground in the storm and he and his friend are wandering on the beach. He approaches Barbara, touches her and speaks to her, but receives no answer. In fact, he is rather appalled by this cold, bloodless, zombie-like figure standing alone; he thinks she is deaf and dumb; her skin feels like fungus. But the captain has arrived to save Barbara, this modern version of Psyche who is standing on the peak waiting for the monster. Barbara and the captain fall in love. She ties up the wad of letters once more, thus strangling the words and the voice of 'A...' (p. 164) and she begins to talk. She speaks to the man, communicates and comes to language, and the new images of her caught in his photographs are a rebirth, a 'small resurrection' (p. 166), hence the significance of 'Lent', and the bath she takes which is a sensuous ritual of purification. When the captain's ship is ready to sail, he asks her to go away with him. On the eve of the departure she wanders around the garden and feels its menace. The garden is sad, like a 'old seducer' (p. 162); the pools of stagnant water are like 'congealed blood', the garden itself 'like a dead man's eye' (p. 179); a tragic silence reigns. She feels threatened by a 'moist shadow'; the wind howls lugubriously and she feels dazed. The vegetation strangles her, night falls, and the trees raise their angry fists. A lizard slips down a tree, a huge hand seems to hold her back in the 'green wall' and she feels 'penned in' (p. 182). Finally, in a fit of anger, she thrashes her way through the garden. Once in the house she locks up carefully, though the moonlight intrudes through the skylight. That night she dreams 'the dragon has enormous, scaly wings which it spreads as if it is about to attack' (p. 185). Waking up with a start, she prepares to flee.

In a gripping scene, the captain meets Barbara on the beach. He sweeps her off her feet and carries her along the beach to his ship. All nature seems to thwart him; the moon shines strangely on that 'landscape of death' (p. 187). He feels perturbed, suddenly exhausted; thousands of crabs line up as if ready for battle, staring at him with 'eyes like daggers' (p. 187). He feels as though he is stealing a strange creature from another world and will incur the wrath of a vengeful god; never before has he felt so anxious. Then he hears footsteps behind him, coming closer every minute. There is nothing except a shadow, a small shadow which resembles a boy. He looks again; after all, he is a scientist, but there is absolutely nothing which could cast such a shadow. Only the distant light of his ship keeps him on course. He runs at break-neck speed with Barbara in his arms towards the ship until, finally, he finds the rowing boat with his men and is saved. The shadow disappears, normality returns. Yet the captain feels 'the feeling of having beaten off a mysterious power, an unknown force that for a moment he felt hovering above his head' (p. 190).

At the end of the fourth part of the novel then, perhaps originally the final part, the Gothic cycle is complete. The point of view of the very sane captain–scientist is crucial in establishing 'A...' as a supernatural phenomenon (not a mere figment of Barbara's imagination) and Barbara as almost dead (the captain notices her cold skin on several occasions). 'A...' must be a very angry ghost–vampire because his loved one has been snatched away from him for a second time. Barbara, on the other hand, has managed to escape 'A...', the garden, the house, her family tree, timelessness, stasis and death. The sea, always presented in contradistinction to the garden, is the pathway to freedom. Only the sea resists the garden (p. 46). It seems that Barbara (soon married to the captain–Prince Charming) will live happily ever after in the world of light, rationality, time, movement and space. Up to the end of Part IV, Loynaz has written what Williams refers to as Female Gothic (a type found more frequently in the twentieth century), and women's Gothic is conservative.[8]

In Female Gothic the story is told from the limited point of view of the heroine. *Jardín* is narrated by a third person who, save on very specific occasions, tells the story always from Barbara's point of view. Female Gothic hinges on terror and the sublime (rather than horror and the nauseous), that is, on an imagined threat which (as in *Jardín*, perhaps) is finally dispelled. Above all, Female Gothic usually ends happily in marriage; marriage provides the heroine with a new birth and a new identity, which seems to be the case at the end of Part IV. However, in the last part of the novel Loynaz suddenly switches genre. After an almost realist interlude, the final chapters follow the pattern of Male Gothic. This is not on account of a change in point of view, but because what was previously considered a harmless threat is shown to be an awful, inexplicable reality ('vampires do exist' in Williams's terms). What was terror turns to horror (the rotting putrefaction of the 'female' garden which threatens the speaking subject with destruction). The plot changes from comic to tragic. The heroine dies and narrative closure is uncertain (A. Williams 1995: 103–4). For Williams, the differences between Male and Female Gothic reflect the different cultural positions of men and women. Male Gothic articulates a fear of the Female other; Female Gothic posits a transformation of the assumptions of what is male and female. *Jardín* does both.

Apart from the suspense and gloomy atmosphere there are several clues in the 'Prelude' to suggest that a Gothic reading is not fanciful. The 'Prelude' (finished at a quarter to seven in the evening, on 21 June 1935) points out explicitly (and with profound irony) that *Jardín* is hardly a novel. If it is a novel, explains Loynaz, it is a lyrical novel. The heroine is implausible; the text is a 'furtive incursion into the world of fantasy', and Loynaz herself is merely dabbling in 'what is prohibited' (p. 7). Loynaz adds that if Barbara's name were 'Psyche', the character might well be read as a symbol, but even this would have been 'too much effort' (p. 8). In her novel, she continues, the reader will find a strange world in which trees are personified and people dehumanized, where the heroine absorbs the 'mystery of vegetation' which imprisons her and where the garden comes alive absorbing her heartbeat in its roots (p. 9). The opening epigraph, taken from Teixeira de Pascoaes, reads 'Only animals find nature natural' (p. 9).

According to Williams, Gothic is essentially poetic. The genre discloses nature in culture or, put another way, it discloses the semiotic in the midst of the symbolic.[9] The Gothic world is a 'virtual reality', an experimental space in which the repressed 'female' might be 'realized' (A. Williams 1995: 95–6). The supernatural marks our anxiety about the usual systems of making sense of the world, logical categories and physical laws. Thus in Gothic the dead return, the non-material materializes, the inanimate becomes animate, and the boundaries between culture and nature, life and death, dissolve. The world as we know it (the symbolic) is shattered, allowing space for the 'female' semiotic to emerge. This genre description seems to fit Loynaz's own description of her work in the 'Prelude'.

The reference to 'Psyche' immediately suggests a psychological reading (psyche means soul, or private inner space) but it also refers to the myth of Psyche and Cupid (or Psyche and Eros) which, in Williams's view, is the founding myth of Female Gothic (as Oedipus is the founding myth of Male Gothic).[10] Certainly the plot in *Jardín* seems to mirror the Psyche myth.[11] According to this reading, Psyche-Barbara is saved by Captain Eros from the encounter with the monster (she stands on a mountain peak/cliff waiting for the monster to take her away). After many adventures Captain Eros takes Psyche away on his ship, aided by the Zephyr's breezes (Euryanthe may be linked etymologically to 'Euros' [winds] and 'anthos' [flowers]) to his castle in Olympus/abroad (possibly the United States) where they marry and live happily ever after. In the legend of Psyche, however, the main antagonist is Eros's jealous mother, Aphrodite, the goddess of love. There is no such figure in *Jardín*, unless we consider Barbara's mother to be the main antagonist. In this reading the (dead) mother sends her son, Barbara's dead brother, ('A...', 'Amor'?) to deliver Barbara to the monster in a marriage of death. But in *Jardín* 'Amor' either does obey his mother's wishes (unlike Eros) or becomes the monster himself.[12] In a psychoanalytic reading, 'A...' might represent both incestuous mother/brother-love (the monster) and the Other ('Autrui'). Either way, Barbara does not transcend immanence other than in death.

There are other clues. For example, the constant pointing up of the inadequacies of written language (the symbolic): the discontinuities, silences, fragments of (lost) letters, embedded tales, ambiguities, curses, strange warnings and texts probably mis-read because the original context is missing. One of the most obvious gaps occurs at the climax of the novel when Barbara musters up the courage to cross the garden at night and escape with the captain who is waiting for her on the beach. Will the garden let her through? It obviously does without any problem because the relevant passage is omitted in a tremendous anti-climax. Barbara leaves the house; then she is in the captain's arms.

More important, in my view, are the consistent references to vampirism. The etymological root of Dracula is dragon, meaning 'sharp sight'. Dracula is eternal; he lives by sucking young women's blood; he comes out at night, has wings and is repelled by silver crosses. When the young Barbara is seriously ill and, she thinks, about to die, she imagines the dragons from the frieze swooping down to take her. After entering the pavilion and reliving, it seems, the great-aunt's fatal illness (except this time she does not die), Barbara feels as if a dragon is biting her (p. 69). Laura, the black servant, warns her, 'you've got the devil in your body; you've always had it [...] for a hundred years or more' (p. 74). In fact, when Barbara does finally die, the creature which falls on her is a dragon. The numerous references to Barbara as a bloodless creature, to women wearing silver crosses, and to a blood-sucking garden reinforces the vampire theme.

(Dracula was presented by Bram Stoker as the dragon fighting [the cross of] St George.) Vampirism is associated with the garden (the dragon, the materialization of the evil spirit) and even with Barbara herself. The vampire dwells within, in the form of the mother: 'The girl was the garden' (p. 49), 'it is the garden of Death that searches for you and will find you always' (p. 51). Barbara feels her great-aunt in her, as though her hands are not her own. The blood on the great-aunt's gown, which she wears, is her own blood smeared all over her because of a cut finger. When she reads the letters, Barbara is bewitched, they are full of 'magic and poison' (p. 110). Reading them brings 'A…' back to life. But love, she realizes, needs a body. While standing in the pavilion she suddenly has a premonition that 'something awful will happen to her if she stayed there' (p. 92). The earth, too, is vampire-like, 'we have to die so she can suck our blood' (p. 111), and the earth is the mother, 'the earth is the terrible, natural mother, the insatiable devourer of her own children' (p. 112). Above all, the vampire embodies Romantic love which assaulted the great-aunt like a crocodile: 'how she must have defended herself from being absorbed, from feeling her whole self converted into the nourishment of another being' (p. 128). Perhaps that is why 'A…' has a surfeit of blood, as noted by the doctors who apply leeches. Dracula, then, is the garden, the mother, and the earth, and none will pardon Barbara's departure (p. 122).

'A…' wrote to great-aunt 'Barbara', 'I'll make you mine, Barbara' (p. 135). He will awaken and reclaim her. Thus the tragedy is written from the first. Barbara will be like the butterfly caught on the pin. He has a 'dark means' to obtain her and Christianity will not stand in the way (p. 151). The sea and the sun (daylight) are Barbara's defences; for 'A…' the sea is a traitor (p. 143), and Barbara has her 'shield of gold', her 'sword of light' (p. 164).

Although *Jardín* may be considered part of the Gothic tradition, it is no mere pulp fiction. Loynaz destabilizes the Gothic types themselves so that the garden, although associated with the mother and the womb, is also associated with the young male 'A…'. The garden includes an element of the male, 'the invasion of the vegetable kingdom allied with dead stone' (p. 51). Conversely, 'A…' is a feminized figure (hence his association with the garden) but, as a consequence, he does not resemble the Byronic demon-like hero nor the gruesome, sexually obsessed vampire (although DeLamotte notes that in modern Gothic the gentle man often turns out to be the villain). On the other hand, the captain – who saves Barbara – does look like the Byronic hero, yet he takes her away and marries her. Above all, there is no 'other' side to the captain; he is not a mysterious figure. In fact, he seems to be the only sane character in the novel. It could be argued, of course, that the vampire narrative itself destabilizes sexual boundaries in that Dracula presents a 'decadent fantasy of reproduction through transfusion […] Dracula's offspring are the daughters of his blood' (Showalter 1991: 179). Thus 'A…' assumes reproductive possibilities.

Most disruptive of all to the Female Gothic pattern is the final part of the novel, Part V. This final part (so far not discussed), consisting of eight chapters, can be divided into two. The first section (two short chapters) covers some twenty years and expands the 'lived happily ever after' formula. Barbara lives in the real world married to the captain. She interacts with other people; she becomes 'normal', wears fashionable clothes and has her hair permed. She entertains, shops, volunteers to be a nurse in the (First World) War. She travels to many countries on planes, boats, cars and trains; she lives in a fine house and has two children. She becomes a modern, possibly 'American' wife, doted on by her husband whom she, in turn, adores. Yet at no time during this long period, which the narrator skips over hastily, does Barbara engage in the deep self-questioning the reader has become accustomed to in the previous four parts. In fact, Barbara seems not to think at all. The artificiality of her lifestyle, marked by the electric lights she has to learn to use, the false lights of civilization, shapes her to the rigid role models reminiscent of the photographs she saw of herself when she was young. Above all, Barbara is still dependent on a man, her husband. Not only does she depend on him for money and guidance, but the captain, a latter-day Pygmalion, remodels Barbara to his liking (the tastes of modern society) so that only a small vestige of her former self remains. He gives her everything she asks for, but he does the giving. She always obeys him, never doubting the legitimacy of his authority.

These chapters pose a problem for the reader. As Verity Smith notes (1993) the lyrical tone becomes strident. On an historical level, Barbara is seen to leave behind the ghosts of her traditional, patriarchal, 'barbaric' past (the jungle-like garden, the home, the family tree) and has relocated in modern civilization, the world of time and space. From timelessness she moves into history; from stasis to movement; from substance to energy. On a psychological level, Barbara leaves behind the world of her childhood, the silent womb–mother–garden, the 'female' which spooks the symbolic, and the family enclosure. She does this by finding an 'other', the captain. She sees herself reflected in his eyes and thus has access to the symbolic, the world of coherent thought and language. But the symbolic is merely another formulation of patriarchy. The happy ending of the Gothic romance is shown to be not so happy. Although Barbara is contented and wants for nothing, she is never a subject in her own right, she is always the 'object' of the masculine same. The captain has effected 'the humanization of Barbara, her metamorphosis, with the triumph of an author' (p. 225). The light of the world, she finally decides, is a sick sun (p. 203); 'this electric light could not show her a better world than the one she had possessed when she was alone' (p. 206). The light of man merely defines, and 'to define is to limit. To reduce the idea with a word' (p. 208). Barbara may have escaped but now she is caught up in a relationship of power in which the male enforces his superiority. She may well have assumed an identity, the only female identity the symbolic allows, but, as Irigaray points out, the gap between female identity and female subjectivity is immense. The point is, and in this respect the novel is perhaps profoundly pessimistic, there is no place for Barbara.

Even so, the reader is hardly prepared for the shattering final section when Barbara's worst fears are realized, when the cycle of eternal return defeats the masculine myth of technical progress, as foretold at the start: 'it is Barbara's garden that [...] searches for you and will find you, to squash out your life between its stones [...] You can run, you can flee, but this knot will not fail' (p. 51). In the last four chapters the Gothic once again asserts itself with a horrific twist. Some time around 1918 (after the war),[13] Barbara decides she would like to return home, to pass by the place where she was born. They return on the *Euryanthe*, and the apocalypse is unleashed because, of course, 'A...' is waiting for Barbara. The feeling of impending doom which pervades the whole novel is thus realized. As the ship approaches the coast, Barbara notices that the garden has grown to immense proportions. It has overgrown the house. Once the ship drops anchor Barbara finds the lure of the garden irresistible.

In a crucial scene, the captain suddenly has strange misgivings and refuses to make for shore with Barbara, despite her insistent requests. She must wait for the light of the new day. But Barbara wants to 'sleep, return, immerse herself again in the warm breeze of the shadow, not yet born' (p. 236). As if in a dark dream, she boards the rowing boat alone and is carried to the shore. On the beach she sees a figure approach her, as she saw the captain long ago. He carries a lamp; he seems to be young and slim, but she cannot see his face. Her house, he says, has been demolished. Barbara follows the elusive figure she can never reach into the garden. Once there she is caught and trapped. They walk all through the eerie night, through the grave-like horrors of 'smell of humidity, of stagnant water' (p. 242) (vampires love graves and have an aversion to running water) until, once again, she finds the pavilion wall. As day breaks, the wall begins to crumble. She sees the face of the young man, grotesquely half-melted in the morning light; she steps back in horror but is transfixed. He stabs her with the look of death and she is drawn towards him like a sleep-walker. She feels his slimy eyes creeping over her like slugs 'his eyes stuck to her skin, soft and wet [...] like slugs' (p. 245). While she stands face to face with death, a high piece of stonework, 'in the form of an animal with great wings' topples over above her. 'Hold the dragon', she asks, but he whispers, 'Don't be afraid, I will show you the path' (p. 246). The wall falls down. She is killed. At least, that is what we are led to believe, although the final words of the novel suggest the spirit or rather

the substance of Barbara is still alive. It seems as though Barbara survives
as a piece of polished metal, crossed with blue veins, which a modern-day
worker throws away. This might refer to the moon, the symbol of the
feminine, which persists. The final words of the novel are: 'Barbara, behind,
above, below, for ever [...] presses her pale face to the iron bars' (p. 247).
But again the novel presents a feminist twist: in the opening pages Barbara
picks up the moon and buries it in the garden. Perhaps 'A...' is killed too,
but a lizard[14] escaping through the cracks in the stone suggests he is not.
The growing strength of the garden has nourished the powers of 'A...'
so that he finally materializes; his presence become substance. As in other
Gothics, Mother Nature takes on the power of God the Father, and the
route to Barbara's roots lead to Death.

   It could be argued that while Barbara assumes her identity as the object
of the same (the captain) in the real world, 'A...' represents the Other,
the face-to-face encounter with which would enable her to transcend
materiality or the 'en soi' and assume subjectivity. In Levinas's (1987: 76)
account, radical alterity can only be the unknowable (Death, Mystery, love
of the Other). It is not Death itself which enables the subject to transcend
his or her self, but the encounter with the approach of Death, the
encounter with Love. In *Jardín* the Other is Love, all-powerful Romantic
love; it is also the mother–garden–nature. Barbara returns to the garden
because she knows that only there can she aspire to subjectivity, transcend
the immanent, in her love-encounter with the absolutely other 'A...' (Amor,
Autrui?). But the encounter with the sublime which overwhelms her is
also the encounter with the mother (dwelling in Barbara herself). If Barbara
is consumed by the Other of Romantic love, she is also devoured by the
death drive, the return to the mother–womb. She is also killed by the
crumbling patriarchal wall. Hence Ileana Rodríguez's perceptive comments
on the fate of the elite woman in Cuba who cannot adapt to modernity
and is crushed by tradition.

   Despite the no-win situation of the heroine, *Jardín* is a feminist novel.
It critiques everyday modern life as we know it from the point of view
of a woman. Modern life is a useless merry-go-round of meaningless
activity in which woman is always man's other, the object which allows
man access to subjectivity. Second, the novel is an even more ferocious
critique of Romantic love and the Romantic genre in general. As is almost
always the case in male-authored Romantic fiction (an obvious example is
Goethe's *The Sorrows of Young Werther*), the man bewails his lover's coldness
and dies of love. What this novel points out is the egoism and tyranny
of a love which will not allow its object to assume subjectivity but controls
and devours it instead. Third, woman is shown to have no place in the
traditional patriarchal family or family line. She is confined to a secluded
part at the back of the house. The family, purportedly providing security,
fails to protect and it is the rotten edifice of patriarchal culture, the wall

of man's making, decrepit civilization, the archaeology of the past, which kill Barbara. Finally, the novel shows that the return to the mother, the womb, and primeval matter results only in silence, non-being and, ultimately, death. There is no comfort in being reunited with mother-earth. For woman, there is no escape, no way out.

The 'female quest romance' is a paradox in terms (DeLamotte 1990: 180). The horror of this novel is that in the midst of beauty, despite the presence of the sea (infinite horizons) and love (transcendence of self), for woman there is only objectification, putrefaction and death. Barbara glimpses other ways of being, she almost becomes a New Woman (hence the tragedy of her story). She sees through the cracks in the symbolic edifice (to the extent that the mother is masculinized, the male Other is feminized, the dead live, living is death, love is evil, death is love) but she is destroyed by the very breakdown of boundaries (walls), by the ghosts of the present and the past. There is no escape from the mother (within) or from the master (outside). Like the intellectually inclined New Woman (Mina Murray Harker in *Dracula*) Barbara is punished for wanting to know (Showalter 1991: 180). Loynaz confirms her view of the tragedy of the non-compliant woman:

> Without the somber anxiety of watchful Eve, listening to the voices surrounding the garden, Adam would still be sleeping in Paradise. He would still be sleeping, good man, happy to eat and obey. Disobedience. Curiosity. These are the first two steps woman takes [...] Her rebellion and disquiet, her struggle with fear, has given rise to the sign of tragedy which is for ever marked upon her brow. (1951: 20)

The pursuit of forbidden knowledge is one of the principal themes of Gothic romance and, as Williams points out, the curious female (Pandora, Eve, Bluebeard's wife) 'must learn her terrible lesson' (A. Williams 1995: 42).

Gothic romance such as *Jardín* inscribes anxieties about boundaries and thresholds (DeLamotte 1990: 20), hence the focus on barriers (doors, gates) and in-between states and positions (twilight zones, pathways, slime, vapours, ghosts, vampires and metamorphosis). For Irigaray it is the female sex itself which constitutes this threshold, 'a threshold into *mucosity*' (Irigaray 1988: 128). The breakdown of barriers includes repressed womb-fantasies. Crucial to an understanding of the novel are dichotomies such as inside and outside, belonging and extraneous. These anxieties reflect a deeper (Romantic) anguish about the boundaries of the self. As Claire Kahane explains, Gothic fear is a 'fear of femaleness', being a woman threatens one's wholeness, the boundaries of self (quoted in DeLamotte 1990: 189). According to DeLamotte (1990) tracing the boundaries of the self is a woman's theme. Danger comes from a kind of 'inner space' or, as Margaret A. Doody points out, from 'the self under attack' (quoted in DeLamotte 1990: 160). The self shuts out what is alien to it. But the

basic Romantic question – what is self, and what is not me or Other –
remains. Gothic horror (rot and slime) brings to mind Kristeva's (1982)
notion of the abject and, again, the threat of bodily integrity. For Kristeva
(1987) love in the feminine is a merging with elemental matter.

In Loynaz's novel the garden, inevitable death, is within: 'What are you
running away from [...] if the garden is you' (p. 52). As DeLamotte
points out:

> Gothic romance by women represents the hidden unspeakable reality of women's
> lives: not just their lives in the private inner world of the psyche, but also their
> social and economic lives in a real world of patriarchal institutions. (DeLamotte
> 1900: 165)

She quotes Simone de Beauvoir who writes in *The Second Sex*: 'the day
when it will be possible for woman to love not in her weakness but in her
strength [...] love will become for her, as for man, a source of life and
not of mortal danger' (DeLamotte 1990: 148). In *Jardín* that day has yet
to come.

Poetry, prose, resurrection

Jardín was Loynaz's only novel but many of the themes and motifs discussed
above may be traced in her poetry and poetic prose. Some recurrent themes,
all redolent of woman's problematic access to subjectivity, are: entrapment
('Prison of Air', 'The Parting'); the containment of (feminine) fluids ('Water
Games'); transgression and forbidden knowledge ('Song to a Barren
Woman'), and women's state of dereliction ('The Last Days of a House').
What is most striking is the recurrence of the fear of 'femaleness' (as in
the Male Gothic) or mother-matter figured in rotten vegetation, nauseous
slime and stagnant water, and identified with non-identity and silence ('The
Mirror', 'The Ponds', 'Imperfect Poem', 'The Forest'). This is particularly
noticeable in the exquisite prose poems *Poemas sin nombre* [Poems without
Name] (1953), lovingly dedicated, ironically, to Loynaz's mother.[15]

In a few poems, interpellation ('Poem XXXVII') by the loved one and
dialogue (with God or the loved one) does bring about resurrection ('I am
Born Again in You'). Recurrent motifs are: in-between states (usually
denoting repulsion); water, rivers and the sea (the majority included in the
collection, *Juegos de agua* [Water Games], 1947, dedicated to her husband
Pablo Alvarez de Cañas); the garden; and threat, darkness and shadow.
Various poems function almost as glosses of the novel, for example,
'Archangel Saint Michael' where the poet asks the warrior angel to protect
her from 'the hidden devil / that sucks my blood' (Núñez 1993: 96) or
'The Game of Death' where the erotic is horrific and the lover's hand 'a
frozen claw, a slow hook / digging in' (p. 91). Vampire motifs and the
identification of love with death is most evident in *Poemas sin nombre*.

What this poetry articulates is a fear of the female (self, mother) identified with non-being and immanence, and an anxious longing for (but also fear of) transcendence and escape. Loynaz's poems inscribe the tension between stasis (garden, circularity, darkness, death) and a potential departure from the self through the other (sea, sun, time, space). As she explains in her own words with reference to the poem 'Woman and the Sea', which begins, 'I threw my hope to the sea; / and even in the sea, was my hope / green-sea [...]' ('Eché mi esperanza al mar: / y aún fue en el mar, mi esperanza / verde-mar [...]' (Núñez 1993: 119), 'it refers to the mood of those who have tried to free themselves from everything, good or bad, that has weighed down their lives for so long' (Simón 1991b: 96). Shut off from the world, without an interlocutor, the poet identifies herself with an island,

Rodeada de mar por todas partes,
soy isla asida al tallo de los vientos
Nadie escucha mi voz si rezo o grito ('Island'; Núñez 1993: 109)

Surrounded by water on every side / I am an island held down by the stem of the winds. / No one listens to my voice if I shout or I pray

and an island is nothing more than lack,

Una isla es
una ausencia rodeada
de agua: Una ausencia de
amor rodeada de
amor ... ('Geography'; Núñez 1993: 68)

An island / is absence surrounded / by water: an absence of love / surrounded by / love ...

The majority of Loynaz's poems voice frustration and negativity. For there to be love, the self and the other must meet in space and time. In Loynaz's poetry, rather than concurrence and recognition more often there is misplacement, mistiming and non-recognition. The encounter which might lead to rebirth seldom takes place.

This is particularly evident in early poems such as 'The Ballad of Late Love': 'Love arriving late, you didn't see me / yesterday ... ' (Núñez 1993: 53); 'Hesitant Love':

Un amor indeciso se ha acercado a mi puerta ...
Y no pasa; y se queda frente a la puerta abierta [...]
Amor semi-despierto, tienes
los ojos neblinosos aún de Lázaro (Núñez 1993: 57)

A hesitant love has arrived at my door / He won't enter in; he stays at the door
which is open [...] Half-awake love, you have still / the cloudy eyes of Lazarus;

'Traveller': 'I am like the traveller – who arrives at port and no one is
waiting' (Núñez 1993: 58); 'Certainty': 'All the rivers will run to the sea! /
And I won't kiss you' (Núñez 1993: 61); 'The Parting':

Voy caminando en línea recta; llevo
las manos vacías, los labios sellados ...
Y no es tarde, ni es pronto,
ni hay hora para mí (Núñez 1993: 86)

I am walking down a straight line; my hands / are empty, my lips are sealed ... /
It's not yet late, or early, / there's no time for me,

'Is It the Lark?':

Vengo
de un ayer sin riberas que es
hoy todavía o que no fue
nunca (Núñez 1993: 74)

I come / from a yesterday without shores / today it still is / or was never

and 'Time':

Es tarde para la rosa.
Es pronto para el invierno.
Mi hora no está en el reloj ...
Me quedé fuera del tiempo! (Núñez 1993: 83)

It is late for the rose. / It is early for winter. / My hour's not the clock ... /
I was left out of time!

Similarly, in 'Love Letter to King Tut-Ank-Amen' (1929) the poet arrives
too late: 'I think [...] I might have been what I'll now never be: a drop
of love. But you didn't wait for me and you departed walking [...] you
didn't wait for me and you went towards death' (Loynaz 1991: 35).

The same kind of atemporality or extemporality is present in *Jardín*
where the meeting (between Barbara and the other) is a central motif.
The non-encounter (with 'A...') leads to a meaningless interlude: life. The
chance meeting that does take place (with the captain) leads to a temporary
transformation too mundane for rebirth. The final meeting (with 'A...')
leads to death. As indicated previously, Barbara, the female subject-in-
process, is faced with a no-win situation. In his theory of the time–space
aspects of narrative, Bakhtin explains how the motifs of meeting/parting
and recognition/non-recognition are central to Greek romance. Thus the

meeting chronotope is a 'unity of time and space (a unity without a merging)', the result of 'random contingency' and 'chance simultaneity' (Bakhtin 1981: 92, 97). This works for *Jardín* if it is read as an inverted romance. In Classical romance the hero meets the heroine, they set out on a long string of meaningless adventures, and finally marry. The 'adventure time' is a mere 'extemporal hiatus', a timeless digression in the biographical time sequence. This description fits the embedded romance in *Jardín* (Barbara meets the captain, marries and embarks on a world of adventures). However, *Jardín* shifts biographical time (dates, historical events) to this meaningless interlude. The real romance, between Barbara and 'A...', who do meet and finally do marry, albeit in death, which should take part according to romance in biographical time, takes place in time marked not by the clock (which is stopped) but by circular, seasonal change. In other words, for Barbara there is no real time in the adventure sequence or in so-called biographical time. Even the house, the 'castle', is no more than a repository of the patriarchal past, a chronotope which Bakhtin refers to as the 'historicity of castle time', 'the traces of centuries and generations and [...] particular human relationships involving dynastic primacy and the transfer of hereditary rights' (Bakhtin 1981: 240). There is no present, no time or place for Barbara, thus the tragic outcome of her failed encounter with the other. In a frustrated meeting ('they did not meet') the 'chrontopicity is retained but one or another member of the chronotope bears a negative sign' (Bakhtin 1981: 97). The female subject of the above-mentioned poems bears this 'negative sign'.

That the 'negative sign' might be gender-specific, that in 'Western' culture it is woman who is condemned to immanence not man (as Simone de Beauvoir stated), is suggested by the prose poem 'The Bride of Lazarus' which was first published in 1991 but written between 1920 and 1955 (Simón 1991a: 7). This short piece of lyrical prose, which destabilizes the androcentric assumptions of Christianity,[16] could well have been included in *Jardín*. It is the lament of a woman (the 'bride', Barbara) addressed to her lover (Lazarus, 'A...') who, after many years, has risen from the dead and, full of passion, comes to reclaim her. He has arisen anew, but she has merely grown old. Again, their meeting is mistimed, 'like people invited to a party who arrive before the house is prepared' (Loynaz 1991: 68). While he was in timelessness, 'like the unborn child in the pool of mother's blood', she had to go on living in time, counting the days, unable to 'move death to compassion' (p. 69). The cause of the woman's sadness, however, is not Lazarus's tardiness but rather that her love and grief were not sufficiently powerful to bring him back to life. 'Someone else did it' (p. 69). Lazarus's resurrection is thanks to His miraculous word, not hers. A woman's words, then, are powerless, unlike the word of the Father, and the Father brings new birth to man, not to woman: 'I have been left out of the wonder' (p. 70). She is the one who has died, 'go and tell him what happened, tell him to return, and to make me rise too' (p. 72); she wants to be included in the miracle.

In the myth of Psyche and Eros the female subject is condemned to death by her mother(-in-law) but is saved by love. It is in Loynaz's poetry, rather than in her novel, where love does triumph and transcendence is achieved, where the encounter with the loved one leads to transformation, development and rebirth. Thus the poet declares in 'I am Born Again in You':

> Vuelvo a nacer en ti:
> Pequeña y blanca soy ... La otra
> – la obscura – que era yo, se quedó atrás
> como cáscara rota,
> como cuerpo sin alma
> como ropa sin cuerpo que se cae ... (Núñez 1993: 94)

> I am born again in you. / I am small and white ... The other one, / the dark one I was before, is left behind / like a broken shell / like a body without soul / like clothes without a body, falling

and in 'Love is ... ', 'Love is to press against the cross, and to nail oneself / to the cross / and to die, and to be reborn ... / Love is to be reborn' ('Amor es apretarse a la cruz, y clavarse / a la cruz, / y morir y resucitar ... / ¡Amor es resucitar!' (Núñez 1993: 73). In her lecture 'My Poetry. Self-criticism', read in the Lyceum in August 1950, Loynaz stated that poetry is, above all, movement, transition and transcendence: 'poetry is transition', 'passage' ['traslación'] (Simón 1991b: 80–81). It is movement upwards because although it is born 'on earth', 'the higher it grows, the less likely it is to be lost in branches'. Poetry, the miraculous word, makes contact with another world: 'through poetry we make the leap from visible to invisible reality', with 'what we do not have yet we know exists somewhere intangible' (Simón 1991b: 81). Poetry is energy, 'capable of bringing about change'. Poetry brings about transformation; if it does not change the housewife, the typist or the philosopher (p. 82), it is not poetry. Furthermore, for Loynaz poetry is freedom. In 'Poem II' she writes: 'I leave my word in the air, without keys or veils [...] There is nothing in her that is not me' (Núñez 1993: 147). Poetry is the voice of the loved one, the other, which interpellates the subject out of silence into language as in 'Poema XLVII':

> Tú me hablabas, pero yo no sabía desde donde. [...] Era tu voz, sí, tu misma voz de fuego y agua y huracán. Pero yo miraba temblando en torno mío, y sólo veía las desnudas paredes del silencio. (Núñez 1993: 165)

> You were speaking to me but I knew not from where [...] It was your voice, yes, your very voice of fire and water and hurricane. I looked around trembling, and I saw only the naked walls of silence.

When the miracle, the encounter with the other through poetry, does take place, the poet is triumphant. Woman has access to speech and social existence. In 'In My Poetry I am Free', she writes, engendering poetry in the masculine:

> En mi verso soy libre: él es el mar.
> Mi mar ancho y desnudo de horizontes ... [...]
> Yo soy libre en mi verso y él es libre
> como yo. Nos amamos. Nos tenemos.
> Fuera de él soy pequeña y me arrodillo
> ante la obra de mis manos, la
> tierna arcilla amasada entre mis dedos ...
> Dentro de él, me levanto y soy yo misma. (Núñez 1993: 94–5)

In my poetry I am free. / My wide sea stripped of horizons ... [...] / I am free in my poetry and he is free / like me. We love each other. We hold each other. / Outside him I am small, and I kneel / before my handiwork, the tender / clay kneaded between my fingers ... / Inside him, I rise up and I am myself.

Poetry is a means of writing the self, creating a space and becoming a subject in a different time.

Notes

1. See D. M. Loynaz (1994) *Fe de vida*, Ediciones Hermanos Loynaz, Pinar del Río, for a detailed acount of their relationship.

2. Her first unpublished work published in Cuba after the revolutionary period was (1991) *Poemas náufragos*, Letras Cubanas, Havana.

3. Of particular interest is the early essay by Emilio Ballagas, '*Jardín*, Biografía simbólica' (1958) (Núñez 1993: 336–8). Not only does Ballagas point to comparisons between *Jardín* and *The Castle of Otranto* and the work of Poe, he also refers to the importance of mirrors and photographs in the 'symbolic biography' of woman. Ballagas does not indicate a biographical reading of the novel, although this is perfectly feasible. Note Loynaz's identification of her younger brother, Enrique (the poet Enrique Loynaz), with shadows, 'it was an omen [...] which made him always run away from the light. He didn't like the sun [...] at any time in his life, and he didn't want it in his work, he preferred to stay in the shade' (Simón 1991a: 69). In an interview with Pedro Simón she states categorically that the love letters sent to her by Alvarez de Cañas provided the inspiration for the love letters in *Jardín* (Simón 1991a: 39).

4. According to V. A. Smith (1993), Loynaz presents a feminist reading of 'Sleeping Beauty' in the novel. As in the tale, a passive woman waits for a Prince Charming to waken her from her sleep. However, in *Jardín* the mundane life the 'prince' offers the woman is inferior to what she experienced previously. Above all, her sortie means she must leave the archetypal mother-goddess behind. Smith also refers to the Garden of Eden and the Apocalypse, suggesting a feminist version of a biblical reading. Her readings of mirror reflections (or lack of), photographic

images and fluid bodily boundaries in the context of Luce Irigaray's work are similarly instructive. Smith also reads *Jardín* as a failed Bildungsroman.

5. I. Rodríguez divides the novel into two parts, one developing the idea of the house–garden–nation and the other the white Caribbean woman's experience of modernity. She reads the garden as laboratory, and woman as explorer and interpreter (I. Rodríguez 1994: 92). Rodríguez develops the idea of Barbara having one foot in national decadence and the other in modern cosmopolitan society (p. 95) where she is transformed from the white savage to civilized woman (although she is impoverished, she has a family name and is thus an object of exchange). It would be interesting to follow through the theme of 'Tropical Gothicism' (p. 97) in relation to Jean Rhys's *Wide Sargasso Sea* and Charlotte Brontë's *Jane Eyre*. In *Jardín* the death of the male child leaves a space for his sister, as in Rhys's novel (and in Rosario Castellano's *Balún Canán*, 1957). However, Rodríguez pays little attention to the horror, fear and threat in *Jardín* and reads incest where it is not (there is nothing in the novel to suggest 'A…' is the father of anyone in Barbara's family, although there is a suggestion, perhaps, that he is the grown-up dead brother).

6. See V. A. Smith (1993) for a study of the significance of the sea as a 'feminine' element representing fluid ego boundaries.

7. The discursive 'Barbara', the great-aunt, is placed here between inverted commas.

8. For Simone de Beauvoir in *The Second Sex*, marriage does not invite woman to transcend herself, it confines her to immanence and 'shuts her up within the circle of herself' (DeLamotte 1990: 148). For de Beauvoir the little girl is always enclosed and blocked by the walls of the male universe, she is confined to the limbo of immanence and contingence (DeLamotte 1990: 173, 176).

9. Loynaz refers to poetry in similar terms: 'the dark chamber that is the substance of poetry, where everything, even light itself, has to be revealed to us necessarily in shadow' (Loynaz 1951: 16).

10. For A. Williams, in Female Gothic the male other is not Satan but Eros. The Psyche myth offers an alternative to the Father's Law (1995: 146), an alternative model for female access to the symbolic (1995: 157). For folklorists the Psyche myth signifies the search for the lost husband and may be the founding myth of 'Sleeping Beauty'. When Psyche is awakened from her coma-sleep, she experiences a transformation from mortality to divinity; marriage is a means to transcendence.

11. See Apuleius (1995).

12. *Jardín* (up to Part V) would fit Williams's diagram of the Female Plot of Gothic Fiction (A. Williams 1995: 256): the heroine (Barbara–Psyche–Beauty) is initiated in the home, lives happily ever after (overseas–Olympus–castle) with her suitor despite the male and/or female antagonist.

13. The chronology of the story is deliberately confusing. If Barbara returns to the garden shortly after the war (the First World War, as the novel was written in the 1920s), and has at the time a sixteen-year-old son, then she left with the captain around 1902 at the very latest (the birth year of Loynaz, the year of the first Cuban Constitution). She is a young woman at the start of the novel, making her about twenty when she meets the captain. So, Barbara was born around 1882. This means the posters she finds in the pavilion (dated 184–) are not so ancient. Barbara's great-aunt would have been born around 1822, and the affair with 'A…' taken place at the time indicated by the posters (1840s). Hypothetically, Barbara was born in 1882 and died in 1918, at the age of thirty-six.

14. Dulce María's fascination with reptiles and insects is evident in her early collection of poems (1993b) *Bestiarium*, written when she was a school girl. Of the nineteen beasts, eight are insects and the rest include the bat, frog, snake and sea-horse.

15. The poems were inspired by her love for Alvarez de Cañas, a relationship forbidden by her mother. I owe this information to V. A. Smith.

16. As does another of the *Poemas náufragos*, 'The First Miracle', where the initiative for Christ's first miracle (turning the water into wine) comes not from the boy himself but from his mother Mary.

CHAPTER 4

Fina García Marruz: Love of Mother and God

Many of the poems written by Dulce María Loynaz are addressed to God. Hers is not overtly religious poetry, but the Lord functions nevertheless as a propitious interlocutor. Sometimes she pleads; more often she reprimands the Father. Dulce María Loynaz belonged to a traditional Catholic family, but not all Cubans were practising Catholics. In fact, because the church consisted of mainly Spanish priests and had sided with Spain in the Wars of Independence, it had relatively little influence in Cuba. One of the main purposes of the Constitution of 1902 was to separate the church from the state. The increasing influence of the USA in the next five decades familiarized Cubans with other religions, particularly the Protestant churches. African Cuban religions were often more significant among the working classes, certainly among black Cubans, than the established Catholic Church. In this respect Cuba was quite different from Spain and many other Latin American countries. It is perhaps surprising, then, that the Catholic religion should have figured at all in the work of women writers prior to the Revolution. Arguably, no matter what the extent of religious belief of the writer involved, religious discourse provided women with a way of writing. This will be discussed in more detail with reference to the poetry of Fina García Marruz.

Critical appreciation of the work of Fina García Marruz has focused on her association with the group of writers and artists who, under the tutelage of José Lezama Lima, collaborated on the review *Orígenes* between 1944 and 1956. While it is true that García Marruz (married to fellow poet and critic Cintio Vitier) was certainly the only woman in the group, unlike her male companions she has not received as much recognition.[1] This is due to diffidence on her part, to the fact that the kind of poetry she wrote did not fit easily into the post-revolutionary Cuban cultural scene, and to the fact that marriage to Vitier, who published her work, nevertheless reduced the scope for independent critical evaluation. A sense of propriety has restrained him from discussing her poetry at length; for example, he does not examine his or his wife's work in *Lo cubano en la poesía* 'for obvious reasons' (Vitier 1970: 501).

García Marruz published her first book of poems in 1942, at the age of nineteen, but it was with the exceptionally beautiful *Las miradas perdidas* [The Lost Gazes] (1951) that she first made her name in Cuba and Spain.[2] It was on the basis of this collection that Carmen Conde included García Marruz in her anthology *Once grandes poetisas hispanoamericanas* [Eleven Great Latin American Women Poets] (Conde 1967), but the book received only a handful of reviews. After the Revolution of 1959 García Marruz remained in Cuba and published a second collection, *Visitaciones* [Visitations] (1970). Apart from a perceptive commentary by Eliseo Diego, the book passed virtually unnoticed. She would have to wait until the 1980s when, in a cultural climate more propitious for women writers, a selection of her poetry (*Poesías escogidas*, 1984) was published. This gave rise to a spurt of critical analyses including the only book-length study of her work to date (Arcos 1990a) published in a series founded by ex-*Orígenes* co-founder José Rodríguez Feo. Some of her essays on poetry and poetics, dating back to 1959, were collected and published in the same decade (*Hablar de la poesía* [Speaking of Poetry], 1986). This volume includes studies of the work of poets such as Gustavo Adolfo Bécquer, Sor Juana Inés de la Cruz, and José Martí as well García Marruz's own reflections on poetry. The quality and significance of her work is now widely acknowledged in Cuba, particularly among younger poets who have rejected social realist paradigms for the more esoteric aesthetics of the 'Orígenes' group. Proof of their enthusiasm are the 200 booklets which include García Marruz's more recent poems (*Créditos de Charlot* [Charlot's Credits], 1990), produced by hand during the 'special period' when publishing in Cuba came almost to a standstill. García Marruz has in press a third major volume of poetry, *Habana del Centro* [Central Havana].

As might be expected from a poet of her generation, García Marruz writes in the tradition of classical Spanish and Spanish American poetry. Like all the 'Orígenes' poets she was influenced by Juan Ramón Jiménez (whom she met when she was thirteen) (Sánchez-Eppler 1986), by María Zambrano who lectured on poetry and philosophy at Havana University in the early 1940s, and José Lezama Lima himself. García Marruz's poetry is always polished and precise. However, unlike Lezama, she prefers lucid simplicity to hermeticism. Many critics have noted substantial differences between her poetry and that of the other members of the 'Orígenes' group. In 1952 Vitier wrote that she gave the group 'the confessional tone it lacked' (Arcos 1990a: 87). What she did share with them was their Catholic faith and their concept of poetry as a pathway to knowledge.

The 'Orígenes' poets, members of the third generation of writers in post-Independence Cuba (1940–59) (Lazo 1974: 268), worked against a background of corruption, violence and anarchy following the fall of the dictator Machado in 1933 and Batista's coup in 1952. These were years of increasing US involvement in Cuban internal affairs, Mafia gangsters in the Hotel Nacional, roulette tables, prostitutes, gun-runners, consumerism and crass vulgarity, and – as far as the educated Cubans were concerned – profound despair. Would there ever be social reform, national and economic independence, political liberty? In a wider context, those same years saw the demise of the Spanish Republic and the upheaval of the Second World War. In the face of such moral decomposition in Cuba, the 'Orígenes' group took an apolitical stance. It is said they took refuge in a world of aesthetic refinement, but what they were attempting to do was to create, at the level of written culture, an alternative idealized world founded on the humanist values, decency and dignity associated with the best of criollo (Cuban, Hispanic and European) culture. They wanted to keep spiritual and human values alive in a regime which destroyed them. Thus they attempted to resist moral degeneracy with an autonomous literary field, what Bourdieu calls an 'accumulation of symbolical capital' (Bourdieu 1993: 75). Unlike their Marxist contemporaries, working on the *Gaceta del Caribe* (for example, Mirta Aguirre and Rafaela Chacón Nardi), the 'Orígenes' group believed that a major historical transformation would begin not in the material base, but in the sphere of culture (in the superstructure), in a corpus of philosophical, religious and ethical ideas and beliefs which would radiate down to effect a revolution in civil society from above, from the realm of poetry.

'Orígenes', then, refers to national, cultural origins and identities. Orígenes also refers to Origen, the second-century Greek Christian theologian.[3] The 'Orígenes' group engaged with concepts of Cubanism but, more importantly, they initiated a dialogue with the European philosophical tradition. Their discursive field is philosophy, theology and poetry: from the pre-Socratics, particularly Plato, through Plotinus, to St Augustine with whom 'Christian philosophy was launched' (Clark 1994: 129), through to European Catholic thinkers (Jacques Maritain, Henri Bergson and Simone Weil), including Spanish poet and philosopher María Zambrano. Zambrano taught both García Marruz and Vitier when they were students at Havana University, and she became a close friend. In this chapter I shall extend this dialogue by reading García Marruz's poetry and poetics alongside Emmanuel Levinas's 1946–47 essays *Time and the Other* (Levinas 1987), and María Zambrano's work of the 1940s and 1950s,[4] bearing in mind contemporary feminist reworkings of the founding principles of Western metaphysics, that is, Luce Irigaray's rereading of Plato and others. I shall argue that the poetry of García Marruz, despite its obvious Catholic foundations, has been (at least partially) misread. Her work traces a maternal genealogy; it also attempts the impossible, to inscribe the kind of 'sensible transcendental' (the transcending body) posited by Irigaray (Whitford 1991: 48). Like Zambrano, García Marruz aims, tentatively, to uncover the mother excluded from Western philosophical discourse (the mother buried in Plato's cave), to uncover and represent the mother–

daughter relationship, in short, to restructure the symbolic thus enabling female subjectivity to be created through language. García Marruz's poetry is informed by a fundamental paradox: her search for God seems to be at one and the same time a search for the Mother.

According to Arcos, the 'Orígenes' group's concept of the world is 'of a religious kind, Catholic and of a neo-Thomist tendency [neotomista] to be precise' (Arcos 1990a: 44). Shortly after the publication of *Las miradas perdidas* José Chacón y Calvo described the book as 'the book of everyday poetry [...] with the clear light of eternity, born, affirmed and exalted in the shadow of Christ' (*Diario de la Marina* [1951], quoted in Arcos 1990a: 87). Twenty years later Francisco de Oraá wrote of the 'Christian ambience' of García Marruz's poetry. Arcos refers to her 'deep Catholic lineage' (quoted in Arcos 1990a: 93); her poetry 'is Divine Creation [...], God, but also the Word made flesh' (Arcos 1990a: 122), and even Marilyn Bobes (1985), a relatively young feminist critic, refers to her 'unquestionable religious cosmovision' (Bobes 1985: 155). It is possible, of course, to read García Marruz as a Catholic poet, particularly bearing in mind her recurrent use of concepts such as 'Exteriority' ['Lo Exterior'], grace, *caritas*, freedom (*libertas*), illumination, resurrection, transfiguration and incarnation. The 'Sonnets of Poverty', the poems in the section 'The Mysteries', including 'Transfiguration of Jesus on the Mount', in *Las miradas perdidas* and the poems in the section 'Anima viva' in *Visitaciones* are, perhaps, the most explicitly religious. García Marruz refers to her conversion to Catholicism as a long and difficult process lasting six years, not because of the conversion itself, which came about after she read the Gospels at the age of seventeen, but because entering the Catholic Church and accepting its dogma and history was less tractable. She did not take her first communion until the age of twenty-four, on the eve of her marriage.[5] From a Catholic point of view, García Marruz's poetry is the revelation of divine grace, the Word made flesh; poetry is a gift which enables the poet to apprehend what is beyond the world of experience, to glimpse the underlying unity behind all diversity and change. Unlike philosophy, poetry is manifested and made substance in the situations and objects of everyday life. In this sense García Marruz's vision is rooted in the transcendental idealism of St Augustine and in St Thomas's reconciliation of reason with faith. Generally speaking, however, her poetry is not overtly devotional. Although a Catholic reading is important, it sometimes seems to miss the point.

A typically Catholic poem, in Arcos's view, is the sonnet 'Una dulce nevada está cayendo' [A Soft Snow is Falling], the first poem in *Las miradas perdidas*,

Una dulce nevada está cayendo
detrás de cada cosa, cada amante,
una dulce nevada comprendiendo

lo que la vida tiene de distante.
Un monólogo lento de diamante
calla detrás de lo que voy diciendo,
un actor su papel mal repitiendo
sin fin, en soledad gesticulante.
Una suave nevada me convierte
ante los ojos, ironistas sobrios,
al dogma del paisaje que me advierte
una voz, algún coche apareciendo,
mientras en lo que miro y lo que toco
siento que algo muy lejos se va huyendo. (García Marruz 1951: 7)

A soft snow is falling / behind each loved one, every thing, / a soft snowfall embracing / all life holds at a distance. / A slow monologue of diamonds / silent behind what I'm saying, / an actor badly playing his role, / gesticulating for ever alone. / A soft snowfall converts me / before ironical, sober eyes / to the dogma of the landscape where a voice / warns me, a car quickly passing by, / while in all I see and all I touch / I feel something distant escaping.

In Arcos's reading, the poet acknowledges something existing behind the appearances of reality. There is no communication between the 'something' and the poet (the poet speaks but the 'something' is silent). The 'soft snowfall', then, is 'something essential that descends to the appearance of things'; what is 'behind' is the essence of appearances. The distance is the space between the poet's eyes and the true reality of things which she can feel and see (through the world of the senses) but which escapes her. What is this essence felt in things but going beyond things, Arcos asks (1990a: 106–5). He gives no answer but refers to García Marruz's essay on poetry 'Lo Exterior en la poesía' [Exteriority in Poetry] (García Marruz 1947), and says that the something is 'lo exterior desconocido' [unkown exteriority] and that this is God or 'the divine as absolute transcendence' (Arcos 1990a: 110). Poetry enables the revelation of God through God's grace; the poet perceives the Good, the God, through poetry, but, frustrated, is rooted in the world of the senses.

Rather than tracing the process of coming to Catholic faith, from the point of view of a philosophy of the Christian religion, this poem confirms Western philosophical narratives. García Marruz's poem is not idealist (the world is more than a mental vision); there is a reality out there waiting to be discovered (by the privileged philosopher or the believer). In the sense that Christian theology is Greek philosophy applied to readings of the Old Testament, the poem inscribes the presence of a One Supreme Form, the Form of Good (Plato) or the One (Parmenides, for whom Truth, the object of knowledge, was single, eternal and indivisible), and St Augustine's God, developed from Platonist and Neoplatonist thought to provide the theoretical framework of Christianity. The Demiurge creates forms, becomes God-the-Father creating forms from matter, and matter and forms from nothingness. Poetry thus enables the revelation of God through God's grace and charity. The 'soft snowfall' is the presence of the eternal, omnipotent One.

These categories and concepts pertaining to metaphysics have been seriously questioned, even dismantled, particularly by feminist critics. María Zambrano herself queried the legitimacy of philosophical thought, or, in Luce Irigaray's terms, Western cultural phantasies, from which the feminine was so evidently excluded. As Irigaray makes clear in her analysis of Plato's Cave, Plato's One (and hence Augustine's God) are defined in terms of the paternal metaphor: the Idea/Father engenders copies of Himself without the need for a female partner. The maternal womb must be left behind, and with it matter, the body, and the senses which must be transcended if Truth/God is to be attained. In Irigaray's view, the 'male projects his own ego onto the world' which becomes a mirror in which he sees his own reflection. This 'structure of specularization' (Whitford 1991: 34) in which woman provides the mirror, the tain of the mirror, thus occupying the object position (the other) in order for male specularization to take place, does not allow woman ever to see a reflection of herself. This way all theories of subjectivity are appropriated by the masculine. The 'Law of the Selfsame', the love of the masculine same, which is nevertheless predicated on love of the feminine other (the other of the same), forms the basis of the metaphysics of presence and is concomitant with the exclusion of woman. Thus eternal sameness and unity, only to be reached by a disembodied intellect free from contingency, reaching for the light away from the body, must necessarily deny and suppress biological origins and the maternal-feminine. The 'other' sex is defined only in terms of its relationship to men, and 'universality' (gendered masculine) becomes the foundations of language, theory and philosophy. According to Irigaray, the mother should be recovered and a 'sensible transcendental' (the immanent made divine, the transcending body, flesh made word) be distinguished, in short, to restructure the symbolic so that women are allowed access to subjectivity. Female subjectivity has to be created through language, that is, given a symbolic form. Rather than confine García Marruz's poetry to Catholic readings, I suggest she attempts just this.

What is most striking about García Marruz's poetry is its curious blend of the homely and the metaphysical. Her poems are firmly grounded in a woman's experience of ordinary, domestic routine, interspersed with moments of profound philosophical insight. In *La miradas perdidas* (García Marruz 1951) the overriding theme is the fragility of memory (see 'Verses of the Forgetful One', 'Imaginary Memories'). The poems in this collection reconstruct a rosy (or rather lilac) vision of the childhood home with its magical interior spaces ('magical interiors' [p. 11]): its lamps, mirrors,

portraits and windows looking out on to symbolical landscapes. The poet's
mother off to the theatre in her feathered hat, her aunt bringing her milk
in the morning, the sound of the piano, the smell of bread and coffee,
walks through the city's parks, or to see the train, 'My aunt used to take
me to see the trains / with her end-of-century bow, and her modern
ways' (p. 37), or a trip on the yellow tram (p. 53) are vivid snapshots,
which, on reflection, offer the poet a dazzling glimpse of the secret essence
of modern life. The home and its contents function as a woman-centred
microcosm of the universe and acquire deep symbolical value. What is of
particular interest is the way the childhood home is reconstructed as a
lost paradise, through objects (chairs, sofas, cups, floor tiles, lamp-shades,
screens, pillows, dresses, hairstyles) and spaces (the garden, terraces,
thresholds, windows, doors, hallways). Similarly intriguing is the presence
of the poet's elusive mother, usually associated with music, colour, openings, the new day and sometimes with the dark interiors. Images of the
mother are built up through repeated and detailed listings of parts of her
body, material attributes (dresses, house coat, teaspoons) and domestic
surroundings, although her face is never described.

Visitaciones (1970) is a more varied collection of poems and poetic
prose and contains García Marruz's widely acknowledged elegy 'On the
Death of Ernesto Che Guevara' written in 1967. Again the presence of
the home and the family (mother, husband, sons and friends) is crucial
although the poet's angle of vision is more panoramic. She describes local
figures (the road sweeper, a drunkard, a child smiling, the housemaid) and
intrinsically Cuban landscapes. She also includes poems to Martin Luther
King and Ho Chi Minh, and poems written in Mexico and Spain. As in
Las miradas perdidas, what is of particular interest is the way in which the
childhood home is reconstructed through objects (clocks, jugs, lamps,
plates) and spaces (patios, windows, doors). Again, the poet's mother
appears bathed in light. In 'Small Songs', for example, the mother's hands
are 'lights so lost / dawn returning / returning, returning' (García Marruz
1970: 333); in 'Happy Short Melodies' she enters the house in her flower-
printed dress, 'How strong the sun was shining! / How you entered the
house!'; her protection and nurturance is represented by her bed, 'in your
wide, soft bed / that is where I want to sleep' and in 'Dreamy Music' by
her hands:

> ¿Qué me sostiene?
> El recuerdo
> de tu mano
> dándome algo
> que he olvidado. (García Marruz 1970: 265)

> What sustains me? / The memory / of your hand / giving me something / I
> have forgotten.

Again, the mother is reconstructed through her many attributes: hands, printed dress, long hair, multicoloured handbag, red sunshade. At times she is no more than the music of her piano, 'the waltzes and songs only memory and love hear now' (p. 264).[6] Julia Kristeva's notion of the maternal semiotic, the music and rhythms of poetic language affording a momentary glimpse of the inexpressible pleasure of the pre-oedipal union between mother and child, is particularly relevant in this context (Kristeva 1980). These are poems of love: love for the cherished but dispersed and fragmented mother; love for the warm, light spaces of the family home. In what way may these poems which attempt to recuperate the mother be related to the more philosophical or Catholic poems, and how do they fit into García Marruz's concept of poetry? If, as the poet states, 'lo entrevisto' [what is glimpsed] is not another reality but 'the illumination of the "other" in the "here and now"', it may be that the Other to which her poetry refers is not exclusively the indivisible God-the-Father.

A theory in which the Other is not the eternal One is found in Emmanuel Levinas's *Time and the Other* (1987 [1948]). For Levinas the Other is the other person to whom we are bound in love. This points to an alternative reading of 'A Soft Snow is Falling'. Levinas's essay 'marks a progression toward alterity rather than toward totality, [...] a desire to break out of the circuits of sameness'; it aims for a 'liberation from rather than the realization of totality, unity, the self-same' (Cohen in Levinas 1987: 1–2);[7] in Levinas's own words, 'a pluralism that does not merge into unity' (Levinas 1987: 42). In this account, the process of identity (identification), demands sameness and disallows difference. The subject's identity needs materiality but its identity is an enchainment to itself. Solitude for the subject is to be 'shut up within the captivity of its identity'. In everyday existence the subject can go out of itself but is 'limited by the object' (Levinas 1987: 63) or, in Irigaray's terms, the other of the same. In other words, human life in the world is tied to the objects that fulfil it. Light (knowledge) does not 'break the attachment' of the ego and the self, because the illuminated object cannot serve as other, it does not have a 'fundamental strangeness' and, as we saw earlier, the 'structure of reason' (Levinas 1987: 64–5) is solipsism. So consciousness enables a person to distinguish self from things but does not make solipsism disappear, 'its element, light, renders us master of the exterior world but is incapable of discovering a peer for us there'(p. 65).

Life as salvation, resurrection and freedom from matter can occur only if the subject 'encounters an event that stops its everyday transcendence from falling back to a point that is always the same' (Levinas 1987: 66). The alterity which allows the subject to transcend matter is the encounter with the absolutely unknowable, what is 'foreign to all light' (p. 71). Radical alterity is the 'absolutely other' which for Levinas is Death, the Future, or the Other person whose mystery and mortality we share. Exteriority is *the radical alterity* of the Other person, and the relationship between self and the Other is love, 'the face-to-face with the Other, the encounter with a face that at once gives and conceals the Other' (p. 79). The encounter with alterity is love without violence ('possessing, knowing, grasping are synonyms of power' [p. 89]), without fusion and without enslavement. Does a situation exist in the everyday world, Levinas asks, in which 'the alterity of the other appears in its purity'?; for him 'the absolutely contrary [...] the contrariety that permits its terms to remain absolutely other, is the *feminine*' (p. 85; his emphasis). The feminine is not only unknowable, but a 'mode of being that consists in slipping away from the light [...] it is a flight before light' (p. 87). Like Irigaray, then, Levinas recognizes sexual difference; the difference between the sexes 'carves up reality in another sense and conditions the very possibility of reality as multiple, against the unity of being proclaimed by Parmenides' (p. 86), but in struggling to define the feminine as transcendence he sees 'no other possibility than to call it a mystery' (p. 88). This I–you communication between two subjects where, in the other's proximity, distance is nevertheless maintained, is where 'the alterity of the good [is] encountered in the face of the Other' (p. 14).

These ideas, developing those of St Augustine, are entirely relevant to García Marruz's poetry and poetics with one major reservation. As Irigaray points out, the Other cannot be feminine for the female subject unless the female subject, the daughter, detaches herself from the mother and represents the mother on her own terms. Hence the frustrated non-communion with the (possibly maternal-feminine) Other of the 'would-be-female-subject' in 'A Soft Snow is Falling'.

Before examining that poem again, it is necessary to decide what García Marruz herself means by Exteriority. In her seminal essay, 'Lo Exterior en la poesía' [Exteriority in Poetry] (*Orígenes*, 1947) she seems to conceive of poetry and the Other in terms similar to those described by Levinas. As mentioned earlier, Arcos suggests 'Lo Exterior' signifies 'the divine as absolute transcendence' (Arcos 1990a: 110). Exteriority does not refer to external reality (García Marruz 1947: 16), and poetry has nothing to do with reason. Poetry is a 'magical activity' related to mysticism and religion. For García Marruz 'unknown Exteriority' is 'inside us and outside us'; it is unknowable reality which is two-fold: God ('our Angel')[8] and ourselves. The poet, she writes, must search for a 'vision of Exteriority' which will not be forced violently but is discovered, or given, in a vision ('vision, or dogma' [p. 17]). Herein lies the poet's true freedom (freedom from violence), 'Freedom, then, should not reside in ourselves, in our choice, but in the exterior vision of our end, in *our loving surrender to an Object*' (p. 17; my emphasis). Solipsistic art for art's sake has lost its freedom and its vision, its 'surrender'. It is obsessed with light, but its 'lucidity' is 'impotence'. Opposed to solipsism is 'what we may call a *magical distance* between the eye and what is seen', that is, the in-between that separates and yet links the subject and the object, which is not devoured in knowledge. It is this positioning of the subject with regard to the object which concerns García Marruz, and which she sees in the doubling, mirroring, ironic look of Velázquez and Cervantes: 'There is no personal or poetic difference that cannot be explained by the distance from which the object is seen' (p. 18). A poem, then, must not be a monologue, this would be its 'destruction'. In Levinas's terms, the speaking subject can assume subjectivity only in a non-violent loving relationship to the non-assimilable Other.

Many of the ideas in this first part of García Marruz's essay pick up on María Zambrano's *Filosofía y poesía* [Philosophy and Poetry] (1939) in which Zambrano makes a clear distinction between the two forms of 'knowing and expression' (Zambrano 1971: 115): philosophy and poetry. I shall return to this later. Particularly significant is the shared view that philosophy appropriates knowledge and fits it into its disembodied thought-systems, while poetry participates in a wisdom which is already there, before philosophy, in man's origins. Poetry is given as a gift, as grace, like love. The idea of 'grace', the gift of love, the gift of poetry, occurs in both Levinas's and Zambrano's work.

In 'Exteriority in Poetry' García Marruz compares the poetry of two Cubans: José Martí and Julián del Casal. In her view, Martí's poetry expresses a need to transcend life while Casal 'does not reach vision, only emptiness' (García Marruz 1947: 20). Exteriority for Martí is the Home; for Casal it is the Snow. 'The vision of the snow' suggests Casal has not encountered the Other. He substitutes 'snow', she writes, then he substitutes 'mysterious King' (God?). Is this what García Marruz is doing, searching for the Other? Is the subject blocked by soft snow in her arrested progress? She refers to Lezama Lima as an example: the 'loving surrender' of Lezama's poetry dissipates because the poet is 'invaded' by the 'body, the enemy of the spirit' which detains him like 'a breath of frozen air' (pp. 20–21). Like the subject in 'A Soft Snow is Falling', the poet is rooted in the world of the senses. Modern poetry, she writes, 'unable to reach Exteriority, the *angelical* [my emphasis], in words [...] keeps the poet, like Hamlet, between the two extremes of reality [being and non-being], alone with his monologue of doubts'. By this she means, like Levinas, that the poet, enchained to materiality, to identity, cannot aspire to the infinite without the Other. What is interesting in her comment on Lezama Lima is that despite the implicit mind/body split here (the body is the enemy of the spirit), alterity can be read as something other than the One, God-the-Father. She writes: 'Only Dialogue can bring about this communication which, in its purest form, is impossible and mystical; when the union with that which surpasses us, that which is *intimate, closed, the "sealed source"*, gives back to us, in its isolation, *the lost family*' (p. 22; my emphasis). Here García Marruz explicitly includes the feminine 'sealed source', and the

entire family (not just the Father but the mother too) in her conceptual-
ization of alterity. What García Marruz understands by Exteriority, in my
view, is the Other (the 'absolutely unknowable', for Levinas, freedom from
the self-same) which in her poetry is attributed, at times, with maternal-
feminine connotations. The relationship between the self and the Other,
the distancing, is in fact poetry and love: in her words, 'true *intimacy*, that
is always extraneous [extraño] like an angel, the true *otherness of Exteriority*
[allendidad de lo Exterior] (p. 16) ['allende' signifying 'on the other side'].
This Other, in us and outside of us, possibly the Other of other (in
Irigaray's terms, the Other of woman positioned as other) is, at times, the
Mother. This relationship is impossible to articulate in what Zambrano
refers to as 'the word [or language] of reason', but it may be possible in
'the word [or language] of poetry'. Reading García Marruz's essay alongside
Zambrano's work helps clarify this point.

In *Filosofía y poesía* (1939) Zambrano pulls apart the inconsistencies of
Plato's account of the Cave and man's aspiration to Truth, as Irigaray
would do some forty years later. Zambrano also condemns Plato for
rejecting poetry (compared to philosophy) in *The Republic*. With Plato 'the
"logos"' is removed from man and nature (Zambrano 1971: 117); its
'appetite for intellectual domination' (p. 119) pursues knowledge with
violence. Everyday life, things and people are cruelly 'squashed' in the
search for unity. Thus begins the 'inquisition of the intellect'. Poets,
however, remained in 'the immediacy' of everyday life; there was no need
to search for what was already available, the limitless world of the senses
and dreams. Poetry pursues heterogeneity, what is and is not yet, and it
descends 'to flesh and blood' (p. 128). Poets did not search for 'that
permanent, identical-to-itself "idea"' (p. 120); they are in touch with something existing before philosophy that Zambrano represents as Atlantis
(and Irigaray as the Womb), 'a wider space [...] whose receding distant
horizon leaves great truths abandoned, with no conditions for visibility,
without presence [...] submerged continents, which man cannot, according
to Plato himself, completely forget' (p. 121). In Plato's Cave whatever
does not respond to reason is the 'shadow of a shadow clinging to the
stony wall' (p. 133). Poetry, then, is dispersion, origins and 'living in the
flesh' (p. 150). It is possible to compare these ideas with Irigaray's account
of the forgotten mother-womb. Zambrano considers it necessary to rescue
what philosophy left behind 'before its very birth [...] so that [philosophy]
may find new life' (p. 129).

For Zambrano, 'the word of reason', the logos of philosophy, is the
word which the philosopher wants to possess. 'The word of poetry', on
the other hand, is 'irrational' (p. 136), a different kind of logos; poetry
'wants to capture the inexpressible' (p. 211).[9] Poetry gestures towards 'what
did not exist, so that it may be' (p. 188); poetry turns to her origins, to
her 'first dream', 'in search of the loving face. The poet wishes to find

again the face behind the dream', poetry turns 'back, to reimmerse herself in the *breast* from whence she came; [...] to discern precisely what was glimpsed. For that reason she is melancholy' (pp. 195–6). Poetry is linked to 'her first dream' by melancholy (p. 196). Poetry is not self-reflexive, 'she could not double up on herself, try to be herself' (p. 165) and is thus unrepresentable according to the structure of specularization. Poetry, writes Zambrano, was never aware of her treasure, 'never turned her eyes, her sad eyes, towards herself. Never, generous and desperate, did she occupy herself with herself, as philosophy did right from the start' (p. 165). Poetry is Love, not desire or possession which consumes its object. In philosophy there is no love, because 'there is no presence, no face' (p. 193).

In short, poetry is not self-regarding, anguished, powerful Cartesian metaphysics. It is a return to the origins and a mourning for their loss. 'The philosopher lives for the future, distancing himself from his origins, searching for "him self" alone, isolated, and distanced from mankind. The poet lives for others [desvive], distancing himself from his possible "self", for love of his origins' (p. 196).

Because 'the word of poetry' has not developed at the same pace as 'the word of reason', it is not yet possible to think 'from the limitless space' of poetry; 'nobody has yet managed to turn into rational thought the "'Logos full of grace and truth'"' (p. 212). What Irigaray calls the unrepresentable maternal-feminine, 'the unthought and the unsymbolized' (Whitford 1991: 5), attached to the body and the senses, left behind by the philosopher in pursuit of the intelligible, Zambrano calls the site of 'poetry'. Like Irigaray, she conceives of this other way of knowing in semi-religious, Catholic terms pertaining to 'grace' and, like Levinas, 'love' of 'the face of the other'. Despite the fact that Zambrano uses the (masculine) universal subject throughout, does not examine the full implications of sexual difference, and does not refer explictly to the mother, she does make the connection between feminine 'poesía' and woman. The poetic word is related to the unconscious, to the shadows of the unrepresentable, to the lost, pre-symbolic realm of undemanding (maternal) love.

If Exteriority is radical alterity (in Levinas's terms), how can it be the 'feminine' (Other) for woman? What is the Other of the other (of woman positioned as other), one of the conundrums posed by Luce Irigaray? Like García Marruz, Irigaray is concerned with female subjectivity, the position of the speaking subject (subject-other) which, she maintains, is incommensurable with female identity (subject-object). She suggests that female subjectivity can be accessed only if woman learns to separate herself off from the mother, only if the maternal-feminine is retrieved in discourses on theory and thought. Her critique of Western cultural phantasies in which women occupy the object position in the 'structure of specularization' has already been mentioned. The origin, the mother, the body, though necessary, is suppressed and denied. For Levinas man needs something to take him out of himself, his material reality, and thus looks to the Other, to mystery and the feminine. This other way of knowing is 'poetry' for Zambrano. For García Marruz Exteriority is radical alterity encountered in poetry. Clearly, if the subject is not neutral a new kind of cultural phantasy is required but this is as yet unthought. For Irigaray, two-way predication and an ironic mimetic strategy (mimétisme) may lead to a shift in the position of the subject of enunciation. Another relationship to language and to subjectivity must be initiated in which the one does not consume the other. Otherwise woman is for ever situated as object, closed off and frozen.[10]

Returning now to 'A Soft Snow is Falling', in terms of an Augustinian theology, the 'soft snowfall' may well refer to God, immutable truth, or wisdom (the 'Selfsame' the *idipsum*, according to St Augustine [Clark 1994: 19]). To participate in Wisdom is to participate in the Word, that is, Illumination. The Ideas of Divine Illumination 'are present to the gaze of the mind in a certain incorporeal light of its own kind' (*De Trinitate*; Clark 1994: 19) and makes for contact with eternal being. As Richard Harries explains, God is 'so intimately present in and through all things [that] the world becomes a sign and sacrament of his beauty' (Harries 1993: 35).[11] But the subject of the poem cannot participate. The 'snow' might signify frozen grace in so far as rain is the symbol of purification and the descent of Heaven to earth. In Zambrano's terms, the grace or gift of poetry (for Levinas, love without violence, the encounter with the Other) has not come about. Snow, a symbol of nothingness and death, also signifies the preservation of fertility (de Vries 1974) and might suggest the frozen maternal-feminine. In this poem a snowfall connotes a murky pane, a frozen screen, offering no means of self-reflection to the subject, a screen that divides the subject from the light (of knowledge) in Plato's schema. The subject is also frozen then; there is no dialogue between her and the (frozen) Other (behind 'each loved one'), the subject can find no 'peer' with whom to communicate, whom she can love, although she intuits the passage between self and other. She looks without seeing her reflection in the 'snowfall', in the face of the Other. In solitude the subject is condemned to wordless mimicry while she is converted violently, perhaps (warned by a voice?) to the vision, the 'dogma', the Other located in God-the-Father, to which she conforms with ironic eyes. As a woman, she is condemned to the world of objects, aware of the transcendental in what she sees and feels, but cut off from transcendence, almost like the prisoner (sex unspecified) in Plato's Cave. This is a poem of unfulfilled yearning, whereas Augustine found the goal of his longing in God.

As Irigaray states: 'We lack, we women […] a God in which to share, a word/language to share and become' (Whitford 1991: 140). In the quasi-religious discourse of Part IV of *An Ethics of Sexual Difference*, where she sets up a dialogue with Levinas's *Time and the Other*, she adds: 'If we are to have a sense of the other that is not projective or selfish, we have to attain an intuition of the infinite.' This will be either 'the intuition of a god or divine principle aiding in the birth of the other without pressure or violence, or the intuition of a subject that remains unfinished, open to the becoming of the other, that is neither simply active or passive' (Irigaray 1993b: 111). García Marruz's poetry suggests both. Irigaray adds:

> God is beyond this world, but supposedly he already ensures its coherence here and now. [He is] fluid [...] that cements the unity of everything and allows us to believe that the love of sameness has been overcome when, in fact, that love has been raised to an incalculable power and swallows up the love of the other – the maternal feminine other – which has been assimilated to sameness [...] This Other, placed as a keystone to the whole order of language, of semantic architecture, has for centuries been scrupulously protected by the word of men, sometimes only by that of the clerics, in a kind of inescapable circularity or tautology. (Irigaray 1993b: 112)

Women should open up a *sensible transcendental* [her emphasis] 'through us, of which *we would be* the mediators and bridges [...] by conjuring [God] up among us, within us, as resurrection and transfiguration of blood, of flesh, through a language and an ethics that is ours' (p. 129). Speaking of the second coming, Parousia, Irigaray writes:

> Why do we assume that God must always remain an inaccessible transcendence rather than a realization here and now – in and through the body? Like a transfiguration that would not be reduced to a moment or like a resurrection that would not involve the disappearance of this world. With the spirit impregnating the body. (p. 148)

In part, this was the agenda of the Orígenes group (Sánchez-Eppler 1986: 88). It was even more imperative for a woman poet.

The plural Other, the face-to-face encounter with the maternal-feminine through poetry offers an alternative to God-the-Father. Contrasting with 'A Soft Snow is Falling' is the sonnet 'I Love You, Words, Sad Mothers' (not mentioned in Arcos's book) which inscribes some of the ideas proposed by Irigaray:

> Yo os amo, palabras, madres tristes,
> intemperie entrañable de la vida.
> Me acompañáis con soledad dormida.
> Yo os amo, palabras, madres tristes.
>
> Con un amor sin grandes esperanzas
> yo me amo, en mi imposible creo,
> con un frío fervor, un desdén fiero,
> con un amor sin grandes esperanzas.

Qué lluvia has de poner sobre mi nada,
con qué has de atar lo que me desamarra,
qué es, muerte mía, lo que rectificas,

si mi amor con tu divisora espada,
o esta enemistad de mi palabra
con tu música ajena y unitiva. (García Marruz 1951: 115)

I love you, words, sad mothers, / the innermost storm of life. / You are with
me sleepy and lonely. / I love you, words, sad mothers. // With a love without
great hope / Me I love, in my impossible I believe, / with cold fervour, fierce
disdain, / with a love without great hope. // What rain must you bring to my
nothing, / with what will you bind my untying, / what do you rectify, death of
mine, // is it my love with your sundering sword, / or this enmity of my
word / with your music, distant, uniting?

A 'would-be-female-subject' is positioned as a voice, a presence, in dialogue
with and establishing a loving relationship with object(s). The objects are
words ('you'), which are also mothers. According to the 'structure of
specularization' denounced by Zambrano and Irigaray, the 'would-be-female
subject' may not engage on a process of subject formation in which the
other is language/mother, a concept which flies in the face of Lacanian
psychoanalytic accounts.[12] The mothers are sad. Is this because the
daughter is mourning and melancholic? Is this a frustrated mother–
daughter relationship or a reformulation of the symbolic couched in terms
of a mother–daughter relationship in which the daughter cannot mourn
the loss of the mother she never 'knew' and the sad, unrecognized mothers
can only appear as 'words'. 'Words' refer to Zambrano's 'word of poetry'
which searches for what is not, the 'first dream', so that it may exist
(Zambrano 1971: 188). Poetry searches for 'the loving face [...] behind
the dream [...] For that reason it is melancholy' (Zambrano 1971: 195–6).
There is a suggestion here that the 'would-be-female subject' originates in
the biological mother ('innermost' indicating flesh and blood, even the
mother's 'innards' [entrañas]) and at the same time has access to subjectivity
through language. In other words, the mother is inscribed in the process
of subject formation. The words of poetry, sad mothers, the dearly loved,
inner workings of everyday life, and memories of origins, accompany the
subject in her solitude. In sleepy solitude the subject is cut off from the
intelligible; she cannot overcome solitude through knowledge (Levinas)
(where the object is absorbed by the subject), nor by ecstasy (where the
subject is absorbed by the object). A duality, maintaining an in-between
position, is needed. In solitude, then, the 'would-be-female-subject' is shut
up, enchained to herself, unable to separate the ego from the self without
the presence of the radical Other.

The problem of self-love or 'love of the self on the woman's side' is posed in the second strophe. It is certainly a problem for the 'would-be-female-subject' because, without an adequate mirror, according to the structure of specularization, without an other woman cannot accede to subjectivity. Here, in this act of autopoesis, the 'would-be-female-subject' nevertheless states self-love defiantly, but without great hope. She also voices a belief in her 'impossible', her transcendence as woman. She voices the impossible ('cold fervour') defiantly, with 'cold disdain', the disdain marking an attitude to those (philosophers? men?) who stipulate otherwise. It is not just a matter of transcending the body, but of creating a transcendent female body. The subject can leave the 'anonymous finality of identity' (Levinas) only by encountering the non-assimilable self, the Other (mystery, God). Here a two-way dialogue, a question and a challenge, is initiated. In the final two tercets of the sonnet then, what attitude is struck up by the speaking subject? Is she questioning or is she ironically defiant? Is she addressing death (in the female), or God? Whatever it is, it has power and uses its phallomorphic, possibly divine, 'sundering sword'[13] to rectify and to straighten; the female imaginary, dispersed, fluid and plural, is put right. 'Rain' is the grace (of God), which ties up or binds the dispersed, fragmented self (Augustine); *caritas* which allows the self access to subjectivity (Levinas); poetry, which attempts to inscribe the unthinkable (Zambrano); and also fertility suggesting the mother. What does the encounter with the Other achieve? 'What do you rectify, death of mine?' First, it imposes a split between self-love, mother, 'the innermost', on the one hand, and love of words which is now the 'enmity of the word', the 'word of reason' (Zambrano 1971: 212); self-love, mother-love, poetry and language can be joined only in the harmony of death. Death (of the female subject) unifies by excluding the mother yet without it identity is not possible. The sword (of the Lord) thus binds the death drives, preventing disintegration, in the name of unity and identity. This poem voices the tension between female subjectivity and female identity, a tension which can be resolved only by abandoning one or the other, according to Irigaray, and can be voiced only outside the thought-systems of reason, in poetry. A 'would-be-female-subject' defiantly voices the love of words, mothers, and self in the face of death, God, or the symbolic, thus restoring connections between the mother and language. Ironically, the distinction between mother and daughter can be effected only by the reader who reads the 'I' as a 'would-be-subject' that is female.

Several poems foreground the struggle with language and autopoesis itself. The poet avoids gratuitous experimentation with language; her poetry is written with maximum poetic economy without a hint of the darker, surreal or oneiric aspects of reality. Rather, García Marruz makes explicit connections between the home, the mother and the mother tongue. The poem 'Spanish' (in the section of *Visitaciones* entitled 'The Yellow Earth' dedicated to Spain) is a eulogy to the Spanish language whose words and rhythms, the music and language of women and of home, are reclaimed and affirmed:

Me rodea aquí el idioma, como a mi isla
el mar. No cual lo oyera, aislado,
entre otras voces. Me envuelve ahora
por todas partes: tropiezo con su roca
de salud, cortada a pico
de eternidad: hínchame, tómame,
me vuelve a no sé que tiempo inmemorial
y ya no huyo: méceme, la gran habla madre,
sentencias y centro de gravedad y arrullo
de las criadas Teresas olvidadas.

¿Cuándo insegura, trémula,
niña aún, sin memoria,
busqué tu pecho de firmeza,
como se hunde la cabeza sollozante del hijo
en el regazo innumerable? ¿Cuántas veces
las marchas y oberturas, los dúos
de la zarzuela que escuchaba
a mi madre, en las tardes habaneras
de distinta nostalgia, me sacaron
de mi secreto huir, me devolvieron
al desafío alegre, el dar a lo hecho pecho,
rompiendo las visiones nocturnas
con el bregar de la casa, la limpieza
del atarco matinal?
[...] brama mi origen, lengua,
poesía: criandera de mi infancia.
Oigo tu canturreo
entre azulejos blancos de cocina
soleadas, en el verdor que tiembla
en la luz: sol y calor primeros. (García Marruz 1970: 376–8).

Language surrounds me, like my island / the sea. Not as it might be heard, isolated, / between other voices. It surrounds me now / on all sides: I stumble on its healthy / rock, hewn with the pick-axe / of eternity: swell me, take me, / return me to I know not what immemorial time / and I shall not flee: cradle me, great mother tongue, / sentences and centre of gravity and the murmuring / of St Teresa's forgotten maids. // When, insecure and trembling / still a girl, without memory / did I seek your firm breast, / like the sobbing child buries his head / in the bountiful mother's lap? How many times / did the overtures and marches, the duets / of operettas I heard / my mother play in Havana evenings / of distinct nostalgia, bring me out / from my secret escape, give me back once again / joyful defiance, to put my best foot forward, / breaking the visions of night / with the noise of the home, the clean / clatter of morning chores? [...] my origin roars, language, / poetry: nursemaid of my infancy. / I hear you humming a song / between the white, sunlit / kitchen tiles, in the trembling green / of light: my first ever sun and warmth.

What Julia Kristeva (1980: 276, 134–6) refers to as 'le sémiotique', the 'repressed, instinctual maternal element' of language overflows here, undermining the symbolic and disrupting its norms of identity. Similarly transgressive is the earlier sonnet 'Words are Too Big or Small for Me' (García Marruz 1951: 122), a poem of frustrated longing. The female subject cannot find fitting words. The word/flesh is neither that of the female body of the everyday world, nor the incarnation of God, the Other:

la carne me hace verbo sin consuelo
y no doy con su tierra ni su cielo
no hay mano que la puerta oscura abra.

flesh makes me the word without consolation / I cannot find its heaven or its earth / and no hand opens up the darkened door.

The words/flesh are unable to transcend because they are rooted in the senses, 'I want to look, and a faithful wall I encounter / of burning grey, impious mass'. These limits are paradoxical because the poet is searching for the impossible. Finally, she becomes habituated to her impotency, to writing her 'essence' (which must be read ironically) on paper, and immerses herself in the tedium and contingency of autumnal death (p. 122):

Me asquea el suave horror de mi impotencia [...]
Y me acostumbro en hojas a mi esencia,
me rodeo de oro lentamente
aprendiendo el estilo del otoño. (p. 122)

The soft horror of my impotence sickens me [...] / And I accustom my essence to leaves, / I surround myself with gold gradually / learning the style of autumn.

The retrieval of the mother involves memory, what Irigaray calls 'moving backwards in search of something that has been erased' (Irigaray 1993b: 141), and memory is the overriding theme in both *La miradas perdidas* and *Visitaciones*. Memory, what is in the mind (mindful), is etymologically linked to mourning (that which is lost) and is not the same thing as reminiscence which is the recovery of knowledge, or the recovery of things known to the soul in another existence. Memory for García Marruz resembles that of St Augustine; it has to do with Plato's *anamnesis* (memory of the divine in a previous life or disembodied existence) which, with St Augustine, becomes the illumination of the soul by God, a soul previously prepared by divine grace, so that the forms (thanks to God's grace) are now visible to the soul's 'inner eye'. Thus, through St Augustine, *anamnesis* is the encounter with God through the memory, a process which needs the body (sense knowledge).[14] As Henry Chadwick explains:

> *Memoria* for Augustine is a deeper and wider term than our 'memory'. In the background lies the Platonic doctrine of *anamnesis*, explaining the experience of learning as bringing to consciousness what, from an earlier existence, the soul already knows. Augustine develops the notion of the memory by associating it with the unconscious, with self-awareness, and so with the human yearning for true happiness found only in knowing God. (Chadwick in St Augustine 1991: 185)

Searching the memory (the unconscious) for knowledge of the happy life, then, is searching for God. Due to her late conversion to Catholicism, García Marruz was particularly affected by the following passage in Augustine's *Confessions*[15] which gives a clear indication of her notion of memory:

> Late have I loved you, beauty so old and so new: late have I loved you. See, you were within and I was in the external world and sought you there, and in my unlovely state I plunged into those lovely created things which you made [...] The lovely things kept me far from you, though if they did not have their existence in you they had no existence at all. (St Augustine 1991: 201)

Augustine adds: 'See how far I have ranged, Lord, searching for you in my memory. I have not found you outside it [...] But where in my consciousness, Lord, do you dwell? Wherein it do you make your home?' (St Augustine 1991: 200–201). In her poetry García Marruz picks up on the domestic and body imagery used by Augustine in his descriptions of memory. He refers to 'memory's store', the 'vast hall of my memory', and 'the treasure-house of memory' (St Augustine 1991: 186–92). Memory is 'the stomach of the mind' (1991: 191); it is also limitless and extends to unknown lands: memory is 'the broad plains and caves and caverns of my memory' (p. 194) where, writes Augustine, 'there also I meet myself'(p. 186). Augustine longed to transcend the body and memory to reach God (the light): 'through my soul I will ascend to him. I will rise above the force by which I am bonded to the body' (p. 185), 'I will transcend even this my power which is called memory. I will rise beyond it to move to you, sweet light' (p. 194). For Fina García Marruz, memory also makes possible the encounter with God, which (unlike for Augustine) is not necessarily always a transcendence of the body nor a search for the light, or the One. Her encounter with radical alterity (Exteriority) is, at times, the retrieval of the mother. The 'pathway' (Zambrano 1971: 120) whereby this is expressed is poetry.

Irigaray refers to memory as pathos; the philosopher willingly forgets the memory of his maternal origins. It is a 'nostalgia that forgets the threshold, the flesh', and the female imaginary is located on thresholds (Whitford 1991: 52). The philosopher, only interested in the light of consciousness, rejects memory (everyday life, dreams, the occult) in favour of reminiscence, she believes, because 'memory risks getting in the way of reminiscence' (Irigaray 1993b: 348). Outside specularization, the mother (like poetry for Zambrano), 'has no eyes [...] no gaze, no soul. No consciousness, no memory, no language' (Irigaray 1993b: 340). But, Irigaray suggests, 'repetition can be a move backward for [...] a better road. It can be the pathetic, urgent call of something cut off from its roots and dying [...] for lack of the sap needed for growth' (pp. 141–2). Through memory the mother may be retrieved. There is no need to seek her; she is already there. In Zambrano's words, the poet is given this 'encounter, gift, finding by grace' (Zambrano 1971: 116).

In Fina García Marruz's poetry the subject's 'previous existence' is clearly the home and the mother, as several examples (from *Las miradas perdidas* [1951]) illustrate. In the sonnet 'And Yet I Know They are but Shadows', the 'caverns' of her memory are rooted in the home and in the world of the senses; the vision of infinity is not the presence of God but the mother's hand disappearing into a car. This way the poet understands the 'senses or meanings of the night' rather than the philosopher's world of light:

Y sin embargo sé que son tinieblas
las luces del hogar a que me aferro
me agarro a una mampara, a un hondo hierro
y sin embargo sé que son tinieblas.

Porque he visto una playa que no olvido,
la mano de mi madre, el interior de un coche,
comprendo los sentidos de la noche
porque he visto una playa que no olvido

Cuando de pronto el mundo da ese acento distinto,
cobra una intimidad exterior que sorprendo,
se oculta sin callar, sin hablar se revela,

comprendo que es el corazón extinto
de esos días manchados de temblor venidero
la razón de mi paso por la tierra. (García Marruz 1951: 18)

And yet I know they are but shadows / the lights of home to which I cling / I hold on to a screen, to buried iron / and yet I know they are but shadows. // Because I have seen a shore I'll not forget / my mother's hand, the inside of a car, / I understand the senses of the night / because I have seen a shore I'll not forget. // When suddenly the world gives a different turn / and its exterior intimacy unsought I find / hidden without silence, revealed without words, // I understand how the extinct heart / of those days with future trembling stained / are the reason for my passing on this earth.

The glimpse of the mother is an encounter with the unknowable Other in the self ('exterior intimacy'). It is this encounter with the Other (the mother, the night, the senses), revealed without words, which allows the subject to find her place in time, in social life (Levinas 1987: 75–9).

'I Want to See ... ' (García Marruz 1951: 22) inscribes memory of the mother, or rather, mother-music in whose dark 'room' the subject is cradled: 'I want to see the evening I once knew / ... I want to hear the music I once heard / in the nocturnal room that rocks me'. Infancy here is not a lost Paradise but a 'fallen garden'; nevertheless it holds the promise of a brilliant future:

[...] Oh qué futuro
en ti brilla más fiel y esplendoroso,
qué posibilidades en tu hojoso
jardín caído, infancia, falso muro.

Oh, what future / shines in you more faithful and splendid, / what a realm of possibilities in your leafy / fallen garden, infancy, false rampart.

The poet rejects the negative associations (passed on through the philosophical and theological traditions) of the 'garden' of infancy and the mother. Memory enables her to return through the 'false' screen (Plato's paraphragm?) to the mother, and therein find another kind of 'light' (knowledge) of future, infinite possibilities. The subject derives her 'Future substance from the dark / evening past!', and that dark instant is the hidden light, the 'veiled star' ('the face behind the dream', for Zambrano [1971: 195]). It seems to be the mother (from whence the poet derives her sustenance) who affords a means of transcendence:

Te quiero, ayer, mas sin nostalgia impura,
no por amor al polvo de mi vida,
sino porque tan sólo tú, pasado,
me encontrarás en la luz desconocida. (García Marruz 1951: 22)

I love you, yesterday, without impure nostalgia / not for love of the dust of my life, / but because you alone, past times, / will reveal me in a light unknown.

Similar links between the mother and origins are inscribed in several poems, for example, 'I love you, landscape that rocks me / the sleep of death, shaded park. / Like a strange inheritance I see you. / I love you, landscape that rocks me' (p. 124).

In 'Like a Bird' (p. 26) the child stays at home while her mother goes out: 'Mummy had gone out, all feathers / her smiling hat, and it was late.'

Aún sin pensamientos, sola andaba
por la cocina, en el olor cerrado.
Sin palabras, podía ver las losas.

Still without thoughts, alone I wandered / around the kitchen, in the stuffy smell. / Wordless, I could see the slab stones on the floor.

Again, the poet remembers the mother and the home, re-encountering the thresholds and dark womb-like interiors ('Remembering you today is to pass through a yard / as high as the watery trees. / I breathe deeply: threshold, House fastened tight'). The encounter is not through reason or knowledge, but through poetry and love: 'Ah, my mind is empty, but the inclination / that joins these two evenings like a bird folds / its wings, is as real to me as a Beggar' (p. 26). García Marruz refers to Love as a Beggar, possibly picking up on the story of Diotima of Mantinea related in Plato's *Symposium*. For Diotima, Love intermediates between the earthly and the heavenly and allows a relation between man and the divine. Diotima denies the separation of body and soul; both take part in the amorous encounter, which is the pathway to the divine. In this relation between the two lovers, both are subjects (Zambrano 1983).

This chapter has attempted to show that the subject in García Marruz's poetry is a 'would-be-*female* subject'. As mentioned previously, readings which are not gender-sensitive often seem to miss the point. A further example is the poem 'Beautiful Child'. This poem is addressed to an 'innocent' child and, in Arcos's view, highlights the innocence of the child, still in touch with eternity when compared to the adult who has lost this contact. But Arcos does not take into account the fact that the child is male. For this reason the 'boy child' may enter the 'park' of culture and knowledge whereas the female subject can enter only unclassified 'greenery, certain leaves and birds'. The male child can take on a sameness, 'wear the absent clothes / of the deceased', and only he 'in this grave and in-dissoluble kingdom / [has] touched the magic of exteriority, things / unspeakable'. The woman, meanwhile, wears 'the malicious clothes / of one familiar with death [contingency]' (García Marruz 1951: 41). The twist, however, is that the female subject knows more outside words, outside systems of thought. For the boy, the light of the sun of knowledge will fade:

Mas, ay cuando lo sepas, el parque se habrá ido,
conocerás la extraña lucidez del dormido,
y por qué el sol que alumbra tus álamos de oro
los dora hoy con palabras y días melancólicos. (p. 41)

But, ah, one day you will know and the park will have gone / and you'll feel the strange lucidity of the dreamer / and why the sun that illuminates your poplars with gold / gilds them today with words and melancholy days.

Eternal night, darkness, suffering and origins are affirmed in the sonnet 'The Night'. Night shows mortals 'the dark light of God' which is not 'the obscure light of men', and Night is feminine. In the poem 'The Lost Gazes', a series of snapshots of the family and the home, after describing 'that dark chest of drawers / where my aunts kept / madcap magazines' the subject states, 'I want no other infinity / to bathe my shadow pure. / If they ask me I will choose / the same dark chest of drawers' (p. 99), that is, the comfortable darkness of the woman-centred world of the home.

Similar reference to dark origins is in 'Strange Portraits' where the subject enters in dialogue with her infancy. Both she and her past self are framed in strange photographs or portraits. As a woman-subject, she has no means of access to subjectivity. She must enter the fate of her 'race' and is condemned to perform as a sad young man:

> Que esta solitaria noche mía
> no ha tenido la gracia
> del comienzo,
> y entré en la danza oscura de mi estirpe
> como un joven tristísimo
> en un lienzo. (p. 66)

> This solitary night of mine / had no delightful / beginning, / I took part in the dark dance of my race / like a sad young man / on a canvas.

She looks at the portraits, but finds no means of self-reflection. This is a 'mutual, strange / missed meeting'. The problematic process of identity and subjectivity is resolved through a shift towards the end of the poem towards another interlocutor. The poet has been addressing her portrait but now,

> Y a veces me parece que me pides
> para que yo te saque
> del silencio,
> me buscas en los árboles de oro
> y en el perdido parque
> del recuerdo
> y a veces me parece que te busco
> a tu tranquila fuerza
> y a tu sombrero,
> para que tú me enseñes el camino

de mi perdido nombre
verdadero.
De tu estrella distante, aparecida,
no quiero la luz tan triste
sino el Cuerpo.
Ahonda en mí. Encúentrame (pp. 66–7)

And at times it seems you ask me / to lift you out of / silence, / you search for me in the golden trees / in the lost park / of memories / and at times it seems I seek you / your peaceful strength / and your hat, / so you may show me the way / of my true, lost / name. / I don't want the light, so sad, / of your distant star appearing, / but your Body. / Delve in me. Find me.

The poet could be addressing God, or the Other (through memory, in the past self) but an everyday object – the hat – suggests, once again, that the interlocutor is the mother. The mother (poetry) asks to be liberated from silence. The mother searches for her daughter (with what Levinas terms the 'gratuitousness of *for the other*' (Levinas 1987: 106), to give her her 'true', matrilineal name, while the daughter subject longs for the body, the incarnation, of the mother in the encounter. As the poet writes in 'Glory of God': 'in my faithless image I can see you / and yet you are not humbled' (García Marruz 1951: 147).

Finally, in 'To Sor Juana, in her cell and deprived of books watching some girls play spinning-top' (pp. 23–4) there is a clear statement that the original cause is possibly God, but also the mother. In this poem Sor Juana [Inés de la Cruz] has no books, comprising the knowledge of philosophers. She has been prohibited 'the *intellectual* accession to the state-of-things' (Levinas 1987: 97), and 'the shadows disputing delusions' (of Plato's Cave?), merely bring her 'harm' (García Marruz 1951: 23). This 'light' may be 'learned', but it denies 'new life'. Sor Juana looks out of the window and sees some small girls playing with a spinning top. They are 'on the borders / of paused light'; while the books are 'silent' on the table the 'distracted gyration' of the spinning top, which one girl's hand has put into motion, remains. The spinning top spins like the stars spin in the sky, forgetful of their original cause: 'Such are the stars of God, forgetful / of the touch of His hand, as the distance increases'. The hand may belong to God, but it also belongs to the girl. The original maternal-feminine is recovered through a veiled reference to God, and the lines (borrowed from Augustine), 'How strange to live lamenting / life that is death, death that is life' (life which according to the philosophers is death, death [of the mother] which is life), take on another sense. Whatever this 'originary trace' is, it is prior to matter and rationality, 'It is known before the body and its measure / not in what remains escaping' [God, whom we can never reach] 'but in what, escaping, still remains' [between the objects of everyday life, materiality, and contingency, that is, the maternal-feminine].

Shy and retiring as ever, García Marruz is still writing today in her Havana home. Her work demands serious critical attention which focuses not so much on Catholic and Cuban issues but on the fact that the voice here is a woman's.

Writing about Lezama Lima and his novel *Paradiso*, Jean Franco concludes that despite his attempts to re-create classical European spiritual and human values, 'colonized society never gains in dignity, autonomy'; 'colonized man can never free his imagination totally from the conditions which limit him' (Franco 1987: 114–15). If these were the conditions limiting the work of the 'Orígenes' group in general, where does this leave the multiply colonized woman?

Notes

1. Members of the 'Orígenes' group include José Rodríguez Feo, José Lezama Lima, Cintio Vitier (poet and critic) and Eliseo Diego (poet, and García Marruz's brother-in-law).

2. At the age of twenty, García Marruz was on the editorial board of the avant-garde review *Clavileño* (1943). She graduated as Doctor in Social Sciences from Havana University, 1961.

3. Origen (185–254) believed the universe is pervaded by symbols of the invisible world. All things have a double aspect, the corporeal/sensible, accessible to all, and the spiritual/mystical, accessible only to the perfect. The latter could ascend beyond faith to contemplation of the Word dwelling in the Father. In the fourth century Origenism was called the 'hydra of all heresies' and his teachings were condemned (Cross 1957).

4. María Zambrano (b. 1904) was lecturer in Metaphysics in the Universidad Central, Madrid, until 1936. She was a staunch Republican during the Civil War. In 1940 she left Spain for exile and in 1939 lectured in Mexico where she published *Filosofía y poesía* (1939). In 1940 she was appointed lecturer in the University of Havana. Apart from three years in Paris (1946–49), Zambrano remained in Cuba until 1953. One of her courses, taught at Havana, 'The Birth and Development of the Idea of Freedom from Descartes to Hegel' was published recently by Cintio Vitier (*Litoral*, 124–6, 1983: 197–207). Vitier writes: 'We all flourished poetically and intellectually in her seminars, that seed-bed of hers, where we discussed the concept of memory from St Augustine to Bergson.' According to the course notes, the course covered 'the development of the idea of the "subject", because the history of the subject is the history of freedom'.

5. In a letter to the author dated Havana, 16 December 1994.

6. In the above letter to the author García Marruz describes poetry as 'musical, ironic, sad'. She adds: 'I have always felt the essence of the real is of a musical nature and it is sad because we cannot possess it really. That is the "oquedad" [hollowness], or lack, to which I referred, or rather not lack but absence, because what we feel as absent communicates a presence to us more than a lack.' Music is strongly associated with the house in which she was brought up, her mother's house (her parents separated amicably). Her mother, Josefina (married three times), was an accomplished pianist; her house was 'very bright, open and light like a birdcage'. She played arias and Italian romanzas, to accompany Fina's brother, Sergio,

who had a beautiful tenor voice; 'her music was the atmosphere of my home'. The poet adds: 'I can truly say that long before I read poetry, I was familiar with the poetry of the moving image in the cinema and with the sound of the piano.'

7. Compare with the description of Augustine's life as 'a journey from multiplicity to unity' (Clark 1994: 129).

8. An angel can be seen as an alternative to the phallus, denoting the in-between process, the interval, which permits the passage between the sensible and the intelligible, betweeen the immanent and the transcendent; a threshold allowing women to move up and down between matter and spirit. The angel is the messenger betweeen heaven and earth, always passing through boundaries. See Irigaray (1988: 126): 'angels […] open up the closed nature of the world, identity, action and history. The angel is *whatever passes through the envelope* […] postponing every deadline, revising every decision, undoing the very idea of repetition.'

9. Poetry ('la poesía') is a feminine word in Spanish (as is 'filosofía'). I have kept this gender to make explicit Zambrano's connections between poetry and the feminine.

10. According to Irigaray (1985) a girl cannot mourn the loss of the mother because she has no representation of what she has lost. She may identify with the lost object that cannot be represented, which leads to dereliction (self-sacrifice). Castration in Freud can be seen as the prohibition that prevents woman from imagining her own relationship with the mother. There is a non-differentiation between mother and daughter. 'Unless one accepts the need for women to be able to represent their relation to the mother and so to origin in a specific way (not according to the masculine model), then women will always be devalued' (Whitford, 1991: 85–9).

11. Harries (1993) quotes Simone Weil: 'The beauty of the world is Christ's tender smile for us coming through matter. He is really present in the universal beauty. The love of this beauty proceeds from God dwelling in our souls and goes out to God present in the universe' (p. 35) (from *Waiting on God*). Christianity, after all, is a revealed religion.

12. For Lacan one becomes a subject through language but the subject must be male; because the structuration of subjectivity is monosexual, one identifies with the father at the expense of the mother who is repressed.

13. The sword often represents the weapon of the Supreme Deity, as in 'the Sword of the Lord'. It is associated with masculine strength and also purification (de Vries 1974).

14. For St Augustine an image of the sensible object is fixed in the memory through sense knowledge (active sensation). For this to happen a sensible thing, a sense, a body and an image are needed but the soul acts upon them, 'the mind's eye is formed from that which the memory retains' (Clark 1994: 17).

15. In a letter to the author 16 December 1994.

CHAPTER 5

Contexts: Women Writers in Post-revolutionary Cuba, 1959–92

Having encountered reworkings of time and space in the work of Dulce María Loynaz and Fina García Marruz, the chronological perspective of Chapter 1 will now be extended. This chapter offers an overview of the incidence of women writers on the Cuban cultural map of the second half of the century. It takes into account literary works published up to the economic crisis of the early 1990s in Cuba by Cuban women but not work published outside Cuba by expatriate Cuban women who live abroad permanently or in exile. This includes the Cuban American population whose work deserves an in-depth study in its own right. In previous chapters I have briefly referred to women writers exiled during the Republic (usually under Machado and Batista) who returned to Cuba later, such as Camila Henríquez Ureña and Mirta Aguirre,[1] because of their influence on younger generations of female students. Similarly, the work of writers such as Lydia Cabrera and Emilia Bernal, who left Cuba but published important work before the Revolution, has been discussed.[2]

Post-revolutionary Cuba: mapping cultural change

The Revolution resulted in the complete restructuring of Cuban political, economic and social organization. In 1959 the government inherited a situation in which about a quarter of the population over the age of ten (one million) was illiterate (Thomas 1971: 1131).[3] There had been no regular university courses since 1956. During the early 1960s all efforts were channelled into the literacy and education campaigns; 1961 was 'Year of Education'. Over 100,000 high-school students volunteered to teach the urban poor and peasants to read and write, half of them young women. Cuban education was transformed. Thousands of new teachers, mainly women, worked in the new primary schools (over 1,000) set up between 1959 and 1961 (Smith and Padula 1996: 83). Private schools were nationalized. Primary school education was made obligatory and between 1965 and 1978 the number of teachers in primary education, mainly women, rose by 62 per cent. The 'Sixth Grade' literacy campaign, aimed at improving the reading skills of adults, resulted in more than 300,000 housewives reaching sixth grade by 1984 (Smith and Padula 1996: 85). By 1977, 80 per cent of women were literate.[4] In the late 1960s the co-educational rural boarding high schools were established providing full scholarships giving priority placement to the children of working mothers (Smith and Padula 1996: 87). By the end of the 1980s, 50 per cent of the students in the prestigious polytechnical boarding high schools were women. Rather than one major university in 1959, by the 1980s there were eight with 280,000 students, over half of whom were women studying mainly to be teachers. By 1986, 145,000 women workers had obtained a degree. The two major results of the education revolution with respect to literature were the formation of a much wider reading public and of a broader catchment area for new writers.

The publishing industry was also restructured (or, more precisely, created) to produce cheap (or freely available) books to cater for this new, multiethnic mass reading public of all ages, from children to grandparents. Schooling was free and compulsory and these new recruits needed books. Before the Revolution there existed no publishers in Cuba, only a printing and binding industry. Most writers published abroad but an author who wanted to publish a book in Cuba paid the printers for a short run (500–750 copies) and then sold the book herself to retailers and friends. The fact that there were no independent publishers in Cuba prior to the Revolution and that most specialized personnel emigrated after 1960 meant that there were innumerable technical difficulties to solve. New books were not forthcoming despite the founding of the Casa de las Américas publishers and the Imprenta Nacional (which used the former *Reader's Digest* presses) in 1959. As Smorkaloff points out, despite the immediate cultural explosion, the 1960s saw

> the laying down of foundations, and the creation – with what already existed, as far as machinery is concerned – of experience, *savoir faire*, the right conditions for the next stage [...] There was not an avalanche yet; not even a little avalanche in Cuban literary production [...] The material production of books was the same as before [...] What had changed was *the reader* and it is the reader who will revolutionize the concept of the book. (Smorkaloff 1987: 103, 105)

The publishing situation improved in the mid-1960s, particularly after the founding of the Instituto del Libro (1967), with novels appearing in editions of 15,000 to 20,000 copies (Smorkaloff 1987: 146). The Ministry of Culture, established in 1976, centralized and increased all publication activities. If in 1967 16 million copies were produced, this number had risen to 31 million by 1977. Of particular interest to creative writers was the founding of the Union of Cuban Writers and Artists [UNEAC] (1961) which published some of its members' works, including those of new writers. More important was Editorial Letras Cubanas, founded in 1977, whose sole task was to publish and distribute works of classical and contemporary Cuban literature. Between 1959 and 1976, 1,544 books written by Cuban authors were published in Cuba; between 1977 and 1986, 958 books were published by Letras Cubanas alone. Most of the literary works published by Letras Cubanas (1977–86) were novels (53 per cent), followed by poetry (20 per cent) and theatre (6 per cent) but few books appeared in second editions (21 per cent) (Smorkaloff 1987: 224–6). The literary and material quality of these books was very uneven. It was not until the 1980s that the long years of trial and error in the publishing industry brought about the desired results. As Smorkaloff wrote in 1987, the "blossoming" of Cuban letters in all genres [...] is being harvested now' (p. 187).

These changes in education and publishing were directed by an eclectic cultural politics which shifted direction over the decades, though usually reflecting the populism and nationalism of the Cuban radical intellectual tradition originating with Martí. The general aim was to rewrite Cuban history and culture from a popular, socialist point of view while making sure books and cultural activities were available to everyone. Art and culture were considered more important than ever before and were encouraged by massive state subsidies. But culture was not perceived as having the same role as it did in the liberal, bourgeois state. The role of the intellectual was to eliminate alienation and further the Revolution. Traditional values were replaced by purportedly revolutionary values: elitism by egalitarianism; the individual by the community; apathy by participation (Moreno 1971). Texts which found fault with these values were not published. Culture was to be national and independent, it was not expected to imitate foreign models but to reflect and create the aims of the Revolution. The instruments and degree of control used by the government to apply these criteria varied over the years, often in response to external factors.

As for women, the material conditions and legal rights of the vast majority improved considerably, particularly with regard to health and education. The legal situation of women was already highly favourable in the 1950s. The Family Code of 1975 recognized the full equality of both partners in marriage, and stipulated shared-parenting and shared domestic labour. Divorce was legal and easy to obtain. The Maternity Law of 1974 guaranteed women maternity leave and pay. Their jobs were kept for them for nine months. The provision of nurseries was written into the Constitution of 1976. Free health and dental care, free education and a myriad of state benefits were provided. Contraception, sterilization and abortion were legal and free. All children were considered equal, whether their parents were married or not. Morality verged on the puritanical. Sexual harassment was punished with one to six years' imprisonment; rape with four to thirty years' imprisonment, or even the death sentence if the victim was a child. By the end of the 1960s a third of the workforce was female; 40 per cent in the 1990s (Smith and Padula 1996: 120). Most women married around the age of twenty and were encouraged to keep their jobs. By the 1980s the average life expectancy for women was seventy-four years (Stubbs 1989: v).

However, it was difficult to eradicate deep-seated masculinist attitudes, either in the family or in the public domain. In education 'a powerful patriarchal ethos still dominated the system much as it did in the first half of the century' (Smith and Padula 1996: 93). The universal socialist subject has always been implicitly male. The priority of the Revolution, it was argued, was the well-being of the collectivity as a whole, not just 'women's sectorial interests' (Azicri 1988: 116):

> The struggle for equality for women in Cuba was seen as inextricably linked to the general process of social transformation, as a part of the socialist revolution and the construction of a classless society. Substantial advances would not be made, it was thought, by means of an isolated struggle or by the independent action of intellectual *élites*. (Larguía and Demoulin 1985: 37)

Socialists considered feminism a white, middle-class phenomenon which had no role to play in Cuba. The early emphasis on morality as a counter to corruption and abuse, studied in Chapter 2, resulted in a male-oriented Revolution which, while verging on the puritanical, implicitly condoned traditional attitudes towards women. Abstinence or sexual restraint was expected outside marriage, particularly of women. Sexual matters were a public embarrassment. Sexuality was not an issue; rape, domestic violence and sexual abuse were 'invisible topics' (Smith and Padula 1988: 156); pornography, homosexuality, the expression of female sexual desire were taboo at least until the 1980s. The main aims and policies of the Revolution, then, with respect to women, were profoundly contradictory. Women were to be incorporated into the workforce and they were to be protected as mothers (and children) in the heterosexual nuclear family. They were producers and reproducers which, many women argued, made their situation intolerable (Smith and Padula 1996; Randall 1992: 119–54).

The Federación de Mujeres Cubanas [Federation of Cuban Women] was established in 1960 under the Presidency of Vilma Espín (Fidel Castro's sister-in-law) to see the revolutionary programme through. In 1990 the FMC had over 3 million members, 80 per cent of the adult female population (Molyneux 1996: 5). Pursuing a 'mobilization-based participatory politics' (Azicri 1984: 267), it mobilized women during the Bay of Pigs and the Cuban missile crises, the literacy campaigns and the sugar harvests and encouraged women to work. Men were expected to share domestic chores and to protect women, due to, as Vilma Espín explained in 1960, 'the physiological inferiority of woman due to procreation' (Sejourné 1980: x).

In practice, no women have held important government posts and few women have any political power. Women are expected to work and bring up a family, and their husbands do not help. Most women work long hours at the workplace and do the housework (the 'double shift') without the benefits of household commodities, aggravated by long queues for food and transport. Women have to contend with food shortages, rationing, housing problems, bureaucratic muddles and constant workplace and neighbourhood meetings which they are expected to attend. Not surprisingly, Cuba has one of the highest divorce rates in the Americas. The profound contradictions of revolutionary attitudes towards women were encapsulated in the delightful front cover of the women's magazine *Mujeres* (May 1981) described by Verity Smith as featuring 'a woman with a baby at her breasts and a Kalashnikov rifle slung round her hips' (Smith 1995: 3). In a later 1991 issue, Smith adds, young men were reminded that they should always walk next to the kerb when in the company of women and 'allow young women (and their Kalashnikov rifles?) to alight first from a bus' (Smith 1995: 4). The atmosphere of these years was captured succinctly by Belkis Cuza Malé (b. 1949) in 'They are Making a Girl for the Times'. Her scathing irony, targeted at the fabrication of a Cuban superwoman, underlines these serious ideological contradictions:

Están haciendo una muchacha para la época,
con mucha cal y pocas herramientas,
alambres, cabelleras postizas,
senos de algodón y armazón de madera.
El rostro tendrá la inocencia de Ofelia
y las manos, el rito de una Helena de Troya.
Hablará tres idiomas
y será diestra en el arco, en el tiro y la flecha.
Están haciendo una muchacha para la época,
entendida de política,
y casi de filosofía,
alguien que no tartamudee,
ni tenga necesidad de espejuelos,
que llene los requisitos de una aeromoza,
lea a diario la prensa,
y, por supuesto, libere su sexo
sin dar un mal paso con un hombre.
En fin, si no hay nuevas disposiciones,
así saldrá del horno
esta muchacha hecha para la época. (Oviedo 1968: 147)

They are making a girl for the times / with lots of limewash, a few tools, / wires, false hairpieces, / cotton breasts and a wooden chassis. / Her face will be as innocent as Ophelia's / and her hands, a ritual to Helen of Troy. / She'll speak three languages / and be skilled in the art of shot, bow and arrow. / They are making a girl for the times, / an expert in politics / and almost in philosophy, / someone who never stutters, / and never needs spectacles, / who fulfils the requirements of an air hostess, / reads the press every day, / and, of course, liberates her sex / without putting a foot wrong with a man. / In conclusion, if there are no more dispositions, / that's how she'll come out of the oven / this girl made for the times.

In 1987 Sheldon B. Liss expressed the hope that: 'Ideally, a generation from now, when someone writes a sequel to this book women will be included among Cuba's most distinguished political and social theorists' (Liss 1987: 187). Unfortunately, his aspiration has not yet been met.

Historical accounts of cultural developments and official policy towards the arts in post-revolutionary Cuba usually distinguish several phases. The first (1959–61) was a wave of frenzied enthusiasm and self-confidence culminating in Fidel Castro's ambiguous 'Words to the Intellectuals' (1961):

> [...] within the Revolution, everything; against the Revolution, nothing. Does this mean that we are going to tell people here what to write? No. Everyone should write what they want, and if what they write is no good, that's their problem ... We don't prohibit anyone from writing on the theme they prefer. On the contrary. And everyone should express themselves in the way they feel is appropriate and they should express freely the idea they want to express. We will always appreciate their creation through the prism of the Revolution. (Menton 1978: 131)

During this period the UNEAC was founded and membership was compulsory. Its members were guaranteed jobs as teachers, translators and editors as well as free time for their creative work. Innovating enterprises, however, were crushed.

During the second phase, the mid- to late 1960s, writers reaped the benefits of the reorganization of the publishing industry and the creation of the Editora Nacional in 1962 and the Instituto del Libro in 1967. University texts were distributed to students free of charge. In 1967 it was decided that copyright should not be respected, mainly because foreign publishers would not grant Cuba licence to publish university teaching texts, and writers' royalties abolished (Thomas 1971: 1465; Smorkaloff 1987: 164), although copyright was reinstated in 1977. This is what literary critics, such as Seymour Menton, call the 'boom' period of the Cuban novel. It may be extended to include four novels of worldwide repute: A. Carpentier's *Explosion in a Cathedral* [1962] 1963; J. Lezama Lima's *Paradiso* [1966] 1974; G. Cabrera Infante's *Three Trapped Tigers* [1965] 1971; and Carpentier's *Reasons of State* [1974] 1976.

The third period, the 1970s, saw the 'boom' years cut short by a hard-line approach brought on by entrenched practices, increasing dependence on the USSR and economic hardship. This tightening up of cultural policy and state control was encapsulated in the words of Nicolás Guillén, who stated in December 1969 in a speech to the UNEAC:

> Cuban writers and artists have the same responsibility as our soldiers in defending the nation [...] he who does not fulfil his duty, no matter what his rank, will receive the most severe revolutionary punishment for his crime. (Menton 1978: 144)

Symptomatic, too, was the storm with *Mundo Nuevo* in Paris, the imprisonment of the poet Heberto Padilla for a month in 1971 for alleged counter-revolutionary activities, his subsequent release and humiliating public 'confession', and Fidel Castro's rousing condemnation of the 'mafia of bourgeois intellectuals' that same year in the First National Congress of Education and Culture. What Thomas refers to as 'an entrenched literary bureaucracy' (Thomas 1971: 1466) manned by undistinguished bureaucrats increasingly curtailed innovation. During the early 1970s the National Council for Culture, run by the army, was in control. The subsequent so-called 'grey quinquennium' lasted until 1976 when the Ministry of Culture was formed under Armando Hart. The year 1980, the year of 'profundización' or 'in-depth analysis', the Peruvian Embassy crisis, the Mariel boat-lift (when 120,000 Cubans left), the suicide of Haydée Santamaría and the death of Celia Sánchez, both distinguished former revolutionaries, was particularly hard. In the fourth phase, the more prosperous mid-1980s, this hard-line, monologic approach was loosened, while monitoring of equal opportunities policies towards blacks and women was taken more seriously (Stubbs 1989: 78–80). In literature, certain genres (for example, social realism and detective fiction, prominent in the early 1970s) were actively encouraged and book production increased.

Women's writing from 1959 onwards

The overall presence of women's writing on the post-revolutionary cultural map is disappointing, both with regard to the quantity and quality of works published. I should qualify this statement. Disappointing suggests high expectations and, given the outstanding literacy and educational achievements of the Revolution outlined above, these expectations are justified. In 1959 there were only 17,000 university students. In 1996 the population was 11 million, 98 per cent of the adult population was literate (*The Economist*, 6–12 April 1996), and there were more than 200,000 university students. One might have expected more publications from women in a self-proclaimed egalitarian society avid for reading material.

By 1985, according to US marketing and publishing consultant Leonard Shatzkin (Shatzkin 1985), there were twelve publishers in Cuba, mostly run by the Ministries of Culture and Education, which published about 2,000 titles per annum, some 50 million volumes. The great majority of these were school textbooks (many authored by women). A relative increase in the publication of women's literature was to be expected. As this book has, I hope, made clear, the woman writer continues a long tradition in Cuba (unlike in other areas of the Caribbean). Cuban first-wave feminism was one of the earliest and most active women's movements in Latin America; Cuban women were given the right to vote in 1934, ten years before their French sisters. For this reason, too, one would expect Cuban women's writing to have flourished since 1959.

Perhaps the most startling feature of the post-1959 literary scene is the lack of novels published by women. Until the late 1980s there were really only two. This figure can be compared to Mexico where, according to Deborah Shaw (1995: 112), fifty women writers published novels and short stories between 1970 and 1987. Ostensibly, in Cuba the lack of female-authored novels is a gender-specific phenomenon. According to Seymour Menton's account of the development of the Cuban novel after 1959, in line with the cultural shifts outlined above, many novels were published in the late 1960s, very few in the 1970s, and rather more in the 1980s. The publication of women's writing does not follow this pattern. The pattern and rate of production of literary works by women writers in Cuba differ substantially from those of men. Women continued to publish right through the 1960s and 1970s at a constant, relatively low, rate. This was not the case of the male-authored novel which, after the 'boom' of the late 1960s (more novels were published in Cuba in 1967 than ever before), suffered a sharp decline in the 1970s: no novels were published in Cuba in 1972, and only five in 1973 (Rodríguez Coronel 1986).[5] Women simply did not participate in the 1960s novel 'boom'. Consequently, they were hardly involved (at least not as publicly) in the acrimonious debates of the early 1970s. The whole Alejo Carpentier, José Lezama Lima, Lisandro Otero, Guillermo Cabrera Infante, Reinaldo Arenas debate passed them by. In other words, it seems that neither the 'boom' nor the 'grey quinquennium' affected women writers to the same extent as their male contemporaries, although several women writers (for example Nancy Morejón and Excilia Saldaña among others) belonged to the El Puente literary group and publishing house which was closed in 1965 for publishing 'bourgeois' literature. On that occasion black poet Lourdes Casal was arrested. Also Heberto Padilla's wife, Belkis Cuza Malé, a fine poet in her own right, was 'denounced' by her husband during his 'confession' and finally went into exile in 1979.

Even taking into account the gender bias of the 'boom' throughout Latin America and Spain, one might have expected more of Cuba. On the other hand, the novel was never a genre favoured by Cuban women writers. The novels women wrote before 1959, such as Ofelia Rodríguez Acosta's *La vida manda* (Madrid, 1929) and Dulce María Loynaz's *Jardín* (Madrid, 1951), were often published abroad. Nevertheless, revolutionary cultural politics might have reversed this trend. Several women novelists or potential novelists felt disaffected towards the Castro government; Lydia Cabrera left in 1960; Hilda Perera (whose novel *Mañana es 26* [Tomorrow is the 26th] was published in 1960) left shortly afterwards. Dulce María Loynaz did not disguise her antipathy for the revolutionary government (which, in January 1959, ordered all copies of her *Un verano en Tenerife* [A Summer in Tenerife], published in Madrid in November 1958, to be returned to Cuba), and declared she would not publish in Cuba again. Seemingly, the white middle-class women writers who left Cuba (in body or spirit) took the novel with them. But it is also true that those who willingly stayed, such as Renée Méndez Capote, might well have published novels but were not encouraged to do so. Renée Méndez Capote took a leading role in the setting up of Gente Nueva publishers for children and wrote several texts for children as well as her autobiography, but she did not write a novel (Smorkaloff 1987: 154).

With regard to other types of narrative prose (short fiction, 'testimonio' and autobiography) women writers fared rather better. The short story was a popular genre and about a dozen or more collections by women were published throughout the period (see Chapter 6). 'Testimonio' and autobiography (often recast as 'testimonio') were particularly important in the early 1960s.

Relatively few plays have been published by women since the Revolution despite the fact that many women wrote plays which were regularly performed on stage in the 1940s and 1950s. No woman has found a place in the Cuban canon of dramatists (Virgilio Piñera, José Brene, Hector Quintero and so on). But women certainly participate in the theatre, as attested by the incidence of leading directors (such as Raquel Revuelta), stage managers and actresses, some of whom are also playwrights. Individual women's names (unlike the names of men, such as Sergio Corrieri) tend to get lost in collective authorship projects. Gloria Parrado, actress, critic and playwright, whose career extends from the 1940s onward, is probably the most important.[6]

The genre in which Cuban women have always excelled is poetry, and post-revolutionary Cuba is no exception. Most Cuban women writing in Cuba are poets; the most outstanding work published is poetry; the greatest number of texts published are collections of poetry. In other words, there exists a solid, exceptionally impressive tradition of Cuban women's poetry throughout the twentieth century which the Revolution has encouraged and expanded. Most of the white, middle-class women writers who had established a reputation before the Revolution, who stayed and continued publishing in Cuba, were poets. Dulce María Loynaz (b. 1902), Fina García Marruz (b. 1923) and Carilda Oliver Labra (b. 1923) are now considered the founding mothers of contemporary women's poetry. These poets, as well as Cleva Solís (b. 1926) and Rafaela Chacón Nardi (b. 1926), constitute what might be termed the first 'generation' (or group) of women poets publishing after 1959. But, as we have seen, periodization based on 'generations' of writers, much favoured by Hispanic critics, hardly applies to women writers. The poets mentioned above belong to at least two generations according to their dates of birth. The earlier generation might include the avant-garde writers publishing in the mid-1920s and 1930s (the generation of Alejo Carpentier and Nicolás Guillén), but these writers (Lydia Cabrera, b. 1900; Camila Henríquez Ureña, b. 1902; Mirta Aguirre, b. 1912; Dora Alonso, b. 1910; and Dulce María Loynaz, b. 1902) can hardly be grouped together other than on the basis of gender and possibly age. A later generation might include the Catholic 'Orígenes' group publishing in the 1940s, but also the Matanzas poet Carilda Oliver Labra, famed for her erotic poetry, and the socialist feminist writers such as Ofelia Rodríguez Acosta.

About a dozen women poets born between 1940 and 1960, usually referred to as the poets of the Revolution, have published continuously throughout the post-1959 period. The most famous internationally is Nancy Morejón; the poet who perhaps commands the greatest repect in Cuba is Reina María Rodríguez. Their work is extremely varied and does not fit into simple categories. Other important names are Lina de Feria, Digdora Alonso, Georgina Herrera, Minerva Salado, Marilyn Bobes, Lourdes González, Elsa Claro and Cira Andrés, some of whom will figure in later chapters. A new generation of women poets born in the 1970s is now attracting interest from critics abroad. Unfortunately, their 'coming of age' has coincided with the economic crisis of the 1990s. Some poets have published abroad, for example, Zoe Valdés in Spain and Nancy Morejón in Venezuela. Others, such as Fina García Marruz, Damaris Calderón and Excilia Saldaña, published in 'plaquettes' or hand-made books.

As noted previously, no black or mulatto woman writer (poet, novelist or dramatist) made a lasting literary reputation in Cuba before 1959. The one exception was educationalist Rafaela Chacón Nardi, whose mother was born in Martinique, but whose poetry, published in the 1940s, did not signal an African Caribbean heritage. Excepting journalists, such as Marta Rojas, the black or mulatto women authors of today who identify with African Caribbean culture are all poets. There can be no doubt that the Revolution made it possible for black women to publish, but given the country's aspirations, one might have expected more. Only about half a dozen black or mulatto women writers, including Rafaela Chacón Nardi, Nancy Morejón and the Cuban American Lourdes Casal who left Cuba in 1961 but returned (not permanently) in the mid-1970s and died in 1981, have established a literary reputation.

The 'boom' in Cuban women's writing came not in the late 1960s but in the mid-1980s. During that decade an unprecedented number of women's works were published (in all genres), by established writers, by young unknown writers, and – the most surprising development of all – by older writers who perhaps had hardly published for twenty years and whose pre-revolutionary works appeared, at long last, in modern editions. No doubt the 'women's boom' was due to increased production all round. As noted previously, few books were published during the 1970s, but during that decade a strong push was initiated to encourage writing at grassroots level, particularly among young people. 'Talleres', or workshops, such as the Hermanos Saíz Brigade, were set up all over the country in schools and universities. The Ministry of Culture provided young people with the opportunity to travel and meet established writers and artists. This encouragement bore fruit in the 1980s. Reina María Rodríguez's poetry, written in the 1970s, was not published until 1980 and 1984 (Bejel 1991: 349). At the same time, there was an undeniable reassessment of the value of women's work due partly to developments following International Women's Year in 1975 (Miller 1991: 188–91) and to the 'Rectification' campaign of 1986 which encouraged more open discussion of social problems, gender issues, sex, education and publishing, at least at a macrolevel. The international 'boom' in women's writing, particularly in Latin America with the works of best-selling authors such as Isabel Allende reaching record sales, could not fail to influence the Cuban cultural scene. Sadly, the women's publishing 'boom' was tragically cut short by the economic collapse of the early 1990s. A virtual standstill in publishing brought on by a lack of paper meant that many women writers did not publish at all during the early 1990s. As Eric Hobsbawm points out: 'there can be no serious doubt that in the late 1980s and early 1990s an era in world history ended and a new one began' (Hobsbawm 1994: 5). It took a long time for literary women of the post-revolutionary period to make a sustained impact, and when they did the paper ran out.[7]

In what follows I shall enlarge the scale of the literary map in order to discern more closely the details of individual texts, particularly novels and plays which are not discussed in subsequent chapters.

NOVEL In 1988 Cuban critic Luisa Campuzano published a seminal essay in *Letras Cubanas*, 'Woman in the Narrative of the Revolution: An Essay on Scarcity' (in Yáñez and Bobes 1996). The statistics she presented were shocking. In the period 1959 to 1983 she could find only twelve novels published by women compared to 170 by men. In fact, of the twelve, two were written by women who left Cuba, three were 'testimonios', three were detective novels, and two were not worth talking about. The remaining two were Dora Alonso's *Tierra inerme* [Defenceless Land] (1961) (based on an earlier radio novel *Tierra adentro* [Interior Land], 1944) which won the Casa de las Américas prize, and *La hora de los mameyes* [The Time of the Mammy Apples] (1983) by Mirta Yáñez. Neither of these rural novels is what the European academy would call a 'literary masterpiece'.

Add to these half a dozen other works which have come to my notice, such as the detective novel *Una vez más* [Once Again] by Berta Recio (1980), Mary Cruz's historical novel *Los últimos cuatro días* [The Last Four Days] (1988), Chely Lima's *Brujas* [Witches] (1990), Soledad Cruz Guerra's *Adioses y bienvenidas* [Goodbyes and Welcomes] (1990), and Daína Chaviano's *Fábulas de una abuela extraterrestre* [Fables of an Extraterrestrial Grandmother] (1988) and the result is a corpus of interesting but not particularly inspiring texts.

Dora Alonso described *Tierra inerma* as 'a panorama of the sorrow, misery and abandonment our people used to suffer' (*Casa de las Américas*, no. 151, 1985, p. 133). According to Méndez y Soto, it won the Casa de las Américas prize because it suggested that communism alone could resolve the dreadful rural problems it depicted (Méndez y Soto 1977: 74); as Menton indicates, 1960 was the year of the agrarian reform. But critics have not read with a woman's eye. One of the novel's main flaws, according to Méndez Soto, is that the conflict centres on a female character, Ernestina. Menton is also critical: 'Ernestina's problems distract from the social criticism' (Menton 1978: 44). For these critics the characters are weak, the suspense minimal, the descriptions strained and the contradictions too plentiful. Above all *Tierra inerme*, a 'rural novel' written in the style of Venezuelan author Rómulo Gallegos, was considered extremely *démodé* in 1961. It simply did not fit the fashionable parameters of the 'boom' novel and was one of the few 'rural novels' published in Latin America at the time: Menton (1978: 43) mentions six (see Shea 1988).

A novel not mentioned by Campuzano which should have been included in the 'boom' of the late 1960s but passed virtually unnoticed was *Sonámbulo del sol* [Sleepwalker in the Sun] (Barcelona, 1972) written by Nivaria Tejera, Seix Barral prize-winner in 1971. Nivaria Tejera was Cuban but her father was Spanish. Her family moved to Spain when she was two years old and her father was imprisoned during the Civil War. In 1944 the family returned to Cuba and Tejera published *La ravine* (Paris, 1958) / *El barranco* (Havana, 1959), based on her memories of the Civil War. She was appointed Cuban cultural attachée in Paris and Rome in 1959 but removed from this post in 1965. She stayed in Paris thereafter. As Menton points out (1978: 82–3), Tejera's novel provides an interesting counterpoint to fellow diplomat Cabrera Infante's *Tres tristes tigres* [Three Trapped Tigers] (which also won the Seix Barral prize in 1964, and was published in 1967). Both deal with the night-life of 1950s Havana but, unlike Cabrera Infante, Tejera shows the down side, the corruption, poverty and decadence as experienced by an unemployed mulatto. The novel, written in the style of the nouveau roman, justifies the Revolution, although only implicitly, through the protagonist's troubled stream of consciousness. It has not been included by Cubans in accounts of their literary history, despite the fact that Tejera's poetry appears in Fernández Retamar's influential 1960 anthology.

Mirta Yáñez's *La hora de los mameyes*, published over twenty years later, like Alonso's novel, exposes the problems of the Cuban countryside: poverty, violence and injustice. In this short novel, framed as a fictional 'testimonio', the male protagonist, Jutío (a teller-character), recounts his life-story to the reader and to Juliana, the love of his life, assisted by an omniscient narrator. This long tale of woe, interspersed with flashes of humour and magical realism, centres on the tyrant, Doctor Lucio Aguirre, who establishes a soap factory in a remote, coastal village and takes over the lives of its inhabitants. It is a historical novel as the action takes place between 1902 and 1959, ending with the advent of the Revolution which puts paid to all previous iniquities. Aguirre, in collaboration with the local priest and the army, represents the corruption and abuse of power of the Menocal, Machado and Batista regimes. He also represents capitalism and its exploitation of workers. His atrocities culminate with the mass slaughter of the entire village which is bombed by Batista's army because they dared to go on strike. Resisting the Doctor is Jutío (whose life has been blighted by his adversary); the matriarch of the village 'granny Eutemia', the source of moral strength; and, finally, the entire village community. Local community action, focused on the family and preceded by the heroic acts of individuals, is shown to defeat individual selfishness. The local rural family, the village (and the Cuban nation) wins out over global capitalism, foreign intervention and corruption in the public sphere.

In his survey of the Cuban novel (1975 to 1987) Menton (1990) notes a marked increase in the number of novels published during those twelve years. In his view this was due to the encouragement of certain genres, in particular the detective or spy novel and the historical novel. Of the eighty novels published in this period, over a quarter are thrillers, detective or spy novels. To a certain extent, this is reflected in women's writing too. As we have seen, Mirta Yáñez's novel is historical. Berta Recio's thriller *Una vez más* (1980), which won the MININT (Ministerio del Interior [Home Office] prize), is almost as good a read as a novel published by Ruth Rendell. But certain aspects of the novel are rather disconcerting for the European reader familiar with thriller formulae. The murder of Bettina Lefevre, a beautiful Belgian citizen, married to a Belgian businessman based in Cuba, results in an investigating police officer uncovering a spy ring intent on destabilizing the Revolution from within. The story is told by the man from MININT (an anonymous teller-character) who is shown to be kind, courteous and, of course, a staunch patriot. The counter-revolutionaries, all motivated by resentment and greed (one leader of the group was a money-lender before the Revolution, another is an ex-military agent under Batista, now in hiding) use foreigners visiting Cuba (here an Australian) to smuggle out secret documents, first to London, then elsewhere. The aim is to ruin Cuba's trade relations and create bad publicity. Needless to say, all the nasties are captured and imprisoned. As in the best murder stories, the reader is keen to know who killed the victim and why, and also who is the informer assisting the policeman. But *Una vez más* is not just a murder/spy story; it is also a novel about rehabilitation. The informer has committed minor offences against the Revolution and is given this golden opportunity to reform. She does so, successfully, thanks to the firm if patronizing guidance of the MININT man. The lesson she and the reader learn is that Cubans should always be on guard against fifth columnists:

> Sloppiness, negligence, carelessness, our own colleagues' lack of vigilance at work all helped us to conspire against them. What a lack of caution! How many secrets were given away! [...] How much harm has been caused by the inopportune comment, by one word too many, by superficial chatter ... (Recio 1980: 139)

Above all, Cubans should be aware of mixing with loose-living, money-grabbing foreigners (particularly Western European and English-speaking ones) who do not understand the situation in Cuba and who are a danger to Cubans and to themselves (the counter-revolutionaries who murdered Bettina for large sums of money). The Cuban baddies all share bourgeois values; they eat in fancy restaurants, are extremely fashion-conscious and wear only designer clothes (for example, lime-green nylon shirts), and spend their time lounging around the bar in the Havana Libre hotel. Interestingly, the worst are women: one, a chemist, puts corrosive substances into the supplies of toothpaste. The informant (a former, but now re-educated baddie), is also a woman. The goodies are the MININT man and Bettina's poor husband who was dragged into her devious schemes unwillingly. Women are objects of suspicion. Equality politics and identity politics, then, are seen to be mutually exclusive, and *Una vez más*, both didactic and entertaining, teaches more than it thrills.[8]

Narrative innovations of a different sort were made by Chely Lima in her short novel *Brujas* (1990) which focuses on a group of young people who, like their peers in Europe and elsewhere, seek a meaning to their disorganized lives. They sit at home playing noisy Vivaldi records, bemoaning their parents' antiquated ideas, and rebelling against the older generation by walking about naked and practising 'free love'. The novel, which consists of snippets of conversations between the female protagonist (Camila) and her friends, stories, and extracts from a diary, has a strong feminist agenda. Camila wants women to whistle cat-calls at men; she ditches one live-in lover for another, and her neighbour – who has divorced and remarried – has a baby by her first husband while accompanied by both men in hospital. A sense of sadness and dissatisfaction pervades the novel. Camila has written the novel after the death of her boyfriend, Mario, killed in a car accident. The fact that the book is dedicated to Mario Bermúdez, *in memoriam*, suggests the novel is semi-autobiographical.

The everyday experiences of young people is also the theme of Daína

Chaviano's 1988 novel which consists of three parallel stories involving fantastic winged creatures, medieval knights and young Cubans, again all searching for meaning in their rather unusual lives.

'TESTIMONIO'/AUTOBIOGRAPHY   The term 'autobiography' is perhaps more appropriate for what Campuzano refers to as 'testimonio'. 'Testimonio' implies an illiterate subject whose oral account of certain events is transcribed by a writer or journalist. Autobiography is an author's first-person, written account of events in her life-story. 'Testimonio' is possibly preferred in a society which does not encourage individualism, but the generic boundaries are further blurred because many Cuban autobiographies centre on personal accounts of crucial, national, historical events. As Vera León writes: 'in post 1959 Cuban literature the forms of narrative and politics intersect most dramatically at the level of self-narrative and lifestory telling [...] self-narrative is a special zone of the post-1959 Cuban social text' (Vera León 1993: 65). Fidel Castro's *La historia me absolverá* [History Will Absolve Me], delivered in 1953, first marked the construction of the revolutionary subject and was followed by *Diario de Che en Bolivia* [Che's Diary in Bolivia], 1968 (Vera León 1993). Oscar Lewis's *Four Women. Living the Revolution: An Oral History of Contemporary Cuba* (1977) is invaluable for charting women's varied experiences of the Revolution. Women journalists have written the 'testimonios' of other women, such as black journalist Marta Rojas's[9] intriguing account of *Tania, la guerrillera inolvidable* [Tania, the Unforgettable Guerrilla] (1970) and Nancy Morejón and Carmen Gonce's 'testimonio' of a nickel-mining community *Lengua de pájaro. Comentarios reales* [Bird's Tongue. Real Commentaries] (1969). Some six or seven autobiographies were published by women between 1959 and 1983; half of these describe the authors' everyday experiences in the literacy campaign of 1961. Daura Olema García's *Maestra voluntaria* [Volunteer Teacher] (1962) (which won the Casa de las Américas prize and which Menton [1978: 35] refers to as 'propaganda') and Dora Alonso's *El año 61* [The Year 1961] (1981) which includes photographs to give the text added documentary value, are cases in point. Olga Alonso González's *Testimonios* (1973) was published almost ten years after her death; she was killed at the age of nineteen when a tractor fell on her when she was on her way to give classes to a group of peasants. Her 'testimonio' consists of pithy diary entries, poems and letters written while she was a volunteer during the coffee harvest of 1962. Araceli Aguililla's *Primeros recuerdos* [First Memories] (1963) recounts the author's childhood experiences of the early 1930s in order to contrast the harsh life of the past with the opportunities offered to the lucky young people of the 1960s. *Donde se nace por casualidad* [Where You are Born by Chance] (1987) by Cynthia Valdés Montes de Oca is the 'testimonio' of a Cuban woman born in 1939 in New York who decides to return to Cuba in the 1960s. It is dedicated to her grandmother 'who left me her Cubanness' and prefaced by a long quotation from José Martí: 'In the North there is no assistance, no roots [...] The rich are piled up on one side and the desperate on the other. The North [...] is full of hatred. We've got to get out of the North quick.'

One of the most enjoyable books in this group is the spirited *Memorias de una cubanita que nació con el siglo* [Memoirs of a Cuban Girl Born with the Century] (1990 [1963]) written by Renée Méndez Capote (b. 1901) and used as a school text. In the eleven short chapters of this autobiography, Renée reminisces about her family life ('our deformed bourgeoisie', according to the book jacket), schooling and childhood adventures, including an early romance at the age of eleven. The book opens with this comical reference to the Platt Amendment of 1902: 'I was born just before the Republic. I was born in November 1901 and she was born in May 1902, but since our birth we have been very different. She was born amended and I was born determined never to let myself be amended by anyone' (Méndez Capote 1990: 1), and casts personal development in terms of the nation's progress. The colourful scenes (her mother's bedroom, her first ride in a car, the menus on offer at official dinners in turn-of-the-century Havana), her account of her shy responses to the suitor who was later killed and, above all, the dreadfully true story of the family of five fishermen all devoured by sharks, except for the youngest who lived to tell the tale, are the moving and totally convincing episodes of a creole woman's life-story.

SHORT STORY Campuzano mentions twenty collections of short stories published by women up to 1986 to which another three published in the early 1960s by writers who left Cuba (Hilda Perera and Ana María Simó) should be added, as well as at least a further dozen since 1986. Dora Alonso is the most prolific female short story writer of the post-revolutionary period (Menton 1975: 34–5; Davies 1993a). She contributed at least one story to each of the twelve anthologies published before 1971, has published four collections of her own stories for adults, and at least five collections for children. Other important short story writers of the older generation (born in the 1940s) are Ana María Simó (who left Cuba in 1965), María Elena Llana, Rosa Ileana Boudet, Omega Agüero, Olga Fernández and Mirta Yáñez. None the less, according to Menton, in the 1960s (1959–71) 115 volumes of short fiction were published by men and only twelve by women. The stories tend to fall into three categories: magical realism, science fiction/fantasy and the Revolution. But, he points out, not one of the three women authors he mentions (Ana María Simó, Evora Tamayo and Angela Martínez) writes about the Revolution directly. Whatever their sub-genre or aesthetic qualities, women's short stories are invaluable for the description they present of the otherwise hidden, unexpressed thoughts, behaviours and lifestyles of women in Cuba.

This is borne out by my study of the short stories published by Dora Alonso and other women writers in the 1970s and 1980s in Chapter 6. The great majority of stories focus on women but not on the Revolution as such. As we shall see, Cuban women's short stories focus predominantly on the lives of women; women from the recent past until today, young and old, rich and poor, black and white. Set in the city or the country, but usually in the home, or in other everyday locations frequented by women, the stories narrate young girls' hopes and old ladies' memories, everyday lives and fantasies. Realism is the most favoured mode; in the early 1970s it was difficult to publish stories that were not realist (Yáñez and Bobes 1996). Women (such as María Elena Llana) preferred fantasy, dream and the uncanny (and tended not to publish in the 1970s). Science fiction and detective fiction are important, officially-condoned genres. Rural settings feature large. Dora Alonso's short stories highlight the misery of the black peasants, in particular the women. Most of the stories she wrote in the 1940s foreground conflict and violence; after 1959 they become increasingly woman-centred.

Omega Agüero's ironically titled *La alegre vida campestre* [The Happy Life of the Countryside] (1973) also denounces rural atrocities endemic before the Revolution: the violence of the Guardia Rural, corruption and poverty. Her later *El muro de medio metro* [A Wall Half a Metre Thick] (1977) dwells on key moments in one woman's life until, in the last story, the woman decides to have the baby her lover does not want. Mirta Yáñez's *Todos los negros tomamos café* [We Blacks All Drink Coffee] (1976), like some of Alonso's and Agüero's short fiction, is part 'testimonio'. The first-person 'testimonio' sections relate the author's everyday experiences during the student mobilization in the coffee harvest. Intercalated in this autobiographical frame are a series of short stories (some realistic, some strange) told by the local country folk, many of African descent, and thumbnail sketches of local characters, such as the Haitian Yulián. It is in her later book of stories *El diablo son las cosas* [What the Devil] (1986) that Yáñez writes with flair, using stream of consciousness, local idioms and a chatty humour which are her hallmark.[10]

Unlike the realist short fiction mentioned so far, most of María Elena Llana's stories, published in *La Reja* [The Gate] (1965) are fantastic and invite psychological, existential or magical interpretations. In 'We Women' a woman dreams her telephone number has changed. The next day she phones the new number and finds she is talking to her self. Frightened, she leaves the empty house but forgets her keys. She rings the bell hoping her self will answer the door; it does. In 'Know Yourself' a woman is concerned because she has lost her personality. Her personality is sitting in the middle of the room where she left it. She realizes that before she can acquire a new personality she needs a spectator, a chorus, and – in the presence of her friend – starts to build a new spiral-shaped (dialectical) personality. Llana's stories all focus on women, usually in the home. The one exception in this collection is the superbly written title story, 'The Gate', which (contradicting Menton) is set in the final days of the Batista regime and relates a meeting of undercover revolutionaries told from the point of view of the youngest and least experienced of the men. The nail-biting suspense comes to an ambiguous end when the narrator, who has managed to leave the meeting house undetected and arrive home safely, thinks he hears in dreams the sound of the gate opening announcing the dreaded visit from Batista's henchmen. Is he dreaming or is it all too real? Almost twenty years passed, however, between the publication of *La Reja* (1965) and Llana's subsequent volume, *Casas del Vedado* [Houses in Velado] (1983), a superb collection of predominantly ghost stories.

Olga Fernández's prize-winning collection *Niña del arpa* [Girl with a Harp] (1989) is indicative of the 1980s tendency away from realism to fantasy. Although the stories, set in nineteenth-century colonial Cuba, are historical they elicit a strange timelessness and magic. In each story, written in polished prose, an object becomes the repository of infinite duration which contrasts with the transience of human life. Thus in the title story a young girl, Leovigilda, escapes the confines of her claustrophobic home by playing the harp. Over the years her harp-playing self develops into a free-standing alter-ego which will not allow her to rest and keeps her eternally youthful. She never marries but waits for love until, finally, the harp – representing eternal life and love – takes on a life of its own, playing for her loved one even when she is dead. In 'First Love' a young boy loves a girl so much that he imagines her into existence, although only he and his mother can see her. 'The Dagame Tree' is the scary story of a tree, the symbol of eternal evil, which appears after the 1804 earthquake and causes a series of tragic deaths in one family, finally outliving them all. In 'Omelé' the action switches to the world of the runaway slave. Jason, formerly an African prince, loves the orisha Oshún Yeyó Moró who is invisible to all but him. He escapes from the plantation to find her. Conjuring her presence with his drum he is transported miraculously to freedom. All the stories in the collection intimate the existence of another dimension, another world of perpetuity, glimpsed by human beings (usually women) but ultimately out of reach except in death.

Among the younger writers – born in the 1950s and 1960s (Chely Lima, Karina Díaz, Aida Bahr, Verónica Pérez Kónina, Ena Lucía Portela) (Yáñez and Bobes 1996) – Daína Chaviano is one of the most prolific and innovative.[11] Her interest in nuclear physics and astronomy has led her to specialize in science fiction and fantasy. Her short stories *Los mundos que amo* [The Worlds I Love] (1980) present an optimistic view of the human encounter with alien life, space stations and inter-planetary mystery tours while the three novellas collectively entitled *Historias de hadas para adultos* [Fairytales for Adults] (1986), set in strange, dangerous landscapes, is dedicated to Steven Spielberg and *ET.* The poems and stories of *Amoroso planeta* [Loving Planet] (1983) are full of unicorns and vampires and *El abrevadero de los dinosaurios* [The Dinosaurs' Water Hole] (1990) collates an ingenious collection of apocrypha – encyclopaedia articles, diary entries, notes – on dinosaurs. Eroticism, a popular thematics among women writers in the 1990s, appears here in the most unlikely places. In *El abrevadero*, for example, the section 'Erotomania' explains the sexual habits of dinosaurs: 'Pure blooded dinosaurs are often very erotic. They have their own Kama Sutra [...] the simple sight of a bed adorned with cherries will make any female dinosaur lose her head' (Chaviano 1990: 112).

By shifting into the past, the future or the supernatural, the stories written by Llana, Fernández and Chaviano tend to avoid representations of contemporary life. They are woman-centred nevertheless. Even when narrated by male or sexually unspecified narrators, read allegorically, they make for indirect commentary on contemporary women's lives and interests. The family and the home still predominate as settings; love, friendship, personal relationships and self-analysis are still preferred themes.

One genre which, unfortunately, has not been singled out by critics and is of particular significance for women writers is poetic prose. Many pieces of lyrical, poetic prose lie hidden in books of poetry, for example, Cleva Solís's *La mágicas distancias* [Magical Distances] (1961), Fina García Marruz's *Visitaciones* [Visitations] (1970) and Lina de Feria's *A mansalva de los años* [Protected from the Years] (1990). A recent revival of poetic prose among younger poets has resulted in some outstanding publications, for example, Reina María Rodriguez's *Páramos* [Moorland] which won the UNEAC 'Julián de Casal' prize in 1993. *Páramos*, according to the panel of judges, is 'a singular, transgressive book, that flows over the frontiers between genres'; it links 'the poem as writing and poetry as lived experience' ('Premio Poesía Julián del Casal 1993', *La Gaceta de Cuba*, no. 1, 1994: 32–4). By the 1990s, women writing their intimate experiences and constructing a transgressive subjectivity in language which defies generic categories was recognized as valuable literary practice.

THEATRE The work of women dramatists confirms that the general trend in post-revolutionary drama was towards realistic settings in pre-revolutionary low-life Havana and characters who are down-and-outs, prostitutes and poor folk. Sometimes the plays present scenes of contemporary Cuba of interest to women. 'Gloria', written by Ingrid González (possibly for young people), published by the Municipality of Marianao in a flimsy pamphlet with two other plays, has no date of publication but is typical. Set in a tenement block in the time of Batista, it recounts the story of Gloria, a prostitute, converted to the revolutionary cause by Mongo who, young and unemployed, wants to marry the daughter of a black worker, Jacinto, but cannot because he has no money. The focus of the play is on community problems and community action. Each of the characters has a problem caused by lack of money. Against a background of gangsterism, racism, pimps and prostitutes, and in the face of the ridiculed 'Jehovah's Witness', Gloria assists young Mongo by smuggling arms in her handbag under the nose of her police client. The play ends happily, thanks to solidarity and the Revolution, and all the characters' problems (employment, education, housing) are solved. As Mongo points out, 'that's how we all helped each other. My friends encouraged me, I encouraged Gloria, Gloria encouraged Jacinto, and Rosita and Ana did what they could' (González n.d: 33).

Possibly the most successful female dramatist of the post-1959 years is Gloria Parrado (1927–86) who staged plays in the 1940s, and continued in the 1950s and 1960s with, among others, 'The Compass' (1959) and 'The Magus' (1950). Her extremely successful 'Peace in the Sombrero' (1960), which won the Casa de las Américas prize in 1961, was performed in the 1960–61 season but not published until 1984.[12] That year Parrado published *Teatro* (three plays, 'Peace in the Sombrero', 'The Compass', 'The Magus') and a further collection *Tríptico* [Triptych] (1984) (three short plays about women in the pre-revolutionary period).

The three plays in *Tríptico* hang together, like a triptych, connected by short intermediate dialogues. The first play, '1905', set in that year, portrays a moment in the lives of three middle-class, middle-aged sisters, who live alone with their maid. The husband of the eldest has just died leaving them penniless; the middle sister is mentally retarded. The claustrophobic atmosphere of the home, the uselessness of the women's lives and their utter despair, indicate the situation of unmarried or widowed women at the time. As the youngest, Casiana, says: 'I feel trapped like a mouse.' Woven into this story of female oppression is that of the oppressed nation for whose independence the women's father fought and died, 'I gave everything for our independence', says Casiana (Parrado 1984: 51). Neither she nor the nation has been emancipated; both are wasted.

The second play, 'Bembeta and Santa Rita', set in a brothel in a run-down part of Camagüey in 1940, focuses on another family: a mother in her sixties and her grown-up daughters. The mother, Lucita, is shown to be a bad mother who left her nine children for a sergeant, who later raped one of the daughters. Two of her daughters are prostitutes, desperate to leave the profession and marry. The other, Luisa, lives in the country and is appalled at what she finds when she visits her mother. Luisa wants a job, but the only work available for women is prostitution. Lucita's excuse, that she was coerced into marriage and did not want children, is rejected by her daughters. Again, an atmosphere of despair and demoraliza-tion pervades the play and, as in '1905', the house and the nation are shown to be in ruins. In the third play, 'Death on the Quayside', set in the 1950s, an ordinary couple Irma and Anselmo have waited twelve years to marry but he has no money or job. He refuses to be a 'kept' man. Unknown to Irma, Anselmo has joined the revolutionaries and is smuggling arms into the city. Running parallel with this drama, functioning as a moralistic contrast, is the story of the pimp and the two prostitutes he treats appallingly. Amidst knife fights, Santería dances, street squalor and the antics of a drunken American sailor, Anselmo is killed by the police while the pimp slips away. The police will not touch the drunken American, who indirectly causes the tragedy, 'don't you know an American sailor is sacred!' (Parrado 1984: 166) but they do kill the good Cuban. Women are shown to be politically ignorant and indifferent, they neither participate in political activity nor try to improve the situation of their country themselves. As an actor spells out in the epilogue, women lost their place in history when Cuba lost its independence to the United States. This situation continued through to the 1950s, but the Revolution has brought it to an end.

Flora Lauten, a member of the Escambray theatre group (1968–76), set up her own theatre project in the peasant community of Yaya where she encouraged peasant women to write and act in their own plays. Herminia Sánchez, also a member of the Escambray group, established a similar People's Participatory Theatre Group in the late 1970s and published several plays (Randall 1981: 108–10). *¡De pie!* [Stand Up!] (1984) is possibly the least woman-centred text encountered in this book, no doubt because it was written as much by the performers as by Sánchez. The play is one long conversation between a group of cane-cutters (all men) who have finished their day's work. Mobilized in the city, they form part of a brigade in competition with others to reach a million tons of cane. They joke and banter about their day-to-day lives while flashbacks re-create past moments with their families and girlfriends. The revolutionary message is forceful: all the benefits of the Revolution (such as extended trips to the USSR) are spelled out clearly, there are declarations of allegiance to the Party and the nation. Self-sacrifice and physical suffering are necessary for the good of the community, measured not in terms of material goods (fridges are on offer as bonuses) but for the welfare of all. The gender values affirmed in the play are extremely traditional; masculinity is identified with strength, endurance and physical suffering. Women, who presumably need 'protecting' normally, must learn to look after themselves at home. Women workers from the USSR are admired for their physique, 'Yes they are women, and what women! [...] Hey, here in the USSR you always offer your seat to a woman' (Sánchez 1984: 46–7). Interestingly, there is no time for poetry, 'Poetry? Let's get to bed. Tomorrow we have to be up at three' (p. 82).

Rather more entertaining is *La muerte acecha en el agua* [Death Lurks in the Water] (1984) by Xiomara Leyva Ojito (b. 1957), a farce set in 1920. Leonora, a despotic sixty-year-old, rich but still a virgin, marries Alfonso, aged twenty-six. Leonora is afraid of frogs and never washes; she is so dirty Alfonso is unable to do his duty and she threatens to annul the marriage and have him imprisoned. He poisons her with arsenic but, haunted by her ghost, finally repents and gives the money he has inherited to the church. Leonora's ill-treated maid, dismissed without pay, finally confesses to having killed the woman by putting a frog in the glass of poisoned water. A statue is built to the 'martyr': the frog. Once again, the play denounces the iniquities of colonial Cuba: class differences, the oppression of domestic servants, the pernicious influence of the church, the collusion of the petty bourgeoisie and US financial control. The maid wreaks revenge without guilt. As she explains to Alfonso: 'You tried to murder her to get hold of some money you hadn't earned with the sweat of your brow, that's why you felt guilty. I did it to receive my payment for ten years' work and humiliation' (Leyva Ojito 1984: 72).

POETRY   After the Revolution more women than ever were given the opportunity to publish poetry. Many of these poets were young authors who had never published before. Some were black and mulatto women, sometimes from very poor backgrounds. After 1959 women voiced not only their intimate feelings about personal and family relationships but also their perceptions of the community and the city, and of current affairs at home and abroad. They wrote about the Cuban missile crisis, the literacy campaign, Cuba's involvement in Africa, and other historical and revolutionary events. In this sense they were continuing the long tradition in which Cuban women wrote about the nation. On the other hand, women's poetry was seldom overtly political or propagandistic. Before 1980 most collections might include one or two politically correct poems and some volumes were published with an explicit political agenda, for example, Nancy Morejón's *Cuaderno de Grenada* [Grenada Notebook] (1983), written after the US invasion of Grenada. Social themes were more usually focused from a personal perspective; political events would be considered significant for their effects on the subject, her family and friends. Whether she is speaking for herself or on behalf of others, the individual female voice rings clear. Hence the importance of poetry. In 1988 Smith and Padula asked: 'How do Cuban women view themselves in society and how has that changed? What do they hope for the future? What do they want changed about the present? How do Cuban women view each other?' (Smith and Padula 1988: 157). The answers to these questions are to be found largely in women's poetry.

The post-revolutionary poets wrote in a language easily accessible to all, although some – for example, Minerva Salado (b. 1944) and Lina de Feria (b. 1945) – preferred a more complex style. Almost all the poets publishing for the first time in the 1960s and 1970s preferred free verse. Few cultivated the sonnet or other classical forms which were associated with the colonial heritage, the bourgeoisie and the intellectual elite. This trend has been reversed in the last ten years. Some poets publishing for the first time in the 1990s (for example, Damaris Calderón) have returned to classical forms, particularly the sonnet.

One of the most impressive books of poetry published by a woman since 1959 is Fina García Marruz's *Visitaciones* (1970) (407 pages long) which includes poems written between 1950 and 1970, several pieces of poetic prose, and her widely acclaimed lament 'On the Death of Ernesto Che Guevara'. As we have seen, García Marruz writes in the tradition of classical Spanish poetry and in this collection she sustains the quality of her writing. Carilda Oliver Labra (b. 1924) won the National Poetry Prize in 1950 for her volume *Al sur de mi garganta* [To the South of My Throat]. After the Revolution she worked as a teacher in her home town Matanzas but, apart from an *Antología de poemas de amor* [Anthology of Love Poems] (1962) the rest of her poetry was not published until the 1980s and 1990s. Oliver Labra is something of a myth in Cuba. She is now in her seventies, married to a younger man. Recurrent themes are her mother, childhood, the search for self identity and, above all, erotic love.

Of the (now middle-aged) poets of the generation of the Revolution, the one who most clearly develops and experiments with the classical tradition of Spanish and Spanish American poetry is Reina María Rodríguez (b. 1952) who grew up in the Revolution and whose first collection of poems, *La gente de mi barrio* [The People of My Neighbourhood], appeared in 1976. Rodríguez would also have to wait until the 1980s and 1990s to have the majority of her poems published. Her outstanding early collection, *Cuando una mujer no duerme* [When a Woman Can't Sleep] (1982), includes love poetry, poems about her friends and her family, her response to a speech by Fidel, a lament for Haydée Santamaría (who committed suicide in 1980) and for Agostinho Neto. *Para un cordero blanco* [For a White Lamb], which won the Casa de las Américas poetry prize in 1984, focuses more intensely on the self. Here the poet takes stock of who she is:

Me estoy buscando
y tengo miedo
casi un miedo fanático
de haber sido cómplice
inacabada
porque también sonreí cuando quería matar
('Remordimientos para un cordero blanco', Ríos 1989: 23)

I am searching for myself / and I am afraid / an almost fanatical fear / of having been an unfinished / accomplice / because I too smiled when I wanted to kill ('Guilt for a White Lamb')

The poems and poetic prose of *En la arena de Padua* [On Padua Sands]

(1992) are more hermetic and intensely melancholic. Here the poet is concerned with time passing from the point of view of a mature woman: 'a girl makes such a long crossing / to arrive / and to be a girl no more' (Rodríguez 1992: 59). Her poetry expresses disappointment, waste, dereliction, dust ('we are tired of spectacle and distribution' [p. 34]), and, above all, self-questioning:

> no sé cómo construir un velero
> nadie me propuso nunca construir
> un pequeño velero
> no traían más que tablas de salvación
> para flotar a la deriva. (p. 15)

> I don't know how to build a sailing ship / no-one ever suggested building / a little sailing ship / all they brought were life belts / to drift on the tide.

Although the négritude movement had wide repercussions in Cuba in the 1930s and both black writers and black aesthetics were assimilated into the Cuban canon from then on (the most famous Cuban poet this century is probably the mulatto Nicolás Guillén), it was not until after the Revolution that a tradition of black women's writing was established. Not until the 1970s, when the shift in cultural perceptions identified Cuban literature with Third World and Caribbean traditions, were black and mulatto women admitted into the canon.[13] As mentioned previously, Rafaela Chacón Nardi's collection of poetry, *Viaje al sueño* [Journey to Dream] (1948) indicated no concern for black or Caribbean themes. Her only reference to an African heritage in her two recent collections of poetry – *Del silencio y las voces* [Of Silence and Voices] (1978) and *Coral del aire* [Air Chorus] (1982) – is a tentative association of her grandmother's voice with a plausibly African or Caribbean landscape. Much of her poetry is overtly political and articulates socialist rather than identity politics.[14]

The black woman writer who has received most critical attention is undoubtedly Nancy Morejón (b. 1944). A fluent linguist and literary translator, she has read widely in Francophone and Anglophone Caribbean literatures. She is also familiar with the work of black American writers, particularly Alice Walker, although her own poetry prioritizes nationalist and socialist political agendas rather than black, feminist identities. In 1966 she published her first major collection of poems, *Richard trajo su flauta* [Richard Brought His Flute] which includes poems to her two grandmothers (one black, one mulatta), to her working-class parents, to African Cuban gods (Elegguá), and to Fidel, Havana and the Revolution. She also writes about the black freedom movement in the United States, the Vietnam War and the Russian cosmonauts, and several poems are dedicated to contemporary black Cuban writers and to women. Since then she has continued to publish. Her 1979 collection, *Parajes de una época*

[Places of a Time] includes her most famous black poem, 'Black Woman', the most translated of all post-revolutionary Cuban poems written by women. *Piedra pulida* [Polished Stone] (1986), is more intimate. Here a slavery thematics is more ostensible, focused from a black woman's perspective: 'Negro', 'Madrigal for Maroons', 'I Love My Master' and 'Worlds', many of which have been translated into English. Nancy Morejón writes love poetry but the tone is muted rather than erotic. The critical bibliography on Morejón is growing.[15] Her most recent books, published abroad, are *Paisaje célebre* [Famous Landscape] (1993) and *Botella al Mar* [Bottle at Sea] (1996). Apart from Chacón Nardi, she is the only black poet of the four mentioned here to have an entry in the official *Diccionario de Literatura Cubana* (1984).

Georgina Herrera (b. 1936), employed as a maid before the Revolution and self-educated, is the oldest black poet in this group. Like Morejón, she published poetry in the 1960s but it was not until *Gente y cosas* [People and Things] (1974) and *Granos de sol y luna* [Grains of Sun and Moon] (1978), that she established a reputation. *Gente y cosas* are poems about her family and neighbours. Her simple poems to her children, especially those written for her daughter, are among the most poignant. In her 1978 collection Herrera shows a new interest in African history and the traditions and the pantheon of African Cuban religions which will be discussed in Chapter 7. *Grande es el tiempo* [Great is Time] (1989), is more confessional and includes her most famous poem, 'Africa', in which she portrays 'Africa' as a loved one with whom she identifies.

Soleida Ríos (b. 1950) first published poetry in 1977 but her two most important collections are *De pronto abril* [Suddenly April] (1979), and *Entre mundo y juguete* [Between World and Toy] (1987). Ríos's poetry searches deep for childhood memories or quizzes the impact of love. In the 1987 collection she focuses on sexual relationships and the female body. *El libro roto* [The Broken Book] (1996) collates short pieces of dream-like poetic prose. Evidently, Ríos is more concerned with female subjectivity, desire and the subconscious than with the African or Caribbean cultural and literary traditions.

The work of Excilia Saldaña (b. 1946) is more explicitly Afrocentric. In 1987 she published a book of five 'patakin' (Yoruba oral traditions) in *Kele Kele* [Suave, suave/Softly, softly] with a short history of slavery, an introduction to the Afro-Cuban orishas and a glossary of Afro-Cuban terms. It is in her autobiographical poetry that Saldaña makes the most powerful connections between female subjectivity and an African, Caribbean heritage. She was born into a black, Catholic family and her dramatic life-story is recounted in her poetry. One of Saldaña's preferred themes is the re-encounter with the female mulatto body as the site of female identity and sense of self. Some of her most endearing poems to her grandmother have been published in a children's book (beautifully illustrated and produced in Berlin) entitled *La Noche* [Night] (1989), where the grand-mother represents the mysteries, magic and dark beauty of the night.

Although a potential black women's literary tradition has been outlined, in Cuba identity politics has not been a burning issue and, generally speaking, black writers show little interest in exclusively black themes (Perez Sarduy and Stubbs 1993). In contrast, white (or non-black) women (such as Minerva Salado) deploy an African thematics and, at times, assume a black persona. Poems written by white women which inscribe African–Caribbean traditions indicate one of the more interesting developments of post-revolutionary women's poetry.[16] These questions will be discussed in more detail in Chapter 7.

Since 1980 women's writing has thrived (see Araújo 1995). The country is criss-crossed with workshops ('talleres') where writers read out and discuss their work. Women of all ages, colours and backgrounds were publishing throughout the 1980s until about 1992. Crafted, home-made plaquettes (unbound booklets) produced in short runs by the 'talleres' constituted a courageous but short-term answer to the problem of the shortages of printing materials in the early 1990s. It is impossible in this short space to cover in any depth women's writing of the 1980s. The 'boom' has been mainly in short fiction (see Yáñez and Bobes 1996; Redonet 1993; López Sacha 1996) and poetry (see Aguilera Díaz 1990), which is more intimist, confessional, erotic and philosophical than ever. Some poets favour metaphysical speculation (Lina de Feria, Reina María Rodríguez), others are irreverent and 'pop' (Marilyn Bobes, Chely Lima). Others prefer the oneiric (Soleida Ríos). Whereas free verse was the predominant poetic form after 1959, there is now a return to the sonnet and poetic prose. There is also a return to and reassessment of the literary mothers and fathers of pre-revolutionary Cuba, primarily the aestheticism of Lezama Lima. Older women writers, whose work had been virtually ignored during the 1960s and 1970s, were encouraged to publish anew (Dulce María Loynaz, Fina García Marruz, Carilda Oliver Labra, Loló de la Torriente), while poems which had remained out of print for many years were collected in anthologies. However, the most significant switch in direction for women poets in the 1980s, discussed in Chapter 8, has been towards erotic poetry.

A crucial question regarding the post-1959 period is why women write poetry rather than novels. Margaret Randall's *Breaking the Silences* (1982), the most important anthology of post-revolutionary women's poetry trans-lated into English, was completed in 1980. It includes not only poems but also comments by a wide range of poets. Eight poets had published the greater part of their work before 1959. An analysis of the comments and information supplied about the other seventeen, their work, attitudes and lifestyles, revealed the following pattern. The ages of the women poets (in 1980) ranged between early twenties and mid-forties. Of the seventeen, eight were divorced (three lived with their parents), five were single and only three married. Eight had children (usually one or two). Most of them worked in the publishing industry, in journalism, radio and the teaching professions or were perhaps actresses and artists as well as poets. Of the seventeen, ten had a university degree or equivalent. Only three did not live in Havana; five were black or mulatto women, including Lourdes Casal who died in 1981. In other words, these were urban, educated women who had full-time jobs and, at the same time, were bringing up their children alone, often in their parents' home.

As Virginia Woolf indicated sixty years ago, to write a novel a person needs time and space. Since the 1960s Cuban women have had no sustained time to themselves, few opportunities to be alone, and no space in which to write without the family (parents, children, husband) being present. The values promoted by the state – egalitarianism, collectivism, altruism, participation and mobilization – have worked against potential women novelists but, and here is the crunch, have hardly affected men. The reasons for this seem obvious. Women are still considered to be primarily responsible for the family and the household. The time of the educated middle-class woman, who employed other women to do her housework, launder her dirty washing and look after her children, who had plenty of free time, and lots of cleaned, empty space, came to a end (barring some exceptions) with the Revolution. In 1953 some 70,000 servants were employed by the Cuban middle classes (Thomas 1971: 1112). It was mainly men who left Cuba in the mass exodus of 1980 (and 1990) leaving the women to cope (Molyneux 1996: 39). At the risk of oversimplifying, it could be said that after 1959 all women were educated, most women worked, many were divorced, most women looked after their families themselves when they were not at work, or looked after their working daughters' families, all women were involved in one way or another with others (the family, the neighbourhood, the community, the union), and most lived in cramped spaces without even a table of their own. As history has shown, working-class women's novels are few and far between. When can working women with a family be alone to think, to think in silence; where do they do their thinking? Add to these factors the endemic reticence to publish women's work as indicated by Campuzano and Yáñez (Yáñez and Bobes 1996), the lack of serious criticism of women's work and the fact that (as Campuzano admits) women do most of the filing, typing and proof-reading in the publishing industry, it is not surprising that women's creative literature is less abundant than might be expected.

Women's writing in Cuba is under-researched (in Cuba and abroad). The important work of the pre-revolutionary years was virtually ignored by the post-revolutionary cultural establishment which disapproved of middle-class feminism. Only recently has the work of older Cuban women been retrieved from collective oblivion. Post-revolutionary women writers have faced the same problems as their male counterparts: problems and delays in publication and difficulties in the distribution of their work to the world markets. Because they are women, these problems have been aggravated (see Chapter 6). This has much to do with the relative inefficiency of the Cuban state publishing industry, Cuban insularity, and the thirty-seven-year US trade embargo to which the island is still subjected. It is still easier to find information on Cuban women writers living outside Cuba than information on those who have stayed at home. Cuban women writers have been marginalized on two counts: in Cuba (because they are women) and in the 'West' (because they are socialist). Current bibliographies on Cuban literature are often incomplete. They give the false impression that few (or no) women writers publish in Cuba today. One of the purposes of this book is to put the record straight.[17]

Notes

1. See V. Antuña (1974: 96–104). Nancy Morejón confirms Aguirre's influence in Bejel (1991: 231–3).

2. I will not refer to children's literature written by Cuban women. This is plentiful and deserves to be studied as a separate topic (particularly the work of Alga Marina Elizagaray). See Bortolussi (1990).

3. An enormous amount of literature exists on educational developments after the Revolution and figures vary slightly. The following account is based on Pérez Rojas (1979); Thomas (1971); and Smith and Padula (1996).

4. Morgan (1993: 214).

5. Menton (1978) gives slightly different figures: one novel in 1972 and none in 1973.

6. Andrade and Cramsie (1991: 63) mention Maité Vera's *Memorias de un proyecto* [Memories of a Project] as of particular interest for women readers. I have not seen this play.

7. For a personal testimony of life during the early 1990s see Reina María Rodríguez, 'En Estocolmo bajo la luna de Animas', in Vázquez Díaz (1994: 66–75).

8. Cuba has withstood numerous terrorist attacks. In 1976 a Cuban civil airliner was blown up with the loss of seventy-three lives.

9. Marta Rojas (b. 1931) is one of Cuba's leading journalists. See Pérez Sarduy and Stubbs (1993) for translated extracts of her novel *El columpio de Rey Spencer* [The King Spencer Swing] (1993).

10. See Mordecai and Wilson (1989), Esteves (1991) and Bush (1997) for translations of some of Agüeros's and Yáñez's stories.

11. Redonet (1993) includes stories by twelve young women born after 1960 and Yáñez and Bobes (1996) include four. The most promising new fiction writers in Cuba are Ena Lucía Portela, Karina Díaz and Verónica Pérez Kónina.

12. For an informative reading of 'The Compass' see Andrade and Cramsie (1991: 62–8). The volume includes a translation of 'The Compass'.

13. See M. Randall (1982) for English translations of a selection of Cuban women's poetry from Loynaz onwards.

14. See Hernández Menéndez (1996).

15. For English translations of poems by Nancy Morejón see: Pereira (1977);

Crowe (1984); Agosín and Franzen (1987); and Hopkinson (1989). See also Busby (1992); Captain-Hidalgo (1990); Pereira (1990); Weaver (1985); Savory Fido (1982); de Costa Willis (1990); Marting (1988). A special issue of *Afro-Hispanic Review* (Spring 1996) was dedicated to her work.

16. See Lina de Feria *A mansalva de los años* [Protected from the Years] (1990); María Elena Cruz (b. 1953) '¿Legado?' (1987) *Letras Cubanas*, Vol. I, no. 4, April–June: 101–2; and Elsa Claro (b. 1943) 'Angola I' (1980) *Agua y fuego* [Water and Fire] with a foreword by N. Guillén.

17. One of the best bibliographical sources is Fenwick (1992). Also valuable is Herdeck (1979) and Martínez (1990). The latter includes seventeen women's names, but not Nancy Morejón.

CHAPTER 6

Women's Short Stories: the Feminist and the Female

In her study of ideology and the cultural production of gender, Michèle Barrett asks why 'feminists should be so interested in literature or what theoretical or political ends such a study might serve' (Barrett 1985: 65). She goes on: 'What is the relationship between women's oppression and the general features of a mode of [cultural] production?' (p. 73). Bearing these questions in mind I shall study some aspects of short story writing by women in contemporary Cuba. I shall argue, in a reading informed by the work of Pierre Bourdieu (1993) on fields of cultural production, that short stories written by women, at least those which represent in a realist mode contemporary social relations or past relations from a contemporary point of view, insert a gender agenda into the production of dominant systems of thought and belief. Given the dearth of novels written by women, short fiction (which is cheap, easy to obtain, easy to consume, particularly by women who are short of time and space, and more readable than poetry) is likely to be the genre most popular among women readers. The importance of its role in the cultural field is unquestionable. I shall then go on to explore Dora Alonso's short fiction to suggest how narrative strategies other than realism test predominant ways of thinking.

The short stories I shall refer to first, taken primarily from *El diablo son las cosas* [What the Devil] (1988) by Mirta Yáñez (b. 1947) and *Ellas de noche* [Women at Night] (1989) by Aida Bahr (b. 1958), communicate to a mass public certain questionings or a certain ventilation of the ways unequal power relations are embedded in daily life from the point of view of women. In so doing, the stories do not present a political challenge but rather seek to explore and unmask how systems of thought, social structures and institutions are perpetuated, and how they go unrecognized and unacknowledged, even though they might well be oppressive for women.

In the light of Bourdieu's theories on culture and power, it could be argued that officially sanctioned cultural production in post-revolutionary Cuba, where high art and prestige value are problematical, has taken the form of large-scale production. The resulting popular or mass culture, dependent on the broadest possible public (not for economic but ideological validation), is characterized by accessibility and attenuated formal experimentation. As Bourdieu shows with reference to works of art, if the level of emission (the degree of complexity of the code required to decipher the work) is low, the level of reception (the degree to which an individual masters the social code) is high (Bourdieu 1993: 224–5). In Bourdieu's words: 'When the message exceeds the possibilities of apprehension or, to be more precise, when the code of the work exceeds in subtlety and complexity the code of the beholders, the latter lose interest in what appears to them to be a medley without rhyme or reason' (p. 225).

Thus, Cuban short fiction, not autonomous art but heteronomous art, subordinated to and dependent not on economic capital but socialist ideology, is often uncomplicated. The language in the short stories studied in this chapter is standard or colloquial, verging almost on orature. In other words, women short story writers may question orthodox traditions but their *prise de position* will be external (political) rather than internal (stylistic) and will have more to do with 'habitus' than governance (Bourdieu 1993: 17). Bourdieu's concept of 'habitus', what has been described as a 'feel for the game', a 'second sense', 'a system of dispositions', is useful in that it indicates whatever inclines agents to act or react in an uncalculated way (due to a lifelong inculcation through the family, education, institutions, and so on). Bourdieu refers to 'class habitus'; 'gender habitus', a 'set of dispositions which generates practices and perceptions' (Bourdieu 1993: 5) regarding gender, would be more appropriate in a feminist critique. Women short story writers target these dominant perceptions, feelings and ideas on gender. In so doing, they produce symbolical capital.

As soon as the stories are recognized as 'literature', a belief in their value as women's writing (rather than the work of an individual woman) is produced. Thus, the stories might achieve a degree of prestige based on the interaction of knowledge (of what they are about) and recognition of their value. In this way female-authored short fiction brings about a shift in the field of cultural production. The stories 'manage to enter the game' (Bourdieu 1993: 111), literary versions of the life experiences of women enter the field of cultural production. The stories also produce cultural capital in the sense that readers have to be trained to decipher them, to be competent in reading them, and in that sense the stories are a form of consciousness-raising. But in raising consciousness they do not transgress the boundaries of consensus too emphatically. What the stories show, in Barrett's words, is 'an indication of the bounds within which particular meanings are constructed and negotiated in given social formations' (Barrett 1985: 80).

It goes without saying that the meaning of a text depends on how it is read and I choose to read these stories not as critiques of socialism but as critiques of the gender habitus in androcentric systems of thought (capitalist or socialist). These stories represent, above all, women's experiences within a male-oriented society, the patriarchal family and the paternalistic state. As Margaret Hymans points out in a different context, women do not write differently because of biological essentialism but 'because their femaleness has meant that they will become mothers and daughters in a culture that separates the needs of a father and son, mother and daughter'. Women attempt in many ways to 'reclaim their own experiences as paradigms for writing'. Like nineteenth-century women writers, post-revolutionary Cuban women short story writers write about women's experiences 'on the assumption that they could do so' (Hymans 1986: x, xi).

In her invaluable 'Panorama' of women's short fiction, Mirta Yáñez (Yáñez and Bobes 1996) argues that the tensions between the official 'predominant tendency' (realism, rural settings, colloquial language) and individual writers' creative imaginations (fantasy, magical realism, subjectivity, experimentation) was most forcefully felt, particularly between 1966 and the late 1970s, in the short story, the most popular and accessible genre. Those who were most seriously affected by the clamp-down, Yáñez insists, were 'the traditionally marginalised groups – women and gays' (Yáñez and Bobes 1996: 32–3). She attacks Cuban (male) critics for either ignoring women's writing or pigeon-holing it as women's writing and, therefore, considering it of secondary importance (p. 26). Perhaps for this same reason women short story writers were the first to break with enforced parameters. In the 1980s,

> from among women short story writers […] a new discourse emerged, sometimes poetic, sometimes crude, which reformulated entrenched values and customs by unveiling the no longer sacrosanct inner world of personal life, and by writing freely about the female (or male) body and sexual relations. […] With the irruption of parody, intertextuality, a greater interest in human relations and the recuperation of the urban environment, short fiction, especially that authored by women, distanced itself from realism and the epic. (Yáñez and Bobes 1996: 37)

The process was gradual and the shift from realism to fantasy often subtle. For example, the distinctions between two stories both featuring mirrors, one fantastic and one realist (included in López Sacha's anthology, 1996) – Llana's 'The Family' (from *Casas del Vedado*, 1983) and Bahr's 'Imperfections' (first published in 1994) – are fine. Llana's is a ghost story in which a girl passes through a mirror into the land of the living dead; Bahr's describes a deranged old woman who cannot bear to see herself in the mirror. Yet Llana's story is told with realist sang-froid, and Bahr's with an uncanny, surreal sense of panic. Similarly, Bahr's 'There's a Cat in the Window' (Bahr 1984: 67–71) wavers between fantasy and reality (is the old woman really threatened by a man with a knife who makes her clean her house from top to bottom?) until it is resolved (satisfactorily for official culture, unsatisfactorily for the curious reader) when a policeman saves the woman and arrests the man, who does exist.

None the less, by focusing on everyday experience, but from a woman's point of view, these writers were increasingly able to challenge the predominant consensus of reality itself. On which modes of social interaction or aspects of social organization do their stories focus? As indicated briefly in Chapter 5, women's realist short fiction tends to confront routine problems affecting women directly. Brief scenes of daily life, typical activities, recounted in the first or third persons from a woman's perspective, dramatized the conflicts faced by individual women in relation to themselves, their family, lovers, colleagues and friends. The stories are selective representations of potentially shared experiences which should provoke readers into questioning whatever they normally take for granted regarding women. What is not said in the texts is important, as is the insistence on women's collusion in the 'internalization of oppression' (Barrett 1985: 81). As we saw in Chapter 5, however, not all female-authored short stories are concerned with verisimilitude or the complexities of modern social life. Many are displaced narratives describing the hypothetical future (science fiction), the remote historical past, or the unreal. My interest for the moment is in realist fiction set in contemporary urban locations, although fiction depicting the recent past provides penetrating glimpses of the changes in women's history. Two examples set the tone.

Ana María Simó's (b. 1943) 'The Party' (Fornet 1967: 224–30), set in the 1950s, tells the sad story of Albertina, the child narrator's aunt, who is watched over so carefully by her mother (the narrator's grandmother) that she never finds a husband. After the grandmother's death Albertina, aged thirty, realizes she has no future. All the family property will be passed on to her brother and his eldest daughter, the narrator. She locks herself in her room, lost in memories of the dances she used to attend at the Lyceum chaperoned by her mother, and eats herself to death. Here the emphasis is on the strict social controls of female sexuality in the past compared with the freer attitudes and opportunities of the 1960s. In Rosa Ileana Boudet's (b. 1947) '¡Alánimo! ¡Alánimo!' ['Bravo! Bravo!'] (1977) (Cámara 1989: 38–43), from the collection of the same name, a woman remembers the time she spent as a young girl in one of the Revolution's boarding schools. This story, set in April 1961, is important for its 'testimonio' value. A detailed description of the daily routine of these girls, brought to Havana from remote rural districts to be educated in 'art and artillery', provides the setting for a young girl's crush on Victor, the military commander in charge.

Mirta Yáñez

Mirta Yáñez's stories (from *El diablo son las cosas*, 1988) focus on contemporary Cuban women in all walks of life. Two prevalent themes are the ways in which women who participated in the Revolution adapt to life in the 1980s, and the effects on ordinary Cuban women of international political events. On the whole, Yáñez's stories confirm and reinforce dominant systems of thought: bourgeois property obsessions are ridiculed in 'We are Nothing' and Santería practices in 'Bird of Ill Omen', but at the same time a distinctly feminist agenda can be discerned. Many stories are told in the first person by a middle-aged female narrator (a possible representation of the implied author herself) who voices concern about the passing of time and oncoming maturity. Adaptation is problematical because these women, like the author, belong to the revolutionary 1960s generation and have difficulty accepting the presence of younger women who might be more rebellious than they were. Thus in 'Beatles against Duran Duran', generational conflict is diffused when mother and daughter each acknowledge the other's taste in popular music as radical for its time. The mother in not wishing her daughter to do military service realizes she is in danger of becoming 'a reactionary old woman' (p. 97) and adopting the same attitudes her own mother took with her when she joined the coffee campaign in the early 1960s. The point here, that revolutionary values are a lifetime commitment (confirmed when the mother lends a helping hand to a revolutionary Sandinista girl in the Nicaraguan coffee harvest in the early 1980s), is articulated in an all-woman scenario (no fathers, husbands or boyfriends appear) and, more importantly, as the latest stage in a long feminist (rather than socialist) tradition of Cuban women challenging social restrictions. More subversive is 'The Blind Buffalo' where the female narrator decides that by leaving her village, studying, working and travelling she has missed out on the most important things in life: 'I had charged through life without seeing it' (p. 43).

Several stories focus on how women are affected by international politics. The Nicaraguan Revolution was mentioned above; two stories focus on the theme of exile and emigration. 'Split in Two' brings together a grandmother, who emigrated to Cuba from Spain when she was a child, and her granddaughter, who was taken from Cuba to the United States by her parents after the Revolution.[1] Complex notions of national identity and belonging are played out at the level of the individual women of different ages and backgrounds, and the resulting emotional and psychological effects are shown to be heart-rending – each woman's heart is torn in two. The effects of the 1980 Mariel exodus on the women who were left behind is the theme of 'What the Devil', narrated by a young man who models himself on James Stewart in the film *Rear Window* and gradually realizes what is going on behind the four walls of his neighbour's flat. A lonely middle-aged woman, Miss Betti, deserted by her third husband who leaves for Miami, unleashes a vindictive campaign against a mouse which has made its home in her kitchen. After many attempts, she finally kills it but is devastated because she has lost her only friend. 'Opera prima', possibly a covert criticism of the lack of sexual education in Cuba, recounts the experiences of a young Cuban gymnast who, when in Moscow, decides to give up her career. Totally ignorant of her own sexuality and facing puberty with utter confusion, she is nursed through the crisis not by her male trainer, whose only concern is for Cuba to win a medal, but by a group of burly Russian women (the hotel staff) who help her to celebrate her first period with bottles of vodka. Women's independence, women's solidarity, sisterhood and understanding between mothers, daughters and grandmothers and the irresponsibility, callousness and insensitivity of men are recurrent feminist themes, but they are always articulated within the bounds of socialist consensus.

The strongest indictment against men and machismo (and, implicitly, the revolutionary establishment) is 'Kid Bururu and the Cannibals' where an old, black boxer (Kid Bururu) is cruelly taunted by the narrator's ex-husband and his friend, the two cannibals in the story. The ex-husband is handsome and elegantly dressed but (only the narrator knows) an impotent brute; their marriage broke up when she went to work in Tanzania against his wishes: 'I don't feel like letting you go. I'm in charge here, I'm the boss' (p. 60). The friend (who, it is implied, gained his revolutionary credentials by literally twisting young boys' arms until they had their hair cut) now wears his own hair long; it floats in the breeze. These two hypocritical cowards, in order to appear manly in front of young girls, ridicule the old boxer where it most hurts: 'Kid Gavilan took your wife from you', 'Kid Bururu, you're not a man' (pp. 62–3). The implication here that the men who were former revolutionaries, and now form part of the establishment, are vicious, cowardly chauvinists is tempered somewhat by the inclusion of a 'nice guy', the narrator's current husband who is caring and helpful.

Reading Mirta Yáñez's stories in *El diablo son las cosas* is like listening in on a conversation. Her prose is full of tags, idiomatic phrases, addresses to her audience – 'don't you think?', 'What a thing to happen, guys' (p. 81), 'you tell me' (p. 82) – which not only increase its accessibility but also give the impression of listening to a documentary in which women narrate their personal experiences. Thus fiction may be said to function as 'testimonio', or is read as such.

Aida Bahr

Aida Bahr (b. 1958) writes lively, gripping sketches of single moments or episodes in an ordinary woman's life and thus presents an invaluable insight into the inner workings of society from a woman's point of view. Her narrative style is more classical, less quirky, than Yáñez's but her feminist challenge more noticeable. 'Blonder, with More Freckles' from *Hay un gato en la ventana* [There's a Cat at the Window] (1984) (Bahr 1984: 41–7;

Cámara 1989: 168–72) is a skilfully written love story narrated by an anonymous woman who is blonde, thin and freckled. Her opening words lead the reader to believe she has just gone through a traumatic experience, the end of a love affair, perhaps, with the young engineer she works with. To the reader's surprise, the narrator turns out to be shocked because the man she loves has just proposed. The views expressed on marriage in this story are of great interest. The narrator claims marriage, 'a piece of paper', is not important; she and Germán live together happily (although her mother is appalled). Her views are confirmed when Germán leaves the narrator to marry and yet is divorced within two years. On the other hand, it is clear that deep down the narrator desperately wants to marry but Germán is hesitant because they have different political views. He volunteers for military service in Angola and she thinks she has lost him for ever, until he pops the question over the phone. This is the happy ending; but she has had to wait for him to propose, and she has had to become more involved in union activities for him to contemplate marriage. 'Monologue in the Capri Hotel' (Bahr 1984: 35–40) on the other hand, focuses on a young woman who comes across a former boyfriend unexpectedly and wonders whether she should have married him rather than her present husband. The process of her stream of thoughts, narrated in the first person, show how she gradually convinces herself her comfortable lifestyle is preferable to a moment of passion with a man to whom she is attracted but who left her to spend five years in the USSR. This is just as well, because he has taken revenge and stood her up.

Bahr's superb collection *Ellas de noche* [Women at Night] (1989) also centres on the problems facing women in Cuba today, particularly with regard to their love lives and family relationships. She depicts conflicts arising in the workplace as well as the family, while the contradictions inherent in the masculinist premises of socialist organization are foregrounded more clearly. In 'Saturday Night' a mature woman, the head librarian in a small town, wishes to be alone with her boyfriend but has nowhere to go. She suddenly hits on the idea of using her office. Just as she and her friend are about to make love she hears noises in the building. She discovers a young girl employee cuddling her boyfriend lorry driver in the store-room. Her reaction is ferocious; she threatens to dismiss the girl and to apply 'Rule 32'. Not surprisingly, the librarian's boyfriend leaves her and she is devastated. Apart from indicating the problem of the lack of private space, the lack of understanding between women, and society's self-destructive hypocritical attitudes towards sex, the story shows how a single woman's sexual desires conflict directly with her professional and public status, and with the small-town mentality and authoritarian hierarchical society in which she lives. In questions of sexual mores, Cuban society had changed little. The only acceptable space for the fulfilment of female sexual desire is marriage.

Other stories point to working women's problems in the home due to men's unchanging attitudes. 'Warning' recounts a middle-aged working woman's reaction to an anonymous phone call telling her her husband is having an affair with a woman half his age. Her familiar daily routine, told in detail, is completely upset; she becomes ill, but when the husband returns from his business trip he shows great concern for her. Is he having an affair or not? The encounter between a man's two girlfriends, one of whom is expecting his child ('Difficult Moments'), a son's boorish behaviour to his mother who, at short notice, goes to great trouble to prepare lunch for him and his friends while they decide to eat in a restaurant ('Details'), are further attacks on the ideology of domesticity and men's selfish behaviour in the home.

Several stories, however, point to women's collusion in their own subordination and their oppression of other women. 'Tadiana' is a poignant sketch of a naive girl who, brought up by her religious aunts, falls in love with Pedro at boarding school. After he jilts her she falls down the stairs, is injured and leaves school. The story, told from the point of view of Tadiana's class-mates, suggests that the girl is rejected by the group because she is old-fashioned (she plays the violin) and too much of an individualist. If she had confided in the other girls and shared their knowledge (of Pedro's past), and if they had helped her, the situation might have been avoided. A mother's over-protective collusion with her (possibly gay) son which involves deceiving his girlfriend ('The Ideal Girl'), a widowed mother's collusion with her selfish teenage daughter who destroys her second marriage ('Conflict of Feelings'), a jilted girl's collusion with her ex-boyfriend who, now married to another, beds her like a prostitute ('To Lose Out Twice'), all point in this direction.

Perhaps the most touching and provocative piece is the pro-life story 'To Be or Not to Be' which voices an unmarried girl's agonizing thoughts on whether to have an abortion. Caught between two modes of thought, the Catholic family values of her grandmother on the one hand, and modern mechanistic attitudes towards abortion on the other, she is unable to decide. In fact, what this girl wishes is to relinquish the freedom and the responsibility of decision to others, 'to know what to do and not to have to make decisions because they were made years ago [...] why was I born at this point in time [...] all I want to do is not to decide' (Bahr 1989: 43). The problem is not only that the girl wants to protect the unborn child, 'I'm going to kill a tiny little thing, that doesn't cry' (p. 45), or that her parents will be outraged because she is pregnant and considering abortion. The greatest obstacle to having the baby she so clearly wants is that there will be no family structure in which the child can grow, 'there won't be a granny wearing glasses [...], mummy won't know how to make milk pudding and there won't be a daddy standing behind the counter, how awful' (p. 44). This girl has no choice. Hence the difficult situation in which young girls find themselves in Cuba today. The story questions the unthinking attitude of young girls, who take the possibility of abortion for granted, as well as socialist birth control policies. It also suggests that, in the absence of any other alternative, young people still need the protection and moral guidelines of the traditional family institution.

Verónica Pérez Kónina's (b. 1968) 'Daily' from *Adolesciendo* [Adolescing] (1988) (Cámara 1989) is a housewife's almost lyrical account of her day-to-day routine. The banality of the scenario – rushing home from work to get the meal ready, a thoughtless husband out drinking somewhere, a daughter out to parties, a son who hardly visits, the woman's lack of leisure time, 'with work and the house I feel penned in, in a cell, from one corner to the other: not even a visit to the cinema, or to take a walk, not even ... ' (Cámara 1989: 243), and, finally, the woman's decision to take a break and watch the latest TV soap at her friend's house – is told with disarming simplicity and frankness with no trace of self-pity. The fact that this story, so familiar in women's lives, could still be written in Cuba in the late 1980s shows how little things had changed in the home.

All these stories negotiate the relationship between a mode of production (the family, the state) and women's subordination, while indicating how a gender ideology is constructed in Cuban society. One answer to Barrett's question as to why feminists should be so interested in literature or what theoretical or political ends such a study might serve, is that these stories (as is the case with works of realism in general) provide potential documentary evidence of women's ways of thinking in Cuba today. Their verisimilitude stands in lieu of the sociological studies on sex and gender which are so evidently lacking. They go towards answering some of the questions posed by Smith and Padula, for example: 'How does the state's identification of salaried production as the route to full sexual equality correspond to women's needs and desires?', 'How does the current state of the Cuban family correspond to cultural and political priorities?', 'How important is the informal role of grandmothers [...]?', 'What role does the myth of male irresponsibility play in Cuban society?', 'Why has the Revolution adopted traditionally conservative views of sexuality [...]?', 'What are the forms of women's interrelationship in Cuba today?' (Smith and Padula 1988: 149–57).

Dora Alonso

The short stories written by Dora Alonso are different, mainly because of their imaginative deployment of prosopopoeia, but no less illuminating. In the rest of this chapter I shall engage with some of the curious paradoxes these stories present which may be resolved to some extent in a feminist reading. But first, how to approach stories in which a frightened old mare, about to be slaughtered for zoo meat, gives birth to a foal; a caring rat feeds her young on merchandise denied by a profiteer to a hungry human mother and her baby; a cat sees her recently-born kittens carried off by her trusted owner to their death; a pampered bitch escapes to find sexual pleasure with a flea-bitten dog, only to be caught and killed by the dog-catcher at the height of her ecstasy; a woman who hates and kills cockroaches dies of shock when one crawls out of the woodwork while she is in her steam bath, stares her in the eye and makes for her neck? These are just some of the eighteen stories, published originally between 1962 and 1987, collected and republished in 1989 in the volume entitled *Juega la dama* [The Lady Plays]. The criterion according to which they were selected, what they all have in common, is the presence of a female protagonist, animal or human. Alonso calls these stories 'stories about females' but insists there is no feminist subtext. Femaleness is a 'literary theme, no more', she says, despite the fact that the original title was *Jaque mate* ('Check mate' or 'Death to the King') which she thought was too aggressive and therefore dropped.[2] This is the first paradox: a text predicated on femaleness which its author denies is feminist. What is striking, however, is that animality is as prominent a feature as feminality. Even in stories not focusing on animals, animals are present and in my view this is the most salient characteristic of Alonso's short fiction in general, written both before and after the Revolution.

Dora Alonso has not been admitted to the sanctum of Latin American literature. Yet she is the only female writer of narrative fiction mentioned in any depth, or at all, in the standard surveys of the post-revolutionary Cuban novel. Menton lists only two women (one is Dora Alonso) who contributed more than one story to the twelve short fiction anthologies published between 1959 and 1971. In the same period 115 volumes of short stories came out by individual authors; only twelve were written by ten women.[3]

Women writers of adult fiction were affected by the censorship and persecution of the difficult 1970s when, as we have seen, certain genres became more acceptable than others for socio-political advancement. According to Desiderio Navarro, 'poetry, "testimonio" and literature for children' were the genres preferred by those who wanted to make a quick name for themselves or simply earn 'the right to present themselves as "writers"'.[4] Dora Alonso could not remain unaffected by this climate and wrote several books for children in the 1960s and 1970s and two 'testimonios' in the early 1980s. But she did manage to publish three collections of short stories for adults: *Ponolani* (Gente Nueva, 1966); *Once caballos* [Eleven Horses] (1970); and *Cuentos* [Stories] (1976).[5] Alonso belongs to the Cuban generation born between 1910 and 1920 which includes Onelio Jorge Cardoso, Virgilio Piñera and José Lezama Lima, but unlike the majority of her contemporaries who, when possible, rejected 'creole' themes for fantastic literature, she kept to the conventions of 'creole realism'. Hence the preponderance of animals.

Tierra inerme [Defenceless Land] (1961) was classified a 'novel of the land' and as such fell outside the main current of Cuban and Latin American narrative of the 1960s. It has been judged harshly. For North American critics it was 'an anachronistic attempt to justify the agrarian reform' and a failed attempt to apply the novelistic formula of the Venezuelan Rómulo Gallegos (1884–1969, resident in Cuba) to the Cuban landscape (Menton 1975: 34). Cuban critics deplored the lack of social realism, the atmosphere of resignation which, in their view, communicated 'an incomplete account of our recent history', and the narrative techniques were considered inappropriate for a new socialist state of collectivized farms (Méndez y Soto 1977: 73).[6] Despite winning the prestigious Casa de las Américas prize then, the novel was dismissed as unoriginal on the one hand and too uncritical to be included in the mainstream of Cuban post-revolutionary social realism on the other. But Luisa Campuzano (1988: 136) takes a different view: 'Dora Alonso writes in the tradition of the "novel of the land", which has a long history in Latin America, and which still had something to say to us at the beginning of this period.' Does she imply here 'us women'? A feminist approach to *Tierra inerme* (Shea 1988) and Alonso's short stories, published over fifty years (between 1936 and 1987), might explain the relative absence of fantasy, experimental techniques and, more surprisingly, urban guerrilla settings and positive social realism, as well as the subsequent lack of serious critical coverage. Why did Dora Alonso continue to privilege rural life, animals and women?

It is clear that the majority of Alonso's short stories exemplify the discourse of the Latin American autochthonous text. The 'rhetorical devices' subsuming such narrative, according to Carlos J. Alonso, belong to nineteenth-century theories of evolution in which culture is conceived of as an organism with a natural development thwarted by the culprits of history:

> the many botanical and biological metaphors that were used throughout the century [in Latin America] ... attest to the organicity that physical and spiritual processes were assumed to have in common; but it is also expressive of the relationship which was presumed to exist between a culture and the physical environment in which it [the culture] obtained. (C. J. Alonso 1990: 8–9, 59)[7]

In other words, a national *volksgeist* was thought to be manifest in the particular way it adapted to an environment. Much of Dora Alonso's short fiction is naturalistic, even Darwinian. Explicit references are made to Darwin and the influence of his *Diary of the Voyage of HMS Beagle* on the young narrator in two metafictional, possibly autobiographical, stories published in 1969 ('The Rain and the Puma' and 'The Siamese Cat'). Her short fiction deals with individuals interacting with a hostile, miserable Cuban environment, usually rural, in which animals – often those associated with human life (dogs, cats, horses, cattle, rats, monkeys) – but many others, including insects (cockroaches, butterflies) and molluscs, abound. Humans are represented as caged wild animals, the passive victims of heredity and other natural forces, their lives meaningless and tragic. Zoo and circus settings are common. From a pre-revolutionary emphasis on conflict between men ('The Knot', 1937; 'Stowage', 1945) or conflict belying profound mutual interdependence between man and beast ('A Philosopher', 1944; 'Paddock', 1945; 'Negative', 1947; 'Tiredness', 1954), the stories become increasingly woman-centred after 1959. Alonso writes about social injustice experienced (in the past) by poor and black women: the misery of a mother losing her child ('Severina', 1965); the dignity bestowed on a dead black woman by her female friends who dress her for burial in the bridal gown she never wore ('The Bridal Gown', 1975). She writes about the problems older women (widows and spinsters) face, such as physical deterioration, loneliness, sexual frustration and sexual fantasies ('One', 1965; 'Sugar Cotton', 1969; 'Fewer than Twenty', 1972; 'Sophia and the Angel', 1973; 'Ana and Her Loves', 1979). Other stories focus on women whose husbands do no housework and are consequently killed off with poisoned food ('Chicken à la Jardinière', 1987) or, worse still, whose husbands emigrate to Miami ('The Return of Abilio Argüelles', 1987) – these being commentaries on much-debated political issues at the time. Particularly interesting are two types of post-revolutionary short story relating to animals: stories where women clash, fatally, with female animals ('The Cats', 1964; 'The Hen', 1978; 'The Strange Death of Juana Urquiza', 1987) and those in which female animals are personified ('The Rat', 1962; 'Cage Number One', 1964; 'Eleven Horses', 1969; 'Happiness', 1983), the plots of some of which have already been described. This brings us to the second paradox in Alonso's narrative fiction: she writes in the naturalist tradition, yet naturalism and biological determinism are anathema to Marxism and progressive ideology generally. Dora Alonso is no dissident. She publicly stands by Fidel and the achievements of the Revolution. It seems the application of standard categorizations is at fault; the pigeon-holes 'naturalism' and 'of the land' applied to discursive modes, concepts or attitudes from a phallocentric optic are inappropriate, certainly insufficient, when dealing with the work of this (or any?) female author.

A different tack is to explore further the implications of the narrative sub-genre. It has been suggested that conventional realist narrative techniques, such as those used by Alonso, imply a mastery of outer reality and a coherent viewpoint concomitant with male hegemony. But Alonso also privileges one trope in particular: allegory, where an animal subject-noun is personified, that is, takes on human predicates (verb/adjective). In these allegories the animal subject is almost always a female endowed with woman-specific attributes, or constituted as woman through the language of the text, by means of a distinctive lexicon or focalization. Taking examples from *Juega la dama* (1989), in 'Eleven Horses' 'the pregnant mare' is 'la parturienta' ['the woman in labour'], feeling 'a mother's [...] fear', 'short of breath' and 'nervous'. Part of the story is told from the point of view of the 'colt' still in the womb, 'the colt prepared himself to leave. He floated in his night of liquid and the mother's fear was a spur in his side' (Alonso 1989: 54). The horses have memories of their past lives, they are ill and asthmatic, and it seems they can read the sign 'No Exit' (p. 51). In 'The Rat', the rat, 'alert', 'flustered', 'nervous', gives birth to 'little babies' and understands language; but she sees only a partial reality, the dehumanized shopkeeper's big feet and arms. The description of the well-fed rat protecting her young ones, 'her fine nose pointed upwards. Her eyes were shining' (p. 33) is juxtaposed with the description of the poor woman feeding her baby, 'a yellow face, with rings under her eyes' (p. 34). Part of the story is told from the point of view of the rat who sees a thick ledger and thinks it must be 'pregnant with ten small ones' and believes the storekeeper 'was good and tolerant' because he allows weevils and ants into the food. Galana the cat in 'The Cats' is also 'the mother', 'the mother in labour' (p. 86) and later 'disconsolate' when Lola – after helping her through labour – takes away her 'babies'. In 'The Strange Death of Juana de Urquiza' the cockroach is 'robust, lustrous, resolved', the implacable 'enemy' of Juana the cockroach-killer. The cosseted bitch of 'Happiness' enjoys perfume, is 'fussy' and 'incapable of knowing who she was' except when on 'burning heat'; she gives up everything, including her life, for sex with her dog – 'the son of no one', 'always ready for intercourse' (pp. 81–2). The correspondences sought on the literal and symbolical levels of the allegories pertain to female animals and female humans; the resulting female essence is synonymous with motherhood and oppression, but also resilience and solidarity, sexual frustration and sexual pleasure. Similarly, the antagonists in the stories are men (not male animals) representing death, violence, victimization and authority: 'the butcher'; 'the man' (the storekeeper); 'the dog catcher', 'the slaughterer'. When a woman adopts masculinist attributes in her dealings with female animals (Lola, Juana) there is a tremendous sense of betrayal. Lola, like the 'butcher' and the storekeeper, functions as the third term splitting the newly-born creature from unity with the mother, representing the law-of-the-father. In Juana's case, the insect, the female underling, wins out, egged on by a kind of Lamarckian concept of cockroach cultural inheritance.

The effect of these stories is unusually powerful and has to do with the working out of the incongruency inherent in allegory. Samuel Levin suggests that the disparity in allegory (between the literal and the symbolical) can be resolved by dispersonification of either the subject or the predicate ('the *mare* [literally, the woman] was inconsolable' or 'the mare was *inconsolable* [literally, nervous or whatever a horse feels]. But in addition, and this is significant for my argument, he points to a third 'higher level' of meaning which involves readers projecting themselves into non-human life and identifying with it, imagining what a mare feels when sad. The reader thus gains insight into life without the constraints of language and the device expands 'our conceptual horizons'. It is far easier, argues Levin, to personify the non-human because language is human-centred, resulting in a 'deficiency in our lexicon' (Levin 1981: 34).

Feminists would argue that the deficiency in language is its phallocentrism; the resulting view of the world is not simply anthropomorphic, but androcentric. The result of Alonso's use of allegory is an all-encompassing gynomorphic worldview. In it the categories male and female are more important than the categories animal and human. In other words, biological sex differences are privileged over and above class, race or any other socio-cultural category, over the nature–culture divide and even anthropomorphism itself. Alonso seems to be attempting to avoid the constraints of the symbolic in order to put the female, the irrepresentable, 'into discourse', engaging in what Alice Jardine terms gynesis, so that the reader can identify with that which cannot be expressed in language as it stands, that is, female experience and woman as unknowable (Jardine 1985: 25).[8] Furthermore, if we take into consideration that these are autochthonous texts then the inevitable 'mediating analytical construct' described by Carlos J. Alonso as existing between a nationalist author and his or her subject is, in this case, that of a woman. What bearing does a female mediation have on representations of national culture? The allegories, inherently ambiguous, can certainly be interpreted as national projections exemplifying the subjugation, resistance and revenge of the underdog, which fits in with the emplotment of Cuban history as a trajectory of human freedom, through slavery, imperialism and capitalism. But the projections are cast through the female lens of the author. Similarly, the stories could be said to textualize 'what is construed as a collective spiritual essence' (indicated in speech, landscape and human activity) as do the 'novels of the land', but again from the female point of view of the protagonists (C. J. Alonso 1990: 5, 61). I have found only one allegory, 'Peace to the Antelope', where the personified imprisoned subject is a young male. The allegories would seem to articulate the woman version (O'Callaghan 1993) of a national culture, of a collective spirit.

Does this assertion of the pre-eminence of biological essentialism have much to do with the apparent paradoxes evidenced so far: a female-centred text yet not feminist; naturalistic discourse yet Marxist; an autochthonous culture yet woman-centred? Paradox too thrives on ambiguity. Rather than foreclose apparent inconsistency I would like to explore it further. The choice of allegory has deeper implications. First, in Cuba the genre is closely associated with the fable, particularly the beast-fable, of West African origins (cf. J. Chandler Harris's 'Uncle Remus' stories of 1879). As the living expression of African Cuban popular oral culture the fable was appropriated and rendered fit for the literate by Lydia Cabrera, as noted previously. Cabrera's collection of twenty-two African Cuban fables, *Contes nègres de Cuba* (Paris 1936), much acclaimed by Alejo Carpentier, gained immediate international recognition; the Spanish version came out in Havana in 1940. A further collection (*¿Por qué? ... cuentos negros de Cuba* [Why? Black Tales from Cuba]) was published in Cuba in 1948, and three more in the United States: *Ayapá. Cuentos de jicotea* [Ayapa. Turtle Stories] (1970), *Yemayá y Ochún* (1980), and, partly, *Los animales en el folklore de Cuba* [Animals in Cuban Folklore] (1988) (Montero 1989: 34; Irizarry 1979). The point is that there is no clear distinction in these stories between oral traditions (documentary and ethnographic writing) and creative fiction; 'What are these stories?' asks one critic, 'the copied stories of a folklorist or artistic creation? They are a bit of both' (Boggs 1977: 15). The syntax is simple, almost as if Spanish were a foreign tongue to the teller, and the stories are interspersed with colloquialisms and exclamations in both Spanish and Lucumi (Cuban Yoruba). 'The Earth gives to Man and He, sooner or later, pays back Earth what He Owes' (Cabrera 961: 17–18), for example, is a creation story describing how Man (Yácara) comes to an agreement with earth (Entoto) but not with the Sea (Kalunga): Yácara will feed off Entoto's offspring until he finally gives himself up to the earth. In 'Chéggue' a young boy disobeys his father and kills the king of the beasts on New Year's Day. When his father searches for him the chorus of animals chants in Lucumi,

> Chéggue! Oh, Chéggue!
> Tanike Chéggue nibe ún
> Chéggue ono chono ire ló
> Chéggue tá larroyo ... (Cabrera 1961: 20)

They have killed him and he is in the stream. In '[Why] the Mosquito Buzzes in the Ear' humans and the body parts are zoomorphized: thus the Ear represents an easy-going woman who will not pay her debts and the Mosquito the unpaid furniture remover who takes his revenge by for-ever buzzing around her at night. Thus it is that mosquitoes most plague us at night screeching '¡Mi Meeeedio! ¡Meee-dio! ¡Meeeeedio! (My half cent) (p. 16).

Cabrera's animals represent human conduct with a moral intention. But her animals (turtle, tortoise, rabbit, crab, lizard, bull, worm, hen, goat, snake, duck) are as indigenous as African (lion and elephant); they have a 'creole' mentality, speech and humour and are placed in a Cuban land-scape. Fernando Ortiz, in his prologue to *Cuentos negros de Cuba* (1961), links Cabrera's stories to Aesop's fables but points out that the contrasting personalities of particular pairings of animals, such as the turtle and the deer, constitute a cycle of local traditions 'very typical of the Yoruban'. In these tales 'the turtle is the prototype of astuteness and wisdom always conquering over brute force and stupidity' (Cabrera 1961: 11). Some of Cabrera's stories, such as 'Papa Turtle and Papa Tiger', Ortiz believes, are entirely Cuban. Dora Alonso's allegories, then, belong not so much to European Naturalism as to a literary tradition which is doubly feminine: Lydia Cabrera incorporated it into the Cuban canon and, more importantly, black women played a key role in its oral transmission.

Like Cabrera, Alonso collected and reworked African Cuban legends, many first-hand accounts from her nursemaid Emilia and other black women on her father's estate.[9] Several were published in the volume *Panolani* (1966) by 'Gente Nueva' [New People] as children's literature. *Panolani* contains conventional beast-fables where anthropomorphized animals, male and female, exemplify a moral ('The Story of the Turtle', 'Tale of the Dog', 'The One that Could not Enter', 'Condioco'). Other fables humanize animals to a greater degree to comment on human family relationships, for example, in 'Father Bull' a father (bull) is jealous of his male child who is protected by the mother (cow) until he grows up. But more moving and personal are the first six stories or lyrical sketches, which pay tribute to the genealogy of black women story-tellers, from the 'grandmother' in Africa, to her daughter Panolani captured as a child and brought to Cuban slavery, and her daughter Emilia who nurses the anonymous white child, the female narrator (a 'doubling' of Dora Alonso) who passes on the tale:

> Perhaps on account of the secret blood she had drunk from the dark breast, she [the narrator] loved the spirit in the well [...] now the seed was sown and, through the blood of Emilia Trias Carol, the force of the river where Panolani appeared searching for butterflies fluttering in the water's depths, for the red parrots' fire, and the round mirror of the lioness's eye. (Alonso 1980: 181)

Alonso added to her later allegories this extra dimension: feminality.[10] Her discourse is rooted in that of black women's culture inextricably bound to African traditions, the institution of slavery and, eventually, to the formation of an indigenous, African Cuban syncretic culture. Black feminist commentary is relevant in this respect. As it points out, women slaves were not considered human but 'simultaneously racially and sexually – as marked female (animal, sexualized and without rights)', excluded from culture, so that 'white women inherited black women [and men]' (Haraway 1991: 145). In a Caribbean culture such as this, indeed, in the whole of Latin America, motherhood, mothering and the family are exceptionally important. Because of it, according to Pat Ellis, women 'have considerable influence and authority and respect' (Ellis 1986: 6; C. Williams 1986: 110). Cuba is no different and this attitude has survived the Revolution intact. But, of course, sex roles considered innate are a double-edged weapon.

This was nowhere more obvious than in the Cuban policies towards women of the two decades following the Revolution, which, like Alonso's short fiction, suggest biological essentialism. Cuba made exceptional advances with regard to women's material conditions, the eradication of sexual discrimination, health, education and childcare on a scale unequalled in Latin America or even in parts of the developed West. An example is the Family Code (1975) which stipulates shared parenting and shared domestic labour. By the 1960s a third of the workforce was female. Yet in 1968 women were prohibited from taking up 500 posts (another 500 were reserved for them) on the basis that they were physically weaker and more vulnerable than men. Referring to interviews carried out in 1970, Margaret Randall writes: 'the consensus still seemed to be that, in Cuba, differences between men's and women's roles were thought to be biological as well as social in origin' (Randall 1981: 29).[11] A deep-seated paternalism seeps through official communications of the 1970s despite the sweeping reforms.

The president of the Federation of Cuban Women, Vilma Espín, explained in 1960 the need for collective action due to the 'physiological inferiority of woman' resulting from her 'procreative nature' (Séjourné 1980: x). In 1975 Fidel declared that freedom for women was liberation from domestic chores and active participation in social production, but then qualified his statement 'with the limitations required by her role as the reproducer of human beings, her august role as mother and the peculiarities of her physical constitution' (Séjourné 1980: xi). Throughout the 1960s and 1970s the stress fell on: woman as 'supermother', heterosexual marriage and the nuclear family as social norm, echoing Marx's view that heterosexuality was the 'most natural relation of human being to human being' (Haraway 1991: 132). Marx did not historicize sex or nature. For Fidel in 1971 woman was 'nature's workshop where life is formed' (Stone 1981: 68); while scorn was poured on 'false intellectuals who attempt to convert snobbery, extravagance, homosexuality and other social aberrations into the expression of revolutionary art' (Arias 1979: 24). So although well-meaning towards women's liberation, nevertheless recommendations such as the following (in Fidel's 1974 speech) constantly undermine the project:

> There must be certain small privileges and certain small inequalities in favour of women. And I say this clearly and frankly, because there are some men who feel they are not obliged to give their seat on a bus to a pregnant woman [Applause] or to an old woman, or to a little girl, or to a woman of any age ... [Applause]. Just as I understand it to be the obligation of any young man to give his seat on the bus to an old man [Applause]. Because it would be very sad if, with the Revolution, there wasn't even the recollection of what certain men in bourgeois society did out of bourgeois or feudal chivalry, there must exist proletarian manners ... [Applause]. And I say this with the certainty ... that

every mother and every father would like their son to be a chivalrous proletarian. (Stone 1981: 68–9)

Castro was not alone, of course; similar supremacist remarks were constantly made by political leaders, a case in point being the Mexican president Luis Echeverría.[12] Despite the view, nevertheless, that in Cuba 'there is no capitalist ruling class which seeks to profit from racism and sexism', it would seem that, as Johnetta Cole states: 'the Cuban case underlines the necessity of on-going attacks on the level of the super-structure even after socialist transformation is in process' (Cole 1988: 545). The corollary is that sex differences are more pernicious, more ingrained than class division.

Biological explanations of sexual differences such as those found in Alonso's allegories and predominant Cuban ideology, originated, as did naturalism and cultural evolutionism, in the natural sciences, in the work of Herbert Spencer and Darwin, and were developed by modern evolu-tionists such as Edward Wilson in the 1970s (sex roles are determined; male dominance is innate). As mentioned earlier, essentialism (that is, biology gives women an essential feminine nature, for example, special maternal instincts) is a double-edged weapon and has been used traditionally to bolster anti-feminist positions regarding women's status and agency (Sayers 1982: 108–9, 130–36; Harding 1986). Is Dora Alonso's position then profoundly conservative inasmuch as it is inscribed in the parameters of predominant ideology, as she implies when remarking that the stories in *Juega la dama* are non-feminist 'stories about females'?

The allegories, however, could be read equally from the radical or cultural feminist standpoint which also upholds essentialism in an effort to avoid phallocentric explanations of feminine sexuality. So female biology (pregnancy, mothering, parturition) and 'virtues' (support, care, nurturance, relatedness, self-reliance), all attributes associated with feminality in Alonso's stories, should be exalted, celebrated as different yet equal to masculine values. For radical feminists, women constitute a class and it is the biological division by sex not the relation to the means of production (but rather to that of reproduction) that forms the first class division in society. More recently, proponents of 'feminité' have put forward ideas in which women's bodies are contrasted to the symbolic in Western thought, the maternal body thus subverting the law-of-the-father. Femininity for Luce Irigaray (1980) is constituted by biology and women have a specific female desire. They should assert their femininity from which they have been alienated in a patriarchal society and which they are unable to express in phallocentric language. Cixous, too, states that 'in women there is always more or less of the mother who makes everything alright, who nourishes and who stands up against separation; a force that will not be cut off' (Cixous 1983: 286).[13]

In my view Alonso's animal allegories express the constructionist view that women are subjected because culture is valued over nature. By persuading the reader to identify with the animal 'hembra' [female] she revalorizes natural femaleness. If human consciousness indicates culture then by endowing animals with such consciousness the nature/culture binary is straddled. Woman is somewhere in the space between the female body (invoking biology) and the language of the narrator, in the space between the literal and symbolical readings of allegory. The body is a given and female sexuality is constituted through the language in which it is expressed. Furthermore, Alonso's interest in the experiences of black women in Cuba and her anti-racist concern would point to the affirmation of 'the primacy of family life' as resistance, stressed by black feminists, 'because we know that family ties are the only sustained support system for exploited and oppressed peoples' (hooks 1984: 37). As the CEPAL (1982: 70) reports point out: 'In this context [the abolition of slavery] it is understandable that the land should have a greater social and mythical value than an economic value. Throughout slavery, the land signified social worth and status. During emancipation, the land was a symbol and a concrete example of freedom.'

Above all, Alonso, in challenging the Western nature–culture divide itelf, challenges the sex/gender distinction, expressing the Marxist–humanist idea that 'neither our personal bodies nor our social bodies may be seen as natural, in the sense of outside the self-creating process called labor [...]. Therefore culture does not dominate nature nor is nature an enemy' (Haraway 1983: 127). Through the ambiguity of allegory, often masquerading as fiction for children or folklore, using the well-worn paradigms of the 'novela de la tierra', she deconstructs false paradoxes from a position of alterity, located within a particular writing practice and autochthonous tradition, itself 'sprung from the land'. By reaffirming the female body detached from the defining limits of culture, nature becomes all-encompassing; it is life itself. The implications of this remain open to interpretation.

Notes

1. 'Split in Two' in Peter Bush (ed.) 1997.

2. In an interview with the author in Havana, 24 July 1990.

3. Dora Alonso is mentioned briefly in Lazo (1974); Arias (1979); and more fully in Méndez y Soto (1977: 68–74); Menton (1975: 34–5); Bernard and Pola (1985); Campuzano (1988); and Menton (1973).

4. Quoted in González Echevarría (1989: 103). See V. A. Smith (1989).

5. Except for the references to *Juega la dama*, the edition used in this chapter is Alonso (1980).

6. Alonso learned her lesson. In 1985 she was quoted as saying, with reference to a book written for children, 'If *Tierra inerme* is a panorama of the sorrow,

abandonment and misery in which our people lived, *El valle de la pájara pinta* [The Valley of the Red Bird] is a song to the joy of living, to the new life which the Revolution has brought' (Elizagaray 1985: 133).

7. Interesting too is the following comment by Doris Sommer: 'positivists tended to favour biology as the hegemonic discourse for predicting and directing social growth. They became the doctors who diagnosed social ills and prescribed remedies [...]. One result was that national history in Latin America often read as if it were the inevitable story of organic development' (Sommer 1990: 72).

8. See Jones (1985: 86–110).

9. Dora Alonso, 'I Kissed the Machine Guns' in Bernard and Pola (1985: 15–30, 16, 26).

10. Alonso and Cabrera's use of animals can be compared to the more conventional insertion of animals in realist fiction in short stories such as 'The Dog' and 'The Cockroaches' in María Elena Llana, *La Reja* (1965) and 'The Golden Cat' (1979) in Loló de la Torriente, *Narraciones de Federica y Otros Cuentos* [Federica's Stories and Others] (1988). Here the animals are loaded with symbolical value (signifying need, resilience, aggression), including human traits, but they are always inscribed as animals.

11. According to Wilkie (1990) 31 per cent of the economically active population in Cuba is female.

12. 'Being interested in world and community affairs, women complemented their natural roles as mothers' (1975), quoted in Lavrin (1988: 3).

13. But see Spivak (1981); Franco (1983; 1986; 1988); and Joseph (1981). Butler (1990: 79–93) argues that the law-of-the-father creates the maternal body through discourse.

CHAPTER 7

Mother Africa and Cultural Memory: Nancy Morejón, Georgina Herrera, Excilia Saldaña

In the Introduction I referred to the ways the conscious act of imagining presents infinite horizons and many possible life-worlds which are not necessarily tied to actuality but are positioned in the interstices between the self and the world. I have also mentioned the fact that a black women's literary tradition in Cuba is a recent, post-revolutionary phenomenon. In this chapter my question is in what ways, if any, does the work of black and mulatto women writers differ from that of their white sisters? Where are the traces, if any, of a black female imaginary? As we shall see, an essentializing binary as crude as this will be seriously troubled throughout the chapter.

Without wishing to dwell too long on the polemical matter of race relations in post-1959 Cuba and at the risk of oversimplifying, it is probably fair to say that Cuba before the Revolution was 'the most racist of the Hispanic Caribbean territories' (Pérez Sarduy and Stubbs 1993: 9). The Revolution attempted to dismantle institutionalized racism, to the extent that racism became associated with anti-communism, but its anti-racist policies, subsumed under socialist thinking rather than identity politics, have not been as effective as expected. Official policy has been 'melting pot' integration. By the late 1980s the Cuban authorities recognized that reassessment of racial policies was long overdue. The nexus with gender issues is even more complex. The 1976 Cuban Constitution (Articles 12 and 13) condemned racial but not sexual discrimination. It allowed women to organize their own groups (Article 53) but not African Cubans or men. Although the 1992 Constitution finally proscribed all discrimination on the grounds of race, skin colour, sex, national origin and religious belief (Smith and Padula 1996: 46), the inconsistent overlapping of equality and identity politics (studied in more detail in the next chapter) had persisted for thirty years. As Smith and Padula comment on the basis of research carried out by Lourdes Casal in 1976, 'female equality was viewed as having a lower priority than eliminating racial and class differences in the early years of the Revolution. It seems that it is still the case' (Smith and Padula 1988: 151). Yet, according to Carlos Moore, 'race' in Cuba is a non-topic, an eloquent absence, silenced by 'negrophobic' policies in the name of cultural assimilation (Moore 1988: 355–6).[1]

Moore's view does not confirm Alice Walker's. Walker visited Cuba in 1977 with a group of African Americans. In *In Search of Our Mothers' Gardens* (1984) she describes how she was entertained by

> what I perceived (with North American eyes, seeing narrowly) as an 'integrated' group [of adolescents]. Such a group! Black, brown, white, yellow, pink, gold complexions [...]. They were happy, open, expectant. Cuban and human from the blackest to the whitest. And then *we* presented ourselves as 'black' Americans [...] and their faces changed. For the first time they seemed aware of color differences *among themselves – and were embarrassed for us*. And I realized that as I had sat listening to them, I had separated them into black and white and 'mixed', and that I had assumed certain things on the basis of my own perverted categorization. And now I saw that these young Cubans did not see themselves as I saw them at all. (Walker 1984: 211–12)

She adds: 'Black Cubans raised in the revolution take no special pride in being black [...] the more we [...] spoke of *black* culture, the more confused and distant they grew. Young white Cubans seem equally unaware of themselves as white' (p. 211).[2] A more troubled view is expressed by black Cuban poet Pedro Pérez Sarduy and his wife Jean Stubbs:

> We both share the conviction that the creolization process has affected all groupings to such a degree that it is difficult to talk of any form of racial purity, whether in physiological or socio-cultural terms. Nonetheless, we also feel that the 'melting pot' approach begs the question of strong racial differences which must be recognized and respected as such if 'assimilation to white' assumptions are to be challenged. (Pérez Sarduy and Stubbs 1993: 13–14)

They add: 'The pervasiveness [of racism] should not be underestimated. The problems facing blacks in Cuba should not be ignored [...] Today Cuba has a blacker population than it had in 1959, a more educated black population and one with a growing sense of pride in being black as well as being Cuban' (p. 26).

Since the 'negrismo' movement of the 1930s black or mulatto poetry has been understood in Cuba as poetry which identifies with African Cuban (arguably Cuban) culture written by authors of all skin colours. In the words of the mulatto poet Nicolás Guillén referring to that period, 'it was not a question of "black" poetry versus "white" poetry, but the search for a *national* [sic] poetry' (Morejón 1974: 46). African and Hispanic cultures 'had mixed so much that they had formed a single, thick syrup in which all Cubans participate to a greater or lesser extent' (Augier quoted in Guillén 1972: xxx). In his prologue to Lydia Cabrera's *Cuentos negros de*

Cuba ([1940] 1961) the anthropologist Fernando Ortiz wrote: 'This book is a valuable contribution to Cuban folklore literature. Which is whiteblack, despite the negative attitudes often adopted out of ignorance' (Cabrera 1961: 12). This is the official version of national cultural identity, and does seem to reflect a consensus; in Walker's words: 'Color remains, but beyond color there is a shared *Cuban-ness*' (Walker 1984: 210). It also develops an idea deeply engrained in Latin America since the first decades of the century in programmes of bourgeois national reconstruction; 'the cosmic race' would be founded on the visionary promise of the redeeming mestizo (as in Mexican José de Vasconcelos's essay *La raza cósmica*, 1925). Particularly since 1959, the mulatto has been perceived to represent cultural synthesis and national unity (L. V. Williams 1995). In the words of René Depestre, 'Epidermis fetishism is the political son of capitalism' (Depestre 1985: 71). Is the Cuban version, then, merely another, albeit socialist, recasting of the Latin American race relations model founded on miscegenation and paternalistic integrationism as some have argued? Caribbean writers and cultural theorists have long debated hybridization issues and the class struggle in colonized or dependent societies, and Cuba is no exception. The debate goes on. The question that interests me, however, is where is *woman's* voice in this collective project, this master narrative of national identity? Although race, class and gender are commonalities, from a woman's point of view all these categories are subsumed under gender. As Vera Kutzinski points out, the most prevalent emblem of Cuba's national ideology of *mestizaje* has been the eroticized body of the performing Cuban mulatta (Kutzinski 1993). The discourse of sex is inextricably linked to discourses of power (RoseGreen Williams 1993: 16–23).

It follows that from the point of view of cultural theory, post-revolutionary Cuba is a disconcerting site of difference. We may surmise that the tensions between identities pertaining to race, sex and gender might be more striking in the writings of black and mulatto women. Several theoretical prisms may seem more appropriate in a critique of this poetry: Afro-American and Caribbean womanism; Latin American theories of nationalism, 'mulatez' and '*mestizaje*', and Marxist cultural theories, although a certain amount of fine-tuning is needed if cultural theory is to take account of Cuban singularity. What meanings can be attributed to the terms 'black', 'mulatto' and 'coloured' in a Caribbean, socialist context? The need to insist on European and North American concepts of 'race' in Cuban cultural analysis is potentially problematical, as the above observations of Walker and others suggest. Implicit in Walker's statement is the question of whether hierarchies of inequality which inform Western academic discourse are entirely meaningful when theorizing Cuban social and cultural configurations. This indicates the need for specificity and what Fredric Jameson calls with reference to Cuba 'charting the paradoxes and dilemmas of the dialectics of otherness' (Jameson 1989: x). Arguably, ridding 'race' of essentialism may be a first step for constructionists (Fuss 1989), but the category 'black women poets' should also be historicized. The assumption made by North American Barbara Smith, that 'black women writers constitute an identifiable literary tradition [...] as a direct result of the specific political, social, and economic experiences they have been obliged to share', should be questioned in relation to Cuba where, for over thirty years, the experience of the whole population has been radically different from that of the USA (B. Smith 1982: 163–4).[3] Yet slavery and the African ethnic and cultural heritage is as intrinsic to Cuban identity as it is to any other part of the Caribbean. Some would argue (for example, Nicolás Guillén) that Cuban 'blackness', indicative of subject position, should be rid of alienation as well as essentialism.

A similar disquiet regarding critical agendas is evident in studies of the work of Caribbean women writers in a wider context. Evelyn O'Callaghan stresses the need for an eclectic multiplicity of critical perspectives (O'Callaghan 1993: 9), arguing that 'no one critical/theoretical position is adequate to deal with West Indian fictions by women'. She suggests an 'aesthetics of pluralism [...] In other words, the writing is theoretically situated within the creole ethos from which it arises' (O'Callaghan 1993: 15). In a recent conference on West Indian women's writing, Alison Donnell regretted the 'critical policing of writers' by cultural authorities and publishers whose marketing strategies and commercial interests lie with particular bodies of scholarship. The issue, she argues, is not black and white (Donell 1996). Likewise, O'Callaghan, referring to the debate between Peter Hulme and Edward Kamau Brathwaite on whether (white, creole) Jean Rhys is a West Indian writer ('which has once again inserted the discourse of race into the notion of regional identity' [O'Callaghan 1996: 10), points up the perniciousness of what she terms 'a reversed Manichean allegory' (O'Callaghan 1996: 22). O'Callaghan deplores the fact that 'an author's racial derivation [...] is still of primary importance in assigning the term "West Indian"' (p. 10). She adds: 'If the texts complicate easy classification, it is counterproductive to employ theoretical approaches which limit themselves to categorical boundaries and tend to homogenization in the interests of certain ideological or formal constraints' (p. 18). Notwithstanding possible hostile reception, critics should 'attempt readings that avoid dogmatic polemic while retaining sensitivity to the historical and social contexts of the texts' (p. 22).[4] To what extent is Cuban 'blackness' a transcendent signified, as either a negative absence or a positive presence in Cuban women's poetry? How does Henry Louis Gates's remark, 'Blackness is produced in the text only through a complex process of signification', apply to their work? (Gates 1988: 238). Aware of the possible critical pitfalls outlined above I shall limit myself to commenting on the inscription of 'Africa' in the work of some Cuban women poets, namely mulatto poets Nancy Morejón and Georgina Herrera. In the second part of this chapter I shall consider the work of mulatto poet Excilia Saldaña who in her long poem 'The Bride's Monologue' takes a different approach and looks not to Africa but to Europe for a sense of cultural memory. However, the fact that non-black poets, such as Minerva Salado (b. 1944), also deploy an African Cuban thematics and write what could be labelled African Cuban poetry should not be ignored.

In her lengthy poem 'Song of the Acana Tree' (*Palabras en el espejo* [Word in the Mirror], 1987), Salado adopts a black (possibly female) persona in three of the fourteen sections. The different sections of this poem recount the epic story of the Middle Passage interspersed with descriptions and invocations of the major African Cuban deities (Elegguá, Changó, Oyá, Oggún, Yemayá, and so on). They are also intensely lyrical expressions of love for Africa and of solidarity with 'My black brothers' (Salado 1987: 53). In the following extract Salado adopts the persona of a slave (woman?) recently brought to Cuba. She establishes an intimate relationship with the island, addressing it as if it were a love object offering maternal protection. But if the island is her future home, she still longs for the voice of the African mother(land). Her body (skin) is testimony of her reconstructed kinship, the family tree, spreading and flowing out across the seas:

'Canto del ácana, III'

Isla,
junto al hueco sereno de tu manto
voy a amar tus misterios con mis manos
y mis hijos profundos verán brotar la luz
como si fuera miel.
Pero mi tierra es otra y su árbol me enciende
a través de la espuma y del horror
mi piel es la vertiente de sus ramas
y el fruto de su hogar
quiebra mi corazón como una concha
frágil en el anhelo de su voz. (Salado 1987: 51)

III

Island / Beside the serene hollow of your mantle / I'll cherish your mysteries with my hands / And my children, deep within me, / Will see the light shine like honey. / But my land is another, her tree enflames me / Across the sea-spray and the dire / My skin is the flowing of her branches / And her fruit calling from home fires / My heart breaks like a fragile sea-shell / Longing for her voice.

As mentioned in Chapter 5, many poems written by non-black women inscribe African–Caribbean traditions and deities, pointing to one of the more interesting developments of post-revolutionary poetry. What is important is the extent to which each poet identitifies as a woman and as a Cuban with 'Africa' as a cultural, historical and political construct and as a trope facilitating memory and self-construction.

Poetry written by Cubans of African descent was published in the mid-nineteenth century, but African Cuban poetry in which these Cubans were constituted as subjects appeared in the 1920s. Characterized by its rhythm and musical qualities, the early blend of myth, magic and social critique had degenerated into sentimental humour by the 1940s. A rich world bibliography traces the impact of the negritude movement on Cuba, the work of black, white and mulatto male poets, including Nicolás Guillén, and representations of women in this tradition. Yet African Cuban poetry written by women was unheard of before the 1959 Revolution. As elsewhere in the Americas, the inner conflict voiced was the prerogative of the male mulatto; the black female (especially the dancer) incarnated unbridled sexuality, emotional release and aesthetic form. The contorting black female body, presented in terms of indigenous or African animals, fruits, vegetables and musical instruments, available to be played and consumed, was dehumanized and commoditized in pre-revolutionary consumer society. As Sander L. Gilman points out, in the nineteenth century 'the female genitals came to define the female [...] The perception of the prostitute [...] thus merged with the perception of the black [...]. Black females do not merely represent the sexualized female, they also represent the female as the source of corruption and disease' (Gilman 1986: 235, 248, 250). This was the perspective of the white, male observer. Black feminine subjectivity could be inscribed only through the gaze of an other. Sections from one of the first 'negrista' poems written in Cuba (by Francisco Muñoz Monte in 1845) and from a well-known poem by Guillén (first published in 1947) exemplify the perspective of the (usually white) male observer. They indicate what black and mulatto Cuban women, the objects of desire and art, would have to contend with when positioning themselves as the lyrical subjects of their discourse:

> elástica culebra, hambrienta boa,
> la mulata a su víctima sujeta,
> lo oprime, estrecha, estruja, enreda, aprieta,
> y chupa y lame y muerde en su furor.

> Y crujen sus elásticas caderas,
> y tocados de intenso magnetismo
> cada ojo revela un hondo abismo
> de apetito, de rabia y de pasión. (Castellanos and Castellanos 1990: 426)

supple snake, hungry boa, / the mulatta twines round her prey, / she pins him down, squeezes, rubs, hugs, entangles, / and sucks, licks and bites with rage. // And as her elastic hips sway, / With magnetic intensity touched / each eye reveals a deep abyss / of appetite, anger and lust.

'Madrigal'

Tu vientre sabe más que tu cabeza
y tanto como tus muslos.
Esa
es la fuerte gracia negra
de tu cuerpo desnudo.
Signo de selva el tuyo,
con tus collares rojos,
tus brazaletes de oro curvo,
y ese caimán oscuro
nadando en el Zambeze de tus ojos. (Guillén 1990: 79)

> Your belly knows more than your head / and as much as your thighs. / That /
> is the strong, black grace / of your naked body. / Yours is the sign of the
> forest, / with your ruby necklaces, / your bracelets of twisted gold, / and that
> dark alligator / swimming in the Zambezi of your eyes.

In 1970, eleven years after the Revolution, Ildefonso Pereda Valdez published a study of African Cuban poetry. Only one woman is mentioned: Nancy Morejón. But in Cuba, the mid-1970s were marked profoundly by two events: International Women's Year (1975) and, more importantly in the context of this chapter, Cuban involvement in Angola (1975–76). Cuban relations with Africa were transformed to a degree unimagined in other parts of the Caribbean when Agostinho Neto, leader of the MPLA, requested assistance to fend off invading South African forces supporting the FNLA-UNITA. Some 30,000 Cuban troops were sent to Angola; the FNLA-UNITA was defeated before the Cubans pulled out. Cuba was similarly involved in Ethiopia between 1977 and 1978 and for many years supported the liberation struggles against South Africa in Namibia, providing aid for SWAPO and the Front Line States (hence Nelson Mandela's visit to Cuba in 1991).[5] These political developments, which led to an increased awareness of African Caribbean identity in the island and the active, official encouragement of perceived cultural and historical affinities, could not fail to affect African Cuban poetry.[6]

Nancy Morejón (b. 1944), until recently director of the Caribbean Studies Centre in Havana, has published over ten books of poetry since the early 1960s and is the most widely translated female poet of her generation (see Chapter 5). I shall discuss poems from three of her collections: *Parajes de una época* [Places in Time] (1979), *Piedra pulida* [Polished Stone] (1986) and *Baladas para un sueño* [Ballads for a Dream] (1989). Morejón worked closely with Guillén who wrote of her in 1972: 'I think her poetry is black like her skin [...]. For that same reason, it is also Cuban, with its root buried very deeply so that it appears on the other side of the planet [...]. I love her smile, her dark skin, her African hair' (Guillén 1972: II, 334–5). Like Guillén, she is concerned with the construction and affirmation of a syncretic Cuban identity. Her poetry inscribes the 'blackness' Guillén refers to through 'Africa' which is a key trope in this public and political project and in the articulation of a more personal African Cuban subjectivity. It exemplifies what Sylvia Molloy refers to as the expression of 'individual *bios*' in terms of 'national *ethos*' (Molloy 1991: 148). Morejón does not privilege 'blackness' as an analytical tool; she believes it is impossible to engage in what she refers to as an exclusively cutaneous critique of literature (Morejón 1974: 78–9). In this respect her poetry continues in the tradition of mulatto poet Marcelino Arozarena (b. 1912), whose collection of poems written between 1933 and 1966 entitled *Canción negra sin color* [Black Song without Colour], at once invites and erases a polychromatic reading. At least until 1990 Morejón was wary of the term African Cuban being of the opinion that an African Cuban identity is subsumed in a national Cuban identity which cannot be understood without the black cultures of America.[7] She wrote:

> We Cubans […] have set out to create an homogenous nation from the nation's very heterogeneity, created for a political purpose (the Cuban Revolution headed by Fidel Castro), rather than for any other purely cultural or racial controversy. We are a melting pot. We are not assimilated. We are not acculturated to either Spanish or African customs […] we produce ourselves, as a mixed 'mestizo' people who have inherited and sustain both components, without being either African or Spanish any longer, just Cubans. (Morejón 1988: 190)

Morejón's is a woman's voice. She accepts Alice Walker's term 'womanist': 'in my literature it is very important that I am a woman. It would be a nonsense to say I am not, or that I think women don't write in a very special mode and with a special experience and charge' (Savory Fido 1990: 266). How does she negotiate the tensions between sexual politics, the class struggle and ethnicity, and how is Africa inscribed in her poetry?

'Black Woman' (Morejón 1979: 18–20), one of the most frequently translated poems of post-revolutionary Cuba, is a good example of female-centred liberating narrative (P. Taylor 1989: 1–6). It is a first-person account of collective Cuban resistance to the exploitation of slavery, colonization and neo-colonialism, culminating in revolutionary apotheosis. The epic journey through time is recounted by a single female slave, the subject of the poem and Cuban history; an anonymous black woman is figured as the symbol of Cuban national independence and voices the collective consciousness. The power and status of black woman is thus legitimated and takes on mythical dimensions. Her story of liberation, from the crossing of the Atlantic to Castro's anti-capitalist guerrilla offensive, is Cuban his(s)tory – recast in female terms. As a worker, a black and a woman (in that order) the black female persona epitomizes the survival and rebellion of the dispossessed who, through their own efforts, finally reap the fruits of the communist tree:

Acaso no he olvidado ni mi costa perdida ni mi lengua ancestral.
Me dejaron aquí y aquí he vivido.
Y porque trabajé como una bestia,
aquí volví a nacer.
A cuánta epopeya mandinga intenté recurrir.

Perhaps I've not forgotten my long lost shore / or my ancient tongue. / They left me here and here I stayed. / And because I worked like a beast / Here I was born again. / Oh, how many Mandinga epics did I look to for strength!

The poem is informed by a Marxist construction of the subject's identity through productive activity: working ('I worked much harder'), rebelling ('I rebelled', 'I rose up'), walking ('I walked on'), and even escaping ('I ran off to the mountains'), thus transform the slave mode of production and lead to being. This process is the forging of a communist Cuban identity, entailing a personal and collective coming to consciousness:

Ahora soy: sólo hoy tenemos y creamos.
        Nada nos es ajeno.
Nuestra la tierra.
Nuestros el mar y el cielo.
Nuestros la magia y la quimera.
Iguales míos, aquí los veo bailar
alrededor del árbol que plantamos para el comunismo.
Su pródiga madera ya resuena.

Now I exist: only now do we own and create. / Nothing is foreign to us. / Ours is the land. / Ours the sea and the sky. / Ours the chimera, the magic. / Compañeros, I see you dancing / round the communist tree / we planted. / Its prodigious wood resounds. (Based on Weaver 1985: 87–9)

The engendering of the nation as feminine in this poem might suggest an androcentric perspective but the more usual sexual configuration of metropolitan violation and domination of a feminized Third World is here overturned. The subaltern fights back and wins, not in some utopian future or mythical African past but in a present Cuban reality. Morejón's poem achieves what Sartre was unable to do in *Black Orpheus*, that is, 'reconcile lived experience with universal history' (P. Taylor 1989: 159) without forgoing cultural specificity. Hence the importance of the references to the mulatto Independence fighter Antonio Maceo, 'I rode with Maceo's troops', and to the Sierra (Maestra), 'I went down to the Sierra'. This discursive strategy relates two historical events, the Wars of Independence and the Revolution of 1959, as stages in the ongoing struggle towards national liberation and social justice. It also presents a non-erotic, ascetic version of the female mulatto as a representation of national cohesion. Yet two contradictions emerge: the poem's closure forestalls any on-going dialectic, history is absorbed into myth, and references to particularly female experiences are sparse. Having foreclosed on female sexuality, only the (re)productive force 'to give birth' and the ancillary 'embroider' identify this narration as that of a woman, hence the paradoxical significance and gradual annulment of the poem's title, 'Black Woman'. Similarly, ethnic roots become less important as the poem develops, 'I no longer dreamt of the road to Guinea. / Was it to Guinea? To Benin? Was it to Madagascar? Or to Cape Verde?' But if ethnicity and gender are subsumed in the dialectic domination–subordination of class relations, it is nevertheless clear that the generally assumed male, white, viewpoint of historical materialism is replaced by one which is female and black.

'Black Woman' may be compared in this respect to a later poem 'I Love My Master' (Morejón 1986: 100–102), where the feminine voice is much stronger. This first-person narration also traces the coming to consciousness of a black domestic slave woman, but this time sexual exploitation (colonial rape) is as significant as racial subjugation. An individualized white master, who demands sexual fulfilment and domestic service from the acquiescent woman, his property, represents patriarchal and colonial hegemony. The despotic law-of-the-father is disguised by an eroticization of the masculinist values of the mode of production and reproduction he represents (violence, domination, control of the word):

> Amo a mi amo,
> recojo leña para encender su fuego cotidiano.
> [...]
> Amo sus manos
> que me depositaron sobre un lecho de hierbas:
> Mi amo muerde y subyuga.
> [...]
> Amo su boca roja, fina,
> desde donde van saliendo palabras
> que yo no alcanzo a descifrar
> todavía. Mi lengua para él ya no es la suya.

> I love my master, / I gather wood to light his fire each day [...] I love his hands / which lay me down on a bed of grass: / My master subjugates and bites. [...] I love his fine, red mouth, / which utters words / I still can't understand. / My tongue is not his own.

Women's collusion with Romantic myth and male sexual desire, their consent in the internalization of oppression, resolves the conflicts inherent in slavery until the black woman is made powerful through knowledge of her material reality. Knowledge (acquired outside the domestic space from the 'old watchmen', the repositories of 'African' cultural traditions), ethnic and class solidarity, and feminist consciousness are all part of this process of awareness of self and other. Black female stereotyped roles are violently rejected and (like a female Caliban) replaced by curses:

Maldigo
esta bata de muselina que me ha impuesto;
estos encajes vanos que despiadado me endilgó;
[...]
este vientre rajado por su látigo inmemorial;
este maldito corazón.

I curse / this muslin gown he makes me wear / this useless lace he wraps around my throat [...] this belly lacerated by his age-old whip; / this cursed heart.

Plots of horrific revenge break and invert the mutual dependence of the master–slave relationship. Thus the poem reverses the 'negrista' commoditization of the female body. Here the black woman represents the white man as a brute animal, to be dissected and, implicitly, consumed:

Amo a mi amo, pero todas las noches,
cuando atravieso la vereda florida hacia
el cañaveral donde a hurtadillas hemos hecho el amor,
me veo cuchillo en mano, desollándolo como a
una res sin culpa.

I love my master, but every night / when I cross the blossoming paths / to the cane-fields where we secretly made love / I see myself with a knife in my hand, skinning him / like an innocent animal. (Based on Weaver 1985: 75–7)

In a Cuban context, a feminist/womanist poem such as this, even one which is firmly situated in a historical period, has wider implications. By analogy, it signals the global rebellion of (neo)colonized nations against (capitalist) exploiters (James 1996).

A less politically committed, more intimate poem, 'Worlds' (Morejón 1986: 106–8), does not reconstruct political and social revolution but the problem of ethnic identity. The previous two poems destabilize temporal boundaries. 'Worlds' is cast in spacial terms, as its title indicates, and undermines the metaphorical revolutionary journey. The central trope, the 'ship', which shifts its meaning from slave-ship, to home, inner space, mulatto identity, the island, is caught in the Middle Passage between Africa and the Americas. The ship which grows roots in mid-ocean, yet sets out reluctantly into virgin seas, at once records and resolves the contradictions of Caribbean ethnic identity:

Mi casa es un gran barco
que no desea emprender su travesía.
Sus mástiles, sus jarcias,
se tornaron raíces
y medusas plantadas en medio de la mar;
[...]
Mi casa es un gran barco
que resguarda la noche.
Quiero los vinos de su espuma.
Quiero los hierros de sus corrales.
Quiero, al fin, la lenta y prístina llanura
derramada en los ojos.
[...]
Viejo mundo el que amo,
nuevo mundo el que amo,
mundos, mundos los dos, mis mundos:

My house is a great ship / loath to set out on its crossing. / Roots are its masts
and rigging / jellyfish planted in high seas. [...] My house is a great ship /
protected by nightfall. / I want the wines of its foam. / I want the irons of its
farms. / I want, above all, the slow pristine plains / in its eyes. [...] Old World
that I love, / New World that I love. / Worlds, two worlds, my worlds [...]

As movement through time and space is restrained (by the present tense
and the dissolution of the dichotomy land/sea), the ship becomes a figure
of stasis, a utopian topos, an imaginary possible world released from
everyday reality. Initial resistance to leave the African mother, 'the name
of the woman on the coast', is overcome through a sexual relationship
between the female subject and a male slave; the strophe describing this
change in tack is emphasized by the inclusion of the man's direct speech:
'"Let's walk", said the slave, / with his amorous breath.' Solidarity between
man and woman, heterosexual love and reproduction dispel doubt and
lead to future hope. It is their joint construction of a collective culture
which forms their new and mature identity enabling a timeless space for
happiness and sexual pleasure; a space which is an island, Cuba.

Vivo en mi casa que es un barco
(qué poderoso barco me cobija)
Vivo en mi casa que es un barco
(qué poderosa espuma me refresca)
Vivo en mi barco vivo
amparada del treno y la centella
Mi casa es un gran barco
digo
sobre la isla dorada

en que voy a morir.

I live in my house, my ship / (what a powerful ship to protect me) / I live in my house, my ship / (what powerful foam to refresh me). / I live in my ship I live / sheltered from the thunder and the lightning's flash. / My house is a great ship / oh yes / on the golden isle / where I'll end my days.

For Morejón, 'polished stone' symbolizes cultural perfection.[8] Yet the poems in the sub-section 'Polished Stone' of the book of the same title are characterized not by Utopianism but by their lyrical intimacy. Another poem from the section is 'Mother' where a possible subtext is indicated: Alice Walker's *In Search of Our Mothers' Gardens*. The poet focuses on the experiences of her own mother, a poor woman, in pre-revolutionary Cuba, and recounts the legacy she left to her daughters, work and hope:

Mi madre no tuvo jardín
sino islas acantiladas
flotando, bajo el sol,
en sus corales delicados.
No hubo una rama limpia
en sus pupilas sino muchos garrotes.
[...]
Mi madre tuvo el canto y el pañuelo
para acunar la fe de mis entrañas,
para alzar su cabeza de reina desoída
y dejarnos sus manos, como piedras preciosas

My mother had no garden / only sheer-cliffed islands / floating in delicate corals / under the sun. / In her eyes there was no clean branch / only shackles. [...] My mother had a headscarf and a song / to cradle a faith in my soul, / to raise her head high, unacknowledged queen / and leave us her hands, precious stones

The intertextual inscription perhaps hints at a need to differentiate between the experiences of black and mulatto women in the Caribbean and those in the United States, yet at the same time – possibly responding to Walker's book – the poem identifies with the possessive pronoun of its title, with womanism, and inscribes the black Cuban woman's experiences into the stories of other black women.

In a more recent collection *Baladas para un sueño* [Ballads for a Dream] (1989) 'Africa' is no longer the assimilable other within the construction of a collective and personal identity, but a contemporary political reality. Here the focus is on political solidarity and the figurative value of 'Africa' as a trope diminishes. Through various personae, the poet addresses the situation in South Africa and writes against apartheid, in support of the ANC. The private female voice is, again, muted. 'Baas' [Boss], asterisked

as 'Master', picks up the themes of 'I Love My Master' projected on to
a contemporary South African scenario:

> Eres el amo.
> Azares y un golpe seco de la historia
> te hicieron ser mi amo.
> Tienes la tierra toda
> y yo tengo la pena. (Morejón 1989: 7)

> You are the master. / Pure chance and the hard blow of history / made you my
> master. / You have all the land / I have the suffering.

Only the lines 'In the middle of the night / you rise like a beast on
heat. / Yours are my sweat and my hands' (Morejón 1989: 7), suggest
sexual exploitation which is here subsumed under racial and class oppression. Similarly, 'Cook' (p. 17), a third-person sketch of a black woman
(whose status is inferior to that of a pet animal), privileges a class and
ethnicity problematic over gender. Particularly interesting is 'Soliloquy of
a Colonist' (p. 9). Here the murderous, white, South African, male settler
who declares to an interlocutor named Peter,

> Acabo de degollar un ovambo.
> ¿Qué es un ovambo?
> Un negro,
> un animal rabioso,
> un monstruo con apenas dos patas
> y dos ojos immensos como de Lucifer

> I've just cut the throat of an ovambo. / What's an ovambo? / A black man, /
> a raging beast, / a two-legged monster / with two huge eyes, like Lucifer

is associated with a 'Mrs Woolf' and even tends her gardens: 'Mrs Woolf's
oleanders are so lovely. / I water them on Sundays when she goes shopping
to Pretoria'. The implications are clear; as far as black men in South
Africa are concerned, white feminism colludes with patriarchal colonialism
and propagates hegemonic power structures. These poems by Morejón,
then, indicate a perception of black, Cuban, female identity constructed
in terms of African and slave liberatory narrative, articulated within a
Marxist framework.

Georgina Herrera (b. 1936), unlike Morejón, does not hold an official
post but lives and works in Havana writing plays for the radio. Her first
book of poetry, *GH* (1962), was followed by *Gentes y cosas* [People and
Things] (1974). The poems discussed here are from two later collections,
Granos de sol y luna [Grains of Sun and Moon] (1978), dedicated to her
children, and *Grande es el tiempo* [Great is Time] (1989). Some translations
are available in Randall (1982), Finn (1988) and Busby (1992). Herrera was

married to the novelist Manolo Granados and one of her two children, Ignacio Teodoro, is himself a poet; her daughter, Anaisa, was tragically killed in a car accident. Such family details are important as Herrera's poetry centres on her role as mother. In this sense her poetry differs in emphasis from Morejón's. However, poems which foreground 'Africa' lend her work a wider historical, international and political dimension. 'Song of Love and Respect for Lady Ana de Souza' (Herrera 1978: 10–12) is a eulogistic address not to a Catholic saint or Mary herself as suggested by the first line, but to an historical figure, Queen Nzinga (or Yinga in the poem) of Angola (1582?–1663), who defied the Portuguese and, later, converted to Catholicism and changed her name to Ana de Souza (Martin 1980: 72):

> En fin, Señora Santa
> y reina de las riberas del río Kuanza;
> madre
> de los principios y la unidad [...]
>
> Al borde mismo de la incendiada tierra
> libre de Ngola vino usted al mundo.
> En medio de los gritos de la guerra,
> el primer grito suyo fue una señal [...]. (Herrera 1978: 10)

So then, Holy Lady, / Queen of the shores of the River Kwanza, / mother / of all oneness and origin, [...] // On the very edge of the burning land / of freedom called Ngola you came into the world. / In the midst of the cries of war / your first cry was a sign.

The poem presents a mythical rather than a historical figure, despite the dates, names and geographical references (historically Nzinga established her kingdom in the face of local resistance to women in politics, but then allied with Dutch slave-traders and pacted with the Portuguese admitting their slave caravans through her territories). The poem clearly privileges the politics of gender rather than class in the struggle against racial and colonial oppression. The double-named, double-voiced Ana de Souza/ Mother Yinga Mbandi is inscribed as a uniquely syncretic Amazon-like figure: African, Catholic, mother, saint, lady, warrior-queen and liberator. She fights a usurping (male) god and king and counters the culture of the written word with collective oral traditions and her physical female presence. She is perceived as the personification of universal resistance which eludes the patronymic and patrilineal:

> Usted, doña Ana,
> con ese nombre occidental, tomado
> por estrategia, usado

sólo en documentos.
Madre Yinga Mbandi para su pueblo.
Vencida a veces, nunca prisionera,
siempre emergiendo
entre los hombres, sin más armas,
que en los ojos,
prendido como llama furiosa, el deseo
de acorralar al enemigo, junto
al mar tremendo de donde vino. (p. 11)

You, Lady Ana, / with that western name, taken / by strategy, used / only in documents. / Mother Yinga Mbandi for your people. / Conquered at times, captive never, / always emerging / from among your men with no more arms / than desire burning / in your eyes like an angry flame, / the desire to round up the enemy / beside the tremendous sea from whence they came. [...]

Contemporary analogies point to Yinga as a symbolic precedent of black (Afro-European) women's resistance to a white (male, alien, exploitative) hegemony. Yinga is partly a historical figure (although hardly recognized as such in present-day Angola), and partly a projection of the poet's imaginary. Yet it is through the historically validated attributes Yinga represents that the poet articulates her own subjectivity:

Yinga,
señora, agua limpia donde quiero
verme reflejada.
En vasijas
de fina güira o calabaza [...].
Pero su tumba es todo el territorio de Angola,
sin más flores, ni lápidas ni señalamiento. (p. 11)

Yinga, / lady, clean water where I want / to see my face reflected. / In vessels / of finest calabash or gourd [...]. / But your grave is the vast land of Angola, / without flowers, or tombstones, or distinction.

What is interesting is that Herrera looks to Africa rather than Cuba for the legitimization of a revolutionary (syncretic) feminist heritage.

In her poetry, Herrera consistently unsettles the demarcations between private and public life. A good example is 'Our Respects, President Agostinho' (Herrera 1978: 48), a tribute to the erstwhile Angolan president and poet. From the first words of the poem global politics are linked to the subject's family, that is, the president (the present political reality) to the 'grandfather' (the collective mythical memory):

Según abuelo, Africa
era un país bonito y grande como el cielo,

desde el que a diario, hacia
el infierno occidental, venían
reyes encadenados, santos
oscuros, dioses tristes.
Usted viene de Africa.
No es santo, rey, ni Dios siquiera,
es simple, grandemente, un hombre bueno.
Un hombre al quien obligaron
a ganarse la paz de guerra en guerra,
'el esperado',
el que toca a la tumba de mi abuelo,
quien lo despierta, le habla
así, con su manera suave, irrevocable,
le explica de igual modo
en qué puntos estuvo equivocado.

According to grandpa, Africa / was a pretty land, as big as heaven, / and, every day, from there / to the hellish West went / kings in chains, dark saints / and saddened gods. / You, sir, come from Africa. / You are no saint, or king, or even god. / You're simply, in a great way, a good man. / A man whom they obliged to earn / his peace from war to war, / 'the long-awaited-one', / the one who touches grandpa's grave, / awakens him and speaks, just so, / in your irrevocable way, / explaining to him softly, / just where he'd got it wrong.

The grandfather's Manichaean vision of Africa and the West as a lost paradise and hell, and his idealization of the slaves as saints, kings and gods, is contrasted to the textual presence of a down-to-earth president. The twist comes in the inscription of the president as Messiah, a miracle-worker, waking the dead grandfather to reassert Africa as reality and not chimera. But in the poem this 'real' Africa is no less an effect of discursive practice and is as susceptible to mythic representations as the grandfather's version. The president thus incarnates the dead grandfather's desire, and the dichotomies set up in the poem, man/god, heaven/hell, war/peace, belonging to the rational order, dissolve as the key oppositions life/death and past/present fail to hold. An idealized past is incorporated into modern myth. Racial identity and political solidarity inform the poem, not gender differences. However, should the first-person narration be considered a female voice, her compassionate, maternalistic attitude towards her forefather suggests light parody of master narratives.

In 'Questions that Only She Can Answer' (Herrera 1978: 37–8) the mother cherishes her small daughter as a lucky charm, drawing an analogy between the child and a religious talisman, a necklace, a sacred amulet. The subject explores maternal feelings of love, wonder and fear through her physical contact with the charm (a metonymic figuration of Africa) and the child, her daughter. Both are physical and spiritual extensions of herself and indicate a mystery the subject can experience but not utter in words. Conversely, the female object of the poem (the daughter) is made potential subject; only she can answer the poet's questions:

Ojos de etíope, dime,
resuelve tú que puedes
este amasijo de ternura
en el que me debato.
¿Por qué te quiero hasta pisar los límites
del llanto?
¿Por qué la lástima
si te estiras derecho hacia la felicidad?
Suave pedazo de lirio y marisposa
hija
de estarme yo juntando, todas
las ganas de vivir, por vez primera [...]
¿Por qué no cruzo el mar
sino contigo, junto al pecho, como
un resguardo?
¿Por qué andas colgada de mi cuello
como un collar?
¿Por qué, si salto de la cama, sin besarte,
regreso con pavor, como si fueras
mi sagrado amuleto?

Ethiopian eyes, answer me, / resolve – you who can – / this perplexity, / this tangled up tenderness. / Why do I love you till I tread the edge of sorrow? / Why the pain / if you stretch out straight to joy? / My daughter, soft fragment of lily and butterfly, / if only I were gathering life's joys / for the first time [...] / Why will I never cross the sea / unless you're with me at my breast / like a lucky charm? / Why are you hanging from my neck / like a string of beads? / Why if I jump out of bed and forget to kiss you / do I return in fear, as if you were / my sacred amulet?

What is significant is that the mystical–maternal experience is written into discourse relating metonymically to Africa: to the sacred objects of African religions, the sea and, above all, 'Ethiopian eyes'. In this trope the daughter is represented through Africa, and Africa through the daughter, in terms of filial love (kinship). The subject thus constitutes her identity in terms of (female) ethnicity, maternity and nurturing, as she does in a later poem, 'Africa', to be discussed shortly.

In the 1989 collection, *Grande es el tiempo*, Herrera returns to women's history. 'Fermina Lucumí' (p. 17) is addressed to a female slave whose syncretic, generic name ('lucumí' is the term given to the Yoruba in Cuba) rescues her from patronymical anonymity. The date is significant. It refers to the slave revolts of November 1843 when some 400 slaves set fire to canefields near Matanzas. The rebellion was put down by Spanish soldiers and the daughters and mothers of the slaves were forced into prostitution. This revolt marked the start of a dreadful period of reprisals against slaves; some 5,000 slaves were killed by torture in 1843 and 1844, and over 100 were whipped to death during the infamous 'Ladder' conspiracy. But the slave rebellions continued until they were assimilated into the fight for independence after 1868 (FAR 1967: 124–8; and Thomas 1971: 204–5). In this poem, once again female slaves are positioned as subjects of their history, which is Cuba's struggle for freedom. The poet focuses on the slave woman's source of inner strength, perceiving her courage as a particularly feminine strategy, associated with love (leading to cunning and anger) and, above all, memory (leading to power):

> El cinco de noviembre
> de 1843, Fermina, cuando
> todos los bocabajos fueron pocos
> para tumbar su ánimo ...
> ¿Qué amor puso la astucia en su cerebro,
> la furia entre sus manos?
> ¿Qué recuerdo
> traído desde su tierra en que era libre
> como la luz y el trueno
> dio la fuerza a su brazo?
> Válida es la nostalgia que hace poderosa
> la mano de una mujer
> hasta decapitar a su enemigo. [...]
> Lástima
> que no exista una foto de sus ojos.
> Habrán brillado tanto. (Herrera 1989: 17)

On the fifth of November, / 1843, Fermina, when / the beatings were too few / to break your courage [...] / What love brought cunning to your mind, / brought fury to your hands? / What memory / from the land where you were free / gave strength to your arm / like a flash of thunder? / Rightful is the nostalgia which lends a woman's hand / power, even to behead her enemy. ...] / Such a pity / there's no photograph of your eyes. / They must have shone so brightly.

Nostalgia (for past freedom) is empowerment; the desire for the past is projected into the future and is at once remembered and anticipated. This way the disarticulated body of woman is re-membered (with brains, hands, arms) sufficiently strong to decapitate the symbolic order of colonial and patriarchal oppression. The force of memory produces metamorphosis; the woman becomes a bird flying ' through the green shafts of sugar cane' to freedom. Despite the historical framework, the slave woman is a subjective re-creation of the poet who presents her as the archetypal revolutionary black heroine around whom she would have wanted to shape her own identity. This writing of selfhood in history, the conflation of the personal and the public, inheres in the word-play of a short poem of the same collection entitled rather pompously 'Oral Portrait of Victory' (Herrera 1989: 22). The 'victory' is the poet's great-grandmother, Victoria, who incarnates women's triumph in the struggle for freedom:

> Qué bisabuela mía esa Victoria.
> Cimarroneándose y en bocabajos
> pasó la vida.
> Dicen
> que me parezco a ella.

> What a great grandmother she was, Victoria. / She spent her life / running away from slavery and in shackles. / They say / she was just like me.

Again, the link with the past and the sense of cultural heritage (female, black, revolutionary) informs the poet's discursive image or verbal reconstruction of her self.

In 'Africa' (Herrera 1989: 14–15), in my view the most moving poem here discussed, the poet's emotional response to 'Africa' becomes a process of self-exploration and self-affirmation. Her identity is both woman-centred and African-centred as she progressively inscribes herself in the object she addresses. The word 'Africa' again takes on sacred connotations signifying adoration and (self-)respect. At the start of the poem, 'Africa' is figured as a familiar god, a loved one, a child, who awakens feelings of protection and unshakeable loyalty and whom the poet cherishes with maternal care. Subject and object are clearly differentiated up to line 7:

> Cuando yo te mencione
> o siempre que seas nombrada en mi presencia
> será para elogiarte.
> Yo te cuido.
> Junto a ti permanezco, como el pie
> del más grande árbol.

> When I speak of you, / or whenever in my presence you are named / I shall praise you. / I'll take care of you. / I stand beside you like the foot / of the greatest tree.

From then on the poet is conscious of the self-perpetuating relationship between herself and 'Africa'; each is of the other's making:

Pienso,
en las aguas de tus ríos y quedan
mis ojos lavados.
Este rostro, hecho
de tus raíces, vuélvese
espejo para que en él te veas.
En mi muñeca
vas como pulsa de oro
– tanto brillas –; suenas
como escogidos cauríes para
que nadie olvide que estás viva.

I think about the water in your rivers / and my eyes are cleansed. / This face, made from / your roots, becomes / a mirror which reflects you. / I wear you on my wrist / like a golden bracelet – / you shine so! You rattle / like chosen cowries / and no one can forget you are alive.

'The dark continent' is recast in terms of purity and enlightenment, but the poet goes further; she *is* 'Africa'. Her face is a self-reflecting mirror in which 'Africa' (the poet) can see herself. Her body (face) represents the female body subsumed in the collective body politic. She carries 'Africa''s sights and sounds with her as ritual objects; 'Africa' constitutes her desire, maternal feelings and pleasure; it is the source of her spiritual life, her jouissance, her destiny:

Todo sitio al que me dirijo
a ti me lleva.
Mi sed, mis hijos,
la tibia oleada que el amor me arrastra
tienen que ver contigo.
Esta delicia de si el viento suena
o cae la lluvia
o me doblegan los relámpagos,
igual.

Each place I make for / takes me to you. / My thirst, my children, / the warm wave sweeping me to love / involves you. / Equally so / this pleasure when the wind howls / or the rain falls / or the lightning sways me.

The poem thus constitutes 'Africa' as a projection of the (black, female) self and the identity of the (black, Cuban) woman is mediated by an imaginary 'Africa':

Amo a esos dioses
con historias así, como las mías:
yendo y viniendo

de la guerra al amor o lo contrario.
Puedes
cerrar tranquila en el descanso
los ojos, tenderte
un rato en paz.
Te cuido.

I love the gods / whose stories are like mine, / coming and going from war to
love and back again. / You can close your eyes, rest quietly, / lie down a
while / peacefully. / I'll take care of you.

These poems of Georgina Herrera articulate a gyno-Afrocentric perspective through paradigms relating to kinship and history, to matrilineage
and woman-centred social formations. In them the boundaries between
personal, family, national and Third World identities constantly shift;
autobiography becomes a theoretical act, and 'family identity' a 'black
national script of empowerment' (Baker and Redmond 1989: 143).

To sum up, the poems by Morejón and Herrera discussed here celebrate
and affirm a black, Cuban, female identity; any potential conflict is
projected to another time or another place. They seem to stress the point
made by Pedro Pérez Sarduy: 'A reformation of nineteenth-century independence struggles as *not* the patrimony of the patricians but a popular
history of resistance [...] has obvious parallels for the 1950s insurrection
and beyond' (Pérez Sarduy 1990: 29). The same could be said of current
liberation movements in Africa. But these poems go further because they
inscribe resistance against sexual, racial and class exploitation from a
distinctively feminine, socialist, multiethnic perspective. At the same time,
the two poets write themselves into this mythical–historical process, which
informs their present-day identity. They create worlds with the poetic
power of imagination. Morejón tends to privilege a Marxist dialectic and
Herrera maternal bonding in an exploration of and identification with the
interrelated histories, myths and politics of Cuba and Africa. For both,
'Africa' is the key trope in their utopian project; it signifies black, Cuban
and feminine self-figuration.

The work of black and mulatto women writers is perhaps best placed
to break with dominant identities and cultural categories in Cuba. Their
poetry charts the crossing of the borders between Hispanic and African
Caribbean cultures and also queries established boundaries of racial and
sexual difference. Such poems can be read as a form of sexual politics
crossing racial, national and international borders. They are also a form
of textual memory or, in the case of the following poem, intertextual
memory. The second part of this chapter is a close reading of a fifteen-
page dramatic poem by Excilia Saldaña entitled 'The Bride's Monologue'.

Excilia Saldaña, born in 1946 in Havana, is the only child of a black,
middle-class family. She was brought up in her grandparents' home with

a submissive mother and a largely absent father. Her family disapproved of the 1959 Revolution. She left home in the early 1960s and has since published several books of stories and poems. Of all the women writers in post-revolutionary Cuba, Saldaña is possibly the one who has shown greatest interest in African Cuban culture. Her book *Kele kele* (1987) ('Softly, softly' in Lucumí) is a collection of short prose pieces modelled on the patakin or oral tales of Nigeria. She also refers widely to African Cuban traditions, particularly Santería ritual, in her children's stories and poetry. But Saldaña is not so interested in 'négritude' or black identity politics, nor would she call herself a feminist.[9] 'The Bride's Monologue' is an example of what Paul Gilroy calls a 'contact zone' (Gilroy 1993: 6) between local and global cultures. The poem voices a plurality of discourses across cultural and gender boundaries primarily through intertextuality. Briefly, the poem relates a bride/wife's coming to consciousness and her rebellion against the restrictive role as wife and daughter in a patriarchal society. It is a poem about the rebellion of black female subjectivity and the re-invention of a cultural space from a dissonant point of view.

Current debates on multicultural and intercultural expression focus on processes of identity formation, the deferred possibilities of identity, which once resolved into words become static, thus losing the sense of ambivalence prevalent in current understandings of hybridity. Borderline moments capture processes in the making. The term acculturation and other assimilationist 'melting pot' theories have largely been rejected on account of the hierarchies of privilege and appropriation they imply. The 'third space' (Bhabha 1994: 218) posits a way out of binarism. It is a space not of fusion or accumulation, but one in which often incommensurable differences are held together (Bhabha 1994: 219). Literary critics focus on such spaces or moments in the text in which multiple readings co-exist simultaneously. Traditionally referred to as poetics or figurative language (association, connotation, pastiche, irony, inference) this reading 'between the lines' (W. Benjamin 1979: 82) is the very stuff of literature. Referring to the visual arts, Jean Fisher suggests the 'chimera' as the rhetorical figure which encapsulates the constant shifting of meaning outside the scope of communicable language. 'The chimera [...] is neither one thing nor another but both simultaneously, and not reducible to either' (Fisher 1995: 7). The 'chimera' suggests to a literary critic the metaphor, or the metaphoricity of language, which – if extended to imply intercultural exchange – implies translation (the movement of meaning).[10] For Bhabha translation is 'the performative nature of cultural communication. It is language *in actu* [...] rather than language *in situ*' (Bhabha 1994: 228). A 'borderline work of culture' creates 'a sense of the new as a insurgent act of cultural translation' (Bhaba 1994: 3). Translation negotiates the disjunctions between cultures and, in the process, creates new possibilities of meaning.

Following through these ideas in relation to 'The Bride's Monologue',

I shall focus on the ways the text 'translates' previous texts and incorporates them into itself. According to Nikos Papastergiadis, in order to map 'the interruptive force of hybridity and [...] to witness the innovative potential of the foreign text [...] we will have to measure the degree to which the memory of the foreign code has been preserved and examine the impact resulting from the insertion of the foreign text' (Papastergiadis 1995: 16).

'The Bride's Monologue' (1985), published in the cultural review *Casa de las Américas* (no. 152: 86–100) and staged in Sweden, had formed part of a book of poetry entitled *Mi Nombre* [My Name]. This book consisted of five sections and was published in Mexico but it was shredded because of numerous typographical errors. Another section of the book, *Mi nombre. Antielegía familiar* [My Name. A Family Anti-Elegy], was published separately in Havana in 1991. The fact that Saldaña, like many Cuban authors, has been unable to publish because of the political and economic crisis in Cuba after 1990, is symptomatic of her marginalization in the global cultural economy and print capitalism in general. According to Saldaña, the shredded book was a rendering in poetry of key moments of her life-story. Like *Mi nombre. Antielegía familiar*, 'The Bride's Monologue' is a confessional psychobiography which ostensibly inscribes what some critics refer to as the double-consciousness of the Caribbean writer. The interplay of constantly deferred self-presentations makes the poem an example of a hybrid text which relates, in Homi Bhabha's words, 'the traumatic ambivalence of a personal psychic history to the wider disjunctions of a political existence' (Bhabha 1994: 10).

In the poem the Bride takes on the guise of a priestess: a Vestal Virgin-santera. Goddess and housewife, she keeps the sacred flame burning in the temple-kitchen (casa-templo). The 'casa-templo' [house-temple] is the Cuban version of the yoruba 'ille-ocha'. In Yoruban religion the worshipping of the orishas may take place in any shrine in the home. Also, kinship is extremely important in Santería ritual as is the 'rey' or king of each local organization or 'cabildo' [religious group] (Brandon 1993). From inside the private place, the home, the Bride summons up her powers and makes them felt. By creating a spell, a vortex of disorder, the speaker-witch conjures up images of the men in her life (lovers, husbands, her father) and wonders why she has failed with them all:

Los crespos de la noche cuelgan del cielo.
Se esparcen por los hombros de la casa las guedejas del silencio.
Yo las peino.
Suavemente yo las peino:
Soy la anónima alisadora de las ondas del sueño.
También soy una niña acúatica
trenzando y destrenzándome

la cabellera del recuerdo.
[...]
Las manos. Las manos. Las manos.
No hay agua suficiente para limpiar mis manos,
para desteñir el estigma de sangre
– de mi propia sangre –
tañendo para siempre mis manos.
[...]
Las manos. Las manos. Las manos.
¿No he de ver limpias estas manos?

Soy yo. La Esposa.
Todo el dolor del mundo vino a pedir mi mano:
'No soy la Novia', dije, 'sino la Esposa,
¿Puedes tu lavarme las manos?
¿Hay dolor suficiente para limpiar mis manos?'
[...]
Las manos. Las manos. Las manos.
¿Con qué detergente arrancar la costra de sange de mis manos?

(pp. 86, 88, 90)

The ringlets of the night hang from the sky. / Long tresses of silence spread across the shoulders of the house. / I comb them. Softly, I comb them: / I am the nameless one smoothing down the waves of dreams. / I am also a water child / binding and unbinding memory's long mane of hair. [...] / *These hands. These hands. These hands.* / *There is never enough water to clean my hands,* / *to unstain the damned spot of blood* / *–* of my own blood *–* / for ever touching my hands. [...] / *These hands. These hands. These hands.* / *What, will these hands ne'er be clean?* // I am the one. The Bride. / All the sorrow in the world came to ask for my hand. / 'I am not the Betrothed', I said, 'but the Bride. / Can you wash my hands? / Is there sorrow enough to wash my hands?' / [...] These hands. These hands. These hands. / With what detergent can I rip off the bloody scab from my hands?

She continually asks 'open questions' (p. 95) and she refuses to remain on the thresholds (p. 87). Her hands are covered in blood. But what is the crime and who is guilty? The Bride solves the enigma with her old rusty key, a syncretic key inherited from her female ancestors:

Pero yo soy la Esposa
y sólo tengo preguntas abiertas
y una llave de plomo
        que no abre, sino cierra.
Antigua llave sin brillo
        en el fulgor de esta llavera.
La usó mi abuela, y mi madre

y las abuelas de abuela
– la frágil carabalí
        de la tersa piel morena
y la adusta castellana,
        rosa fiel, flor marfileña –.
En la recámara de piedra y cristo
y en la choza de engorde y selva,
        la misma llave,
la misma, que no puede ya cerrar ninguna reja.
Mi vieja llave herrumbrosa (p. 96)

But I am the Bride / and I only have open questions / and a key made of
lead / which locks and does not open. / Ancient lustreless key / in the glow of
this key-keeper. / My grandmother used it and my mother / and the grandmothers of my grandmother / – the fragile Kalabari / with taut black skin /
and the stern woman from Castile, / faithful rose, ivory flower –. / In the
dressing-room with stone and Christ / in the hut with cattle and jungle, / the
same key / the same, that will not now close any gate. / My old rusted key […]

The key (to racial and gendered identity) reveals the mulatta's own hybrid
sexuality disavowed because of a past traumatic experience: she was
sexually abused by her father.[11] Discovering the repressed trauma and
responding to it enables the decentred subject to reconstruct a sexualized
self.

Contrary to expectations, the foreign texts in 'The Bride's Monologue'
are not African but belong to three literary canons pertaining to three
powerful imperial cultures: the Greek, the Spanish and the British. There
are numerous allusions to consecrated Hispanic authors such as Cervantes,
García Lorca, José Martí and Rubén Darío, to popular songs and tango
lyrics, to Sappho and Oscar Wilde. But the most significant texts underlying
Saldaña's palimpsest are two classical tragedies: Shakespeare's *Macbeth* and
Aeschylus's *Oresteia*. Particularly important are the two female protagonists,
Lady Macbeth and Clytemnestra. The poem is rich in embedded levels of
meaning which may or may not be set in motion by the hypothetical
reader, depending on the positionality of the reader and his or her
familiarity with other cultures/translations. Two questions arise: how do
these foreign texts interrupt 'The Bride's Monologue' and does the poem
affect readings of the canonized classics? I will concentrate on the first.

In the poem the much repeated refrain 'My hands. My hands. My
hands', 'Will I never see these hands clean?' (p. 89), the references to the
viper, and the line 'what man not born of woman' (p. 98) (cf. 'for none
of woman born / shall harm Macbeth' [*Macbeth* IV, i, 80]) point explicitly
to *Macbeth* and to Lady Macbeth's cry 'What, will these hands ne'er be
clean' (V, i, 35). Similarly, the references to the serpent and, more specifically, Saldaña's lines 'with no oxen on my tongue' (p. 91) (cf. 'an ox

stands huge upon my tongue' spoken by the watchman in *Agamemnon*) and 'I carpeted / the house to the bathroom' (p. 91) refer directly to the *Oresteia*, to Orestes' description of Clytemnestra as 'some water snake, some viper' who sets a trap with a 'bath curtain' (Aeschylus 1953: 129):

> me toqué
> con orquídeas y violetas
>   calcé
> berenjenas moradas,
>   alfombré
> la casa hasta la bañadera.

I wore / orchids and violets, / I put on my feet / purple aubergines, / I carpeted / the house to the bath chamber.

What, then, do Lady Macbeth and Clytemnestra share and how do they relate to the Cuban Bride? 'The Bride's Monologue' tells of a violent crime which has stained the Bride's hands with blood and involves feelings of guilt and retribution. The crime on the 'surface' level of the poem is, as previously mentioned, the father's rape of the daughter and this is heightened by allusions to the work of García Lorca where 'blood' (*Blood Wedding*) connotes kinship and death. The line 'I don't want to see it!' (p. 98), alluding to Lorca's *Lament for Ignacio Sánchez Mejías*, refers in 'The Bride's Monologue' ('I don't want to see it [la]!') simultaneously to the girl, the shame and the blood. For this reason the Bride needs to 'exorcize' (p. 98) the demonized father from her memory through ritual. The poem, then, voices the subject's attempts to free herself from the trauma caused by the violation of her body (hence the virgin's blood) and the violation of kinship taboos (the blood-line) by the father. The poem's scope is the domestic sphere (the family, the kitchen). The woman/housewife is a victim (of male violence), her guilt is self-directed, and the father is the victimizer. Does the poem inscribe, then, yet another example of the kind of 'universal [...] male dominance and female exploitation' which Chandra Mohanty (1988: 74) believes obsesses First World feminists?

Certain features of the poem suggest more complex subtexts. First, the Bride is not meek. She is a powerful, desiring subject invested with agency, a witch/priestess conjuring up supernatural forces to help rid her of the father-figure (note the scattered references to Santería ritual: ebbó (ceremony), omiero (sacred water or herbal bath), apetedbí (assistant to the priest). In a rewriting of Freud, the daughter must rid herself of the father. The intertextual, intercultural references – to *Macbeth* and the *Oresteia* – take the drama one step further. They indicate a second crime which is not made explicit on the 'surface' level of the poem. What Lady Macbeth and Clytemnestra have in common is that they kill the king, the father/king of the family/state, the husband (Clytemnestra) or the father look-alike (Lady Macbeth), the 'king' of the Santería 'cabildo'. These domestic tragedies, therefore, have a highly political subtext. The two women, queens in effect, are noble in status, cunning in statecraft and ambitious for power. They are not merely wives, or even regicides, but decisive power-brokers in the public sphere. In order to be this they must divest themselves of feminine sensitivity and assume 'male strength of heart' (Lattimore in Aeschylus 1953: 15). Their prime strategy is flattery and seduction: they lure their victims into their castle/homes and offer them feasts. They are assisted by supernatural, irrational female forces – the witches/'weird sisters' (in *Macbeth*) or the Furies (in *Oresteia*). In both cases the king is stabbed and his blood stains the women's hands, and both women are plagued by subsequent nightmares of guilt, 'torture of the mind' in the words of Lady Macbeth (Macbeth, III, ii, 21). All these heterogeneous motifs are embedded in the shifting temporal frames of 'The Bride's Monologue'. Of significance, too, is Clytemnestra's motive for slaying her husband, the king: he killed their daughter, Iphigenia, as a sacrifice to the gods in order to hasten the progress of the invading fleet. In Clytemnestra's words, 'he slaughtered like a victim his own child, my pain / grown into love' (Aeschylus 1953: 81). In 'The Bride's Monologue' the crime, then, is two-fold: violation (read killing) of the daughter is followed by parricide or, more precisely, regicide, and the effects of the crime extend well beyond the family. The poem is subversive inasmuch as it inscribes publicly two social taboos: incest and parricide. The political connotations of killing the king in a domestic Cuban context are, of course, suggestive but perhaps simplistic. This is because the target of retribution in the poem is not just the father-figure but all social categories of men and these, unlike the king, are explicitly associated with a Cuban domestic culture by means of localizing vocabulary.

The Bride, who refers to herself as the 'goddess of Dolores Avenue' (Saldaña 1985: 88) (Saldaña's home address is 'Avenida de Dolores') invites these men to her home; they knock at her door, she dresses as a priestess and lets them in, carpeting 'the house to the bath chamber' (p. 91) (just as Clytemnestra welcomed Agamemnon before she stabbed him in the bath). The suitors present her (in her kitchen-temple) with their distinctly Cuban promised offerings: pawpaw, two-star apple fruit, cowrie shells and gourds. Then, it seems, the Bride kills the men (or imagines she does) and lays them to rest on a clothes-line where they hang out 'in a democracy of wire and rope' (p. 90) until she takes them in to iron them:

No, los muertos no descansan en los cementerios.
Su lugar de reposo son las tendederas,
en la democracia del alambre y la soga
– donde conviven el paño lujoso y el jirón maltrecho. [...]
¡Qué acto de amor incomparable es plancharlos luego!

Almidonados y lisos
– colgados
    por orden de colores
en los pecheros –
listos están siempre en mi armario, para usarlos [...]

> No, the dead do not rest in cemeteries. / Their place of rest is on clothes-
> lines, / in a democracy of wire and rope / – where luxurious cloth hangs out
> with worn rags. [...] / What an act of uncomparable love it is to iron them
> later! / Starched and uncreased / – hanging / in order of colour / on the coat
> hangers – / they are in my cupboard, ready to use [...]

The figures, hierarchically arranged according to colour, represent the many
facets of masculinity in a national, multiethnic context. The poem, then,
is a feminist text, an indictment of patriarchy at the level of the home
and the state, in which a female subject fights back, but then feels guilty.

    The tension in this love–hate relationship is communicated through
one word, 'hypsipyle', which also denotes a postcolonial dimension. The
Bride's suitors pin 'hipsipilas' (p. 91) on her dress; this word is taken from
a famous poem, 'Sonatina', by Rubén Darío, founder of South American
'modernismo'. In Darío's line 'Oh to be a hypsipyle which has left the
chrysalis' the neologism 'hypsipyle' suggests an insect in a chrysalis half-
formed between the larva and the imago, and, in 'Sonatina', the final,
perfect stage of the creature (princess/insect) freeing herself/itself from
the confines of the castle/chrysalis (Darío 1987: 98). This confirms a
feminist reading. But 'The Bride's Monologue' refers also to the original
proper noun or name – Hypsipyle – who, in Greek mythology, saved her
father (the king's son) from the women of Lemnos who wanted to kill all
the men on the island. An ambiguity is set up between the suitors who
want the Bride to save the father (in a Greek reading) and the Bride who
wants to kill off the father (in a Latin American reading). 'The Bride's
Monologue', then, is about killing the father on both a local and interstatal
scale (in *Macbeth* Scotland and England; in the *Oresteia* Argos and Troy)
and at a postcolonial level. Furthermore, the King of Scotland and
the King of Argos represent not only the patriarch but also the Imperial
King and the White King who in Saldaña's poem, reading between the
lines, is killed off by the black, female, subaltern subject. Tentative intertextual connections can thus be made between a feminist and a postcolonial
agenda. An obvious subtext in this respect is the section which reads,

Todo mujer ama lo que mata.
Ay,
mis muertos,
la pobre mulatica bizca,
    centro de le burla del colegio,

que quiso ser *princesa* de un exótico reino
que custodian cien blancos con sus cien alabardas,
un sijú que no duerme y un otá colosal
es ahora la reina viuda [...] (p. 92)

Yet each woman loves the thing she kills. / Ah, my dead ones, / the poor little
cross-eyed mulatto girl, / target of laughter at school, / who wanted to be the
princess of an exotic kingdom / guarded by a hundred *white* men with their
hundred halberds, / an *owl* that never sleeps and a colossal *sacred stone*, / is now
a widow-queen [...] (emphasis added)

which is almost word for word a copy of two famous lines from Rubén
Darío's poem 'Sonatina'. In 'Sonatina' the fair-haired, blue-eyed princess
is 'guarded by a hundred black men with their hundred halberds / a
hound that never sleeps and a colossal dragon' (Darío 1987: 98).[12] In
Saldaña's poem Darío's fairy-tale princess has been replaced by the cross-
eyed mulatta who is guarded (and served) not by black men but by white
men, and not by a (European) hound and dragon but an indigenous
Cuban 'sijú' (owl) and a African Cuban 'otá' (sacred stone). This marked
reversal of Western aesthetic paradigms and the insertion of a black Cuban
identity into a canonical poem which epitomizes Spanish American
'modernismo' (the cultural movement which emulated the conquest culture
of the Western cosmopolitan elites) is undermined by the black, female,
subject who refuses to be sub-altern, under another. In 'The Bride's
Monologue' the Freudian 'dark continent' finally rids herself of the colonial
master and the mysogynistic texts of the West are retold by what Sara
Sulieri refers to as the 'female racial' voice (Sulieri 1994: 246).

In the next chapter I shall briefly discuss the ways in which Saldaña
reclaims the repressed, female hybrid body in her autobiographical poem
Mi nombre. Antielegía familiar (1991) where she inscribes the transformation
of the rejected black female body in terms of black revolutionary history.
Unlike Morejón and Herrera, Saldaña does not look to an imaginary or
real Africa for tropes of self-reconstruction. In 'The Bride's Monologue'
she constructs an imaginary domestic space from which she is able to
reappropriate and reverse colonial paradigms for her feminist agenda, and
in *Mi nombre* she queries the psychic dismemberment of the mulatto
woman resulting from these unresolved tensions at home.

Notes

1. Moore later qualified this view. His version of events has been seriously
questioned. See Pérez Sarduy (1990: 29): 'We Cubans, especially black Cubans, who
defend the revolution, at home and abroad, know full well who we are and why we
do so. [...] As Cuba enters the 1990s, affirmative action programs in place for
blacks, women and religious believers [...] have to be seen as indicative of new

social and political forces in an ongoing struggle.' For a thorough examination of African Cuban culture and racism in Cuba before the Revolution, see Castellanos and Castellanos (1990).

2. This view was put forward in several conversations with young black Cuban poets: Victor Fowler, Soleida Ríos and Ignacio Granados in Havana, 1992.

3. For a different viewpoint see Martínez Echázabal (1990).

4. I would like to thank Evelyn O'Callaghan for allowing me to read her paper. For the Peter Hulme/Edward Kamau Brathwaite polemic, see *Wasafari*, Vol. 20, 1994: 5–11 and *Wasafari*, Vol. 22, 1995: 69–78.

5. See LeoGrande (1980); Levine (1983); and Moore (1988). Castro has, of course, visited South Africa since 1994 (see Mandela and Castro 1991).

6. In 1987 two important African monarchs visited Cuba, the Asantehene (Ghana) and the Ooni of Ife, sacred capital of the Yoruba (Nigeria). See Pérez Sarduy and Stubbs (1993: 10).

7. Comments to the author in 1990.

8. Conversation with the author in Havana, September 1992.

9. Conversation with the author in Havana, September 1992.

10. Etymologically 'translate' means 'to bear/across' (Latin), to 'trans/fer'. Similarly, 'metaphor' means 'to transfer a word from its literal signification' and derives from the Greek for 'trans/fer', 'meta' (change)/'phor' (fer/to bear).

11. Conversation with the author in Havana, September 1992.

12. 'Pobrecita princesa de los ojos azules / Está presa en sus oros, está presa en sus tules, / en la jaula de mármol del palacio real, / el palacio soberbio que vigilan los guardas, / que custodian cien negros con sus cien alabardas, / un lebrel que no duerme y un dragón colosal.'

CHAPTER 8

The Mother and Female Desire: Poetry in the 1980s and Early 1990s

The figure of the mother admits ambivalent interpretations. As a symbol of biological determinism and woman's traditional role in society it is associated with gender conservatism, anti-feminism and right-wing politics. Note, for example, the words of Auguste Comte:

> It is in order to better develop her moral superiority that woman must gratefully accept the rightful practical domination of man [...] First, as a mother, and later as a sister, then above all as a wife, finally as a daughter, and possibly as a maid-servant, in these four natural roles woman is destined to preserve man from the corruption inherent in his practical and theoretical existence.[1]

For radical feminists the mother represents nurturance, women's moral superiority, and resistance to androcentric values and patriarchal social structures. As we have seen in this study, the mother-figure in Cuba has been inscribed in female-authored texts as a symbol of both moderate reform and radical change throughout the twentieth century. K. L. Stoner explains how almost all the feminists of first-wave feminism revered motherhood and thus pursued sexual difference politics rather than equality politics. Motherhood was a divine right which justifies women's political participation (Stoner 1991: 2, 10). For the socialist and Marxist feminist writers of the 1920s motherhood was sacred. Ofelia Rodríguez Acosta wrote in 1932, 'giving birth is [...] the proof of women's biological capacity to construct' (1933: 21) and Mariblanca Sabás Alomá in 1930, 'women create men and make them like they want them' (Sabás Alomá 1930: 35). The mother represented family unity, probity, abnegation and virtue. Motherhood as myth or, in María Corominas's words, 'sublime role' (González Curquejo 1919: 144), stood for the nation's progress. As Pedro García Valdés explained in 1952: 'The history of the Homeland is that sacred treasure chest in which the secrets and memories of the Cuban family are kept' (García Valdés 1952: 6). After the Revolution this symbolical value of the mother persisted:[2] 'veneration of motherhood is a cornerstone of national culture' (Smith and Padula 1996: 122).

The idealization of motherhood *qua* national icon in conservative and progressive Cuban cultural politics invalidates to some degree the debate between feminist proponents of a politics of identity and those who propose a politics of equality. I refer to 'identity politics' in the context of feminist discourse as a politics of autonomy[3] and self-determination predicated on notions of female sameness, be that sameness essential, attributed or performative. Feminist theory has also coined the terms difference politics or special value. The special differences are perceived to be particularly 'womanist' attributes (nurturing, motherhood and sisterhood) which differentiate women from men. 'Politics of equality' here refers to the ideal of universal (rather than sectional) emancipation associated with Enlightenment thought. By exploring the equality/difference divide, related to the often acrimonious debates between essentialists and constructionists, psychological and political feminists, radical and socialist feminists, as inscribed in Cuban women's writing, I hope to suggest that such dichotomies, if they are considered mutually exclusive, are not entirely appropriate in this context. In Cuban women's writing, a textual negotiation takes place between the two positions, suggesting another discursive space which possibly indicates new theoretical and political directions for feminism. As Nancy Soporta Sternbach states: 'Just as North American or European feminism once provided crucial insights for the second wave of feminism in Latin America, perhaps now Latin American feminisms can enrich and inspire our own movements' (Soporta Sternbach et al. 1992: 434).

Drawing on the work of Chantal Mouffe, Spanish feminist philosopher Celia Amorós questions the premises of difference politics despite the fact that she is a self-declared difference feminist who affirms positive feminine values which are, in her view, necessarily 'antipatriarchal' (Amorós 1991: 311). With reference to the idea that the women's movement has nothing to learn from other liberation movements or discourses, Amorós states 'it is at this precise point that I would vindicate the refreshing shade of the Marxist tree and I suggest we should lean on its venerable branches' (p. 312). Feminists should remember Marx's words: it is not consciousness that determines social being but social being that determines consciousness (from Marx's 'Preface' to the *Critique of Political Economy*). Difference feminism, she writes, is in danger of becoming 'mystification' (p. 312): feminism is an ethics and it should take into account 'all other forms of exploitation and alienation' (p. 328). Many difference feminists who uphold special feminine values recognize the need for an effective political model to bring about change. Grassroots organizations, associated with radical feminism, are often advocated by former members of communist parties. It would seem that, at least in Spanish and Latin American cultures, identity politics must be inflected by equality politics to be taken seriously. Similarly, the cultural transposition of the sex/gender system and the essentialist/constructionist distinction is problematical. As Teresa de Lauretis (1989:

4–5) pointed out some years ago in her study of the construction of gender as 'both the product and the process of its representation', Romance languages do not have a term which corresponds to the English word 'gender'. Moreover, the grammatical genders (masculine and feminine) do not always designate animals and people of the male and female sex. In Spanish America gender is not immediately perceived as constructed but as natural. Picking up on these points, Amy Kaminsky makes a case for a radical materialist feminism and oppositional politics. She warns against traditional scholarship which 'simply imposes the analytical categories central to its own intellectual enterprise when they have no counterpart in the field of study' (Kaminsky 1993: 3). In Latin America there is a 'cultural resistance' to constructionism, to the notion of constructed difference between men and women, because the word 'sexo' collapses gender and sex and essentializes both (p. 7). In Kaminsky's view, if it is to survive, Latin American feminism must be both 'politically progressive and locally motivated', but it need not be bound to the European Enlightenment (including Marxist philosophy) if the term feminism indicates a recognition by women of all times and places of their own oppression and their strategies for change (p. 21).

Mexican feminist Francesca Gargallo claims that all Latin American women are marginalized by poverty but also by 'the elitism of the minuscule groups of female intellectuals in the Women's Movement who have absolutely no political influence' (Falcón 1992: 491). Indeed, the tensions mapped by Soporta Sternbach in her survey of the Latin American feminist biennial 'Encounters', held from 1981 to 1990, show that the early Latin American feminist groups (white, middle-class and university-educated) were very much divided between 'activists' of 'double militancy' persuasion on the one hand and independent 'feminists' on the other (Soporta Sternbach et al. 1992: 407). However, the 1987 meeting in Taxco was attended by 1,500 women from all over South America, many were poor, many did not accept the feminist label, and for the first time representatives came from Cuba. Current tensions in Latin America are not between difference and socialist feminists but between the (educated, middle-class) veteran 'feminists' and the broad-based, multiracial, politically organized, all-women's, 'women's movement' (Soporta Sternbach et al. 1992: 414). Latin American feminism, a social movement (p. 394) (not a political organization) emerged through clandestine class resistance to the military regimes of the 1970s. Soporta Sternbach believes Latin American feminism is unique in its praxis and organization of women: 'Latin American feminists [...] not only challenged patriarchy [...] but also joined forces with other opposition currents in denouncing social [...] and political oppression' (p. 397). They broke with the Left as far as organization is concerned due to sexist practice, but remained Left politically and ideologically. In a supposedly 'postfeminist' era, Latin American feminisms are 'clearly a powerful, vibrant, energetic, creative, and exuberant political force' (p. 432). European and North American feminism can learn from Latin America by mobilizing its own grassroots women's movements using the strategies of both radical and socialist feminism.[4]

Difference feminism has been suspect in Latin America because of the emphasis placed on the family and women's role as mother by authoritarian regimes. This was not the case in pre-revolutionary Cuba, as we have seen, where the mother symbolized moral superiority and national independence. In post-revolutionary Cuba the situation is further complicated because feminism is understood as radical feminism and is associated with bourgeois ideology and cultural imperialism. Since 1959 a complex socialist–Latin American–Caribbean cultural space exists resulting in the deliberate blurring of differences (of race, class and gender). Cuba is not a pluralistic political system where opposing interest groups compete for achievement and status; the values promoted are egalitarian and collectivistic. In this matrix there is no place for identity politics or difference feminism. But, as we have intimated, Cuba is no socialist feminist panacea. Until the mid-1970s Marxist strategies for women's liberation (following Engels's *The Origin of the Family, Private Property and the State*): the incorporation of women into the labour force, the abolition of the family as an economic unit, and the socialization of domestic work (with, for example, nurseries), were adhered to. The position of women in Cuba was improved by legislation aimed at removing class, racial and gender inequalities. In 1960 the Federation of Cuban Women, broad-based, politically organized and multiracial, was founded to promote 'mobilization-based participatory politics' (Azicri 1984: 271). Women were men's equals, not their opponents; the movement was 'feminine not feminist'. But, as we have seen, the FMC made few inroads into traditional Hispanic 'machismo'. The most significant step in this direction was the Family Code of 1975, passed on International Women's Day in International Women's Year, which aimed to enforce shared parenting and domestic work by law. It marked an important shift in policy from the social to the individual, from the public to the private, but 'men resisted' (Harris 1992: 185).

During the late 1980s (the period of rectification), it was recognized that Marxism had to be refocused to encompass feminism. Fidel Castro declared in the Third Party Congress, 1986, that efforts to correct 'historical injustices' such as racial and gender inequalities had been inadequate (Harris 1992: 186). It is clear, then, that neither under individualistic, liberal capitalism nor collective socialism were Cuban women able to live outside patriarchal formations and a masculine economy.[5] Neither social system questioned heterosexuality as the norm, nor the nuclear family as the basis of social organization. Without consciousness-raising, gender relationships were not revolutionized. The family unit is still the building block, a central institution, of the socialist polity and although 'open' and socialist, it is, in the words of one commentator, as conservative as it is revolutionary.[6] In Cuba the collective (sectorial) experience of women was assimilated into the wider collective experience of the developing nation. Despite the redrawing of the map of social relationships *vis-à-vis* class, gender and race (but not sexuality), feminine subjectivity is still largely hidden and unspoken. This has partly to do with the idealization of motherhood which results in 'woman's desexualization and lack of agency' and the preservation of a gender system in which 'man expresses desire and woman is the object of it' (J. Benjamin 1990: 86). The tensions in Cuba, then, are not so much between radical and socialist feminisms, or grassroots movements and elitist feminist top-down organizations; the tensions are between a collective, patriarchal, national ideology on the one hand and women's personal experiences, desires and feminine subjectivity on the other. Little space has been given to matters private or psychological, much less to the sexed female body outside the reproductive role. Unfortunately, in Cuba – as elsewhere – a politics of equality has not resulted in a new order, what Campioni and Grosz refer to as 'a completely different perspective on problems of truth, reason, reality, and knowledge' (Gunew 1991: 392). The anxieties, desires, and fantasies associated with female sexuality and woman's selfhood are articulated outside masculinist, hegemonic discourse in one of the few autonomous spaces remaining for women, creative writing.

The marked shift in post-revolutionary women's writing (in poetry especially) from a thematics linked to the collective enterprise and national identity towards the inscription of the self and personal identity occurred in the mid-1980s. Part of the writers' strategy, as we shall see, involved a demystification and even derogation of the idealized mother-figure (see Chapter 2), be it the subject's mother or the subject as mother. This was necessary (from a psychological point of view) because, as Jessica Benjamin explains: 'the child can only perceive the mother as a subject in her own right if the mother *is* one [...] the mother's subjectivity (in contrast to the maternal ideal) must include imperfection to be real [...] real subjectivity does not require her to be self-sufficient, perfect, omni-competent' (J. Benjamin 1990: 214). Possibly the most important new direction taken by these writers was to focus on female sexual desire in erotic poetry and thus counter the 'de-eroticization' of women in the prevailing socialist gender system (p. 92). Female-authored erotic literature, which had flourished in the Republic (and even earlier), clashed with the revolutionary idea of woman as responsible mother and self-sacrificing worker. In part, this was a puritanical response to what was perceived as the profligacy and moral corruption of the previous decades and as such had at least countered the sexual objectification of the female mulatto. Could the mulatto woman writer now afford to re-eroticize the hybrid female body on her own terms? In an ascetic climate, female-authored erotic poetry might be considered potentially subversive; the eroticized mother was perhaps the most subversive image of all.

In what follows I shall first discuss representations of the mother and the home in the work of older and younger women poets. I shall then look at erotic poetry written by women, primarily in the last decade. All these poets supported revolutionary equality politics – though not uncritically – and at the same time inscribed difference in their work. By focusing on their personal lives and sexual relationships above all, these poems articulate female specificity in such a way as to subvert and yet also to affirm the socialist feminist discourse the poets publicly espouse.

The dynamics of twentieth-century family life in Cuba are complex and are indicative of the ambivalent relationship between the public and private spheres. The home functions as both affirmation of and resistance to dominant discourses, possibly in response to shifts in generational attitudes. This blurring of binary divisions, the process whereby 'the private and public, past and present, the psyche and the social develop an intersticial intimacy' is referred to by Homi Bhaba as the 'unhomely moment' (Bhaba 1994: 13). As I suggested in an earlier study (Davics 1996), which focused on the individual responses of Cuban women poets (particularly Excilia Saldaña) to the 'unhomely moment', the work of several poets evinced a noticeable disavowal of house and home. This seemed surprising in view of the interest in promoting family organization in socialist Cuba. Many poems which reconstruct childhood memories recriminated mothers and fathers, although not grandparents. This perspective was more manifest in the poetry of some first-generation post-revolutionary black and mulatto women born in the 1930s and 1940s (Georgina Herrera, Soleida Ríos, Excilia Saldaña) whose disavowal of the parents and the home might well be read as a rejection of pre-revolutionary capitalist society, although the continuation of the trend in the work of younger poets born in the 1960s suggests this interpretation may be too simplistic. Before looking at this poetry in detail a brief consideration of the work of an older generation of poets, poets who were born in the 1920s and have continued to publish in Cuba until today, is enlightening.

As is to be expected, these older poets are educated women belonging predominantly to the white (rural and urban) middle classes. Notwithstanding the ambivalent attitude towards the mother noted in the work of Dulce María Loynaz, their recollections of childhood homes and families are imbued with harmony, light and love, which – given that the lifestyle they enjoyed has probably disappeared – might hint at contemporary alienation.[7] Cleva Solís (1926–97) writes in 'Loved Ones' (1974) in a book dedicated to her mother,

El sol de la familia
era todo,

era lo que venía siempre,
lo que estaba allí
y no se iba [...]
La Madre iba
serena y apacible
en su gala de amorosa veste (*Los sabios días* [Days of Wisdom], 1984: 32)

The sunshine of the family / was everything / she used to always turn up / she used to always be there / she never left us [...] / The Mother was / peaceful and serene / dressed up in her costume of love [...]

In a sonnet 'My Mother' (*Sonetos* 1990), Carilda Oliver Labra (b. 1924) also describes her mother in images of light and nurturance:

Mi madre es esa niña sin padre y sin muñeca
que nos hizo la carne y el alma del verano.
Usa vestidos serios y ya no toca el piano,
pero aquí en esta casa ha sembrado una areca. [...]
Mi madre es esa única criatura diferente
que para darme un beso, raro y resplandeciente,
me ha zurcido la herida que llaman corazón (Oliver Labra 1990: 50)

My mother is the girl without a doll or a father / who cooked us meat and gave us the summer's soul. / She wears formal clothes and no longer plays the piano, / but here in this house she sowed a butterfly palm. [...] / My mother is a singular creature, without compare, / who, to give me a kiss, resplendent and rare, / has darned up my wound that some would call heart.

As mentioned in Chapter 4, it is in the poetry of Fina García Marruz (b. 1923) that the inscription of the childhood home as a lost paradise affectionately reconstructed through material objects and spaces is most strongly sustained. As in Cleva Solís's poetry, here the mother is associated with light, music, openings, comings and goings, and the dawn. In 'Good Morning' (*Visitaciones*, 1970) she prepares milk and bread for breakfast and opens the balcony shutters to let in a stream of light:

Ya mamá se ha levantado.
Ya coge la leche y el periódico.
Ya tuesta los panecitos.
Ha abierto el balcón
y cae una franja de luz
sobre las losas de colores
de la sala: un polvillo
de luz bailando en lo oscuro
aún, atraviesa las puertas
del cuarto. Se oye
la llave del agua. (García Marruz 1970: 111)

Mama has risen early. / She takes in the paper and milk. / She's already toasting the rolls. / She has opened the balcony doors / and a shaft of light bursts in / on the colourful tiles / in the parlour: a dust of light / still dancing in the dark / crosses the doors / of the room. You can hear / the tap running.

The mother's protection is represented by her 'wide soft bed' (García Marruz 1970: 333) and in 'Dreamy Music' by her hands (p. 265). Images of the elusive mother are built up through repeated and detailed listings of parts of her body, attributes and domestic objects but her face is never mentioned. She is, after all, no more than the 'dreamy music'. In 'Aimable fille du printemps' (1962), a moving poem lamenting the death of 'my little mother', the sick mother is carried away out of the house, 'you were waving your hand clumsily, your failing hand, your hand / that was really waving goodbye' (p. 264). The perspective in these poems is that of the loving daughter watching intently the somewhat distant and cherished mother she addresses in the confines of the home. The mother comes and goes while the subject stays inside. But the house itself is strangely intangible, consisting of bright, unbounded interior spaces, thresholds and other intermediate areas. The housetop terrace in 'Small Songs' is one such space 'which is still home / and begins to be the place / of another encounter' (p. 338). In such lucid poetry there is little sense of a distraught Caribbean double consciousness. What is important is the fluidity of ego-boundaries articulated as retrospective projections of house and family suggesting the appropriateness of Eurocentric models of motherhood in literary analysis. Despite allusions to spectral figures there is no dark uncanny, no sense of threat. As discussed in Chapter 4, the poem 'Spanish', a homily to the Spanish language, underlines this point. Here explicit connections are made between the home, mother, mother country and mother-tongue reclaimed and appropriated by the poet in the process of identity formation. The Spanish language surrounds her like an amniotic fluid, filling her with jouissance as she recovers the mother tongue, the source of her strength:

poesía: criandera de mi infancia.
Oigo tu canturreo
entre azulejos blancos de cocina
soleadas, en el verdor que tiembla
en la luz: sol y calor primeros. (p. 378)

poetry: nursemaid of my infancy. / I hear you humming a song / between the white, sunlit / kitchen tiles, in the trembling green / of light: my first ever sun and warmth.

It could be argued that the lack of contention in Fina García Marruz's poetry is because she is white. This may be so, but it is interesting to note neither is there tension in the work of the mulatto poet Rafaela Chacón

Nardi (b. 1926). In the poem 'Serenade of Snow' (*Coral del aire* [Air Chorus], 1982) Chacón Nardi addresses her mother in terms similar to those noted above. Her mother represents light, the dawn, and music:

Madre, si mi vida fuera
sombra de tu sombra fiel,
de tu sueño mirabel
abierto a la luz primera;
si la firme primavera
que aún asoma tu morada
y la música callada
que fluye siempre de ti
pudiera quedar en mí
como nieve serenada; [...]
Manos tuyas, madre mía,
celestes madrugadoras,
manos para abrir auroras
o pulir la luz del día. [...] (Chacón Nardi 1982: 78–9)

Mother, if this life of mine / was shadow of your shadow true, / bellflower of your sleeping dreams / open to the morning blue; / if the constant spring-time / still shining in your home / and the silent music / that through you ever flows / could stay a while in me / a serenade of snow; [...] / Mother, your hands are / celestial early rising / hands for opening new dawns / and polishing daylight. [...]

Like the mother in García Marruz's poems, in Chacón Nardi's work too the mother's voice, 'softly / moderato cantabile' (*Del silencio y las voces* 1978: 30), is identified with European music. The significant factor seems not to be ethnic origins but middle-class family structures. A discrepancy does appear, however. In another poem ('Of Dew and Smoke') Chacón Nardi identifies the mother with the songs of her native Martinique:

con tu olor a café nuevo,
con tus buenos-días-hija-
despiértate-que-ya-es-hora [...]

Mar
Martina
Martinica
suaves raíces,
sal pura,
ligerísima caña.

Agua ceñidora,
madre,

hidromiel, isla y guitarra,
bella razón de mi sangre,
alba remota. (Chacón Nardi 1982: 133, 135).

your smell of fresh coffee, / your-good-morning-daughter / wake-up-it's-getting-
late [...] // Marine / Martine / Martinique / soft roots, / pure salt, / lightest
sugar cane. // Wrap-around water, / mother, / honey mead, island and guitar, /
my blood's perfect reason for living, / remotest dawn.

Whereas for García Marruz the mother (tongue) signifies the metropolis,
Chacón Nardi in 'About Silence and Voices' (*Del silencio y las voces* [Of
Silent Voices] 1978) tentatively associates the voice of her grandmother
with Africa: 'She speaks to me / – in her native tongue – / of fishing
nets and sun, / volcanoes / the jungle at dawn' (Chacón Nardi 1978: 30–
31). This is the only reference to a Caribbean African heritage in her two
recent collections of poetry. In the work of all four poets mentioned here
(Solís, Oliver Labra, García Marruz and Chacón Nardi), portraits of the
mother and home are complemented by rarer but equally positive representations of the father and other members of the family.[8]

This nostalgic reconstruction of a childhood paradise in the work of
older poets can be usefully compared with the less idealized representations
of the mother and the family by younger poets, born in the decade before
and after the Revolution. This group of poets includes black and mulatto
poets raised in poverty and publishing for the first time after 1959. More
surprisingly, younger poets born in the 1950s and 1960s, that is, who grew
up in socialist Cuba, also renege on the mother and the family.

Lina de Feria (b. 1947), in her prize-winning and aptly entitled collection
Casa que no existía [House that Never Existed] (1967), was one of the first
(white) poets to debunk the myth of the protective home:

alquilamos la casa desconociendo que era
una sucursal del infierno en la calle reina
donde no habitaban cosas como la amabilidad
el favor grandioso
o las reales visiones de la gente [...]
desconociendo que el lugar sería
el sabio aniquilador de la inocencia. (de Feria 1967: 12)

We rented the house without knowing / it was a subsidiary of hell in queen
street / where nothing like friendliness stayed / or generous favours / or the
splendid visions of people [...] / not knowing the place would be / the wise
destroyer of innocence.

In a later collection (*A mansalva de los años* [Protected from the Years],
1990) dedicated to her mother and son, she describes the home as a
continually weeping blister, 'home hardly sweet like a blister from a burn /

that always burst when it was time to get dressed and start walking '(de
Feria 1990: 38) and the mother thus:

> si mi madre llegara hasta mí
> – la racha buena el bien de pronto –
> echará en cara que amasó poco tiempo mi vida
> y sentiré tan verdadero lo que dice
> que tendré que inmolar en su honor
> el defecto de mi ternura
> tan escondida en la sobrevivencia
> en la ráfaga del tiempo
> que parece imposible de salir a flote. (p. 61)

if my mother ever reached me / – good times, sudden fortune – / she will
accuse me of a half-baked life / and I will feel her words so true / I'll have to
sacrifice in her honour / my defect, tenderness, / hidden so deep to survive /
the gusts of time / impossible, it seems, to ever float out safely.

'Mami', written by Georgina Herrera (b. 1936), is also a poem addressed
to her mother:

> ¿Cómo pudo existir tan grande espacio
> entre las dos? ¿Cómo
> vivimos tantos años, sin que nada
> fuese a ambas común?
> Ahora
> es que puedo entender. Y te agradezco
> el desamor, la angustia,
> el desamparo. Y
> la total ausencia de esa sustancia
> elemental que me hace
> vivir sin nadie, en medio
> de mil manos, deseando
> una mano que impida
> mi perenne caída inevitable (Herrera 1989: 36)

How could a void so great exist / between us? How could / we live together
so many years, / with nothing in common? / Now / I can understand. And I
thank you / for the unlove, the anguish, / the neglect. And / for the total lack
of that elementary / substance that makes me / live alone, among / a thousand
hands, wanting / just one hand to stop / my everlasting, inevitable fall.

Here the mother is inscribed as lack. The mother's hand, which indicates
her presence in the work of the above poets, merely confirms her absence
in Herrera's poem. The lack of mother-love leads to a fearful anxiety,
inscribed in other poems. In 'Family Scene' the mother deliberately creates

fear in her children and a peaceful family scene turns to horror. The man of the house is drinking in the bar with other men discussing politics and work. The mother remains at home with her children. But rather than provide protection, she tells them ghost stories that fill them with dread:

En casa quedan la mujer
y los chiquillos, alrededor
de la lámpara de luz brillante.
Ella hace uso de su soledad.
Cuenta
historias de aparecidos, de cantos de lechuza
siempre anunciando lo que no se quiere. [...]
Despavoridos, vamos
a dormir.
Y así, las noches y los sueños
se nos fueron poblando
de sensaciones que, aún a veces, siguen
al acecho del momento propicio
para impedirnos la felicidad. (Herrera 1989: 56)

The wife stays at home / with the little ones, round / the lamp shining brightly. / She uses her loneliness well. / She tells them / ghost stories, hooting owls / always foretelling what we don't want to know. [...] / Frightened, we all / go to bed. / And so our nights and our dreams / were filled with / feelings that still sometimes now / are ready to pounce on a happy moment / threatening our joy.

In the same collection, an ironic gloss of a Spanish children's song, the speaker describes the yard of her childhood home as bare and neglected as the young girl in it:

Nadie adornó su espacio con arecas [...]
Patio sin otro ruido
que el silencioso andarlo
de mis pies descalzos.
Sitio para mí sola, donde la ternura
y su modo simple de crecer y darse
como la hierba fina,
me fue vedado.

No one adorned its space with palm plants [...] / Yard without a sound / save for the silent pattering / of my bare feet. / A place for me alone, where tenderness / and its simple way of giving and growing / like fine young grass / was kept away from me.

An enclosed space, 'as wide as a cell', it returns to haunt her like 'a gap in my childhood' ('The Yard of My House', p. 55). As if to compensate for lack of love the poet writes at length, in this and other collections, about her own children, charting their development and the strong affective ties which bind them to her. She also seeks strength in her great-grand-mother ('Oral Portrait of Victory', p. 22) (see Chapter 7), in 'grandfather's lap' ('Thunder', p. 20) and in black history.

The first poem in *Entre mundo y juguete* [Between the World and Toy] (1987), published by the mulatto poet Soleida Ríos (b. 1950), is entitled 'House'. Like the 'hand' for Herrera, 'house' signifies lack, the negation of the referent, 'painful word I did not live / I have not seen' (Ríos 1987: 7). Yet in Ríos's poem, despite the absence of the home, the mother does function as a unifying and compensating presence: 'I give thanks / crossing it from wall to wall / is my mother's wet skirt' (p. 7). These fissures in the decentred self, split between past and present, are more evident in 'Autumn Water' where the speaker negates the possibilities of writing a poem about her childhood home and, in so doing, writes a poem. She knows her mother is weeping in the yard and the memory of the 'hungry scorpion' is too hurtful to reconstruct, yet the poem is written. Her very disavowal of the home and the mother affirm their presence:

Yo la llamo de noche
y quiero regresar a su lugar
como cuando venía de la escuela.
Perdóname madre mía
pero me he dado cuenta que esto
no fue posible (p. 11).

I call her at night / I want to return to her place / like when I used to come home from school. / Forgive me, mother / but I realize now / it could never be.

In Ríos's poetry the subject is not disparaging towards the mother but does not idealize her either. The mother is represented as as real, imperfect person. The mother of 'Rose of the Winds' from *De pronto abril* [Suddenly April] (1979), dedicated to the poet's mother Gloria, is figured as the subject's only hope and inspiration, 'there was no other good health / no other revelation / than the dream of your sheet' (Ríos 1979: 15). The adjacent poem, 'First Letter', is written to an absent father whose presence (the word in the poem) is mere scriptural 'invention'. A biological father exists, 'Certainly I came from you and mother / and a night of copulation and then birth' but the poet lives 'dangling waiting for you' while her mother takes on both roles, 'fills both mirrors'. It is the mother's song that gives courage while the missing patronymic is compensated for by writing in 'fictive' kin: 'but I still construct you / with the poverty of my name / and everything about you I create with pencil and paper' (p. 14). This way the poet writes herself into a traditional nuclear family home. In 'For Gloria' (*El libro roto* [The Broken Book] 1996), written shortly after her mother's death, the fluid ego boundaries of the subject merge with those of the dead mother as she watches her mother's body and her own in the mirror. She remembers her mother's memories, and she remembers herself as a young child afraid because of her mother's absence. Yet these small distances between mother and daughter become insurmountable in death. From the same collection, 'Some Order in the House' elicits a double reading. Here the house can be seen to represent the nation and the father Fidel or God, 'my father the father of the one who can do all things / has he lied to me?' Thus the unreliability of the biological father of 'House' is extrapolated to all fathers and to the law of the father in general.

Disavowal of the home and/or the mother is evident, therefore, in the work of some black and mulatto women poets born before the Revolution. However, this trend continues in the work of younger women raised in socialist Cuba. In their poetry there is a shift away from the home as a physical space; there are few references to houses as such and even fewer to the material objects contained in them. Interiors are replaced by exteriors (parks, streets, public places). Emphasis is placed on the emotional and moral ties between individual people (family and friends) in sexual or family relationships. The mother is portrayed with ambivalence; she is figured as hard-working yet unfulfilled, supportive yet with little time for her daughter. Fathers tend to be absent or disliked. María Elena Cruz Varela (b. 1953), for example, in a poem dedicated to 'mama', asks her mother for help, 'Help me once again to solve life's problems', but adds a rider indicating her own and her mother's isolation, 'Wherever I see you, you are as lonely as the parks'. She denies the connection between her own anguish and '[...] your hurried hands / your disagreeable way of saying: / **you'll be the end of me yet**' but her negation merely affirms the contrary ('It Couldn't be the Sea', *Afuera está lloviendo* [It's Raining Outside], 1987: 50). Similarly, Zoe Valdés (b. 1959) in 'Infancy' describes her mother arriving to collect her, 'My mother arrived with night trembling in her body / she never had a song, yet she always had a kiss' (*Respuestas para vivir* [Answers to Live], 1986a: 10) and Elena Tamargo (b. 1957) refers to her hard-working, 'remote little mother' as a woman who never paused for love but who nevertheless gave her children nurturance and knowledge, 'your story and your greenery' (in Ríos 1989: 150). For Damarís Calderón (b. 1967) in 'A Woman Alone and Bitter' the dehumanized mother is dried up and out of reach,

> mi madre me paría en una sala sórdida
> de una clínica desconocida
> boqueaba como un pez [...]

Mi madre era un seto cerrado
que tuvo alguna vez su pequeña fuente
una empalizada
que asolaron los perros y los años. (Calderón 1992: 19–20)

My mother gave birth to me in a sordid room / in an unknown clinic / she
gasped like a fish [...] // My mother was a hedged-in fence / that once had a
little spring / a stockade / the years and the dogs demolished.

The mother's hands have been cracked by fire, yet it is out of her 'worn out wood' that the daughter reconstructs her own house: 'from her worn out, rotten wood I remake the ropes of my house' (p. 19). The poet summarizes her mixed feelings towards her mother in the final three lines: 'I shot out from between her legs / as if in a bomb attack. / I've been the hero and the traitor' (*Duras aguas del trópico* [Hard Waters of the Tropics], pp. 19–20). 'Snapshot of My Father', from the same collection, is a devastating reproach of the revolutionary father's hypocrisy:

Comunista, pudo haber sido masón o cuáquero.
Igual le habrían cortado los nudillos,
igual habrá partido su tazón con nadie.
En deplorables noches montaba a mi madre
como quien coge un tren equivocadamente (p. 21)

He was a Communist but he could have been a Mason or a Quaker. / They would have cut his knuckles just the same, / just the same he would have shared his bowl with no one. / In the dreaded night he mounted my mother / as if he had caught the wrong train.

Cira Andrés (b. 1954) in 'Paper Boats' describes the mother who still makes paper boats, but the stream representing the fluid mother–daughter bonds of childhood has now become a dividing window-ledge (*Sobre el brocado de los ojos* [On the Eyes' Brocade], 1991: 7). In an earlier collection, Andrés presented herself as 'the mother of my mother', '[...] she is the most beautiful birth I have ever had / I've created her like a poem' ('If I Told My Friends', *Visiones* [Visions], 1987: 35). Biological paradigms of mothering are reversed when the poet teaches her mother to read.

One poem that does describe a house interior clearly rejects remnants of pre-revolutionary middle-class family models. 'Ash Saturday' by Reina María Rodríguez (b. 1952) opens with the statement, 'here private property does not exist / yet my children still detest their family'. This is expanded through descriptions of a bounded, deathly, dilapidated space filled with items denoting middle-class mores and pretensions (large cushions that ought not be touched, a cheap, empty jewellery-box). Its female inhabitants are what remains of the bourgeois family: a spinster aunt, an invalid great-grandmother, and 'a grandmother, widowed by a dead man who had a mistress'. The windows are low; even the 'flowers on the floor tiles' cannot find space to grow. The poet reviews these surroundings critically from inside, but her children, the new generation, 'scratch the walls' in their attempts to escape the confines the house and family represent (*Cuando una mujer no duerme* [When a Woman Can't Sleep], 1982: 36).[9]

In these poems the stability and reliability of the mother, the family, the home and, by extension, the nation are troubled. Representations of the father are particularly negative. On the other hand, the demythification of the mother and the home allows the mother to acquire subjectivity in her own right, as a person separate from the daughter who may or may not identify with her. Another strategy for inscribing female subjectivity is writing women's sexual desire. This may be of two interrelated types: the female subject's encounter with her own body and desires, and her response to or appreciation of the male body. The tone can vary from the ironic and jocular to the deadly serious.

As we have seen, it would be a mistake to suggest that eroticism is new to Cuban women's writing. Far from it: Cuban women have published erotic literature throughout the century. The sonnet, 'I'm disarranged, love, I'm disarranged', written by Carilda Oliver Labra in 1946, expresses an effusive erotic delight which was certainly not encouraged in the first decades following the Revolution:

Me desordeno, amor, me desordeno
cuando voy en tu boca, demorada;
y casi sin por qué, casi por nada,
te toco con la punta de mi seno. (Oliver Labra 1992: 76)

I'm disarranged, love, I'm disarranged / When I stay in your mouth, delayed; / And for no reason at all, nothing less, / I touch you with the tip of my breast.

Other poems by Oliver Labra, such as 'I've Lost Me a Man', 'Men Who Served Me for a Summer' (1979), and 'Eve's Speech' (1965), which reads,

Por eso, cuando nos mordemos,
de noche,
tengo como un miedo de madre a quien dejaste sola.
Pero no importa,
bésame,
otra vez y otra vez
para encontrarme.
Ajústate a mi cintura,
vuelve
sé mi animal,
muéveme (p. 39)

That's why, when we bite each other / at night, / I'm frightened like a mother left alone. / But it doesn't matter, / kiss me, / again and again / so I'll find myself once more. / Fit yourself round my waist, / come back, / be my animal, / move me.

are further expressions of female desire which did not surface again in Cuba until after the mid-1980s. Oliver Labra's erotic poetry was not republished until then.[10]

What is new is black and mulatto women's erotic literature, the self-portrayal of women as dominant, active, even aggressive agents of the sexual act, and political dissent couched in sexual terms. Women's appropriation of erotic writing is a form of empowerment and literary emancipation, a way of shocking a complacent audience. Interestingly, in Cuba this renewed interest in erotic literature is not a response to the same kind of market demand experienced in capitalist economies where female-authored erotic literature is big business and may merely serve to reinforce a male-oriented consumer economy. Cuban erotic poetry has not been promoted by publishers but by the women writers themselves, although it does form part of a wider trend, in revolutionary Central America (particularly Nicaragua), towards literature of the 'izquierda erótica' (erotic left) (O'Shaughnessy 1995). The younger Cuban writers, born after 1959, have experienced a sexual revolution in Cuba (as in most parts of the world). As Ian Lumsden (1996: 21–2) writes: 'Since 1959 young Cubans have become much more open and liberal about sex. They have probably become more sexually active as well […] premarital sex is commonplace […] Young women seem very much at ease with their sexuality.' They have also benefited from the wide-ranging sex education programmes initiated by the FMC in 1977 but which did not have a wider impact until the early 1980s (Leiner 1994: 93–116).[11]

The daring and, for some, outrageous poetry of Chely Lima (b. 1957) describes bedroom scenes which feature the poet and her husband (*Terriblemente iluminados* [Terribly Illuminated], 1988). In 'Counterversion of a Poem by a Contemporary' the poet describes the kind of men she prefers and ends with a political jibe:

Casi, en un final
me gustan los hombres como loco
– que es decir
          de una manera quizás altamente censurable –
Y para acabar
               bocas
                    nalgas
                         ojos
                              penes
                                   manos aparte,

me gustan aquellos escasos, deliciosos, que
                                        me aman. (Lima 1988: 24)

Almost, in conclusion, / I like men madly / – that's to say / in perhaps a highly
censurable way – / To conclude at last / mouths / buttocks / eyes / penises /
and hands apart, / I love the few, the delicious few, who / love me.

'Psalm', from the same collection, celebrates the objectified or sanctified
lover's body in eroticized Catholic discourse,

Bienaventurado el color y la hechura de tus ojos
cuando cesan de morirse en el orgasmo.
Bienaventurada tu boca
porque ella ha traído su mansa higuera a mi sed. (p. 107)

Blessed be the make and colour of your eyes / when in orgasm they no longer
die. / Blessed be your mouth / it has brought its calm figtree to quench my
thirst [...]

In 'Carnal Recount' the poet describes in detail her lover's body as she
kisses it full-length: throat, cheek, back, waist, buttocks, chest, legs, thighs,
the 'secret ways' under 'pubic grasses' where 'the fish sleeps in the palm
of my hand / closed up tightly in its ancient amphibian rings' (pp. 108–
9). Her 1992 plaquette, *Rock sucio* [Dirty Rock] is more varied in theme
but still as ironically and, some might say, tastelessly frank. The poet
wants:

Un hombre que me diga tómame y haz conmigo lo que quieras.
Un hombre que se quite la ropa mirándome a los ojos.
[...] Un hombre que me deje ir y me reciba luego como a una hostia
consagrada.
[...]
Un hombre sensual como un gato con hambre. (Lima 1992: 17)

A man who says to me take me and do what you will. / A man who takes his
clothes off looking me in the eyes. [...] / A man who lets me come and takes
me in like a holy communion wafer [...] / A man as sensuous as a hungry cat.

Soledad Cruz Guerra (b. 1952) writes in 'Public Declaration of Love'
(*Documentos de la otra* [Documents of the Other Girl], 1991),

Amo a este hombre que cabalgo,
que monto sin arreos.
Montura, bridas,
ni siquiera estribos para el salto.
El duda y se defiende [...] (Cruz Guerra 1991: 32)

I love this man I ride, / I mount him without reins. / No saddles or bridles / or even stirrups for the jump. / He is doubtful and tries to defend himself […]

Cira Andrés's (b. 1954) two poems addressing her own body reveal a new awareness not so much of sexuality but of the materiality of the embodied self. In 'The Body' (*Sobre el brocado de los ojos*, 1991), her thirty-five-year-old body still keeps

Memoria de una bestia feliz
resbalando
resbalando
hermoso
ardiente en el incendio del mediodía
humillado en la noche que te pudre. […] (Andrés 1991: 11)

the memory of a happy beast / slipping / slipping / beautiful / burning in the mid-day fire / humbled in the putrid night […]

and again in 'Naked' (*Palabras de María* [Mary's Words], in press),

Cuerpo mío […]
yo te regalo a las cámaras fotográficas,
a la luz, a los ojos que quieran contemplarte,
me deshago de tí, me burlo
porque no sabes conducirme
más allá del momento donde estoy. […]
En ti entran los forasteros, los ladrones
que miro concierta repugnancia y placer.

Body of mine […] / I offer you up to the cameras / to the light, to the eyes of those who want to see you / I shed you off, I laugh at you / you can take me no further / than the moment where I am now. […] / Strangers and thieves enter in you / I watch them with repugnance and pleasure.

Desire appears in the least expected places, as a facet of everyday life. In Reina María Rodríguez's poem 'He wipes his spectacles with my skirt' (*En la arena de Padua*, 1992), a rare and subtle excursion into eroticism, the decently dressed woman is unexpectedly aroused when a man cleans his glasses with her skirt:

bajo mi saya están las piernas oscuras.
él limpia los espejuelos con mi saya,
yo fragmento las hojas de un árbol
aparentemente distante.
bajo mi saya están sus manos
sólo el roce de la tela tratando de pulir el cristal

limpia mis piernas
él no sabe lo que hace
como si mis piernas no lo fueran
alguna vez a devorar.
perdió el sentido común
por un instante
mi saya sus ojos el cristal
pero volvió a esconder su pupila.
yo estaba meditando ser un árbol
ser cualquier cosa
y desaparecer
aparentemente distante. (Rodríguez 1992: 69)

under my skirt my legs are dark. / he wipes his spectacles with my skirt, / while I crumble the leaves on a tree / apparently distant. / under my skirt are his hands / just the touch of cloth trying to polish the glass / he is wiping my legs / he has no idea what he's doing / as if my legs could not even once / devour him. / he lost his common sense / for a moment / my skirt his eyes the glass / but he lowered his pupils again / I was thinking of being tree / or anything at all / and disappear / apparently distant.

Zoe Valdés (b. 1959), who spent several years in France and in an interview stated she was obsessed by 'the woman question', is disarmingly frank in her descriptions of the female body and female reproduction. 'Poem in Full Moon' (*Todo para una sombra* [All for a Shadow], Barcelona 1986b) celebrates menstruation, 'How lucky I am to have stained the sheet tonight / [...] How lucky I am to be a woman and not a wolf-man' (Valdés 1986: 39). 'A Poem for When You are not Here' voices passionate, ubiquitous, excessive female desire:

Déjame hacer el amor con tus objetos personales:
Darle un beso libido a tu reloj
restregar mis senos con tu almohada [...]
Escribir un verso caliente en mi vagina
con tu stylo asombrado. [...] (Valdés 1986b: 38)

Let me make love to your personal belongings: / Give your watch a libidinous kiss / Rub my breasts across your pillow [...] / Write a hot poem in my vagina / With your astonished pen.

Of particular interest is the pro-life poem, 'Abortion':

Aunque no esté encinta
un niño se está muriendo dentro de mí,
nadie puede quererlo como yo,
ni tú que has olvidado el avaricioso minuto.

Mientras se va formando,
su mirada atraviesa sangre y tejidos
y en el espejo me ha anticipado que tendrá ese color
que yo no sabría definir.
Tú llegas para salvarlo,
y si me acaricias él se estira de placer.
Los senos se me llenan y algo suave y sin olor
gotea de ellos.
Dicen que las brujas lloran por los pechos
y que el pelo se les pone plateado de tanta magia.
El niño está embrujando un espacio de mi cuerpo,
yo te lo digo,
qué lástima mis senos vacíos,
mi útero sangrando cada luna llena
y tu semen cayendo al precipicio. (p. 53)

Although I'm not pregnant / a baby is dying in me. / No one can love it as I do, / not even you, the greedy moment forgotten. / As it slowly develops / its gaze crosses tissue and blood / and in the mirror it has told me its colour, / one I could never define. / You are here in order to save it / and if you stroke me it shivers with joy. / My breasts fill, a soft, odourless substance / drips down. / They say witches cry from their breasts / and that their hair turns to silver with magic. / The child is casting a space in my body. / Yes, it is. / What a shame my empty bosom, my uterus bleeding each full moon / and your semen down a precipice falling.

This is not a poem demanding women's right to abortion, as the title might suggest. In a country where abortion and contraception are readily available it would make little sense. The poem is about women's control of reproduction; it laments the denial of conception. Motherhood is at once celebrated and disavowed. Consider the poem in the light of the third objective of the Second National Congress of the FMC in 1974: to educate woman to fulfil her role 'as the one who constructs a new society, in her roles as worker, mother, and former of the new generations' (Wasmer 1977: 224). Woman, in a socialist context, is expected to be incorporated into productive and reproductive activity. The Cuban family unit is strengthened, and is destabilized inasmuch as it is 'open' (allowing for divorce and cohabitation). The woman in the poem is emancipated, yet confesses a natural, maternal instinct, a biologically-determined desire to conceive, to save the child. The inscription of the female body and its reproductive potential, female subjectivity and agency, the casting of conception in magical, mystical terms, and the recognition of the man's role in the process, suggest 'a multiple, shifting and often self-contradictory identity' indicated by Teresa de Lauretis (1986: 9) in feminist writing. Similarly, in Reina María Rodríguez's *Páramos* [Moorlands] (1993), in a section entitled 'Strong is Love like Death', the desiring, maternal female subject is written as a (textual, sexual and cultural) transgression:

Freddy Mercury dead on his bed – not round, not Japanese – and I, without green make-up (Christian Dior) and the smell of child's urine on my blanket. outside a peaceful February sun. your sex in your hand defying misery and eternity. flaccidity and vanity and even love, and I, amazed, petrified beneath you, touching tentatively and conquering the cross. the jump of my belly against yours [...] (under cross-fire between the gynaecologists' surgery and the television screens we have buried love in the inconfessable, on the altar of pleasure, desire ... on the altar of Politics) the end of utopia is not revitalized with technique ... the end of love is not saved by sex ... what would it be without utopia? what would it be without my excess of womb? (quoted in *La Gaceta de Cuba*, 1994, no. 1: 34)

All of these poems describe heterosexual love. Only one or two feature a female love object, as for example Nancy Morejón's beautifully understated 'The Unfaithful Plant' (Morejón 1986: 23),

La planta que más
amé,
pulposa en sus hojuelas,
alga de sol
en sus amplias cabezas,
nunca tendió sus luces
hacia mí.
Sólo clamó en su sitio
por el transeúnte que
la miraba, distraído,
sin percibir el amado fragor
de su belleza.
[...]
Y yo aún buscando trasplantarla,
viendo que no tenía raíces,
ni una sola raíz,
en donde sostener tanto cariño.

The plant I loved / the most / juicy her leaves / seaweed of sun / on full heads of flowers / never spread out her lights / towards me. / She just clamoured from where she stood / for the passer-by who / glanced at her aimlessly / not seeing the dearly-loved blaze / of her beauty [...] / And I'm still wondering how to transplant her / since she has no roots / not one single root / wherein to hold so much affection.

By focusing on their intimate lives in this way, particularly on sexual relationships and erotic desire, these women inscribe feminine difference into their poetry. This practice opens fissures in Cuban revolutionary ideology, the discourse of equality, but often affirms it at the same time. *Mi nombre. Antielegía familiar* (1991), an autobiographical poem by Excilia Saldaña (b. 1946), both denies the traditional role of the mother and the bourgeois family while extolling woman's role as mother and creator in revolutionary Cuba (Davies 1996). This same poem foregrounds the reconstruction of the sexed mulatto female body. It charts the mulatto girl's rejection of her hybrid body and yet, at the point of total abjection (when she compares her body to that of the white baby Jesus), a process of self-reconstruction begins. Her repressed body resurfaces as the process of production (not reproduction) inextricably linked to the plantation economy through which it is defined:

A través de la mulatez del melado
oteo un cuerpo:
me regodeo
en el cañaveral inédito del pubis
en el penacho de la cabeza
en el desmoche de las axilas
en el breve trapiche de los pechos
en las piernas espesas
en el tacho de bronce del ombligo
en la centrífuga de los ojos
en los dientes refinos. (Saldaña 1991: 5)

Through the mulatto shades of cane syrup / I see a body: / I take cruel delight / in the unedited cane-fields of the pubis / in the crest of a head / in the cane-cut arm pits / in the brief sugar-press breasts / in the thick legs / in the bronzed round-bottomed boiler of a navel / in the centrifugal force of the eyes / in the refined teeth.

The mulatto woman recovers her agency and subjectivity by recuperating her body through psychic re-memberment. Women recover not only their bodies but also their names. In *Mi nombre* [My Name] the poet refers to her own name, Excilia, meaning possibly 'exsilia', 'those who are banished', in positive terms while rejecting the family name, the name-of-the-father, Saldaña:

mi nombre de decir sí
mi nobre de llenar el espacio
mi nombre palabra
mi nombre poema [...] (pp. 32–3)

My name to say yes / My name to fill space / My name word / My name poem [...]

This poem is interesting inasmuch as it is an 'anti-elegy', a non-lament, for the family from which the subject is 'exiled'. The family here is pre-revolutionary, bourgeois and patriarchal. The subject, clearly inserted in a revolutionary social context, rewrites her new, autonomous self in terms of Cuban national liberation. The construction of subjectivity is perceived to be grounded in collective experience and difference is made possible by equality. Although both poems focus on the inscription of the woman's name, Saldaña's is quite unlike the following untitled poem published by the young writer Damaris Calderón (b. 1967) in *Duras aguas del trópico* (1992) where there is much less enthusiasm for the name:

Un nombre tengo. ¿Y si fuera
rosa sangrada, adversario?
Un nombre ¿ves? necesario
– dijeron. Y así anduviera.
Ama al nombre aunque te hiera
o no la carne nombrada.
Ama al nombre, lastimada
aún la carne. No le asombres
Pues son demasiados nombres
en tanta carne extraviada. (Calderón 1992: 35)

One name I have. And if it were / bleeding rose, adversary? / A name, you see, necessary / – they said. And that's how I should be. / Love the name though it wounds / or not the flesh named. / Love the name, though it hurts / your flesh still. Don't scare it away. / For there are too many names / in so much body astray.

Here the name and the body must perforce go together even if the fit is painful; such is the law. If the name were otherwise ('bleeding rose', for example, connoting the female body and female sexuality) it would be considered conflictive, a contravention, or 'adversary'. The unitary subject must accept the imposition of one name. Otherwise, the female body and its superfluous, multiple identities would be 'astray', dispersed, meaningless and misled. The name, order in language (replicated in the classical poetic form), is necessary for signification yet at the same time it is the containment of superfluous feminine excess.

What emerges in these texts featuring uncaring mothers, dysfunctional families, desiring women and rampant female sexuality is an identity that is 'at odds with language' (de Lauretis 1986: 9), at odds with categorization and symbolical representation, and at odds with the revolutionary establishment, certainly until the late 1980s. The construction of subjectivity is always problematic in feminist writing, more so in works where a discourse of difference might be seen insidiously to destabilize projects of equality. Nevertheless, whether at the level of grassroots theory or the writing of the self, feminist discourse should also be political critique. Capitalism may well be patriarchal but patriarchy is immemorial. That feminism must move beyond Marxist politics (the most radical of political theories) and incorporate difference, while retaining a political strategy, has become increasingly apparent during the 1980s and 1990s in Europe and the United States as well as in Cuba. As Ana Rubio Castro (1990: 207) notes:

> Difference feminism does not ignore the usefulness and the necessity of the struggle for legal rights; it simply states that this struggle is not enough [...] Access to legal equality and to full rights of citizenship are not sufficient without having already established other models, other purposes, other objectives, another life project and another culture.

The malaise in the British socialist feminist camp was apparent in the Editorial of *Feminist Review* in Spring 1992. The collective admitted that since the founding of the review in 1979 it had had to rethink its agenda because 'the period of optimism about feminism and socialism, and the possibilities for socialist feminism' had passed. Their strategies must incorporate a 'pluralistic or pluralized tolerance of categories of difference' in cross-cultural studies. As Sarah S. Hughes wrote elsewhere: 'Feminist scholarship in the US has now widely come to recognize the deficiencies of a white, middle-class framework' (Hughes 1992: 389). To explore 'the gendered meanings of race and class' led feminist research to, among other places, the Caribbean and Latin America (p. 389). 'How can anyone ask me to say goodbye to "emancipatory metanarratives" when my own emancipation is still such a patchy, hit-and-miss affair?' asked Sabina Lovibond (1989: 12). She suggested that a decentralized women's movement should keep to its political programme, the 'abolition of the sex-class system' (p. 28), as its objectives converge with other egalitarian or liberationist movements. These words echoed exactly those of Celia Amorós in 1985 and Amy Kaminsky in 1992. Radical feminism may be, like postmodernism, a phenomenon of late capitalism: Susannah Radstone asked (1992) if, in the light of postmodernist anti-essentialism, women's collective action was still desirable at all, and if it was how women might be thought of outside biology. Essentialism is not a 'thing in itself' but qualities to which women are bound (Radstone 1992: 89).[12] All these women are socialists who, like their Cuban counterparts, try to interrelate identity politics and equality politics in their writings, to construct what Rubio Castro terms a dialectics between feminist theory and feminist practice (Rubio Castro 1990: 193). Knowing and representing reality is one step towards cultural transformation, but profound change is possible only 'if we create a theoretical base which is capable of being alternative, if we create, ultimately, a new utopian horizon' (Rubio Castro 1990: 207). As we have seen, in their creative writings Cuban women invent those imaginary possible worlds, related to but released from empirical reality and objective time. Women writers invent new spaces, ask different questions, open other doors. Their effect on Cuban culture and society has been profound.

Notes

1. Auguste Comte, *Système de politique positive*, Vol. II, quoted in Michèle Le Doeuff (1988: 190).

2. For a survey of the manipulation of the mother icon in connection with Antonio Maceo's mulatto mother Mariana Grajales, the 'Mother of Cuba', between the 1920s and 1950s, see Jean Stubbs (1995). The process of converting Grajales into matron-saint began in the late 1920s at the same time as the cult to Martí. Similarly, Maceo's wife, María Cabrales, symbolized the revolutionary 'compañera'.

3. What Lynn Segal (1991: 85) describes as a 'commitment to notions of the absolute autonomy of each oppressed group to organize itself and assert its own needs and identity'.

4. There exists a large bibliography on the feminist/women's movements in Latin America. See, for example, Radcliffe and Westwood (1993).

5. However, Azicri (1988: 55) refers not only to the pre-revolutionary patriarchal upper- and middle-class families, but also to the matriarchal lower-class family where women were the heads and breadwinners.

6. Azicri (1988: 56): 'The concern with safeguarding the family as a central institution in a socialist polity was and still is paramount to the regime.' The official view is that the family, as ideological superstructure, is socialist, egalitarian, politically mobilized and integrated into the revolutionary process. The bourgeois family, based on private property, the submission of women and discrimination against illegitimate children, was replaced by the socialist family based on public ownership, socialist production and the legal equality of all members and descendants.

7. I should mention here Dulce María Loynaz's wonderfully moving poem 'Ultimos días de una casa' (1958) in which the house is personified as an old woman abandoned by her family and, ultimately, destroyed by men. The house voices the mother's version, her incredulity, pain and despair.

8. See, for example, Rafaela Chacón Nardi, 'Del silencio y las voces'; Carilda Oliver Labra, 'Sonetos a mi padre'; Cleva Solís, 'En la exposición de Angel Acosta León'.

9. For a more recent view of the home and family in Rodríguez's poetry, see 'Vigas' in *En la arena de Padua* (1992).

10. Carilda Oliver Labra, *Calzada de Tirry 81* (1987); *Antología poética* (1992); *Sonetos* (1990).

11. Leiner (1994: 102–3) mentions the publication of a series of books originally published in East Germany starting with *El Hombre y La Mujer en la Intimidad* [Man and Woman in Intimacy] (1979). All 100,000 copies of *¿Piensas ya en el amor?* [Thinking already about Love?] (1981) were sold out in a single day.

12. For a full account of 'those who stress the similarities and those who stress the differences between men and women', see Snitow (1990) and Segal (1987).

One Hundred Years of Hard-won Independence. Women Writers and the Special Period

It is an incredibly beautiful island, filled with hard-working, intelligent people. It is richly endowed with an enormous variety of natural resources and it is a veritable tropical Garden of Eden. (Viscount Montgomery of Alamein. *Hansard* [Lords], 22 January 1997, 780)

I start by emphasising that the Cuban people are our friends, and I wish them well – I have no desire to tell them what to do, or to interfere with their freedom to make political and economic choices according to their preference [...] It is quite intolerable in the modern world, at the end of this century, after having fought for 200 years for free trade that, of all people, the US, the great leaders in our time in matters of free trade, should adopt this kind of policy. (Lord Preston. *Hansard* [Lords], 22 January 1997, 786, 788)

The above comments were made in a debate in the British House of Lords on the subject of the most recent crisis in Cuban foreign affairs, the attempted imposition by the US administration of the Helms–Burton legislation which aims to sanction companies of any nation in the world if they dare to trade with Cuba. The comments illustrate the rejection of this ridiculous policy even in the most entrenched sectors of the British establishment and indicates renewed international interest in the island.

Between 1990 and 1995 Cuba went through one of the most critical periods of its 100 years of independence when, following the collapse of the Soviet bloc in 1989, economic aid was brought to an end and the trade blockade imposed by the USA since 1960 was further tightened (Molyneux 1996: 1–5). The Helms–Burton legislation is the latest move in that irrational saga of retribution. Over those five years Cuba experienced a 50 per cent collapse in national output; real GDP growth rate dropped to minus 20 per cent in 1993. The Cuban population underwent conditions (acute shortages of all materials, foodstuffs and energy) not unlike those experienced in a war zone. Recovery began in 1994 and has since strengthened due to a gradual opening up of a market economy, foreign investment and tourism (Yamaoka 1997).[1]

Cuban culture and society has changed a great deal over the last seven years. Although the polity remains in control (its nadir being the Havana riots of August 1994 and the subsequent Miami-bound sea exodus), the arts and the economy are now more open and pluralistic. Fissures in hegemonic ideology and structures leave openings for contestatory discourses, including those of women and, even more spectacularly, gays. Sexuality is very much on the Cuban agenda (Leiner 1994; Lumsden 1996; Smith and Padula 1996). The most effective sources of renewal seem to be at the micropolitical level, in the areas of the private, personal and domestic. It is largely thanks to the multitude of sacrifices and the heroic resilience on the part of Cuban women that Cuban society has weathered this latest storm. In saving the nation, yet again, women might argue, they have made their voices heard.

The effect of the special period on women writers was tremendous. First, there was no paper, glue or ink. All publishing other than the absolutely necessary (for example, school books) came to an end. Works in press remained there. Only the hand-made 'plaquettes' of enterprising arts and crafts workers kept the home-grown literary scene alive. Second, there was no petrol; transport ground to a halt; there were constant electricity cuts; few machines, fridges or cookers functioned properly. Factories and industry stopped. Third, there was strict food rationing. People survived on handfuls of beans and rice for weeks; there was no soap for washing. The burdens placed on women in the family were immense. But all this was not enough to stop women writing.

With the collapse of industry, working women now had more time at home or in the workplace, where there was nothing to do. Education and women's rights, for example to paid maternity leave, remained intact. If women could find pen and paper they could write. Many sought publishers outside Cuba, primarily in Spain and Latin America. At the same time Canada, socialist Spain, Italy – released from US competition – looked increasingly to Cuba for ecomonic and cultural investment. A stronger rapprochement between women writers in Cuba and expatriates in the USA was forged (Vázquez Díaz 1994; de la Hoz 1994). Increasing interest in the fortunes of Cuba led to increasing demand on the world markets for works by or about Cubans, including women (Pérez Sarduy and Stubbs 1993; Trives 1990). Joint publishing ventures have opened up new opportunities. So it was that women were able to continue publishing in the 1990s: Nancy Morejón in France (*Le Chainon Poétique*, 1994), Venezuela (*Paisaje célebre* [Famous Landscape] 1993), Spain (*Botella al Mar* [Bottle at Sea], 1996) and the USA (*Afro-Hispanic Review*, Spring 1996); Dulce María Loynaz in Spain (her complete works); several writers – especially the youngest – in the various anthologies published in Spain (López Sacha 1996), Mexico (Aguilera Díaz 1990; and Padura 1993) and Puerto Rico (Bejel 1991). Zoe Valdés has left Cuba for Spain and has made a reputation for herself by criticizing the Cuban government and writing novels that some would call erotic and others pornographic (*La nada cotidiana* [Everyday Nothingness], 1995; *Te di la vida entera* [I Gave You My Life], *La hija del embajador* [The Ambassador's Daughter], and *Sangre azul* [Blue Blood], all published in 1996). Conversely, Olga Fernández has left for Ecuador but finds writing away from home increasingly difficult. Daína Chaviano, Chely Lima and the critic Nara Araújo are in Mexico, the latter publishing in the United States. Marilyn Bobes spent some time in Puerto Rico. The great majority of women writers have remained in Cuba and, as the economic conditions improve, their works are published: Lina de Feria, Carilda Oliver Labra, Reina María Rodríguez, Mirta Yáñez, Marilyn Bobes, Olga Fernández, Analuz García Calzada, Fina García Marruz, and recently Marta Rojas, Soleida Ríos, Georgina Herrera and Nancy Morejón are all cases in point. Marilyn Bobes won the Casa de las Américas Prize (1995) for her book of short stories *Alguien tiene que llora* [Someone has to Cry]. Long overdue critical works on women writers are appearing (Hernández Méndez on Chacón Nardi, 1996; Yañez and Bobes, 1996). Particularly gratifying is the recent success of Lina de Feria, who was imprisoned for three years after events leading to the Mariel exodus in 1980, and released thanks to the efforts of UNEAC (the Writers and Artists' Union). She has been awarded the National Critics' Prize twice in recent years for her books *A mansalva de los años* (1991) and *El ojo milenario* [The Millennial Eye] (1995), and has since published *Los rituales del inocente* [Rituals of the Innocent] (Unión, 1996), which sold out in a month, and a bilingual edition of her poetry is planned with Gallimard in France. De Feria shared the 1996 National Critics' Prize with Reina María Rodríguez and, significantly, Serafina Núñez, who was born in 1913 and published her poetry in the 1930s. Cuban women writers have staked their claim for a hard-earned place in the sun in their nation's next 100 years of independence.

Note

1. According to the International Planned Parenthood Federation (IPPF) in 1996 Cuba still had 'the best development and reproductive health statistics in the whole of Latin America, some of them as good as those of many industrialized countries'. Life expectancy was 75 years and there was a 95 per cent literacy rate. Yet women were again hit hard: although family planning provision was good, only 40 per cent of contraception was acceptable in terms of quality 'partly because of the economic embargo affecting the country (IPPF 1997: 16–17).

Bibliography

Aeschylus (1953) *Oresteia*, translated by R. Lattimore, Chicago University Press, Chicago.

Agosín, M. and C. Franzen (eds) (1987) *The Renewal of the Vision. Voices of Latin American Women Poets 1940–1980*, Spectacular Diseases, London.

Aguilera Díaz. G (1990) *Un grupo avanza silencioso*, 2 vols, UNAM, Mexico.

Alfonso, V. (1988) 'Del mar a la piedra. *Piedra pulida*', *Letras Cubanas*, Vol. 7, January–March: 268–70.

Allen, R. F. (1987) *Teatro hispanoamericano: una bibliografía anotada*, G. K. Hall, Boston.

Alonso, C. J. (1990) *The Spanish American Regional Novel: Modernity and Autochthony*, Cambridge University Press, Cambridge.

Amorós, C. (1991; 1st edn 1985) *Hacia una crítica de la razón patriarcal*, Anthropos, Barcelona.

Andrade, E. and H. Cramsie (eds) (1991) *Dramaturgas latinoamericanas contemporáneas*, Editorial Verbum, Madrid.

Antuña, V. (1974) 'Camila Henríquez Ureña. In memoriam', *Casa de las Américas*, Vol. 14, no. 84, May–June: 96–104.

Apuleius (1995) *The Golden Ass*, translated by P. G. Walsh, Oxford University Press, Oxford.

Araújo, N. (1993) 'Naturaleza e imaginación: el *Bestiarium* de Dulce María Loynaz', *Anthropos*, no. 151: 65–7.

— (1995) 'Literatura femenina, feminismo y crítica literaria feminista en Cuba', *Letras Femeninas*, Vol. 11, nos 1–2: 165–71.

Arcos, J. L. (1990a) *En torno a la obra poética de Fina García Marruz*, UNEAC, Havana.

— (1990b) 'Obra y pensamiento de Fina García Marruz', *Revista Iberoamericana*, Vol. LVI, July–December: 1195–202.

Arias, S. (1979) 'Literatura cubana (1959–75)', *Casa de las Américas*, no. 113, March–April: 14–26.

Astica, F. (1986) *Homenaje a Emilia Bernal en su centenario*, Instituto Costarricense de Cultura Hispánica, San José de Costa Rica.

Azicri, M. (1984), 'Women's Development Through Revolutionary Mobilization: A Study of the Federation of Cuban Women', in I. L. Horowitz (ed.), *Cuban Communism*, Transaction Books, New Brunswick and London, pp. 267–300.

— (1988) *Cuba*, Frances Pinter, London and New York.

Baker Jr, H. A. and P. Redmond (eds) (1989) *Afro-American Literary Study in the 1990s*, University of Chicago Presss, Chicago and London.

Bakhtin, M. M. (1981) *The Dialogic Imagination*, ed. M. Holquist, University of Texas Press, Austin.

Barnet, M. (1963) 'Las memorias de Renée Méndez Capote', *La Gaceta de Cuba*, Vol. 22, no. 4, July.

Barrett, M. (1985) 'Ideology and the Cultural Production of Gender', in J. Newton and D. Rosenfelt (eds), *Feminist Criticism and Social Change*, Methuen, New York and London.

Bejel, E. (1991) *Escribir en Cuba*, Universidad de Puerto Rico, Ríos Piedras.

Benjamin, J. (1990) *The Bonds of Love*, Virago, London.

Benjamin, W. (1979; 1st edn 1955), *Illuminations*, Fontana Collins, Glasgow.

Bergmann, E., J. Greenberg and G. Kirkpatrick (eds) (1990) *Women, Culture and Politics in Latin America*, University of California Press, Berkeley and Oxford.

Bernard, J. L and Pola, J. A. (eds) (1985) *Quiénes escriben en Cuba*, Letras Cubanas, Havana.

Bhabha, H. K. (1994) *The Location of Culture*, Routledge, London and New York.

Bobes, M. (1985) 'Fina García Marruz. Elogio a la serena perfección', *Casa de las Américas*, no. 149, March–April: 155–6.

Boggs, R. S. (1977) 'Testimonio', in R. Sánchez and J. A. Madrigal (eds), *Homenaje a Lydia Cabrera*, Universal, Miami.

Bortolussi, M. (1990) *El cuento infantil cubano: Un estudio crítico*, Pliegos, Madrid.

Bourdieu, P. (1993) *The Field of Cultural Production. Essays on Art and Literature*, Polity Press, Cambridge and London.

Brandon, G. (1993) *Santeria from Africa to the New World*, Indiana University Press, Bloomington and Indianapolis.

Brooksbank Jones, A. (1996) 'Latin American Feminist Criticism Revisited', in A. Brooksbank Jones and C. Davies (eds), *Latin American Women's Writing. Feminist Readings in Theory and Crisis*, Oxford University Press, Oxford and New York.

Busby, M. (ed.) (1992) *Daughters of Africa*, Jonathan Cape, London.

Bush, P. (ed.) (1997) *The Voice of the Turtle*, Quartet Books, London.

Butler, J. (1990) *Gender Trouble: Feminism and the Subversion of Identity*, Routledge, New York.

Cámara, M. (ed.) (1989) *Cuentos cubanos contemporáneos 1966–1990*, Universidad Vera-cruzana, Xalapa, Mexico.

— (1991) 'Adiós a los ochenta: ajuste de cuentas con la joven literatura cubana', *Plural*, no. 238, July: 66–71.

Campuzano, L. (1988), 'La mujer en la narrativa de la Revolución: ponencia de una carencia', *Letras Cubanas*, Vol. 7, January–March: 132–49.

Captain-Hidalgo, Y. (1990) 'Nancy Morejón (1944). Cuba' in D. Marting (ed.) *Spanish-American Women Writers. A Bio-Bibliographical Source Book*, Greenwood Press, Westport.

Carbonell, J. M. (1928) *La poesía lírica en Cuba*, Siglo xx, Havana.

Castellanos, I. and J. Inclán (eds) (1987) *En torno a Lydia Cabrera (Cincuentenario de 'Cuentos Negros de Cuba' 1936–1986)*, Universal, Miami.

Castellanos, J. and I. Castellanos (1990) *Cultura Afrocubana. El negro en Cuba 1845–1959*, Universal, Miami.

Castellanos, R. (1988) *Meditation on the Threshold*, translated by Julian Palley, Bilingual Press, Tempe, Arizona.

Castro-Klarén, S., S. Molloy and B. Sarlo (eds) (1991) *Women's Writing in Latin America. An Anthology*, Westview Press, Boulder.

CEPAL (1986) *Cinco estudios sobre la situación de la mujer en América Latina: estudios e informes de la CEPAL*, Naciones Unidas, Santiago de Chile.

Cervantes, C. A. (1985) 'Juana Pastor: La primera poetisa cubana', in Oscar Fernández de la Vega (ed.), *Sobre la poesía negrista*, New York, 1985, pp. 11–16.

Cixous, H. (1983) 'The Laugh of the Medusa' in E. Abel and E. K. Abel (eds), *The Signs Reader. Women, Gender and Scholarship*, Chicago University Press, Chicago, pp. 279–97.

Clark, M. T. (1994) *Augustine*, Geoffrey Chapman, London.

Cole, J. B. (1988) 'Women in Cuba: The Revolution within the Revolution', in J. B. Cole (ed.), *Anthropology for the Nineties: Introductory Readings*, Free Press–Macmillan, New York and London.

Conde, C. (1967) *Once grandes poetisas hispanoamericanas*, Cultura Hispánica, Madrid.

Cross, F. L. (ed.) (1957) *The Oxford Dictionary of the Christian Church*, Oxford University Press, London.

Crowe, M. (ed.) (1984) *Woman Who Has Sprouted Wings: Poems by Contemporary Latin American Women Poets*, Latin American Literary Review Press, Pittsburgh.

Cudjoe, S. R. (ed.) (1990) *Caribbean Women Writers*, Calaloux, Wellesley, MA.

Darío, R. (1987; 1st edn 1896) *Prosas profanas y otros poemas*, ed. I. M. Zulueta, Castalia, Madrid.

Davies, C. (1993a) 'Beastly Women and Underdogs. The Short Fiction of Dora Alonso', in C. Davies (ed.) *Women Writers in Twentieth-Century Spain and Spanish America*, Edwin Mellen Press, Lewiston, Queenston and Lampeter, pp. 55–69.

— (1993b) 'Writing the African Subject. The Work of Two Cuban Poets (Georgina Herrera and Nancy Morejón)', *Women. A Cultural Review*, Vol. 4, no. 1: 32–48.

— (1995) 'Women Writers in Cuba 1975–1994. A Bibliographical Note', *Bulletin of Latin American Research*, Vol. 14, no. 2: 211–15.

— (1996) 'Cross-cultural Homebodies in Cuba: The Poetry of Excilia Saldaña', in A. Brooksbank Jones and C. Davies (eds), *Latin American Women's Writing: Feminist Readings in Theory and Crisis*, Oxford University Press, Oxford and New York.

de Costa Willis, M. (1990) 'The Caribbean as Idea and Image in the Poetry of Nancy Morejón', *Journal of Caribbean Studies*, Vol. 7, nos 2–3: 233–43.

de la Hoz, L. (ed.) (1994) *La poesía de las dos orillas. Cuba (1959–1993)*, Libertarias Prodhufi, Madrid.

DeLamotte, E. C. (1990) *Perils of the Night. A Feminist Study of Nineteeth-Century Gothic*, Oxford University Press, Oxford and New York.

de Lauretis, T. (ed.) (1986) *Feminist Studies/Critical Studies*, Indiana University Press, Bloomington.

— *Technologies of Gender: Essays on Theory, Film, and Fiction*, Macmillan, Basingstoke.

Depestre, R. (1985) *Buenos días y adiós a la negritud*, Cuadernos Casa de las Américas, Havana.

de Vera de Lens, A. (1930) *Pro la mujer cubana*, Alberto Soto, Havana.

de Vries, A. (1974) *Dictionary of Symbols and Imagery*, North Holland, Amsterdam and London.

di Stefano, C. (1991) *Configurations of Masculinity: A Feminist Perspective on Modern Political Theory*, Cornell University Press, Ithaca and London.

Donnell, A. (1996) 'An Ambiguous Inheritance. The Poetry of Una Marson and Contemporary Criticism', paper presented to the Second International Caribbean Women Writers' Conference, 'The Centre of Remembrance', Goldsmiths College, University of London, 28 June.

Elizagaray, A. M. (1985) 'Una pájara pinta para los niños latinoamericanos', *Casa de las Américas*, no. 151, July–August: 132–3.

Ellis, P. (ed.) (1986) *Women of the Caribbean*, Zed Books, New York.

Esteves, C. and L. Paravisini-Gebert (eds) (1991) *Green Cane and Juicy Flotsam: Short Stories by Caribbean Women*, Rutgers University Press, New Brunswick, NJ.

Fabian, J. (1983) *Time and the Other: How Anthropology Makes Its Object*, Columbia University Press, New York.

Falcón, L. (1992) *Mujer y poder político*, Vindicación feminista, Madrid.

FAR (Fuerzas Armadas Revolucionarias) (1967) *Historia de Cuba*, FAR, Havana.

Feijóo, S. (1964) *Sonetos en Cuba*, Dirección de Publicaciones Universidad Central de Las Villas, Santa Clara.

Fenwick, M. J. (1992) *Writers of the Caribbean and Central America*, Garland, New York and London.

Fernández Retamar, R. (1954) *La poesía contemporánea en Cuba (1927–1953)*. Orígenes, Havana.

— (1960) *Poesía joven de Cuba*, Editora Popular de Cuba y del Caribe, Lima.

Fernández Robaina, T. (1985) *Bibliografía de la mujer cubana*, Biblioteca Nacional José Martí, Havana.

— (1990) *El negro en Cuba 1902–1958*, Ciencias Sociales, Havana.

Finn, J. (1988) *Voices of Negritude*, Quartet Books, London and New York.

Fisher, J. (1995) 'Some Thoughts on "Contaminations"', *Third Text*, Vol. 32, Autumn: 3–9.

FNAF (1923) *Memoria del Primer Congreso de Mujeres Organizado por la Federación Nacional de Asociaciones Femeninas, Abril 1–7*, Havana. Stoner Collection, Reel 2.

— (1949) *Homenaje de las asociaciones femeninas al honorable presidente de la República, Dr. Carlos Prío Socarrás*, P. Fernández, Havana. (See Stoner Collection, Reel 4).

Fornet, A. (ed.) (1967) *Antología del cuento cubano contemporáneo*, Era, Mexico.

Franco, J. (1983) 'Trends and Priorities for Research on Latin American Literature', *Ideologies and Literature*, Vol. 4, no. 16: 107–20.

— (1986) 'Apuntes sobre la crítica feminista y la cultura hispanoamericana', *Hispamérica*, Vol. 45: 31–43.

— (1987 [1974]) 'Lezama Lima. En el paraíso de la poesía', in E. Suárez Galbán, *Lezama Lima*, Taurus, Madrid.

— (1988) 'Beyond Ethnocentrism: Gender, Power, and the Third-world Intelligentsia' in C. Nelson and L. Grossberg (eds), *Marxism and the Interpretation of Culture*, Illinois University Press, pp. 503–15.

Fuss, D. (1989) *Essentially Speaking. Feminism, Nature and Difference*, Routledge, London and New York.

García Lorca, F. (1982) *Llanto por Ignacio Sánchez Mejías*, Instituto Cultural de Cantabria, Madrid.

García Valdés, P. (1952) 'Prólogo', in V. E. Rodríguez de Cuesta, *Patriotas cubanas*, Talleres Heraldo Pinareño, Pinar del Río.

Gates, H. L. (ed.) (1986) *'Race', Writing and Difference*, Chicago University Press, Chicago.

— (1988) *The Signifying Monkey*, Oxford University Press, Oxford.

Gell, A. (1992) *The Anthropology of Time: Cultural Constructs of Temporal Maps and Images*, Berg, Oxford and Providence.

Gilman, S. L. (1986) 'Black Bodies, White Bodies: Towards an Iconography of Female Sexuality in Late Nineteeth-Century Art, Medicine and Literature', in H. L. Gates (ed.), *'Race', Writing and Difference*, Chicago University Press, Chicago.

Gilroy, P. (1993) *The Black Atlantic. Modernity and Double Consciousness*, Verso, London.

González Curquejo, A. (1910, 1913, 1919) *Florilegio de escritoras cubanas*, 3 vols, La Moderna Poesía, Havana.

González Echevarría, R. (1989) 'Cuban Criticism and Literature: A Reply to Smith', *Cuban Studies*, Vol. 16: 101–6.

González Freire, N. (1961) *Teatro cubano 1927–61*, Minex, Havana.

Guillén, N. (1972) *Obra poética*, 2 vols, ed. A. Augier, Arte y Literatura, Havana.

— (1990) *Summa Poética*, Cátedra, Madrid.

Gunew, S. (ed.) (1991) *A Reader in Feminist Knowledge*, Routledge, London and New York.

Haraway, D. J. (1983) 'Animal Sociology and a Natural Economy of the Body Politic, Part 1: A Political Physiology of Dominance', in E. Abel and E. K. Abel (eds), *The Signs Reader. Women, Gender and Scholarship*, University of Chicago Press, Chicago, pp. 123–38.

— (1991) *Simians, Cyborgs and Women. The Reinvention of Nature*, Free Association Books, London.

Harding, S. (1986) 'The Instability of the Analytical Categories of Feminist Theory', *Signs*, Vol. 11, no. 4: 645–64.

Harries, R. (1993) *Art and the Beauty of God. A Christian Understanding*, Mowbray, London and New York.

Harris, R. (1992) *Marxism, Socialism and Democracy in Latin America*, Westview Press, Boulder.

Harter, H. A. (1981) *Gertrudis Gómez de Avellaneda*, Twayne, Boston.

Harvey, Sir P. (1984) *The Oxford Companion to Classical Literature*, Oxford University Press, Oxford.

Henriques Ureña, M. (1978 [1963, 1st edn]) *Panorama histórico de la literatura cubana*, 2 vols, Editorial Arte y Literatura, Havana.

Herdeck, D. E. (1979) *Caribbean Writers. A Bio–Biographical–Critical Encyclopedia*, Three Continents Press, Washington, DC.

Hernández Menéndez, M. (1996) *La poética de Rafaela Chacón Nardi*, Letras Cubanas, Havana.

Hiriart, R. (1978) *Lydia Cabrera: vida hecha arte*, Eliseo Torres and Sons, New York.

Hobsbawm, E. (1994) *The Age of Extremes*, Michael Joseph, London.

hooks, b (1984) *Feminist Theory: From Margin to Center*, South End Press, Boston.

Hopkinson, A. (ed.) (1989) *Lovers and Comrades. Women's Resistance Poetry from Central America*, Women's Press, London.

Hughes, S. S. (1992) 'Beyond Eurocentrism: Developing World Women's Studies', *Feminist Studies*, Vol. 18, no. 2: 389–404.

Hymans, M. (1986) *Bearing the Word. Language and Female Experience in Nineteenth-Century Women's Writing*, Chicago University Press, Chicago and London.

Instituto de Literatura y Linguistica de la Academia de Ciencias de Cuba (1984) *Diccionario de Literatura Cubana*, 2 vols, Letras Cubanas, Havana.

IPPF (International Planned Parenthood Federation) (1997) *Annual Report 1996–1997*, Banson, London.

Irigaray, L. (1980) 'When Our Lips Speak Together', *Signs*, Vol. 63, no. 1: 69–79.

— (1985) *Speculum of the Other Woman*, translated by G. C. Gill, Cornell University Press, Ithaca and New York.

— (1988) 'Sexual Difference', in T. Moi (ed.), *French Feminist Thought. A Reader*, Basil Blackwell, Oxford.

— (1993a) *Je, tu, nous. Toward a Culture of Difference*, Routledge, London and New York.

— (1993b) *An Ethics of Sexual Difference*, translated by C. Burke and G. C. Gill, Athlone, London.

Irizarry, E. (1979) 'Lydia Cabrera, fabuladora surrealista' in R. Minc (ed.), *The Contemporary Latin American Short Story*, Senda Nueva de Ediciones, New York, pp. 35–43.

James, C. (1996) 'Patterns of Resistance in Afro-Cuban Women's Writing: Nancy Morejón's "Amo a mi amo"', in J. Anim Addo (ed.), *Framing the Word. Gender and Genre in Caribbean Women's Writing*, Whiting and Birch, London, pp. 159–68.

Jameson, F. (1989) 'Foreword', in R. Fernández Retamar, *Caliban and Other Essays*, translated by E. Baker, University of Minnesota Press, Minneapolis.

Jardine, A. A. (1985) *Gynesis: Configurations of Woman and Modernity*, Cornell University Press, London and Ithaca.

Jiménez, J. R., C. Henríquez Ureña and J. M. Chacón (eds) (1937) *La poesía cubana de 1936*, Fernández Cía., Havana.

Jones, A. R. (1985) 'Writing the Body: Toward an Understanding of "l'écriture feminine"' in J. Newton and D. Rosenfelt (eds), *Feminist Criticism and Social Change* Methuen, New York, pp. 86–101.

Joseph, G. (1981) 'The Incompatible ménage à trois: Marxism, Feminism and Racism', in L. Sargent (ed.), *Women and Revolution: A Discussion of the Unhappy Marriage of Marxism and Feminism*, Pluto Press, London, pp. 91–107.

Kaminsky, A. (1993) *Reading the Body Politic: Feminist Criticism and Latin American Women Writers*, University of Minnesota Press, Minneapolis.

Kapcia, A. (1982) 'Revolution, the Intellectual and a Cuban Identity: The Long Tradition', *BLAR*, Vol. 1, no. 2, May.

— (1997) 'Ideology and the Cuban Revolution', in W. Fowler (ed.), *Ideologues and Ideologies in Latin America*, Greenwood Press, Westport, CT.

Kearney, R. (1991) *The Poetics of Imagining from Husserl to Lyotard*, Routledge, London and New York.

Kedourie, E. (1951, 2nd edn) *Nationalism*, Praeger, New York.

Kirkpatrick, S. (1989) *Las Románticas. Women Writers and Subjectivity in Spain 1833–1850*, University of California Press, Berkeley and London.

Kostia, Conde (ed.) (1904) *Arpas cubanas*, Rambla y Bouza, Havana.

Kristeva, J. (1980) *Desire in Language*, translated by T. Gora, A. Jardine, L. Roudiez, Columbia University Press, New York.

— (1982) *The Power of Horror. An Essay in Abjection*, translated by L. S. Roudiez, Columbia University Press, New York.

— (1987) *Tales of Love*, translated by L. S. Roudiez, Columbia University Press, New York.

— (1989; 1st edn 1986) 'Women's Time', in T. Moi (ed.), *The Kristeva Reader*, Basil Blackwell, Oxford.

Kutzinski, V. (1993) *Sugar's Secrets: Race and the Erotics of Cuban Nationalism*, University of Virginia Press, Charlottesville.

Larguía, I. and J. Demoulin (1985) 'La mujer en el desarrollo: estrategia y experiencia de la Revolución', *Casa de las Américas*, no. 149, March–April: 37–53.

Laurenzi, E. (1985) *María Zambrano. Nacer por sí misma*, horas y HORAS [sic], Madrid.

Lavrin, A. (1988) *Female, Feminine and Feminist: Key Concepts in Understanding Women's*

History in Twentieth-century Latin America, Department of Hispanic, Portuguese and Latin American Studies, Bristol.

Lazo, R. (1973; 1st edn 1954) *La teoría de las generaciones y su aplicación al estudio histórico de la literatura cubana*, UNAM, Mexico.

—— (1974; 1st edn 1966) *Historia de la literatura cubana*, UNAM, Mexico.

Leal, R. (ed.) (1963) *Teatro cubana en un acto. Antología*, Ediciones Revolución, Havana.

Le Doeuff, M. (1988) 'Women and Philosophy', in T. Moi (ed.), *French Feminist Thought*, Basil Blackwell, Oxford.

Lefebvre, H. (1991) *The Production of Space*, Basil Blackwell, Oxford.

Leiner, M. (1994) *Sexual Politics in Cuba. Machismo, Homosexuality and Aids*, Westview Press, Boulder, San Francisco and Oxford.

LeoGrande, W. M. (1980) *Cuba's Policy in Africa 1959–1980*, University of California Press, Berkeley.

Levin, S. R. (1981) 'Allegorical Language' in M. W. Bloomfield (ed.), *Allegory, Myth and Symbol*, Harvard University Press, Harvard, pp. 23–38.

Levinas, E. (1987; 1st edn 1948) *Time and the Other* [1948], translated by R. A. Cohen, Duquesne University Press, Pittsburgh.

Levine, B. B. (1983) *The New Cuban Presence in the Caribbean*, Westview Press, Boulder.

Lewis, O., R. M. Lewis and S. M. Rigdon (1977) *Four Women. Living the Revolution. An Oral History of Contemporary Cuba*, University of Illinois Press, Urbana, Chicago and London.

Liss, S. B. (1987) *Roots of Revolution. Radical Thought in Cuba*, Nebraska University Press, Lincoln and London.

Lizaso, F. and J. A. Fernández de Castro (eds) (1926) *La poesía moderna en Cuba (1882–1925)*, Hernando, Madrid.

López Sacha, F. (1996) *La isla contada. El cuento contemporáneo en Cuba*, Tercera Prensa-Hirugarren Prensa, Donostia.

Lovibond, S. (1989) 'Feminism and Postmodernism', *New Left Review*, Vol. 178: 5–28.

Lumsden, I. (1996) *Machos, Maricones and Gays. Cuba and Homosexuality*, Temple University Press, Philadelphia.

Mandela, N. and F. Castro (1991), *How Far We Slaves Have Come*, Pathfinder, New York.

Martí, J. (1955) 'Nene travieso', *La Edad de Oro*, Ministerio de Cultura, San Salvador.

—— (1961) *Obras Completas*, Vols XXIII, XXI, Patronato del Libro Popular, Havana.

Martin, P. M. (1980) *Historical Dictionary of Angola*, Scarecrow Press, London and New Jersey.

Martínez, J. (ed.) (1990) *Dictionary of Twentieth-Century Cuban Literature*, Greenwood, Westport.

Martínez Echázabal, L. (1990) *Para una semiótica de la mulatez*, Porrúa Turranzas, Madrid.

Marting, D. (1988) 'The Representation of Female Sexuality in Nancy Morejón's "Amor, cuidad atribuida"', *Afro-Hispanic Review*, Vol. 7, nos 1–3: 36–8.

Masiello, F. (1992) *Between Civilization and Barbarism. Women, Nation, and Literary Culture in Modern Argentina*, University of Nebraska Press, Lincoln and London.

Méndez y Soto, E. (1977) *Panorama de la novela cubana de la Revolución (1959–1970)*, Universal, Miami.

Menéndez, N. R. (1993) 'No Woman is an Island. Cuban Women's Fiction in the 1920s and 1930s', unpublished PhD thesis, Stanford University.

Menton, S. (1973), 'El cuento de la revolución cubana: una visión antológica y algo más', in E. Pupo-Walker (ed.), *El cuento hispanoamericano ante la crítica*, Castalia, Madrid, pp. 338–55.

— (1975) *Prose Fiction of the Cuban Revolution*, Texas University Press, Austin.

— (1978) *La narrativa de la Revolución cubana*, Playor, Madrid.

— (1990) 'La novela de la Revolución cubana, fase cinco: 1975–1987', *Revista Iberoamericana*, Vols 152–3: 913–32.

Miller, F. (1991) *Latin American Women and the Search for Social Justice*, New England University Press, London and Hanover.

Ministry of Culture (1989) *Flor Loynaz*, Ministry of Culture, Havana.

Mohanty, C. T. (1988) 'Under Western Eyes. Feminist Scholarship and Colonial Discourses', *Feminist Review*, Vol. 30: 61–88.

Molloy, S. (1991) *At Face Value. Autobiographical Writing in Spanish America*, Cambridge University Press, Cambridge.

Molyneux, M. (1996) *State, Gender and Institutional Change in Cuba's 'Special Period': The 'Federación de Mujeres Cubanas'*, University of London, Institute of Latin American Studies, No. 43.

Montero, S. A. (1989) *La narrativa femenina cubana 1923–1958*, Academia, Havana.

Moore, C. (1988) *Castro, the Blacks and Africa*, University of California, Center for Afro-American Studies, Los Angeles.

Mordecai, P. and B. Wilson (eds) (1989) *Her True-True Name. An Anthology of Women's Writing from the Caribbean*, Heinemann, London.

Morejón, N. (1974) *Recopilación de textos sobre Nicolás Guillén*, Casa de las Américas, Havana.

— (1988) *Fundación de la imagen*, Letras cubanas, Havana.

Moreno, J. A. (1971) 'From Traditional Values to Modern Values', in C. Mesa-Lago (ed.), *Revolutionary Change in Cuba*, Chicago University Press, Pittsburgh, pp. 471–97.

Morgan, R. (ed.) (1993) *Mujeres del mundo. Atlas de la situación femenina*, Hacer Editorial/Vindicación Feminista, Madrid and Barcelona.

Nasta, S. (ed.) (1991) *Motherlands. Black Women's Writing from Africa, the Caribbean and South Asia*, Women's Press, London.

Núñez, A. R. (ed.) (1993) *Homenaje a Dulce María Loynaz*, Universal, Miami.

Núñez Machín, A. (1989) *Mujeres en el periodismo cubano*, Oriente, Santiago de Cuba.

O'Callaghan, E. (1993) *Woman Version. Theoretical Approaches to West Indian Fiction by Women*, Macmillan, London.

— (1996) '"Ancest/hers?": "Politically Correct" Marginalization and Early Narratives of the West Indies by White Women', paper presented to the Second International Caribbean Women Writers' Conference, 'The Centre of Remembrance', Goldsmiths College, University of London, 29 June.

Oliver, M. R. (1964) 'La literatura del testimonio', *Casa de las Américas*, Vol. 4, no. 27, December.

Osborne, P. (1995) *The Politics of Time: Modernity and the Avant-Garde*, Verso, London and New York.

O'Shaughnessy, L. (1995) 'Songs of Iphigeneia. Strategies for Survival in Post-Sandinista Nicaragua', *Poetry Ireland*, Vol. 48, November: 19–28.

Oviedo, J. M. (ed.) (1968) *Antología de la poesía cubana*, Ediciones Paraíso, Lima.

Padura, L. (1993) *El submarino amarillo (Cuento cubano 1966–1991)*, UNAM, Mexico.

Papastergiadis, N. (1995), 'Restless Hybrids', *Third Text*, Vol. 32: 9–18.

Pereda Valdez, I. (1970) *Lo negro y lo mulato en la poesía cubaña*, Cuidadela, Montevideo.

Pereira, J. R. (ed.) (1977) *Poems from Cuba*, University of the West Indies, Mona.

— (1983) 'Image and Self-image of Women in Recent Cuban Poetry', in Lloyd King (ed.), *La mujer en la literatura caribeña. Sexta conferencia de Hispanistas*, University of West Indies, St Augustine, Trinidad, pp. 51–68.

— (ed.) (1990) *Ours the Earth. Poems by Nancy Morejón*, University of the West Indies, Institute of Caribbean Studies, Mona.

Pérez Rojas N. (1979) *Características sociodemográficas de la familia cubana 1953–1970*, Ciencias Sociales, Havana.

Pérez Sarduy, P. (1990) 'Open Letter to Carlos Moore', *Afro-Hispanic Review*, Vol. 9, nos 1–3: 25–9.

Pérez Sarduy, P. and J. Stubbs (eds) (1993) *Afrocuba*, Ocean Press, Melbourne.

Picón Garfield, E. (1994) *Poder y sexualidad en la obra de Gertrudis Gómez de Avellaneda*, Rodopi, Amsterdam.

Pollock, G. (1988) *Vision and Difference. Femininity, Feminism, and the Histories of Art*, Routledge, London.

Portuondo, J. A. (1981; 1st edn 1958) *La historia y las generaciones*, Letras Cubanas, Havana.

Radcliffe, S. and S. Westwood (eds) (1993) *Viva. Women and Popular Protest in Latin America*, Routledge, London and New York.

Radhakrishnan, R. (1996) *Diasporic Mediations. Between Home and Location*, University of Minnesota Press, Minneapolis and London.

Radstone, S. (1992) 'Postcards from the Edge: Thoughts on the "Feminist Theory: An International Debate" Conference held at Glasgow University, Scotland, 12–15 July 1991', *Feminist Review*, Vol. 40: 85–93.

Randall, M. (1974) *Cuban Women Now*, Women's Press, Toronto.

— (1981) *Women in Cuba. Twenty Years Later*, Smyrna Press, New York.

— (1982) *Breaking the Silences*, Pulp Press, Vancouver.

— (1992) *Gathering Rage. The Failure of 20th Century Revolutions to Develop a Feminist Agenda*, Monthly Review Press, New York.

Redonet, S. (ed.) (1993) *Los últimos serán los primeros*, Letras cubanas, Havana.

Remos y Rubio, J. J. (1969) *Historia de la literatura cubana*, Vol. III, Mnemosyne, Miami.

Rice Cortina, L. E. (ed.) (1983) *Spanish American Women Writers. A Bibliographical Research Checklist*, Garland Publishing, New York and London.

Rine Leal (ed.) (1963) *Teatro cubana en un acto*, Ediciones Revolución.

Rocasolano, A. (1985) (ed.) *Poetisas cubanas*, Letras Cubanas, Havana.

Rodríguez, I. (1994) *House/Garden/Nation*, Duke University Press, Durham and London.

Rodríguez, M. C. (1990) 'Women Writers of the Spanish Speaking Caribbean. An Overview', in S. R. Cudjoe (ed.), *Caribbean Women Writers*, Calaloux, Wellesley, MA.

Rodríguez Coronel, R. (1986) *La novela de la revolución cubana*, Letras Cubanas, Havana.

RoseGreen Williams, C. (1993) 'The Myth of Black Female Sexuality in Spanish Caribbean Poetry: A Deconstructive Critical View', *Afro-Hispanic Review*, Vol. 12, no. 1: 16–23.

Rubio, L. (1914) *Consideraciones sobre feminismo*, A. Molina, Havana.

Rubio Castro, A. (1990) 'El feminismo de la diferencia: los argumentos de una igualdad compleja', *Revista de Estudios Políticos*, Vol. 70: 185–207.

Ruddick, S. (1989) *Maternal Thinking. Toward a Politics of Peace*, Beacon Press, Boston.

Ruíz del Vizo, H. (1972) *Poesía negra del Caribe y otras áreas*, Universal, Miami.

St Augustine (1991) *Confessions*, translated by H. Chadwick, Oxford University Press, Oxford and New York.

Salgado, M.A. (1989) 'La poesía tradicional y el compromiso ideológico en la creación femenina de la Segunda Promoción de la revolución cubana', in *La historia en la literatura iberoamericana*, R. Chang-Rodríguez and G. de Beer (eds), Ediciones del Norte, New York, pp. 179–87.

Salper, R. (1970) 'Literature and Revolution in Cuba', *Monthly Review*, Vol. 22, no. 5.

Sánchez, R. and J. A. Madrigal (eds) (1977) *Homenaje a Lydia Cabrera*, Universal, Miami.

Sánchez-Eppler, B. (1986) *Habits of Poetry; Habits of Resurrection. The Presence of Juan Ramón Jiménez in the Work of Eugenio Florit, José Lezama Lima and Cintio Vitier*, Tamesis Books, London.

Santí, E. M. (1975) 'Lezama, Vitier y la Crítica de la Razón Reminiscente', *Revista Iberoamericana*, Vol. 41: 535–46.

Savory Fido, E. (1990) 'A Womanist Vision of the Caribbean. An Interview with Nancy Morejón', in C. Boyce Fido and E. Savory Fido (eds), *Out of the Kumbla. Caribbean Women and Literature*, Africa World Press, Trenton, New Jersey.

Sayers, J. (1982) *Biological Politics: Feminist and Anti-feminist Perspectives*, Tavistock, London and New York.

Segal, L. (1987) *Is the future female?*, Virago, London.

— (1991) 'Whose Left? Socialism and Feminism in the Future', *New Left Review*, no. 195: 81–91.

Sejourné, L. (1980) *La mujer cubana en el quehacer de la historia*, Siglo XXl, Mexico.

Shatzkin, L. (1985) 'Book Publishing in Cuba. How It Works', *Publishers Weekly*, 12 April.

Shaw, D. (1995) 'The Mexican Woman Writer: a Critical Invention?', in K. Duncan and E. Karidis (eds), *Beyond Solitude: Dialogues between Europe and Latin America*, University of Birmingham, Birmingham.

Shea, M. E. (1988) 'A Growing Awareness of Sexual Oppression in the Novels of Contemporary Latin American Women Writers', *Confluencia: Revista Hispánica de Cultura y Literatura*, Vol. 4, no. 1: 53–9.

Showalter, E. (1991) *Sexual Anarchy. Gender and Culture in the Fin de Siècle*, Bloomsbury, London.

Simón, P. (1991a) 'Al lector', in Dulce María Loynaz, *Poemas náufragos*, Letras Cubanas, Havana.

— (ed.) (1991b) *Dulce María Loynaz*, Casa de las Américas, Havana.

Smith, B. (1982) 'Toward a Black Feminist Criticism', in G. T. Hull (ed.) *But Some of Us Are Brave*, Feminist Press, New York.

Smith, L. M. and A. Padula (1988) 'Twenty Questions on Sex and Gender in Revolutionary Cuba', *Cuban Studies*, Vol. 18: 149–58.

— (1996) *Sex and Revolution. Women in Socialist Cuba*, Oxford University Press, Oxford and New York.

Smith, V. A. (1989) 'Recent Trends in Cuban Criticism and Literature', *Cuban Studies*, Vol. 16: 81–99.

— (1991) 'Dwarfed by Snow White: Feminist Revisions of Fairy Tale Discourse in the Narrative of María Luisa Bombal and Dulce María Loynaz', in S. M. Hart and L. P. Condé (eds), *Feminist Readings on Spanish and Latin-American Literature*, Edwin Mellen Press, Lewiston, Queenston and Lampeter.

— (1993) '"Eva sin paraíso": una lectura feminista de *Jardín* de Dulce María Loynaz', *Nueva Revista de Filología Hispánica*, Vol. 41, pp. 263–77.

— (1995) 'What are Little Girls made of under Socialism?: Cuba's *Mujeres* [Women] and *Muchacha* [Girl] in the Period 1980–1991', *Studies in Latin American Popular Culture*, Vol. 4: 1–15.

Smorkaloff, P. M. (1987) *Literatura y edición de libros. La cultura literaria y el proceso social en Cuba*, Letras Cubanas, Havana.

— (1997) *Readers and Writers in Cuba. A Social History of Print Culture 1830s–1990s*, Garland, New York.

Snitow A. (1990) 'A Gender Diary', in M. Hirsch and E. Fox Keller (eds), *Conflicts in Feminism*, Routledge, London and New York.

Sommer, D. (1990) 'Irresistible Romances: the Foundational Fictions of Latin America' in H. K. Bhaba (ed.), *Nation and Narration*, Routledge, London, pp. 71–98.

Soporta Sternbach, N., M. Navarro-Aranguren, P. Chuchryk and S. E. Alvarez (1992) 'Feminisms in Latin America: From Bogotá to San Bernardo', *Signs*, Vol. 17, no. 2: 393–434.

Spivak, G. C. (1981) 'French Feminism in an International Frame', *Yale French Studies*, Vol. 62: 154–84.

Stone, E. (ed.) (1981) *Women and the Cuban Revolution*, Pathfinder Press, London.

Stoner, K. L. (1991) *From the House to the Streets. The Cuban Woman's Movement for Legal Reform 1898–1940*, Duke University Press, Durham and London.

Stubbs, J. (1989) *Cuba. The Test of Time*, Latin American Bureau, London.

— (1995) 'In Search of an Unchaperoned Discourse on Mariana Grajales Coello. Social and Political Motherhood of Cuba', in B. Brereton and V. Shepherd (eds), *Engendering History. Caribbean Women in Historical Perspective*, James Curry, London.

Suardíaz L. and D. Chericián (eds) (1984) *La Generación de los años 50. Antología poética*, Letras Cubanas, Havana.

Suchlicki, J. (1974) *Cuba. From Columbus to Castro*, Charles Scribner, New York.

Sulieri, S. (1994) 'Women Skin Deep. Feminism and the Postcolonial Condition' (*Critical Inquiry*, Vol. 18, 1992), in P. Williams and L. Chrisman (eds), *Colonial Discourse and Post-colonial Theory. A Reader*, Harvester Wheatsheaf, Hemel Hempstead.

Taylor, D. (1985) *Women: A World Report*, Methuen, London.

Taylor, P. (1989) *The Narrative of Liberation*, Cornell University Press, Ithaca and London.

(1962) *Teatro cubano. Teatro contemporáneo*, Aguilar, Madrid.

Thomas, H. (1971) *Cuba or the Pursuit of Freedom*, Eyre and Spottiswoode, London.

Toledano Sande, L. (1985) 'José Martí, hacia la emancipación de la mujer', *Casa de las Américas*, no. 151, July–August: 25–41.

Torrents, N. (1990) 'Cuba's *Mujeres* [Women] Magazine. The First Twenty-five Years', *Studies in Latin American Popular Culture*, Vol. 9: 223–35.

Trives, T. (1990) 'Race, Gender and Humanism in Cuba's Socialist Theatre', unpublished PhD thesis, UCLA.

Valdés Roig, C. (1930) *María Luisa Milanés*, Archipiélago, Santiago de Cuba.

Valdiva, A. (ed.) (1904) *Arpas cubanas*, Havana.

Vázquez Díaz, R. (ed.) (1994) *Bipolaridad de la cultura cubana*, Skogs Grafica, Stockholm.

Vega, J. (1989), 'Aparición poética de Minerva', *Letras Cubanas*, Vol. 11, January–June: 319–23.

Vega Ceballos, V. (1978) *Emilia Bernal (poetisa de la inconformidad y la rebeldía)*, Universal, Miami.

Vera León, A. (1993) 'Jesús Díaz: Politics and Self Narration in Revolutionary Cuba', *Latin American Literary Review*, Vol. 21, no. 41: 65–78.

Versényi, A. (1993) *Theatre in Latin America*, Cambridge University Press, Cambridge.

Vitier, C. (1970; 1st edn 1958) *Lo cubano en la poesía* [Universidad Central de las Villas, Santa Clara], Instituto del Libro, Havana.

Walker, A. (1984) *In Search of Our Mothers' Gardens*, Women's Press, London.

Wasmer, G. (1977) *La mujer en Cuba socialista*, Ministerio de Justicia, Havana.

Weaver, K. (ed.) (1985) *Where the Island Sleeps like a Wing. Selected Poetry of Nancy Morejón*, Black Scholar Press, San Francisco.

Whitford, M. (1991) *Luce Irigaray. Philosophy in the Feminine*, Routledge, London and New York.

Wilkie, J. W. (ed.) (1990) *Statistical Abstract of Latin America*, Vol. 28, UCLA Latin American Center Publications, Los Angeles.

Williams, A. (1995) *Art of Darkness: A Poetics of Gothic*, Chicago University Press, London and Chicago.

Williams, C. (1986) 'The Role of Women in Caribbean Culture' in P. Ellis (ed.), *Women of the Caribbean*, Zed Books, New York, pp. 109–14.

Williams, L. V. (1995) 'The Emergence of an Afro-Cuban Aesthetic', *Afro-Hispanic Review*, Vol. 14, no. 1: 48–57.

Women in Cuba: Twenty Years Later, Smyrna Press, New York.

Woolf, V. (1984) *A Room of One's Own* (1st edn 1929) and *Three Guineas* (1st edn 1938), Chatto and Windus, London.

Yamaoka, K. (1997) *Cuba's Survival. Socialism with Reality*, Institute of Developing Economies, Tokyo.

Yáñez, M. (1993) 'Poesía femenina en Cuba' in C. Davies (ed.), *Women Writers in Twentieth-Century Spain and Spanish America*, Edwin Mellen Press, Lewiston and Lampeter.

Yáñez, M. and M. Bobes (1996) *Estatuas de Sal. Cuentistas cubanas contemporáneas*, UNEAC, Havana.

Yglesias, J. (ed.) (1984) *Poesías escogidas*, Letras Cubanas, Havana.

Zambrano, M. (1939) *Filosofía y poesía*, Universidad de Morelia, Morelia.

— *Filosofía y poesía* in *Obras Reunidas. Primera entrega*, Aguilar, Madrid.

— *La Tumba de Antigona. Diotima de Mantinea*, Vol. I, *Papeles para una Poética del ser*, Vol. II, *Litoral*, 121–6.

Zavala, I. (1992) *Colonialism and Culture: Hispanic Modernisms and the Social Imaginary*, Indiana University Press, Bloomington.

Cuban women writers. A select bibliography

Agüero, O. (1974) *La alegre vida campestre*, UNEAC, Havana.

— (1977) *El muro de medio metro*, UNEAC, Havana.

Aguililla, A. (1963) *Primeros recuerdos*, Ediciones Unión, Havana.

Aguirre, M. (1938) *Presencia interior*, n.p., Havana.

— (1948) *Influencia de la mujer en Iberoamerica*, P. Fernández, Havana.

— (1970) *Canción antigua a Che Guevara*.

— (1974) *Juegos y otros poemas*, Gente Nueva, Havana.

— (1980) *Ayer de hoy*, UNEAC, Havana.

Alonso, D. (1980) *Letras*, ed. I. Alvarez García, Letras cubanas, Havana.

— (1981) *El año 61*, Letras cubanas, Havana.

— (1989) *Juega la dama*, Letras cubanas, Havana.

— (1989) *Palomar*, Gente Nueva, Havana.

Alonso González, O. (1973) *Testimonios*, PCC, Havana.

Andrés, C. (1987) *Visiones*, Letras cubanas, Havana.

— (1991) *Sobre el brocado de los ojos*, Editorial Unión, Havana.

— (in press) *Palabras de María*.

Bahr, A. (1983) *Fuera de límite*, Uvero, Santiago de Cuba.

— (1984) *Hay un gato en la ventana*, Letras cubanas, Havana.

— (1989) *Teatro*, Ediciones Caserón, Santiago de Cuba.

— (1989) *Ellas de noche*, Letras cubanas, Havana.

Bernal, E. (1916) *Alma errante*, Rambla Bouza, Havana.

— (1922) *¡Como los pájaros!*, García Monge, San José de Costa Rica.

— (1925a) *Nuevos motivos*, Calpe, Madrid.

— (1925b) *Layka Froyka*, Calpe, Madrid.

— (1925c) *Vida. Poesías*, Calpe, Madrid.

— (1928) *Exaltación. Poema sinfónica*, Hernando y Galo Sáez, Madrid.

— (1928) *Cuestiones cubanas para América*, Hernando y Galo Sáez, Madrid.

Bobes, M. (1979) *La aguja en el pajar*, Ediciones Unión, Havana.

— (1989) *Hallar el modo*, Letras cubanas, Havana.

Bobia, A. (1923) *Ofertorio*, in (1993) *La Canción del agua. Poesía escogida*, Vigía, Matanzas.

Cabrera, L. (1936) *Contes Nègres de Cuba*, Gallimard, Paris.

— (1940) *Cuentos negros de Cuba*, La Verónica, Havana.

— (1948) *¿Por qué? ... cuentos negros de Cuba*, C.R., Havana.

— (1957) *Anagó: vocabulario lucumí*, C.R., Havana.

— (1961) *Cuentos negros de Cuba*, Popular, Havana.

— (1970) *La sociedad secreta 'Abakuá'*, C.R., Miami.

— (1971) *Ayapá. Cuentos de Jicotea*, Ediciones Universal, Miami.

— (1974) *Yemayá y Ochún. Kariochas, Iyalochas y Olorichas*, C.R., Madrid.

— (1986 [1954]) *El Monte*, Ediciones Universal, Miami.

Calderón, D. (1992) *Duras aguas del trópico*, Ediciones Matanzas, Matanzas.

Chacón Nardi, R. (1948) *Viaje al sueño*, Cofre, Havana.

— (1978) *Del silencio y las voces*, Letras cubanas, Havana.

— (1982) *Coral del aire*, Letras cubanas, Havana.

Chaviano, D. (1980) *Los mundos que amo*, UNEAC, Havana.

— (1983) *Amoroso planeta*, Letras cubanas, Havana.

— (1986) *Historias de hadas para adultos*, Letras cubanas, Havana.

— (1988) *Fábulas de una abuela extraterrestre*, Letras cubanas, Havana.

— (1990), *El abrevadero de los dinosaurios*, Letras cubanas, Havana.

Cruz Guerra, S. (1991) *Documentos de la otra (archivo incompleto)*, Editorial Capitán San Luis, Havana.

Claro, E. (1980) *Agua y fuego*, UNEAC, Havana.

Cruz Varela, M. E. (1987) *Afuera está lloviendo*, Letras cubanas, Havana.

de Feria, L. (1967) *Casa que no existía*, Ediciones Unión, Havana.

— (1990) *A mansalva de los años*, Ediciones Unión, Havana.

— (1991) *Espiral en tierra*, Ediciones Unión, Havana.

— (1995) *El ojo milenario*, Sed de Belleza Editores, Santa Clara.

— (1996) *Los rituales del inocente*, Ediciones Unión, Havana.

de la Torriente, L. (1988) *Narraciones de Federica y otros cuentos*, Letras cubanas, Havana.

de Vera de Lens, A. (1930) *Pro la mujer cubana*, Editorial Alberto Soto, Havana.

Díaz Parrado, G. (1984) *Tríptico*, Ediciones Unión, Havana.

Domínguez Navarro, O. (1937) *La vida en las prisiones cubanas*, Abella, Mexico D.F.

— (1971) *50 años de una vida*, Instituto Cubano del Libro, Havana.

Fernández, O. (1989) *Niña del arpa*, Ediciones Unión, Havana.

García Calzada, A. L. (1995) *Minimal Son*, Letras cubanas, Havana.

García Marruz, F. (1942) *Poemas*, Ucar García, Havana.

— (1947) 'Lo exterior en la Poesía', *Orígenes*, Vol. 4, no. 16: 16–22.

— (1951) *Las miradas perdidas (1944–1950)*, Ucar García, Havana.

— (1970) *Visitaciones*, Instituto del Libro, Havana.

— (1984) *Poesías escogidas*, Letras cubanas, Havana.

— (1986) *Hablar de poesía*, Letras cubanas, Havana.

— (1990) *Créditos de Charlot*, Vigía, Matanzas.

— (1992) *Los Rembrandt de l'Hermitage*, Ediciones Unión, Havana.

— (in press) *Habana del Centro*, Ediciones Unión, Havana.

Gómez de Avellaneda, G. ([1841] 1993) *Sab and Autobiography*, translated by Nina M. Scott, University of Texas Press, Austin.

— (1973) *Sab*, edited by Mary Cruz, Instituto Cubano del Libro, Havana.

González, I. (n.d.) *Gloria*, Municipio de Marianao, Marianao.

Henríquez Ureña, C. (1985) *Feminismo y otros temas sobre la mujer en la sociedad*, Editorial Taller, Santo Domingo.

Hernández, M. E. (1991) *Donde se dice que el mundo es una esfera que Dios hace bailar sobre un pingüino ebrio*, Ediciones Unión, Havana.

Herrera, G. (1974) *Gentes y cosas*, Ediciones Unión, Havana.

— (1978) *Granos de sol y luna*, Ediciones Unión, Havana.

— (1989) *Grande es el tiempo*, Ediciones Unión, Havana.

— (1996) *Gustadas sensaciones*, Ediciones Unión, Havana.

Leyva Ojito, X. (1990) *La muerte acecha en el agua*, UNEAC, Havana.

Lima, C. (1988) *Terriblemente iluminados*, Ediciones Unión, Havana.

— (1990) *Brujas*, Letras cubanas, Havana.

— (1992) *Rock sucio*, Editorial Unión, Havana.

Llana, M. E. (1965) *La reja*, Ediciones Revolución, Havana.

— (1983) *Casas del Vedado*, Letras cubanas, Havana.

Loynaz, D. M. (1947) *Juegos de agua*, Editora nacional, Madrid.

— (1951) *Poetisas de América*, Academia Nacional de Artes y Letras, Havana.

— (1953) *Poemas sin nombre*, Alianza, Madrid.

— (1958) *Ultimos días de una casa*, Colección Palma, Madrid.

— (1991) *Poemas náufragos*, Letras cubanas, Havana.

— (1992 [1958]) *Un verano en Tenerife*, Gobierno de Canarias, Madrid.

— (1993a [1953]) *Jardín*, Letras cubanas, Havana.

— (1993b) *Bestiarium*, Editorial José Martí, Madrid and Havana.

— (1993c) *Dulce María Loynaz. Poemas escogidos*, ed. Pedro Simón, Fondo de Cultura Económica and Universidad de Alcalá de Henares, Madrid.

— (1994) *Fe de vida*, Ediciones Hermanos Loynaz, Pinar del Río.

Méndez Capote, R. (1990 [1963]) *Memorias de una cubanita que nació con el siglo*, Editorial Pueblo y Educación, Havana.

Morejón, N. (1967) *Richard trajo su flauta y otros argumentos*, Instituto del Libro, Havana.

— (1971) and Carmen Gonce, *Lengua de pájaro*, UNEAC, Havana.

— (1979) *Parajes de una época*, Letras cubanas, Havana.

— (1983) *Octubre imprescindible*, UNEAC, Havana.

— (1984) *Cuaderno de Granada*, Casa de las Américas, Havana.

— (1985) *Where the Island Sleeps like a Wing. Selected Poetry by Nancy Morejón*, trans. by K. Weaver, Black Scholar Press, San Francisco.

— (1986) *Piedra pulida*, Letras cubanas, Havana.

— (1989) *Baladas para un sueño*, Ediciones Unión, Havana.

— (1990) *Ours the Earth. Poems by Nancy Morejón*, trans. J. R. Pereira, University of the West Indies, Mona.

— (1992) *Elogio a la danza*, UNAM, Mexico.

— (1993) *Paisaje célebre*, Fundarte, Caracas.

— (1994) *Le Chainon Poétique. Nancy Morejón*, Imprimerie Municipale, Champigny-sur-Marne.

— (1996) 'Pierrot y la luna', *Afro Hispanic Review*, Vol. 15, no. 1, 1996: 56–9.

— (1996) *Botella al mar*, Olifante-Ibercaja, Zaragoza.

Olema García, D. (1962) *Maestra voluntaria*, Casa de las Américas, Havana.

Oliver Labra, C. (1949) *Al sur de mi garganta*, Talleres El Imparcial, Matanzas.

— (1990) *Sonetos*, Letras cubanas, Havana.

— (1992) *Antología poética*, Letras cubanas, Havana.

Papastamatíu, B. (1986) *Paisaje habitual*, Letras cubanas, Havana.

Perez Konina, V. (1989) *Adolesciendo*, Ediciones Unión, Havana.

Recio Tenorio, B. (1980) *Una vez más*, Letras cubanas, Havana.

— (1989) *Cuentos para una noche lluviosa*, Letras cubanas, Havana.

Ríos, S. (1979) *De pronto abril*, Ediciones Unión, Havana.

— (1987) *Entre mundo y juguete*, Letras cubanas, Havana.

— (ed.) (1989) *Poesía infiel. Selección de jóvenes poetisas cubanas*, Editora Abril, Havana.

— (1996) *El libro roto. Poesía incompleta y desunida 1987–1989*, Instituto del Libro, Havana.

Rodríguez, R. M. (1982) *Cuando una mujer no duerme*, UNEAC, Havana.

— (1984) *Para un cordero blanco*, Casa de las Américas, Havana.

— (1992) *En la arena de Padua*, Ediciones Unión, Havana.

— (1994) *Páramos*, UNEAC, Havana.

— (1995) *Travelling*, Letras cubanas, Havana.

Rodríguez Acosta, O. (1922) *Evocaciones*, Graphical Arts, Havana.

— (1929) *La vida manda*, Biblioteca Rubén Darío, Madrid.

— (1933) *La tragedia social de la mujer*, Genesis, Havana.

Rojas, M. (1970) *Tania la guerrillera inolvidable*, Instituto del Libro, Havana.

— ([1993, Santiago de Chile] 1996) *El columpio del Rey Spenser*, Letras cubanas, Havana.

Rubio, L. (1914) *Consideraciones sobre el feminismo*, A. Molina, Havana.

Sabas Alomá, M. (1921) *La Rémora*, Siglo XX, Havana.

— (1930) *Feminismo: cuestiones sociales-crítica literaria*, Hermes, Havana.

Salado, M. (1987a) *País de noviembre*, Letras cubanas, Havana.

— (1987b) *Palabras en el espejo*, Ediciones Unión, Havana.

Saldaña, E. (1987) *Kele Kele*, Letras cubanas, Havana.

— (1985) 'Monólogo de la esposa', *Casa de las Américas*, no. 152: 86–100.

— (1989) *La noche*, Gente Nueva, Berlin/Havana.

— (1991) *Mi nombre. Antielegía familiar*, Ediciones Unión, Havana.

Sánchez, H. (1984) *¡De pie!*, Ediciones Unión, Havana.

Solís, C. (1961) *Las mágicas distancias*, Imprenta Nacional, Havana.

— (1984) *Los sabios días*, Ediciones Unión, Havana.

Tejera, N. ([Paris 1970] 1972), *Sonámbulo del sol*, Seix Barral, Barcelona.

Valdés, Z. (1986a) *Respuestas para vivir*, Letras cubanas, Havana.

— (1986b) *Todo para una sombra*, Taifa, Barcelona.

— (1995) *La nada cotidiana*, Emecé, Barcelona.

Valdés Montes de Oca, C. (1987) *Donde se nace por casualidad*, Gente Nueva, Havana.

Vian, E. (1986) *La immensa mujer, el hombrecito y la madreselva*, Letras cubanas, Havana.

Villar Buceta, M. (1927), *Unanimismo*, Hermes, Havana.

Yáñez, M. (1976) *Todos los negros tomamos café*, Editorial Arte y Literatura, Havana.

— (1981) *La Habana es una ciudad bien grande*, Letras cubanas, Havana.

— (1983) *La hora de los mameyes*, Letras cubanas, Havana.

— (1988) *El diablo son las cosas*, Letras cubanas, Havana.

Index